WESTERN WORLD COSTUME

COSTUME

An Outline History

Anatole France on Fashion*

In his old age Renan would have liked to lift the veil from the future. And why?—To satisfy his scientific curiosity! "Ah," he declared, "How I would have turned with emotion the pages of the little book, the elementary manual of science, which will be carried by the school children a hundred years after my death."

And I, also, would like to lift this mysterious veil. I, too, have my scientific curiosity. But it is not so fanciful as that of the aged devotee. I scorn retorts and alembics, steam, and electricity. I had for too long the delusion of science. Today I am freed from these follies. I no longer believe in this science which arrogates to itself alone, the privilege of being exact. This presumption suffices to condemn it.

If I were permitted to choose from the rubbish which will be published a hundred years after my death, do you know which I would take?

A novel? No, it is always the same rhapsody: a man loves a woman who does not love him; or a woman loves a man who does not love her; or both love each other madly or detest each other furiously. This offers a certain number of combinations, but it does not exceed, even by introducing another lover, more than ten situations.

No, it is not a novel which I would pick in this library of the future, nor a work on history—when it offers something of interest it is only another novel.

I would take simply a fashion magazine in order to see how women will dress themselves a century after my death. And their fantasies would tell me more about future humanity than all the philosophers, the novelists, the preachers, or the scientists.

* From *Anatole France Himself,* by J. J. Bronsson, translated by James R. Hopkins. Reprinted by permission of the publishers, J. B. Lippincott Co.

Western World Costume
An Outline History

Carolyn G. Bradley

DOVER PUBLICATIONS, INC.
Mineola, New York

Bibliographical Note

This Dover edition, first published in 2001, is an unabridged republica-
tion of the work originally published in 1954 by Appleton-Century-Crofts,
Inc., New York.

Library of Congress Cataloging-in-Publication Data

Bradley, Carolyn, G. (Carolyn Gertrude), b. 1901.
    Western world costume : an outline history / Carolyn G. Bradley.
       p. cm.
    Originally published: New York : Appleton-Century-Crofts, 1954.
    Includes bibliographical references.
    ISBN 0-486-41986-X (pbk.)
     1. Costume—History. I. Title.

GT510 .B69 2001
391'.009—dc21

                                  2001028858

Manufactured in the United States of America
Dover Publications, Inc., 31 East 2nd Street, Mineola, N.Y. 11501

Preface

It is hoped that this volume will be a mine of information for students of costume, fashion designers, theater producers, artists, and that it will give, as a whole, a kaleidoscopic view of the development of dress from primitive times to the present. A glance through various chapters should likewise demonstrate how closely related fashions are to the social climate of various eras—for example, the cool simplicity of Grecian garments, the elaborate styles of the Restoration in England, the emphasis on freedom of movement in modern American clothes.

The book is not a narrative history of costume but is presented in outline form to facilitate reference to the vast store of material that it contains. Each historic period is treated as an entity but chapters are arranged under uniform topics so that the reader can, for instance, easily trace the development of "Footwear" from Thebes to present-day New York, and make quick comparisons with other periods. Short historical sketches and chronologies introduce each chapter, but the meat of the book is in the sections entitled "Dress" (for both Men and Women) where all the distinctive features of costume of a given era are listed under: Garments, Hair, Headdress, Footwear, Accessories, Jewelry, Typical Colors, Typical Materials, and Make-up. Most of these items are also contained in a Glossary at the end of the chapter. *Words in italics in the text indicate the first appearance of a style.*

Additional features of individual chapters include short listings of "Significant Motifs" of a specific period, "Influences on Later Costumes," bibliographies, and (beginning with the Renaissance) the names of artists whose works reflect the fashions of their times. An extensive general bibliography and other helpful references are provided at the end of the volume.

Many drawings, of both the full costume and characteristic details, illustrate the book, with cross references in the text. The maps included show the geographical and political background of significant historic epochs. More information is presented on the 19th and 20th centuries than for previous periods on the assumption that the recent past is of especial interest to the reader today.

My acknowledgments are due to Ruth Bradley Smith, F. Meredith Dietz, and Dorothy Perkins Lyon for suggestions and assistance in the realization of this book; to Lois Lampe for her helpful criticism and careful reading of the manuscript; to Olga Krill for locating the sources of many illustrations; to the New York, Indianapolis, and Columbus Public Libraries, the Ohio State Library, the Library of The Ohio State University, and for the graciousness of their librarians, especially Ralph Janeway, Esther Stroedter, and Nellie Jennings; to the illustrators, Phyllis Lathan Stoner, Marjory Stewart, and Eleanor Smith Johnson; to James R. Hopkins, Director Emeritus of the School of Fine and Applied Arts of The Ohio State University, who has always been a source of encouragement; and to Ruth D. Keener, editor of this volume, who has given freely of her time and energy in preparing it for publication.

C. G. B.

Contents

CONTENTS

Primitive and
Aboriginal Peoples

CHRONOLOGY

PALEOLITHIC PERIOD (*Old Stone: earliest times-8000 B.C. or later*): Oldest man-like remains *Pithecanthropus erectus* (Java) may be as early as 550,000 B.C. *Homo Heidelbergensis* (Germany) 150,000 B.C. or earlier. *Homo Neanderthalensis* (western Europe to Palestine) *c.* 100,000-25,000 B.C. *Cro-Magnon, c.* 8000-4000 B.C. Man a nomad, lived in crude huts and caves, followed food supply, hunted and collected vegetables for food. Tools of chipped stone, wood, bone. Development of culture during Ice Age.

NEOLITHIC PERIOD (*New Stone: c. 4000-2500 B.C.*): Man located in one place, accumulated possessions; practiced agriculture, domesticated animals. Made pottery and tools of polished stone. Growth of large communities, social organization. Possible migration of people from a central locality in Asia to parts of Europe and Africa.

BRONZE AGE (*3000-1000 B.C.*): Bronze implements.

IRON AGE (*after 1000 B.C.*): Examples of iron tools date back as far as 2500 B.C. in Mesopotamia. In many cases this civilization resembled that of various present-day cultures.

PRIMITIVE PEOPLES OF TODAY: Indian tribes of Latin America. Natives of Africa, Asia, Australia, South Pacific Islands, and islands off the coast of Alaska.

CHAPTER 1

Primitive and Aboriginal Peoples

HISTORY

There is much difference of opinion about the chronology of the early periods in the story of mankind, but it is generally agreed that man first appeared at a very remote date, possibly 550,000 B.C. The oldest human-like remains within our knowledge is the *Pithecanthropus erectus,* found in Trinil, Java. The next stage in development is represented by the *Homo Heidelbergensis* and other human skeletal remains from Java, China, and Europe. Evidence from the *Homo Neanderthalensis* (*c.* 100,000-25,000 B.C.) indicates a new type of man who used numerous and diversified instruments of bone, finished with skill, and lived in caves and rock shelters. It is thought that he painted his body and possibly practiced *tattooing,* as well as fashioned materials for dress. This race, which disappeared quite suddenly, was replaced by a fourth type of man—the Cro-Magnon (*c.* 8000-4000 B.C.). From evidence which has been found the latter possessed a very different kind of culture and apparently had unusual artistic ability as shown in little bone implements, crude needles and coloring materials, the latter denoting a development in costume.

Paleolithic culture reached its peak in the last part of the Old Stone Age or Reindeer Period. In the Neolithic Period or New Stone Age, more highly developed men occupied Asia, Africa, and western Europe some 4000 years ago. They wore garments of skin and ornaments, and left us important contributions from their culture: the bow and arrow, the boat form, the wheel, pottery making, and the art of weaving. Body painting and tattooing were popular. Necklaces of shells also date from this period.

The Bronze Age followed the Neolithic Age and continued from *c.* 3000-1000 B.C. These dates may vary greatly since in some locations the Bronze Age was not arrived at and in others this period was never

3

terminated. Costume at this time was highly developed and accompanied by beautiful accessories.

Our knowledge of the clothing of primitive man may be obtained through archaeological evidence, and from peoples living under like conditions at the present time.

Less than a hundred years after Columbus discovered America, John White recorded in water color paintings the life of the Indians on the Carolina coast, and Jacques Le Moyne, a Frenchman, made memory sketches of Florida, after he returned to England. These records give an excellent idea of the primitive costume of the North American Indian.

Opinions vary in regard to the origin of clothing, but the most important may be classified: (1) as a protection against the elements; (2) to satisfy the aesthetic sense; (3) as an expression of modesty.

Exception has been found to the first theory. Nude natives have been seen in cold climates with sleet frozen on their bodies. The natives in the extreme south of South America wear very little clothing.

Throughout centuries man has justified decorating himself in various ways in order to attract the opposite sex. The owner of a *bear's-tooth necklace*, for example, was able to attract the object of his affection, not only because the teeth were thought beautiful, but also because possession of such a necklace signified bravery. He would be considered a valiant man and be recognized as a good provider.

There are arguments against modesty as a reason for donning clothing. Tribes that wear the most clothing are not necessarily the most modest. The costumes of some tribes show the marital status of the individual, such as skirts of coconut leaves worn by Yap women of the Caroline Islands and the longer skirts of the Indian women of Chichicastenango, Guatemala.

As the centuries of various costume unfold before us we are impressed with the repetition of certain costumes and new accessories suggested by those of ancient times. Permanent waving and straightening of the hair, in common use now, was considered an innovation a number of years ago, although these arts had been practiced by women for centuries. The primitive hairdresser when straightening hair used about two hundred sticks and a bowl containing paste made of black powder mixed with an oleaginous substance. First, the operator took a strand of hair, stretched it out to the length of a stick and

4

then rolled the two between the palms of the hands. The application of paste caused the hair to adhere to the stick, and after drying, to be straighter.

The position of woman in primitive cultures is usually that of homemaker. She often has a servile attitude toward her husband, sometimes helping him in the field. At other times, she may take charge of the financial affairs of the house and make decisions in important transactions. In one Indian tribe in the southwestern part of the United States, the wife asserts her authority by placing her husband's belongings outside of the door when she has become tired of him and does not wish to have him around the house any more.

Primitive man is an excellent hunter and often a very good agriculturist. He is accomplished in the handicrafts; the man of an Indian tribe in Guatemala does the expert weaving and embroidering and works with woolen fabrics, whereas the woman weaves only cotton.

The costume historian is never surprised to find a counterpart of a costume of today in an illustration of primitive man in Africa, Australia, or other parts of the world, the difference being that the higher the stage of development, the greater the variety of costumes, and the greater the individual freedom with which they are worn.

DRESS

A. *Sources of information:* tomb relics and frescoes, statues and statuettes of ancient tribes; present-day tribes.

B. MEN AND WOMEN
  1. Garments:
    (PEOPLES OF WARM CLIMATE)

    Outer upper and outer lower: body painting and tattooing by light colored tribes, *scar-tattooing* by dark-colored tribes; social standing shown by amount of tattooing used by Yap Islander and native of the Amazonian section; tattooing by Maoris of New Zealand, after first successful fight, a fresh design for each ensuing exploit; loose garment woven from fibre worn by Maoris; *loin cloth;* upper part of body nude; full skirt resembling *broomstick skirt* of 1945, or *wraparound skirt, refajo,* by Guatemalan Indian woman; *huipil,* used by Aztec, or Mayan woman.

5

(PEOPLES OF COLD CLIMATE)

Outer upper and outer lower: trousers usually worn by both man and woman; sometimes hide and skin sewed with bronze needle; wraparound skirt and simple upper garment with opening for head; *fur skirt,* having fur on inside or outside of garment sometimes sewed on linen or wool; *poncho;* clothing made from wool, skin of livestock, horse, sheep, goat or camel, by nomad of steppe region in western Turkistan; long skirt of feathered bird skin worn by man in Aleutian Islands, fur of seal or sea otter by woman; waterproof raincoat of seal intestine with decoration of feathers with drawstring on hood and at wrist, by man and woman of Aleutian Islands; *rebozo* worn by Mexican woman of the highlands; *perraje* used by Guatemalan Indian woman; *capizaje,* by Guatemalan Indian man.

2. **Hair:** woman's head sometimes shaven in British East Africa; elaborate arrangement used by some African women, twisted and plastered topknot or hundreds of hanging curls by Zulu woman; gum and mud mixture used in twisting hair into curls and unusual shapes, such as *cockscomb spike* and knob with an added decoration of *cowrie shells* and feathers; numerous permanent plaits solidified with palm oil and cornwood dye keeping them in place for several months, by some African tribes; hair oiled and buttered, then set in waves by Tigré woman; decorative coils by Nigerian woman; loose flowing hair sometimes symbol of mourning by Mayagasy woman; hair dressed over an elaborate wire frame by some tribes in Africa; elaborate hairdress used as carrying place for precious objects by messenger; braids and more simple hairdress usually worn in cold climates.

3. **Headdress:** simple headband of animal skin; narrow band of iron later used as a symbol of royalty; various *masks,* insect-like mask with pendant tassels, worn with tunic of palm fibre, and helmet when initiating young man to manhood, by South Kukuruku in Africa; white headband used to attract object of affection; shawl worn as head covering; fur turban by man in cold climate; feathers by various Indian tribes; *tzut* worn by Guatemalan Indian man.

4. **Footwear:** woman usually barefoot; man often barefoot; *sandal;* low shoe or *moccasin* by man or woman; fur stocking and leather boot in Fox Islands; fur-lined boots worn in cold climates, also soles of shoes made especially for walking on ice; stocking of woven grass and salmon skin by Eskimo; *zapato* worn by Guatemalan Indian man; *huarache* worn by Mexican Indian.

1. Earring   2. Wraparound Skirt   3. Tattoo   4. Baldrick   5. Fur Skirt
6. Bear's-tooth Necklace

5. **Accessories:** *faja* worn by Guatemalan Indian woman; walking stick; ceremonial mask; torque or twisted rod of gold as mark of dignity; *baldrick;* hairpins; buttons; feathers worn as decoration by Indian tribes; beaded decorations, by Eskimo and Indian; fur gloves and mittens, by Eskimo.

6. **Jewelry:** amber worn as ornament in Neolithic times; intricate charm and *amulet,* sometimes of amber; shell, bone, teeth, polished stone, and bangled copper wire necklace; flint bracelet; *earring;* nose, ear, arm and leg ornaments; girdle of brass rings worn by Dyak woman of Borneo. Additional forms of jewelry found in this Chapter, *Section 9.*

7. **Typical colors:** many bright colors, in warmer climates: red sometimes used as symbol of blood of sacrifice, green, blue, yellow, orange, and sometimes purple, symbol of royalty; white used for war and black for mourning in north and west Australia, whereas white used for mourning in the south of that country; red used as symbol of mourning in some sections of Africa; red, brown, yellow, white, black, gray, and blue by Bushman; red, yellow, ochre, black and white and sometimes purple and salmon pink by Polynesian, tuft of red feathers indicating presence of Supreme Being; subdued colors of fur combined with bright colors in cold climates.

8. **Typical Materials:** bark cloth, the tapa cloth of the Hawaiian, the balassor cloth of the Polynesian; leaves; handwoven cloth of fibre, wool, cotton or linen; cloth decorated with embroidery; tassels and fringe; animal skin, ordinarily softened and made pliable, used by Indian tribes and the Eskimo; shoe of hide, wood, fibre or other plant products.

9. **Make-up:**

Body Painting: in hot climates, to ward off perils of warfare, evil spirits, illness, and death; to prevent excess sleeping (a superstition of the Moroccan man); as an aid in obtaining food; for courtship; during funeral rites; also coconut and palm oils used as protection from burning rays of sun.

Decoration and mutilation:

Lips: huge disks inserted; piece of wood put through wife's lip as symbol of husband's authority by Saras-djingas; labret worn in perforation of lip and cheek by Eskimo.
Teeth: filed to a point; blackened in order not to resemble teeth of a dog; sometimes two upper teeth knocked out during a special initiation ceremony in Australia.

CHAPTER 1: DRESS

Nose: ivory *nose plug* worn by members of some tribes in Africa; quills, beads, plugs and rings inserted in nose among some Eskimo tribes; nose ring through one nostril worn by tribesman in South America, by woman of the Sudan, by Zouia child; wedding ring in nose of woman to distinguish social rank; porcupine quills pulled through nostrils, fashionable in French Equatorial Africa; broken, flattened nose of Polynesian distinguished him from European with unbroken nose, called "canoe nose" by natives.

Eyes: crossed eyes considered beautiful by ancient Mayan, ornament dangled on forehead helped to cause this defect.

Eyebrows: plucked by members of some African tribes so that they would not resemble the ostrich.

Ears: ear lobes weighted with an ornament in childhood, reaching to shoulder in adolescence, by members of some Peruvian tribes; weight or jampot in lobe of each ear by Kikuyu native; tooth earrings along edge of ear by members of some African tribes; rings in ear lobes worn by woman until death of husband in Masai tribe in British East Africa; ears sometimes pierced in several places by members of some Eskimo tribes.

Neck: series of brass rings around neck progressively added to increase its length by Padaung woman of the hill tribes of Burma; necklace of wire with copper bangles, wire coils, seeds, and beads.

Fingers: mutilated to show distinguished person of a certain profession in an Australian tribe; finger cut off as a sign of mourning or cure for illness by Bushman, Hottentot, and Kaffir.

Legs: huge anklet plates used by tribesman of African tribe, also bands of brass or other metal.

SIGNIFICANT MOTIFS

Designs of the huntsman from the Stone Age were evident; in the Bronze Age geometrical designs were used; and in the Iron Age motifs of birds and horses have been found. The designs used by various Indian groups of the United States and Mexico include the stylized human figure, deer, frog, monkey, bird, lizard, *snake, bow, scalp,* pine cone, seed-pod, cloud, cyclone, *lightning,* rain, scroll, moon, star, cross, crossed sticks, *whirling sticks, sling shot.* Among the most popular motifs in Guatemala are: *double-headed eagle,* stylized human figure, *figure of girl, bat,* gadfly, *bee, wasp, peacock* and *turkey,* deer, *monkey, tiger,* armadillo, *sun, moon, star, cross, scroll,* lightning, *rain, fields, hills and trees, plumed serpent;* designs of the Polynesian include geometric decorations named morning star, light of the sea, bloodstain or honey-sucker; very small realistic designs are used by Eskimo.

9

INFLUENCES ON LATER COSTUMES

Bustle, 1931 and 1940's, showed influence of certain African tribes; wrap-around skirt, middle 1940's, developed from the primitive skirt, broomstick skirt also reflected influence of the Mayan Indian whose skirt is dampened and pulled into pleats and then dried; costume jewelry including that made with shells, from primitive jewelry; saddle bag, 1949-52; decoration on side of hose, 1949, might be compared to tattooing.

BOOKS OF REFERENCE

(See also GENERAL BIBLIOGRAPHY, p. 433)

Boaz, Franz, *Anthropology* (New York, W. W. Norton and Co., 1928)

Buschan, G., *Illustrierte Volkerkunde* (Stuttgart, Strecker and Schröder, 1922-28)

Cordry, Donald Bush, *Costumes and Textiles of the Aztec Indians of the Cuetzalan Region* (Los Angeles, Southwest Museum, 1940)

———, *Costumes and Weaving of the Zoque Indians of the Chiapas, Mexico* (Los Angeles, Southwest Museum, 1941)

Hiler, Hilaire, *From Nudity to Raiment* (London, W. G. Foyle, Ltd., 1929)

Kamps, Norman, and Adrian, Rupert, *Aztec Costumes and Customs* (Norman Kamp, 1949)

Lewis, A. B., *New Guinea Masks* (Chicago, Field Museum of Natural History, 1922)

Meyrick, Samuel Rush, *The Costume of the Original Inhabitants of the British Islands* (London, J. Dowding, 1815)

O'Neale, L. M., and Kroeber, A. L., *Textile Periods in Ancient Peru* (Berkeley, University of California Press, 1930-48)

Suarez, Galvez, *Guatemala Indians* (Guatemala, C. A., B. Zadick and Co., n.d.)

Vanoverbergh, Morice, *Dress and Adornment in the Mountain Province of Luzon, Philippine Islands* (Washington, D. C., Catholic Anthropological Conference, 1929)

GLOSSARY

Amulet—charm worn as a protection against disease or evil, and to bring favorable results.

Baldrick—strap of hide or fur worn over shoulder; usually supported a bag in which articles were carried. *Pl. I, 4.*

Bat—represents the ancient ruling house of the Cakchiquel.

CHAPTER 1: GLOSSARY

Bear's-tooth Necklace—necklace made of bear teeth. *Pl. I, 6.*

Bee, Wasp and Tiger—symbols which represent the legendary origin of the Maya.

Body-painting—method of painting the body with various ochres.

Bow—shown with 2 triangles touching a straight line resembling a bow.

Broomstick Skirt—after washing, skirt is pulled into pleats on a stick and then dried.

Capizaje—long or short piece of blue, black, or brown fabric having an opening for the head, usually with fringed ends; worn in Guatemala.

Cockscomb Spike—crestlike shape in which hair was twisted.

Cowrie Shell—beautifully colored shell of the genus Cypraea.

Cross—symbol of the 4 corners of the earth.

Double-headed Eagle—two meanings are given to this design by the Mayan Indian: the 2 heads representing faces, 1 looking toward good and the other toward evil; 1 head looks upward to heaven and the other downward to earth. Another form of the double-headed eagle signified the reigning house of Charles V of Spain.

Earring—small or large metal ring worn in lobe of ear, *Pl. I, 1.*

Faja—narrow or wide sash worn by Guatemalan Indian.

Fields—represented by parallel lines.

Figure of Girl—some have thought this figure represented a Mayan princess, others have said it represented a Spanish princess.

Fur Skirt—short or long skirt of fur; sometimes resembling a loin cloth. *Pl. I, 5.*

Hills and Trees—zigzag lines topped with vertical lines.

Huarache—sandal woven of leather strips worn by Mexican Indian.

Huipil—blouse worn by Aztec or Mayan woman in Mexico and Guatemala, often of exquisite handwoven fabric.

Lightning—represented by sharp, zigzag lines.

Loin Cloth—cloth worn around the loins.

Mask—covering for face or head, often shaped to represent an animal or a human head; made of papier maché or carved of wood.

Moccasin—soft leather shoe.

Monkey—first known as a messenger between men and the gods.

Moon—represented by a small disk surrounded by a black silk circular area, the symbol of darkness.

Mutilation—method of mutilating or changing the shape of a part of the body.

Nose Plug—piece of wood, metal, or quill drawn through the nose.

Peacock or Turkey—symbol of Tlaloc, god of fertility.

Perraje—shawl worn in Guatemala.

Plumed Serpent—represented by an *s* lying on its side.

Poncho—rectangular piece of material or blanket with central or near central opening for the head and worn as a protection from the elements.

Rain—represented by fringe; purple fringe worn by royalty.

Rebozo—shawl worn by Mexican woman.

Refajo—wrapped or pleated skirt worn by Guatemalan Indian woman.

Sandal—type of footwear with a sole and 1 strap over the instep and another between the 1st and the 2nd toes.

Scalp—represented by 2 equilateral triangles with the sharp angles touching each other.

Scar-tattooing—method of scarification in which a series of cuts are arranged in a design and filled with clay or similar material to give them the desired prominence when healed.

Scroll—symbol of the unspoken word.

Sling Shot—2 equilateral triangles, short sides connected by their narrow bases.

Snake—sometimes represented by zigzag lines, or by a figure similar to a dart.

Star—shown by dots and circles which are symbols of the spirits of Mayan ancestors.

Sun—circle with long-pointed rays, symbol of virility and the divinity.

Tattooing—the practice of making colored designs, usually dark blue or red, on various parts of the body. *Pl. I, 3.*

Tiger—refer to *Bee.*

Turkey—refer to *Peacock.*

Tzut—square piece of fabric, folded diagonally and worn as headdress, often beautifully embroidered in meaningful symbols, worn in Guatemala.

Wasp—refer to *Bee.*

Whirling Sticks—represented by a symbol similar to a swastica.

Wraparound Skirt—earliest skirt worn by woman, consisting of straight piece of material wrapped around the lower part of the body from right to left in front, then across the back from left to right, allowing the surplus to cross the front again and to be tucked under the top of the skirt. *Pl. I, 2.*

Zapato—shoe worn in Mexico and Guatemala.

Egypt

CHRONOLOGY

PREDYNASTIC PERIODS (*c. 5000-3700* B.C.): Introduction of calendar, *c. 4241.*

ANCIENT KINGDOM (*Dynasties I-X*): *Dynasties I-II, c. 3700-3150* B.C.: The two kingdoms of Upper and Lower Egypt united under rule of Menes. Writing used. Arts and crafts developed. Pharaoh deified in life and death. *Old Kingdom, Dynasties III-V, c. 3150-2600* B.C.: Arts and crafts highly developed. Excellent painters and sculptors. Stone architecture, erection of colossal pyramids. Literature flourished. *First Intermediate Period, Dynasties VI-X, c. 2600-2300* B.C.: Breaking up of kingdom, decline of arts and crafts.

MIDDLE KINGDOM (*Dynasties XI-XVII*): *Dynasties XI-XII, c. 2300-1927* B.C.: First Theban Dynasties, feudal period, revival of militarism, great prosperity, high development in the arts and crafts; classical age of Egyptian literature. Temple builders. *Second Intermediate Period, Dynasties XIII-XVII, c. 1927-1580* B.C.: Disunion, invasion of Hyksos. Horse introduced by invaders.

NEW KINGDOM (*Dynasties XVIII-XXX*): *Dynasties XVIII-XIX, c. 1580-1200* B.C.: Great prosperity of Theban Dynasties. Foreign conquests, period of cultural advance, Temple of Luxor. *Dynasty XX, c. 1200-1090* B.C. *Dynasty XXI, c. 1090-945* B.C.: Priest kings at Thebes. *Dynasty XXII-XXIV, c. 945-750* B.C.: Egyptianized Libyan settlers, kings of Egypt. *Dynasty XXV, c. 750-661* B.C.: Conquest of Egypt by Assyria. *Dynasty XXVI, c. 661-525* B.C.: Saite Period. *Dynasty XXVII, c. 525-404* B.C.: Persian Period. *Dynasties XXVIII-XXX, 464-332* B.C.

PTOLEMAIC PERIOD (*332-20* B.C.) Cleopatra committed suicide, *30* B.C.

CHAPTER 2

Egypt

HISTORY

A dearth of rain forced the prehistoric ancestors of the Egyptians to desert the plains on either side of the Upper Nile. For thousands of years the watershed had provided a rich country, but when game became scarce due to lack of rainfall, these people abandoned the life of the hunter, became agriculturists and settled down in the lower valley of the Nile. Since that time the Egyptians have been greatly influenced by this river.

The Egyptians made such progress in civilization that by 3500 B.C. they were producing stone vessels, decorated pottery, figurines carved of bone or ivory, or modeled in clay, and woven linen cloth. Finally, metal tools came into general use.

Economic developments also advanced political progress. Formerly divided among many small states, the people of Egypt now formed two clearly defined kingdoms—the Kingdom of Upper Egypt in the Nile valley in the south; and the Kingdom of Lower Egypt in the Delta at the north.

About 3000 B.C., after bitter wars, the powerful but backward people of the South and those of the northern kingdom united as a nation composed of nobles, the masses, and slaves, under rule of the first supreme *pharaoh*, Menes. King Menes moved his capital from the South to a few miles above the Delta, and the city was named Memphis.

Our rich knowledge of this important country is due to the Nile valley's dry climate, which has preserved materials for 3000 to 4000 years. Even the texture and color of fabrics and paints have remained intact through the centuries.

The Old Kingdom covering ten dynasties was followed by the Middle Kingdom consisting of Dynasties XI-XVII. The gigantic pyramids were a product of the Fourth Dynasty. The Middle Kingdom was the classic period of Egyptian history in which literature and

15

poetry, sculpture, and architecture flourished. There were Semitic invasions, and the effects were reflected in art and dress after the fall of Dynasty XII.

The New Kingdom and the Late Period, embracing Dynasties XVIII-XXX, had a brilliant beginning but not so glorious an end. At the height of prosperity during the time of Rameses II many great temples were built; but in 525 B.C. Egypt met defeat from the Persians, and in 332 B.C. was conquered by Alexander the Great of Macedonia. Upon the latter's death, Ptolemy, a Macedonian general, was made governor and for almost three hundred years the country was ruled by his descendants. The last of the Ptolemies was Cleopatra, the best known queen in Egyptian history. Roman rule followed for nearly five hundred years. Since that time the Arabs, Turks, French, and English, in turn, have ruled Egypt.

The Egyptian believed that in his future existence life would continue and he would enjoy all of the comforts he had known in his stay on earth. For that reason a permanent abiding place, huge and awe-inspiring, was erected for the dead and the body was preserved by mummification. Scenes depicting everyday life in the field and in the papyrus swamp, and every known trade and occupation, were portrayed on the walls of the tombs. These familiar scenes showed the brewer, the baker, the potter, and the scribe.

The costumes of men and women were similar during the Old and Middle Kingdoms. The style of dress showed the wearer's wealth and importance. In the New Kingdom, beginning with Dynasty XVIII, changes in costume occurred as a result of commercial interests and contacts with other peoples. Among these changes were the innovation of the shirt; and many variations of skirts, one type shorter in front than in the back, another type looped up to show the pleated inner skirt, and another with a full pleated skirt.

Mirrors of highly polished metal aided the beauty-conscious lady of the Nile in applying powder, rouge to the lips, and paint to the eyelids and corners of the eyes in order to enhance their brilliance and to make them appear longer. The male likewise was particular about his appearance. The slave applied unguents to the master's face and then shaved him with a bronze blade, ground very sharp with emery and stropped with soft ox-skin. The length of the beard indicated his station in life. It was the king who set the fashion for men in dress.

The king had to acknowledge his wife as his equal, if not his superior. Egyptian history includes queens who were great leaders. The woman of Egypt enjoyed social freedom and achieved legal advantage. She fought on the battlefield, entered alliances, and exerted much power. The Egyptian woman could hold property, a wife had complete control of the joint estates. A man was responsible for any irregular conduct of his wife. In the later years of Egyptian civilization when life became more secure the woman of a wealthy family was not permitted to work nor to fight. The position of woman became subordinate as is usual in a military society. There were two types of marriages: one without a full written contract, another with a full written contract. The latter included a dowry and the contract mentioned conditions in regard to property in case the marriage would be dissolved.

Various tasks occupied the men. In the palace there were wigmakers, sandalmakers, perfumers and special officials in charge of cosmetics. In the towns and cities, there were merchants, ceramists, jewelers, coppersmiths, and professional writers or scribes. Agriculture and weaving were important occupations.

In November, 1922, after Lord Carnavon and Howard Carter made the spectacular discovery and excavation of the tomb of Tutankhamen, the fashion world showed how much archaeological finds may affect costume. Shops were flooded with Egyptian-style textiles and costume jewelry, and dresses were draped in Cleopatra-like fashion. These influences continue to invade present-day styles from time to time.

DRESS

A. *Sources of information:* temples, Theban and other tombs, sculpture of the Pyramids of Gizeh, portrait statues, mural paintings, mummy cases, papyri manuscripts, colored *hieroglyphs* showing merchants, laborers, and kings.

B. MEN (*Ancient Kingdom, Dynasties I-X*)
   1. Garments:
      Outer upper: nude populace, until Dynasty V.
      Outer lower: short skirt of white linen worn by nobility; skirt wider and longer, Dynasties V and VI; triangular erection at side; soft material draped in different ways with large, stiff box pleat or fullness draped under belt at front; royal skirt with front rounded

off and wide strip hanging from under girdle worn by king; loin cloth worn by peasant.

Under: loin cloth worn by nobility in later part of period.

Cloaks and overgarments: skins of wild beasts; long, elaborately draped *robe* worn by king for official business.

2. **Hair:** black *wig;* round bob arranged in little curls; long hair falling from crown of head to shoulder worn later in period.

3. **Headdress:** red wickerwork crown of Lower Egypt; tall, white, helmet-like crown of Upper Egypt; *pshent,* after 3700 B.C.; *helmet* headdress with *royal snake* or *symbol of royalty* worn also by pharaoh; close-fitting hood with *lappet* at each side; *claft; badge* ending with gold fringe; simple *fillet* worn by man not of royal birth.

4. **Footwear:** sandal of plaited or woven papyrus or palm leaves, worn out-of-doors.

5. **Accessories:** ornamental girdle of painted leather or embroidered linen; walking stick ornamented with color and gold, inscribed with owner's name.

6. **Jewelry:** bracelet inlaid with paste or precious stones, for the upper or lower arm; anklet of colored embroidery or of gold and silver; necklace with pendant figure of god or sacred animal; gold, silver, bronze, or *faïence* ring; official seal ring of red carnelian used by pharaoh; beads in profusion, of emerald lapis lazuli, agate, carnelian, amethyst, onyx, jasper, garnet, rock crystal, and turquoise; pearl and amber also popular.

7. **Typical Colors:** usually white; mineral dyes used at first, later vegetable dyes.

8. **Typical Materials:** cloth of coarse texture; skirt of matting, worn by peasant.

9. **Make-up:** *postiche* or artificial beard; various lords of the royal toilette important, called "superintendents of the clothes of the King," "washers of the Pharoah," etc.

C. **WOMEN** (*Ancient Kingdom, Dynasties I-X*)
1. **Garments:**
   Outer upper and outer lower: tight *tunic* with 1 or 2 shoulder straps, bare breast.
   Cloak and overgarments: opaque and transparent shoulder *cape.*
2. **Hair:** cut short to accommodate wig; wig of real hair worn by well-to-do, of wool, by lowest class; wig set low on forehead; fringed wig sometimes reaching to shoulder; black wig ornamented with gold; gold wig sometimes terminating in braids; coiffure supports worn; straight hair in 2 long tresses or rolls hanging to breast; hair

18

1. Pectoral   2. Kalasiris   3. Lily or Lotus
4. Apron   5. Cross or Key of Life   6. Transparent Outerskirt
7. Loin Cloth   8. Hieroglyph   9. Collar

also worn loosely; lotus flower often intertwined in the hair; *horus lock.*

3. **Headdress:** miter-shaped cap with long ear-tabs; type similar to claft worn by man; helmet-like cap; thin bonnet of soft material with hood effect; small *toque;* festive coiffure resembling hawk or guinea head; *vulture* with outspread wings, symbolic of Maati, Goddess of Truth; *vulture cap; feather or plumed headdress* of Isis worn by the queen; stiff turban with uraeus worn by royalty; perfumed *cone,* 4 to 6 inches high; gold *circlet* around wig worn by royal concubine.

4. **Footwear:** barefoot or sandal.

5. **Accessories:** cane, 4 to 6 feet long, often gilded and inscribed with owner's name; mirror of bronze with handle forming a design of a flower or a human being; fan made of dyed feathers and leaves, having handle 5 to 7 feet long.

6. **Jewelry:** many strands of beads sometimes extending to waist; jeweled *collar;* jeweled belt sometimes connected to jeweled collar by straps; at first, anklet of beadwork or woven material, later of gold and silver; upper and lower *arm bands.* Refer to B. 6.

7. **Typical Colors:** white, green, yellow, and red for tunic.

8. **Typical Materials:** softer linen than fabric used for man's costume.

9. **Make-up:** oils and unguents; *stibium* for eye; green or black eye shadow; *kohl;* veins of chest sometimes outlined in blue; lips painted with carmine; fingertips and toes colored with *henna.*

D. MEN (*Middle Kingdom, Dynasties XI-XVII*)

1. **Garments:**

   Outer upper: sleeved tunic of heavy or transparent linen, unbelted and reaching to knee; belted tunic of opaque, soft material.

   Outer lower: continuation of older types; transparent outerskirt over underskirt, both skirts same length at first, then outerskirt narrow, and longer in back than in front.

   Under: loin cloth.

   Cloaks and overgarments: *shawl;* draped robe with opening for head, side forming draped sleeve, sometimes left unsewed.

2. **Hair:** wig set low on forehead covering ears; long-haired wig with hair falling back from crown.

3. **Headdress:** pshent; badge; claft, helmet-like cap ornamented with royal asp.

4. **Footwear:** sandal often lined with cloth, embroidered in gold and decorated with enamel and jewels, sometimes ornamental clasp over instep, heelless sandal with turned-up toe worn by upper class; enemy sandal with picture of enemy on inside of sole; mourner unsandaled.

1. Symbol of Royalty   2. Claft   3. Vulture Cap   4. Asp   5. Mantle
6. Sacred Beetle or Scarab   7. Feather Headdress
8. Horus Lock   9. Fillet   10. Cape   11. Cone   12. Badge

5. **Accessories:** waist belt with elaborate, long, narrow *apron;* royal apron decorated with colored feathers, asp, lion's head, and polychrome glass, attached to girdle; apron with master's name worn by slave; lion's tail sometimes worn at back of skirt of royalty, cross, or key of life; walking stick about 6 feet long, and with head resembling flower or other ornament.

6. **Jewelry:** refer to *B. 6.*

7. **Typical Colors:** green popular; white generally used by upper class triad of colors used—black, yellow, and red; red, blue, and white; dark blue, light blue, and white; cream, blue, and black; dark red, medium yellow, and blue; also dazzling white, red, saffron, blue, or black costume; colors in manuscripts distinguish types: woman (yellow); man (red); deified king (black); nobleman (usually white); god (green); slave (blue).

8. **Typical Materials:** wool, considered unclean by priest, worn by layman; costliness of material used in costume distinguished class; heavy and transparent linen used in tunic; fine linen of natural color, bleached, or dyed, often embroidered with gold, silver, and purple by upper class; cotton or linen cap; leopard skin worn by priest; papyrus plant or matting for tight, short costumes used by lower class; woven palm leaves or papyrus, wood or leather used for sandal.

9. **Make-up:** skin painted or dyed; unguents and oils used; false ceremonial beard, with or without slender line along jawbone, length determining rank of person.

E. WOMEN (*Middle Kingdom, Dynasties, XI-XVII*)

1. **Garments:**

    Outer upper: tunic with strap across shoulder or with kimono sleeve; robe of opaque, soft material, similar to a man's garment although draped differently and girded.

    Outer lower: transparent outer skirt; wraparound skirt with fullness at front; skirt longer than the man's and belted higher; plain wraparound skirt, the garment of slave.

    Cloaks and overgarments: shawl; shoulder cape; *rectangular cape.*

2. **Hair:** short bob similar to type worn by man; sometimes rather long with curled ends, worn behind ears; black wig ornamented with gold, having 2 tresses extending to the breast.

3. **Headdress:** elaborate, or merely a circlet of gold worn by royalty; vulture cap, uraeus, plumed or feather headdress; crown of Lower Egypt worn over crown of Upper Egypt by queen; fillet with naturalistic lotus; decorated cloth over wig; perfumed cone 4 to 6 inches high.

1. Wig   2. Winged Globe   3. Pshent   4. Arm Band
5. Wraparound Skirt   6. Tunic   7. Papyrus or Reed

4. **Footwear:** sandal with turned-up toe.
5. **Accessories:** parasol used on chariot and for ceremonial procession; fan of leaves, palmetto, or dyed feathers; walking stick, 4 to 6 feet long; hair comb of wood or ivory; stick of ivory, wood, bronze, or glass used for applying make-up; container of alabaster for kohl; mirror of highly polished metal.
6. **Jewelry:** breast plate; elaborate girdle clasp; gold, silver, bronze, faïence, and enamel earrings; rings; *pectoral;* bead necklace with pendant in form of amulet or sacred animal; flat bracelet and arm bands; sometimes anklet. Refer to *C. 6.*
7. **Typical Colors:** green very popular at first, white, yellow, and red also worn; white very fashionable later.
8. **Typical Materials:** very fine linen.
9. **Make-up:** body oils of various kinds, including castor oil; eye and brow made longer with kohl; eyeshadow of blue or green made of *malachite;* ochre used on cheeks; henna used to color fingertips and toes; superfluous hair plucked; special care given to teeth; bone or ivory false teeth held in place with gold wires; false beard attached by a gold chin strap sometimes worn by queen.

F. MEN (*New Kingdom, Dynasties XVIII-XXX*)

1. **Garments:**
   Outer upper: many changes in style of clothing for man; shirt introduced in Dynasty XVIII, tucked under girdle; tunic sometimes with sleeve for left arm only, right arm free for movement; *kalasiris.*
   Outer lower: length of skirt from just below the knee to the ankle; many variations of skirt, including looped puffs, giving first suggestion of drapery worn in latter part of Dynasty XVIII; underskirt longer and wider, sometimes with pleating; short skirt, similar to antique type, worn by great lords of Egypt, gold ornament added to this skirt; pleating resembling *accordion pleating* becoming popular in Dynasty XIX; slave with scanty clothing.
   Under: loin cloth.
   Cloaks and overgarments: large, loose *mantle,* fashionable about 1350-1090 B.C.; later, a kind of fringed shawl.
   Additional garments: highly decorated garment worn by the pharaoh; official robe elaborately draped.
2. **Hair:** artificial wig; long wavy hair; sometimes longer wig ending in corkscrew curls; after 1150 B.C. wig sometimes dyed blue or red; wig with hair parted in middle and rippled to shoulder; one type showing the ears and with neat rolls hanging down below collarbone, resembling the claft.
3. **Headdress:** simple fillet sometimes worn by man not of royal blood; uraeus used on front of headdress.

4. **Footwear:** shoe and boot worn. Refer to *D. 4.*
5. **Accessories:** sash worn in various ways in this period; golden clasp at girdle on festive occasions. Refer to *D. 5.*
6. **Jewelry:** refer to *B. 6.*
7. **Typical Colors:** refer to *D. 7.*
8. **Typical Materials:** linen in a variety of weaves, fineness of texture of great importance. Refer to *D. 8.*
9. **Make-up:** refer to *B. 9.*

G. **WOMEN** (*New Kingdom, Dynasties XVIII-XXX*)
1. **Garments:**
   Outer upper and outer lower: tunic, tight or full, with or without sleeve or shoulder strap, belted higher than man's, length to calf of leg, to ankle, or to ground; at beginning of Dynasty XVIII, left shoulder only, covered by dress; bell-shaped tunic; kalasiris; transparent outer skirt, often with drapery, pleating resembling accordion pleating.
   Under: thick undergarment in Dynasty XX.
   Cloaks and overgarments: long mantle, shawl with embroidered hem, clasped at the breast.
2. **Hair:** stiff conventional form, parted in middle, falling in curls; in Dynasty XVIII; many styles after Dynasty XVIII; hair or wig in heavy mass to waist in Dynasty XX; dyed in fantastic colors such as blue and red after 1150 B.C.; black wig, ornamented with gold plaques or spirals.
3. **Headdress:** refer to *E. 3.*
4. **Footwear:** refer to *E. 4.*
5. **Accessories:** refer to *E. 5.*
6. **Jewelry:** ends of bracelets in design of lion's head, after Dynasty XX. Refer to *E. 6.*
7. **Typical Colors:** refer to *E. 7.*
8. **Typical Materials:** refer to *E. 8.*
9. **Make-up:** refer to *E. 9.*

SIGNIFICANT MOTIFS

The *zig-zag* form, *sacred beetle* or *scarab*, royal *asp*, royal snake or *uraeus*, *ostrich feathers*, *hawk* and vulture, the *cross* or *key of life, fret, lily* or *lotus*, *winged globe, papyrus* or *reed, scroll*.

INFLUENCES ON LATER COSTUMES

High-waisted garment and long narrow skirt of French Directory, 1795-99; lotus and scarab in designs after opening of Tutankahem's tomb, 1922;

extreme make-up, late 1920's; accordion pleating, 12th century, 1920, '21, '37, '39, '40, '47-'52; handbag, 1929, using shape of rush skirt as a suggestion; cape in various periods from Egyptian cape of 3000 B.C.; drapery in 1936, '37, '48, '51, and '52, showing influence of Egyptian period; walking stick carried in Middle Ages, about 1800, and in later times; right sleeve only, sometimes used in evening dress, 1949 (left sleeve only used in Egyptian costume).

BOOKS OF REFERENCE

(See also GENERAL BIBLIOGRAPHY, p. 433)

Breasted, James H., *Egyptian Servant Statues* (Washington, D. C., The Bollingen Press, 1948)

―――, *A History of Egypt* (Chicago, Univ. of Chicago Press, 1906-7)

Budge, Sir E. A. Wallis, *The Book of the Dead* (London, Routledge and Kegan Paul, Ltd., 1949)

Glanville, S. R. K., *Daily Life in Ancient Egypt* (London, George Routledge and Sons, 1930)

Hope, Thomas, *Costume of the Ancients* (London, Henry G. Bohm, 1841)

Houston, Mary G., and Hornblower, Florence S., *Ancient Egyptian, Assyrian, and Persian Costumes and Decorations* (New York, The Macmillan Co., 1920)

Maspero, G., *Art in Egypt* (New York, Charles Scribner's Sons, 1930)

Müller, W. Max, *Egyptian Mythology* (Boston, Marshall Jones Co., 1923)

Petri, Flinders, *Arts and Crafts of Ancient Egypt* (London, Methuen and Co., 1926)

Ross, E. D., *Arts of Egypt Through the Ages,* Chap. II (London, The Studio Ltd., 1931)

Thackeray, Lance, *The People of Egypt* (London, A. and C. Black, Ltd., 1910)

GLOSSARY

Accordion Pleating—small, tight pleats at right angles to the plane of the fabric resembling the folds of an accordion.

Amulet—small object to which magical powers were attributed. Refer to *Chap. 1.*

Apron—ornament of elaborate tabs of leather, metal, or enamel, hanging from king's girdle. *Pl. II, 4.*

Arm Band—wide metal bands worn on upper and lower arm. *Pl. IV, 4.*

Asp, Royal Snake or Uraeus—symbol of royalty and of blessing given by the king, used on headdress of rulers. *Pl. III, 4.*

Badge—emblem worn by a prince on side of head, extending as far as the shoulder. *Pl. III, 12.*

CHAPTER 2: GLOSSARY

Cape—sleeveless garment worn over shoulder. *Pl. III, 10.*

Circlet—narrow metal band worn around the head.

Claft—headcovering of heavy material falling backward loosely over the shoulder, known as the headdress of the sphinx. The greatest pharaohs were represented with this head covering. Claft trimmed with lotus flowers, or decorated with gold worn by woman. *Pl. III, 2.*

Collar—round, flat neckwear made of beads, shells, faïence, semiprecious stones, and gold; sometimes made of papyrus or fabric, with geometric and lotus designs embroidered in bright colored wool. *Pl. II, 6.*

Cone—ornament containing perfume worn on top of the head. *Pl. III, 11.*

Cross or Key of Life—emblem of eternity. *Pl. II, 5.*

Faïence—fine, richly colored, glazed earthenware.

Feather or Plumed Headdress—symbol of Isis and royalty. *Pl. III, 7.*

Fillet—band worn around the hair or wig by both man and woman. *Pl. III, 9.*

Fret—ornamental pattern representing wanderings of the soul.

Hawk—symbol of royalty.

Helmet—close-fitting cap, low on the sides, usually extending over the ears and decorated with royal symbol.

Henna—shrub or tree whose leaves give a red-orange dye used as a cosmetic.

Hieroglyph—character in the writing of the ancient Egyptians. *Pl. II, 8.*

Horus lock—braid of false hair worn behind right ear by fashionable woman. *Pl. III, 8.*

Kalasiris—long-sleeved or sleeveless robe. *Pl. II, 2.*

Kohl—preparation from galena or dark gray lead ore which was used to stain the eyelids and the eyebrows.

Lappet—folded part which extended down each side of headdress.

Lily or Lotus—flower, symbol of fertility and immortality; also symbol of the Kingdom of the South. *Pl. II, 3.*

Loin Cloth—straight piece of cloth held in place by a girdle wrapped around the body from right to left, with the ends extending down the front or at the side. Refer to *Chap. 1. Pl. II, 7.*

Lotus—refer to *Lily.*

Malachite—green ore of copper.

Mantle—cape-like garment draped under 1 arm and over the other, sometimes falling over both shoulders and fastened in front. This mantle developed into the short mantilla which was sometimes edged with fringe. *Pl. III, 5.*

Ostrich Feathers—emblem of a god or royalty.

Papyrus or Reed—standard of the Kingdom of the North; also paper made from the papyrus plant. *Pl. IV, 7.*

Pectoral—ornaments made of gold and enamel, with a cut-out design, which hung on a breast-length gold chain over the collar. This semiofficial ornament was worn by royalty and other important people. *Pl. II, 1.*

Pharaoh—royal title given the ruler in ancient Egypt.

Plumed Headdress—refer to *Feather Headdress.*

Postiche—false beard attached usually by a gold strap, worn as a sign of dignity.

Pshent—state headdress which combined the headdresses of the Northern and Southern Kingdoms. *Pl. IV, 3.*

Rectangular Cape—transparent cape clasped at the breast.

Reed—refer to *Papyrus.*

Robe—very full, rectangular-shaped garment which formed dolman-like sleeve when girded.

Royal Snake or Uraeus—refer to *Asp.*

Sacred Beetle or Scarab—symbol of immortality. Red carnelian, carved in design of sacred beetle, used as official seal by the pharaoh in place of lock and key. *Pl. III, 6.*

Sandal—refer to *Chap. 1.*

Scarab—refer to *Sacred Beetle.*

Scroll—symbol of the Nile River.

Shawl—rectangular-shaped fabric of varying size.

Stibium—mixture used for staining eyelid and eyebrow.

Symbol of Royalty—design significant of the nobility; realistic snake, or bird often worn on headdress. *Pl. III, 1.*

Toque—close-fitting cap.

Transparent Outerskirt—linen skirt lengthened in the back and looped up in puffs, used in latter part of Dynasty XVIII. *Pl. II, 6.*

Tunic—long, scant garment varying in length and reaching from the bust to the ankle, worn by man and woman. 1 or 2 straps over shoulders held tunic in place. *Pl. IV, 6.*

Uraeus—refer to *Asp.*

Vulture—sacred bird which was the protector of the king in time of war.

Vulture Cap—headdress topped with the outspread wings of a vulture. *Pl. III, 3.*

Wig—artificial headdress built upon a net-like surface which served as a protection from the heat of the sun. *Pl. IV, 1.*

Winged Globe—symbol of the sun carried on wings through the heavens. This motif, shown over the entrance of the temples and tombs, signified the protection of the sun-god. It was also used as a decoration on garments, accessories and jewelry. *Pl. IV, 2.*

Wraparound Skirt—refer to *Chap. 1. Pl. IV, 5.*

Zig-zag—symbol of the Nile River which gave life to the crops.

Asiatic Empires

CHRONOLOGY

SUMERIAN PERIOD (*3175-2425* B.C.): First Dynasty of Ur, *2575-2425* B.C. Royal tombs of Ur, epoch of city kingdoms.

DYNASTY OF AKKAD (*2425-2270* B.C.): Founded by Sargon.

SUMERIAN AND AKKADIAN EMPIRE (*2270-2150* B.C.): Guti supremacy in Babylon.

FIRST BABYLONIAN EMPIRE (*1900-1600* B.C.): Hammurabi, a great ruler. Code of 285 laws, practically every kind of legal document found, mortgages, deeds of sale, guarantees, promissory notes, etc. Canal built.

KASSITE RULE IN BABYLONIA (*1600-1150* B.C.): Much art destroyed.

PHRYGIANS SETTLED IN ASIA MINOR (*1100* B.C.).

HEBREW KINGDOM UNDER DAVID (*c.* 1000 B.C.): Kingdom of Jews divided into Kingdom of Judah and Kingdom of Israel, *975* B.C. Famine in Israel. Israel, an Assyrian province, *741* B.C. Jews under Ptolemies, *323-198* B.C.

MEDIAN EMPIRE (*835-750* B.C.)

ASSYRIAN EMPIRE (*884-606* B.C.): First Period, *884-745* B.C. Second Period, *745-626* B.C. Kingdom of Israel destroyed by Sargon II, King of Assyria, *722* B.C. Assurbanipal, *668-626* B.C. Library founded in Nineveh, *630* B.C. Art highly developed. Fall of Nineveh, the Assyrian capital, *612* B.C. End of Assyrian Empire, *606* B.C.

CHALDEAN OR SECOND BABYLONIAN EMPIRE (*625 c. 550* B.C.): King of Babylon (Nebuchadnezzar) destroyed Jerusalem, *586* B.C.

PERSIAN EMPIRE (*550-330* B.C.): Cyrus, *550-530* B.C. Cambyses, *530-522* B.C. Egypt became Persian province, *528* B.C. Darius, *521-485* B.C. Persian conquest of Ionia, *494* B.C. Defeat of Persians, *479* B.C. Alexander conquered Babylon and destroyed Persepolis, *331* B.C.

CHAPTER 3

Asiatic Empires

HISTORY

Before 3000 B.C. the Sumerians—original inhabitants of Assyria—had founded walled cities and developed an elaborate civilization, but they were conquered by invading Semitic Akkadians, who took over political control about 2300 B.C. The wealth of precious metals that have been excavated denotes a prosperous civilization flourished in this section of the world.

The first Babylonian Empire, spreading over the valleys of the Tigris and Euphrates rivers, was founded by Hammurabi, a Semite, about 1900 B.C. About 1600 B.C. Babylon, its leading city, was harassed by the Kassites who brought with them the horse and war chariot and established their own kingdom. In the meantime, a settlement of Ashur, in the northern part of the valley, had become very strong and assumed leadership, while Babylon became a lesser power. For centuries the power swayed back and forth between the two capitals, Nineveh of Assyria and Babylon of Babylonia.

Assyria became an empire as early as 884 B.C. and later was the most powerful Asiatic state. The private life of one of its rulers, Assurbanipal, and his queen is depicted on many bas-reliefs of this period.

In the 8th century B.C., under a line of strong kings beginning with Sargon II (who was also a Semite), Assyria dominated western Asia but maintained her supremacy for only about 150 years. The empire fell in 612 B.C. when the Chaldeans (a Semitic tribe that had already captured Babylonia), assisted by the Medes and Persians, took Nineveh. Two kingdoms were established, the Medo-Persian in the north and the Chaldean in the south. During the Chaldean (or second Babylonian) Empire, Babylon was rebuilt until it surpassed Nineveh. This great new empire, under Nebuchadnezzar and his successors, lasted until about 550 B.C. when it was defeated by Cyrus.

Under Cyrus, the lands of the Medes, the Lydians, and Asia Minor

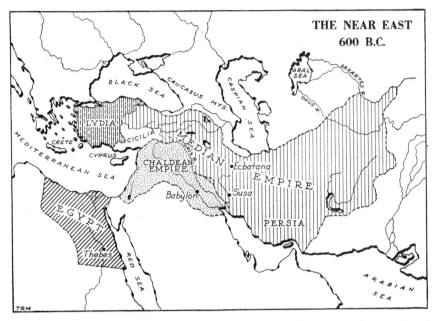

THE NEAR EAST
600 B.C.

(which included the Phrygians, Syrians, Parthians, and Amazons), were all conquered and thus the Persian Empire was established. Further conquest between 530 and 522 B.C. under Cyrus' son Cambyses, resulted in the acquisition of most of Egypt. The Persian Empire passed into the hands of Greece when defeated by Alexander the Great about 331 B.C.

Arts and costumes of Babylonia, Assyria, Mycenae (a Greek city), and even of Egypt in the early centuries, were so merged that it is very difficult to distinguish them individually.

In contrast with the simple garments of wool worn by the Sumerians, the costumes of Babylonian and Assyrian monarchs were very extravagant. During the most prosperous times, garments were practically covered with jewelry and woven embroidery.

The expression "to tie the nuptial knot" originated among the Babylonians. The priest, when conducting a wedding ceremony, would take two threads from the outer garment of the bride and two from that of the bridegroom and tie them together as a symbol of union.

About 550 B.C., Cyrus brought the long robe or sleeved tunic of the Medes to Persia and encouraged his people to adopt it. The Persians brought pantaloons to the other civilizations.

The Phrygian cap was used as far westward as Venice and the Doge wore it until the last days of Venetian independence in 1797.

CHAPTER 3: HISTORY

The myth of King Midas, a Phrygian ruler, no doubt was due to the wealth of gold in that country.

The Hebrews, who were inhabitants of Palestine, a territory situated to the Southwest of Syria in Asia Minor, adopted a costume with drapery and fringe which showed the influence of Babylonia, Assyria, and Persia. The costume worn by the Greeks after their Persian victory was dominant until 164 B.C. when Rome took over Palestine.

In most of the Asiatic countries the woman had very little freedom. Marriage at an early age originated as a protective measure since the conqueror of a country usually carried off many of the women and girls to his native country. Gradually this protection became an enslavement of the Hebrew woman. She was veiled and not permitted to uncover her head before any man who was a stranger. Before the exile of the Hebrew people, a daughter might be sold either as a concubine or a slave. In spite of these rigid rules, a woman was able to excel in certain professions; judges are listed among women of that time.

Greater freedom was enjoyed by the woman of Babylon since her role in this country was an influential one. In more ancient times she was esteemed as a prophetess, performed the religious ceremonies, and had authority to manage the property of the deity. The famous code of laws of Hammurabi lists laws of marriage similar to those of today. Although the father of the bridegroom paid the price of the bride, marriage was really more like a contract between man and wife. It is true that there were slaves, but a woman usually had economic independence and a good legal position with the right to be a scribe, judge, or witness. A married woman was permitted to take her husband's place and property. Some of the women who lived in the city of Babylon achieved considerable power and some girls became secretaries. The making and using of dyes were important household duties of a woman. Research work was carried on by both men and women. The wealthy woman was philanthropic and sometimes bestowed sums of money on each citizen of the city in which she lived. She gave money for the construction of public buildings and made contributions for the enjoyment of her fellow citizens. At times she presided at public games and over religious ceremonies.

The man in the Asiatic countries engaged in agriculture and in the arts and crafts, which were well established. The title of shepherd taken by the early Chaldean princes shows the importance given to the pastoral habits of the people. The traveling salesman held an essential place in life; raw materials brought into the country were manufactured into finished products and sold in the countries farther to the north and west. The banker was also very important and was vital to the successful financing of the various businesses of the country.

The Sumerian slave was not considered as an inferior since he had been usually a freeman captured from another country. He was given many rights, including that of purchasing his freedom.

DRESS

A. *Sources of information:* coins, engraved gems, monuments, sculpture from palaces, temples, tombs, and stelae, bronze, marble, and *fictile* vases, illustrations by J. J. J. Tissot, the French artist who visited Palestine in the 19th century and made a series of water colors of the life of the Old and the New Testament, from the landscape and people of the time and suggestions from ancient and new manuscripts.

B. MEN (*Early Babylonian, 1900-1600* B.C.)
   1. Garments:
      Outer upper: nude torso.
      Outer lower: skirt reaching to calf or ankle, sometimes of sheep skin.
      Cloaks and overgarments: shawl with or without fringe, of soft material worn over left shoulder.
   2. Hair: shaven head and upper lip, short chin-beard.
   3. Headdress: cap similar to fez.
   4. Footwear: barefoot.
   5. Accessories: walking stick or staff; wide belt; sword.
   6. Jewelry: gold and bronze bracelets and ornaments; chain with pendant of coin-like seal.
   7. Typical Colors: no doubt indigo, madder, and purple.
   8. Typical Materials: finely woven cloth of flax or wool.
   9. Make-up: apparently none.

C. WOMEN (*Early Babylonian, 1900-1600* B.C.)
   1. Garments:
      Outer upper and outer lower: scant garment to ankle; low neckline; unbelted tunic, short tight sleeve; later, ankle length dress with flounce.
      Cloaks and overgarments: fringed cape, gathered and tied at neck.
   2. Hair: low on forehead, separated in bandeaux and held down on the

34

forehead by a ribbon; elaborate coils or braids; thick, short braids pinned up over nape of neck when wearer was away from home; hair drawn back from ears occasionally, falling down in ringlets over shoulder; sometimes long hair braided with gold bands.

3. **Headdress:** crown with gold rings across forehead and triangular decoration in back composed of 7 long thin points each topped by a gold rosette; close-fitting cap with linen band or veil rolled around it; elaborate conical *tiara* worn by wealthy woman.

4. **Footwear:** usually barefoot.

5. **Accessories:** belt; hairpins.

6. **Jewelry:** gold rings, necklace of fine workmanship, beads of lapis, agate, onyx, and carnelian; gold and bronze bracelets, earrings and ornaments; brooch.

7. **Typical Colors:** Refer to *B. 7.*

8. **Typical Materials:** Refer to *B. 8.*

9. **Make-up:** eye emphasized by use of kohl on lid and at corner; skin made smooth with finely powdered pumice; white lead used on face.

D. MEN AND WOMEN (*Phrygian, 1100* B.C.)

1. **Garments:**
   Outer upper and outer lower: long, flowing or close-fitting tunic with long sleeve worn by woman; 2 tunics worn by man, knee-length undertunic with sleeve, outertunic reaching to hip or to knee; tight or loose *pantaloons* terminating at ankle.
   Cloaks and overgarments: fringed mantle fastening at right shoulder with brooch.

2. **Hair:** short bob, bang over forehead, full beard and mustache, by man; hair low on forehead with long curl on side extending almost to shoulder by woman.

3. **Headdress:** richly ornamented helmet with 2 or 4 flaps in the back. *Phrygian bonnet* or *cap* with band around head, point of cap made of leather or metal.

4. **Footwear:** half-boot laced across the front, sometimes with flying flaps.

5. **Accessories:** belt.

6. **Jewelry:** brooch; bracelets; silver, and gold ornaments.

7. **Typical Colors:** beautiful rich colors including purple.

8. **Typical Materials:** fine linen often embroidered in harmonious colors; mantle edged with beautiful designs or an all-over pattern; exquisite needlework; leather or skin of animal used for cap; flap on each side of cap or helmet often made from skin of leg of animal.

9. **Make-up:** apparently none.

D. MEN (*Hebrew, c. 1000 B.C.*)

    1. Garments:

        Outer upper: loin cloth only in the early part of the period; short-sleeved, ankle-length tunic, girded, fringed around the lower edge, later, 2 tunics; long outertunic with long sleeve, short undertunic; sleeved *cafton* or *kafton* with fringe or purple tassels; robe unseamed, left side held in place by cord.

        Outer lower: breeches of fine linen worn by priest and Levite.

        Under: long shirt-like tunic.

        Cloaks and overgarments: rectangular shawl, fringed along lower edge for king or high priest; mantle with purple tassel at each corner; voluminous mantle used for many purposes including covering of body, as a carpet, and carryall.

    2. Hair: ointment used to make hair glossy; semilong, sometimes braided in many braids or left in curls or waves; fairly long, neatly trimmed beard.

    3. Headdress: headcloth worn by shepherd; *miter;* cap with pointed top falling backward or forward, sometimes with brim, or drapery in back; *turban.*

    4. Footwear: barefoot; sandal; shoe extending to ankle.

    5. Accessories: inscriptions on parchment worn on forehead and wrist by devout man; highly ornamented girdle.

    6. Jewelry: usually none, sometimes in prosperous times of the Jewish kingdom, nose rings, necklaces, and gold chains adopted by some men.

    7. Typical Colors: many hues, especially purple.

    8. Typical Materials: goat's or camel's hair first used, later fine wool or very fine cotton; rich cloth woven with gold; stripes popular; first tunic of linen, second of wool; leather girdle, later of metal adorned with precious stones; richer and finer fabrics in the time of King David, 1000 B.C.

    9. Make-up: hair powdered with gold dust, worn by pages preceding Solomon on ceremonial occasion.

E. WOMEN (*Hebrew, c. 1000 B.C.*)

    1. Garments:

        Outer upper and outer lower: simple loose tunic to ankle, sometimes fringe or rich embroidery at neckline, girded at hip; sometimes tight-fitting tunic with girdle worn indoors; short sleeve or sleeveless; gown with long sleeve; later more voluminous costume, outergarment with sleeve to middle of hand.

        Cloaks and overgarments: large cape-like garment having huge sleeve.

        Under: undertunic or chemise to knee.

1. Mantle   2. Tunic   3. Shawl   4. Cidaris   5. Kandys
6. Kalasiris   7. Tiara   8. Phrygian Bonnet or Cap   9. Sandal

2. **Hair:** elaborate braids.
3. **Headdress:** head always covered; low or high cap covered with gold ornaments; very thin or coarse *veil*, sometimes covering entire head and face, with eyeholes permitting wearer to see, sometimes forehead and throat wrapped; cap of net, wool, cotton or gold thread, tassels at back, sometimes interspersed with gold beads or precious stones; cap also decorated with pearls.
4. **Footwear:** barefoot; sandal; shoe.
5. **Accessories:** sometimes fold of girdle served as purse; mirror of polished metal, including silver and copper; silver, gold, or ivory stick used for applying make-up to eyes.
6. **Jewelry:** gold, silver and other metals used in ornaments; rings set with rubies and emeralds, worn on all fingers; series of bracelets of gold or ivory sometimes worn from wrist to elbow; anklets; earrings sometimes worn along upper edge of ear; often drop earrings, cluster of grape-shaped ornaments on earring; necklaces of many rows of pearls; nose ring, sometimes a number worn; dangling ornaments of gold in hair; gold or silver pendants.
7. **Typical Colors:** purple or scarlet mantle, rich colors popular; purple border on outer tunic, gold embroidery; white or cream also used; yellow, purple, or crimson belt; sometimes gilt sandal; dark somber tones used by common people.
8. **Typical Materials:** linen, wool, and silk (the latter may have been introduced into Bible lands by merchants who brought it from India whence it had come from China); costliness of material distinguishing rank of wearer; thin muslin used first for outer garment, silk used later.
9. **Make-up:** custom of painting margins of eyelid with kohl adapted from Egyptian woman; eyebrows arched with inner ends meeting each other; hands colored with henna; perfumes and oils used.

F. MEN AND WOMEN (*Medes, 835-750 b.c.*)

1. **Garments:**
   Outer upper and outer lower: long-sleeved *kandys* of man held by girdle; foot-length tunic, gathered at front and side; coat-like garment; long tunic worn by woman.
   Cloaks and overgarments: purple cape worn by chief priests, the cut varying with rank.
2. **Hair:** enormous quantities of false hair.
3. **Headdress:** miter, sometimes highly embroidered; *aigrette* worn as ornament in hair by woman; hood with 2 strips, 1 falling over shoulder, and 1 down the back.
4. **Footwear:** shoe slit at instep and fitted with a tongue; richly embroi-

dered, laced boot worn by wealthy; leather boot, by common people.

5. **Accessories:** girdle; staff with gold knob used by priest.
6. **Jewelry:** chain; ankle bells worn by woman.
7. **Typical Colors:** brilliant colors including purple; white worn by priest with blue and white cord around cap; blue and white cord around cap also signified relative of the royal family; often light-colored boot.
8. **Typical Materials:** leather; coarse fabric; fine cloth of cotton and silk often beautifully embroidered.
9. **Make-up:** eyelid and eyebrow painted.

G. MEN (*Assyrian-Babylonian, 884-606* B.C.)
1. **Garments:**
   Outer upper and outer lower: girded tunic, low neckline; sleeved kalasiris for nobleman, long; short tunic for slave.
   Under: loin cloth.
   Cloaks and overgarments: richly embroidered shawl, sometimes worn without tunic, rectangular piece drawn under one arm, fastening with clasp on shoulder; sometimes, with opening for head and one arm; large, draped shawl for king; narrow fringed scarf similar to baldrick; extravagant use of fringe and tassels toward end of period; fringe indicative of rank; long fringed scarf crossed over breast, worn by prime minister; double fringed scarf, by master of ceremonies; short fringe, by king's attendants; scarf not worn by lesser officials.
2. **Hair:** black curly bushy hair, or wig, to shoulder; bang; fairly long, square-cut, bushy beard; mustache curled at ends.
3. **Headdress:** fillet; headbands crossing on temple forming a kind of bonnet; flat rings of graduated size with rosettes at center front, side, and back; bandeau with 2 cords descending from a rosette; pointed fez-like tiara of gorgeous fabric trimmed with scarlet; ornamental bands sometimes extending to waist, often trimmed at side with double bullock horns fastened against a lily; dome-shaped turban or miter for king or god; crown; white striped *diadem* and white claft; Phrygian bonnet or cap; fez worn by nonroyal person.
4. **Footwear:** barefoot, sandal, and high-laced boot; gold tassels or buckle on sandal.
5. **Accessories:** high collar; narrow belt over wide close-fitting leather belt; baldrick; girdle usually with tassels; mace or stick, 2 feet long with ornamental knob; fan; fly whisk; ebony comb; umbrella; long apron worn by some members of the priesthood.
6. **Jewelry:** large, heavy earrings; bracelet; armlet; rings; gold collar.

7. **Typical Colors:** white, black, Tyrian purple, red, and gold; all-over pattern and border.
8. **Typical Materials:** elaborately embroidered cloth; linen; wool; dressed leather. Assyria famous for beautiful weaving.
9. **Make-up:** eyelids and eyebrows no doubt painted.

H. WOMEN (*Assyrian-Babylonian, 884-606* B.C.)
1. Garments:
   Outer upper and outer lower: long tunic with 3-quarter length sleeve, belted or unbelted, low neckline, similar to type worn by man.
   Cloaks and overgarments: fringed, rectangular shawl draped over right shoulder.
2. **Hair:** Grecian influence; braids and waves; long bushy bob; sometimes arranged in a knot, mass of curls, or in symmetrical rolls.
3. **Headdress:** veil; fillet or crown for royalty.
4. **Footwear:** barefoot or sandal; high laced boot for hunting.
5. **Accessories:** belt with clasp.
6. **Jewelry:** close-fitting necklace resembling *dog collar;* gold collar similar to the one worn by man; large heavy earring; bracelet; armlet.
7. **Typical Colors:** refer to *F. 7.*
8. **Typical Materials:** refer to *F. 8.*
9. **Make-up:** rare perfume; pungent oils and cosmetics; hair, hands, and nails colored with henna.

I. MEN (*Persian, 550-330* B.C.)
1. **Garments:**
   Outer upper: tunic belted or unbelted, extending to knee or longer, sleeveless or with wrist-length, set-in sleeve.
   Outer lower: tight-fitting trousers.
   Cloaks and overgarments: girded long or short robe, similar to the one worn by the Egyptian, fullness often under the arm.
2. **Hair:** enormous bushy wig of curled hair, shorter than Assyrian; sometimes with long braids worn over shoulder; round or pointed beard joined to thick mustache.
3. **Headdress:** band or fillet 3 inches wide sometimes worn low on forehead; king's crown wider at top; domed hat with ribbon hanging in the back; also deep cap covering neck and entire head except the face; later, turban; *cidaris;* hood with peak standing straight up, falling back, or omitted entirely by servant, warrior, or hunter.
4. **Footwear:** barefoot, soft shoe, or moccasin having turned-up toe; sometimes piece of leather wrapped around foot and tied over instep; type of low heel shoe protected the foot from the burning sands.

5. **Accessories:** walking stick; umbrella; fly whisk; cane rod carried by priest; javelin; knife.
6. **Jewelry:** used sparingly; earrings; chain; gold collar.
7. **Typical Colors:** purple robe lined with white; yellow, yellow-green, blue, or blue-green.
8. **Typical Materials:** tanned hide used at first, later, linen.
9. **Make-up:** perfume.

J. WOMEN (*Persian, 550-330 B.C.*)

1. **Garments:**
   Outer upper: longer and wider tunic than that worn by man, closed in front and girded with fringed sash; very voluminous in latter part of period.
   Outer lower: breeches to knee or ankle at first; very full pantaloons in later period.
   Cloaks and overgarments: fringed scarf or cape; scarf fringed on both ends and side.
2. **Hair:** hair falling about shoulders, usually covered by a veil.
3. **Headdress:** fully veiled; head and shoulder covered.
4. **Footwear:** barefoot, or soft shoe with turned-up toe.
5. **Accessories:** sash with fringe.
6. **Jewelry:** necklace, bracelet, earrings, ring, ankle bells.
7. **Typical Colors:** refer to *I. 7.*
8. **Typical Materials:** leather; thin fabric used for full trousers. Refer to *I. 8.*
9. **Make-up:** eyelid and eyebrow painted.

K. MEN AND WOMEN (*Scythian*)

1. **Garments:**
   Outer upper: coat open in front and held by girdle or tucked under trousers; low neckline; sleeve full but tight at wrist.
   Outer lower: lower leg of breeches confined in top of boot.
   Cloaks and overgarments: large shawl.
2. **Hair:** man wore rather long hair and beard.
3. **Headdress:** pointed cap or cap-shaped piece of cloth worn by man; long veil worn by woman.
4. **Footwear:** soft boot laced in front; sandal.
5. **Accessories:** bow and arrow, spear, dagger, and sword used by man.
6. **Jewelry:** bracelet of gold for wealthy; torque; brooch.
7. **Typical Colors:** blue, green, red, yellow, and purple.
8. **Typical Materials:** leather, fur, wool and felt; fringe trimming; fine cloth in voluminous costume of woman.
9. **Make-up:** face painted.

L. MEN AND WOMEN (*Amazon*)

1. **Garments:**
   Outer upper: short vest with long sleeve; outertunic, sleeveless, close-fitting or full; clasp on shoulder; tunic girded if too long or when fighting.
   Outer lower: pantaloons of same material as vest, held in top of shoe or sandal; skirt worn over long pantaloons by woman; short skirt worn in the home; pantaloons of skin worn during warfare.
   Cloaks and overgarments: voluminous mantle.
2. **Hair:** medium length.
3. **Headdress:** similar to Phrygian bonnet, metal helmet of same shape, jagged crest of ancient animal of mythology on back of cap; helmet ending in shape of bill of a griffin.
4. **Footwear:** richly ornamented shoe encircling entire foot, laced up front.
5. **Accessories:** girdle; bow and arrow; spear.
6. **Jewelry:** brooch.
7. **Typical Colors:** likely similar to those of neighboring Asiatic countries.
8. **Typical Materials:** fine fabric embroidered or painted in stripes, zigzags, dots or checks.
9. **Make-up:** apparently none.

M. MEN AND WOMEN (*Parthian*)

1. **Garments:**
   Outer upper: sleeved coat, sleeveless shirt.
   Outer lower: trousers.
   Cloaks and overgarments: many coats worn at one time; very long sleeve.
2. **Hair:** man with long hair and beard.
3. **Headdress:** miter or cylindrical cap, wider at top than bottom; Phrygian cap; round or pointed headdress; veil fastened to headdress and falling down the back, worn by woman.
4. **Footwear:** leather sandal, shoe, or boot.
5. **Accessories:** refer to *I. 5.*
6. **Jewelry:** emblematic ornament; refer to *I. 6.*
7. **Typical Colors:** reddish purple shoe; gay colors worn by upper class.
8. **Typical Materials:** softer and finer fabrics used by woman than by man.
9. **Make-up:** man with elaborately curled beard; woman noted for her beauty, no doubt used eye shadow and paint.

CHAPTER 3: MOTIFS

SIGNIFICANT MOTIFS

Motifs of the various countries can scarcely be distinguished from each other. The Assyrian designs included the bull, lion, and eagle; palm, date, fig, and fir trees; vine, fern, and tall grass; also copies and variations of the winged globe, lotus or lily, and rosette found in Egyptian ornamentation. The Chaldean and Babylonian ornamentation included the winged bull with a human head and other designs characteristic of those found in Assyrian decoration. The Persian designs showed adaptations of the motifs found in Egyptian, Assyrian, Babylonian, and Grecian decoration. In addition to designs which showed the influence of those of Egypt, Assyria, Babylon, and Persia, the Hebrews used stripes and geometrical designs.

INFLUENCES ON LATER COSTUMES

Beautiful fabrics of gold and other costly material; color and line of garment shown later in medieval dress; trousers and fitted jacket of all later periods; aigrette worn in hair, 1775, shows influence of Asia Minor; fringe, 1850, 1907, and late 1920's, '30's, and '40's; printed fabrics of various periods; turban; shoe with heel in later centuries; stocking cap, 20th century, shows influence of Phrygian cap; dog collar, 5th-11th century, 1850's, '90's, 1900's, '40's, and '50's.

BOOKS OF REFERENCE

(See also GENERAL BIBLIOGRAPHY, p. 433)

De Quincy, Thomas, *Theological Essays and Other Papers,* Chapter on "Toilette of the Hebrew Lady," Vol. II (Boston, Ticknor, Reed and Fields, 1854)

Hope, Thomas, *Costume of the Ancients* (London, J. Murray, 1908)

Houston, Mary G., and Hornblower, *Ancient Egyptian, Assyrian and Persian Costumes and Decorations* (London, A. and C. Black, Ltd., 1920)

Tissot, J. J. J., *The Life of Our Lord Jesus Christ* (New York, American Art Assn., 1902)

——, *The Old Testament* (Paris, M. de Brunoff, 1904)

Wright, Marion Logan, *Biblical Costume with Adaptations for Use in Plays* (London, Society for Promoting Christian Knowledge, 1936)

GLOSSARY

Aigrette—feather or plume of the egret, a kind of heron.

Baldrick—strap or narrow scarf worn over shoulder and across body, usually to support a sword. Refer to *Chap. 1*.

Cafton or Kafton—coat-like, fringed garment sewed down each side and tied in front, worn by Hebrew.

Cape—refer to *Chap. 2*.

Cidaris—truncated cone-shaped headdress, ornamented with a band or fold at its base. *Pl. V, 4*.

Claft—refer to *Chap. 2*.

Diadem—mitre-like headdress wider and higher toward front, having decoration of rosettes. A white, striped diadem was worn by the royalty.

Dog Collar—close-fitting necklace, worn later in 18th, 19th, and 20th centuries.

Fictile—molded pottery.

Kalasiris—close-fitting one-piece shirt of very fine cloth, fastened with a girdle and worn by the Babylonian and Assyrian. Refer to *Chap. 2. Pl. V, 6*.

Kandys—extremely long garment, with funnel-shaped skirt held by girdle, worn by Mede. *Pl. V, 5*.

Kohl—refer to *Chap. 2*.

Lotus—refer to *Chap. 2*.

Mantle—loose, sleeveless outergarment. Refer to *Chap. 2. Pl. V, 1*.

Miter—high headdress, wider at the top than at the bottom.

Moccasin—refer to *Chap. 1*.

Pantaloons—full, long trousers, gathered at ankle.

Phrygian Bonnet or Cap—cap with point which bent forward. *Pl. V, 8*.

Sandal—type of shoe with sole strapped to foot. Refer to *Chaps. 1, 2. Pl. V, 9*.

Shawl—oblong outergarment, draped diagonally from left shoulder and under right arm. Refer to *Chap. 2. Pl. V, 3*.

Tiara—very elaborate, miter-like headdress worn on important occasions. One type of tiara was decorated at the base with a band of jewel-framed rosettes, and had 1 or 2 bands set on top. Another tiara was cylindrical and covered with rosettes. *Pl. V, 7*.

Tunic—body garment of various lengths and fabrics. Refer to *Chap. 2. Pl. V, 2*.

Turban—headdress of cloth, wound around the head.

Veil—thin cloth draped over the head and occasionally over the face; an expression of modesty.

Winged Globe—refer to *Chap. 2*.

Greece

CHRONOLOGY

MINOAN OR CRETAN PERIOD (2800-1200 B.C.): The Aegean Civilizations. Two dynasties, Cnossus and Phaestus. Hieroglyphic writing, c. 2300 B.C. Linear script replaced the hieroglyphic, after 1600 B.C. Portrayal of this civilization in the *Iliad* and *Odyssey*. Dorians came, c. 1100 B.C., introduced the Iron Age.

HOMERIC OR ARCHAIC PERIOD (1200-510 B.C.): Monarchies replaced by aristocracies except in Sparta. Land monopolized by nobles. Alphabet introduced. Greek colonization. Homeric poems, c. 800 B.C. Olympic Festival founded 775 B.C.

HELLENIC PERIOD (510-336 B.C.): Persian Wars 499-478 B.C. Golden Age 450-400 B.C. High perfection reached in architecture, art, and poetry. Great dramatists in Athens. Temple of Athena Niké erected, c. 435 B.C. Erecktheum, 435-408 B.C. Peloponnesian Wars between Sparta and Athens. The First War, 460-446 B.C. The Great Peloponnesian War, 421-404 B.C. Downfall of Athens. Defeat of Greeks by Philip of Macedon at Chaeronea, 338 B.C.

HELLENISTIC PERIOD (336-146 B.C.): Including Alexandrian Period, 337-323 B.C., named for Alexander the Great. 4th Century distinguished by great orators and philosophers. Italy invaded by Hannibal of Carthage, who crossed the Alps, 218 B.C. Conquest of Greece by Romans, 146 B.C.

CHAPTER 4

Greece

HISTORY

The early Cretans, also known as Minoans, dominated the peninsula of Greece and nearby islands. A wealth of material has been found in Cnossus in Crete which gives us an idea of the life of these people. Some of the Neolithic remains found at Cnossus are even older than the predynastic remains in Egypt. During Dynasty XII in Egypt, there was extensive trade between these two centers of civilizations; goods were transported by ships propelled by sails and oars.

The Cretans were seafarers as early as 3000 B.C. As a people, they did not come to full development until unified under one ruler, about 2500 B.C. Free from invasion, they were able to develop their culture, and made great contributions to civilization in architecture, pottery, jewelry, and fine textiles. Bathrooms, drain pipes, and other conveniences indicate their high degree of advancement. Under King Minos, whose palace was in Cnossus, Cretan civilization reached its climax. Their culture spread, and such cities as Mycenae, Tiryns, and Troy were founded. There were trade relations with Egypt, Syria, and Mesopotamia. This splendid era came to a close, however, when the Dorians, a less civilized and more warlike people, swept across Crete and by 1100 B.C., conquered the Aegean world.

The costume, found on the island of Crete, was different from that of any other Grecian period. Except for the low neckline, woman's dress can be identified with a similar garment worn in the middle of the 19th century.

As the Dorians conquered the lands about the Aegean Sea, they assimilated many elements of Cretan civilization. Their voyages brought them in contact with the Egyptian, Babylonian, and Assyrian cultures. A monumental architecture developed in the early part of the period, and sculpture and pottery also reached a high state of excellence. The Ionians settled in Attica and evolved an individual art. They

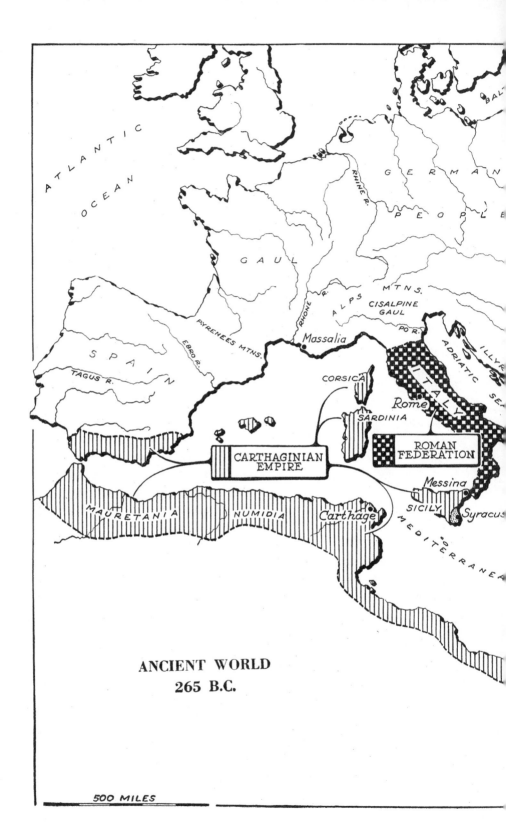

ATLANTIC OCEAN

GERMAN PEOPLE

BALT

RHINE R.

GAUL

MTNS.

ALPS

CISALPINE GAUL

PO R.

ILLYR

RHONE R.

Massalia

PYRENEES MTNS.

EBRO R.

SPAIN

TAGUS R.

CORSICA

SARDINIA

ADRIATIC SEA

ITALY

Rome

CARTHAGINIAN
EMPIRE

ROMAN
FEDERATION

MAURETANIA

NUMIDIA

Carthage

Messina

SICILY

Syracus

MEDITERRANEA

ANCIENT WORLD
265 B.C.

500 MILES

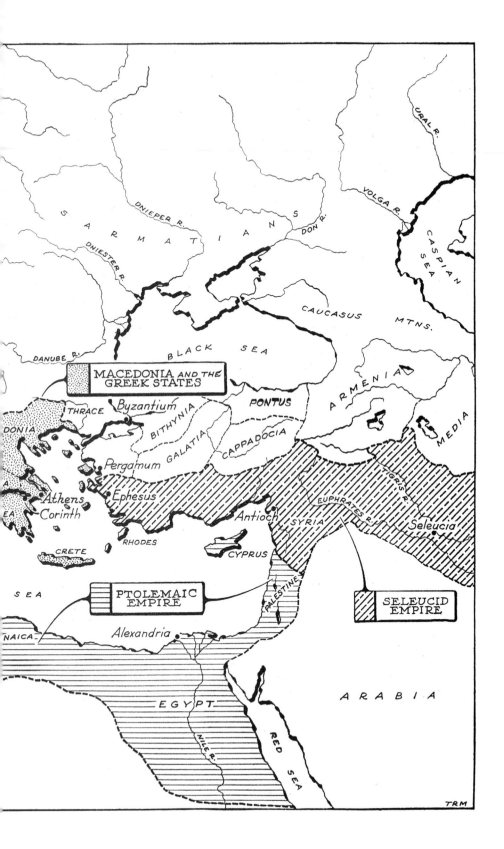

were artists, poets, and philosophers in contrast to the Dorians who were soldiers and practical men of affairs.

The Homeric Period (1200-510 B.C.) was marked by the introduction of the alphabet, the beginning of Homeric poetry, and the great Greek colonization which was encouraged by the aristocrats and landowners. Due to the discontent among the landless people, the leaders in Greece advised them to settle on distant shores. The colonies that were established not only engaged in agriculture but developed commerce enterprises. In the Hellenic Period (510-336 B.C.) Athens became the center of Western civilization, and art and culture reached its highest development. Commerce and industry flourished. History lists many important names of this time: Herodotus, historian; Aeschylus, Euripides, Aristophanes, dramatists; Myron and Phidias, sculptors; Socrates and Plato, philosophers. The Hellenistic Period that followed (336-146 B.C.) included the Alexandrian era (337-323 B.C.). The latter was dominated by Alexander the Great, Macedonian King, who founded the city of Alexandria in 331 B.C. and became King of Persia after his successful invasion of that country. The great cultural era of philosophy, literature, and art ended with the death of Alexander. His general, Ptolemy, founded the Ptolemaic Dynasty which lasted in Egypt until the death of Cleopatra in 30 B.C. The Gauls from the West raided Macedonia and Greece about 277 B.C., crossing Asia Minor to settle in Phrygia. The Romans appeared later and conquered Corinth, bringing Greek independence to an end.

Throughout the Grecian period the lines of the costume remained similar. The exquisite quality and beauty of cloth distinguished the Homeric Age; the cut and manner of wearing garments were significant later. Although many tunics were often worn at one time, a sumptuary law regulated the number of tunics to three or less when they were worn to funerals or festivals. The influence of the luxury of the Orient and of Byzantium was reflected in elaborate embroideries and jewels.

During Homeric times, the life of the woman was free and dignified. She stayed close to her household where she exercised a certain amount of authority, taking charge of the affairs of her husband when he was off at war. A woman was forbidden to enter the professions. A case is cited of one woman who posed as a man and became a famous physician but when she was found out by jealous male rivals they brought a lawsuit against her. This resulted in an amendment to the law which made it legal for women to practice medicine. The making of clothes, weaving, and embroidery occupied the time of women of high rank.

As life became more luxurious and intellectual interests dominated Athens the woman did not have the opportunity to participate in the social life of her husband. By the time of the Golden Age of Pericles, her life had become that of a cloistered slave. Before she was married at the age of sixteen or seventeen she had seen and heard little of life. She seldom left the house and if she did, she was always accompanied. Although she could attend religious festivals and family gatherings she seldom was allowed by her husband to be in the public eye. While keeping his wife sequestered the husband sought more intellectual and lively companionship with the hetaerae, a class of independent, educated women of Athens. These women were usually foreigners who were not permitted to marry men who were citizens of Greece. One of the most famous of this class was Aspasia whose salon was frequented by all the great men of the time. She was not only intelligent but a charming personality and a leader of fashion who wore her costume in a distinctive way. It is said that a few of her male friends introduced their wives to her and that she urged them to seek to improve themselves intellectually so that they could be better companions of their husbands.

The Dorians were only at the pastoral stage of development when they invaded the Cretan territories. Soon after they were in their new environment, the Dorian man took over the duties of farming, various types of handicraft, and engaged in commerce. The majority of the inhabitants worked in agriculture, producing animal products, vegetables and grains, cultivating olive trees for oil and grape vines for wine. All forms of manual labor, commerce, and business were considered degrading by the aristocratic Athenian; work of this kind was left to their social inferiors.

DRESS

A. *Sources of information:* frescoes from Cnossos, frieze of the Parthenon, and temple of Zeus, paintings, pottery, sculpture, monuments, Tanagra figures, medals, and literature.

B. MEN (*Minoan or Cretan Period, 2800-1200* B.C.)
   1. Garments:
      Outer upper and outer lower: loin cloth.

Under: loin cloth.

Cloaks and overgarments: short mantle or cape fastened at one shoulder.

2. **Hair:** hair often concealed by helmet; looped and knotted with hair-pin at top extending through metal helmet; short hair signified mourning.
3. **Headdress:** helmet and broad-brimmed hat.
4. **Footwear:** richly embroidered shoe and half-boot with heel of moderate height.
5. **Accessories:** dagger inlaid with golden figures worn in broad belt.
6. **Jewelry:** necklace; rings; bracelets for wrist and upper arm; jeweled pin on mantle.
7. **Typical Colors:** gay colors; blue-black, purplish-brown, white, yellow-green, gray, and white.
8. **Typical Materials:** patterned fabric used for loin cloth.
9. **Make-up:** apparently none.

C. WOMEN (*Minoan or Cretan, 2800-1200* B.C.)
   1. **Garments:**
      Outer upper: short-sleeved bodice, low neckline, very small waist.
      Outer lower: ankle-length, bell-shaped skirt with flounces.
   2. **Hair:** several strands of curled hair to waist, remainder of hair in elaborate knot.
   3. **Headdress:** tall-crowned, narrow-brimmed hat.
   4. **Footwear:** shoe with moderately high heel; often barefoot.
   5. **Accessories:** ornamental stick pin; beautiful gold buttons.
   6. **Jewelry:** long string of beads; golden necklace; ring; bracelet for wrist or upper arm.
   7. **Typical Colors:** refer to B. 7.
   8. **Typical Materials:** patterned cloth.
   9. **Make-up:** apparently none.

D. MEN (*Homeric or Archaic, 1200-510* B.C.)
   1. **Garments:**
      Outer upper and outer lower: long *chiton* worn by young and old at first; then knee-length Ionic chiton, sometimes open down one side with the edges fringed; later, open side sewed; by 5th century B.C., similar to woman's Ionic chiton with portion on upper arm gathered; later, long chiton worn only by older man, by the 5th century B.C., short chiton for young man; double-girded Doric chiton, worn by athlete; chiton shaped or cut away under arm; crinkled chiton also used; *kolpos; apotygma; kolobus.*
      Cloaks and overgarments: himation sometimes worn alone with no

1. Caul   2. Cap with Small Brim   3. Phrygian Cap   4. Pilos   5. Fillet
6. Doric Chiton   7. Ionic Chiton   8. Ephebi, Sandal   9. Ceryphalos

other garment, the only garment worn by philosopher or very learned man; *chlamys* introduced, c. 500 B.C.; *ephebi.*

2. **Hair:** long hair usually done up in braids, knot, curls, or coil, and held by band; long braids crossed in back, the 2 ends fastened in front; short hair above forehead combed to conceal ears; long hair worn by elderly man; hair cut in honor of the dead; short hair worn by athlete; beard of soft wavy curls or stiff and pointed, without mustache, young man beardless.

3. **Headdress:** *petasus; pilos;* Phrygian cap; fillet, net or kerchief, or wide bands worn by athletes and charioteers; purple petasus draped with white scarf, signifying royalty; brim of petasus sometimes in 4 sections, with 2 turned up; small skull cap under helmet of warrior; himation and chlamys often thrown over head, *stephane.*

4. **Footwear:** generally very elaborate; barefoot, or sandal worn in the house; sandal with straps wrapped around leg; ankle-height shoe, often laced from foot to top of shoe; shoe probably made on last, construction of right and left shoes followed the shape of the foot; high boot for horseman and hunter; boot with large tongue; *buskin; cothurnus; carabitina.*

5. **Accessories:** long walking stick; utilitarian glove for boxing, gardening, eating hot food and kneading bread; wax tablet or roll and stylus; olive wreath over woolen fillet signifying victor in Olympics; ivy wreath for winner of recitations honoring Dionysus, and victor in dramatic contests; laurel and parsley for bard, orator and poet; myrtle wreath for Aphrodite, goddess of love, and as an emblem of peace and plenty; olive for Athena, goddess of the arts; oak leaves for Zeus, king of earth and air, also worn at religious festival; garland of wild parsley worn at funeral; wreath of fresh flowers, worn by man at banquet; sunshade sometimes used by dandy.

6. **Jewelry:** beautiful workmanship, yellow gold, silver, and bronze; usually not set with jewels; plain gold band worn by royalty, jeweled band for king, lord, and various divinities; *fibula* and stephane decorated with jewels; seal ring; gold pins and ornament worn in hair, before 5th century B.C.

7. **Typical Colors:** various bright colors for chiton and himation, saffron, blue, and Tyrian or red-purple dye from the mullusk; red and yellow, at border of apotygma and tunic; other colors used were dark red, brilliant red, and vermilion; blue, in paintings, but not in dyes; indigo, yellow ochre, emerald green, veridian, apple green, gray, brown, and black; white for aristocracy; black, purple, dark green, and gray for mourning; green, gray, and brown worn by peasant; white, real gold, and silver used in embroidery; later, colors in the Hellenic Period less vivid, spotlessness, sign of good breeding;

plain colors or all white used; gold, saffron, and purple, purple cothurnus; gilded sandal worn by nobility; yellow, white, red, and natural-colored sandal, by others.

8. **Typical materials:** expertly woven cloth, horizontal and upright looms used; linen, wool, and hemp for chiton; Doric chiton, at first of wool, Ionic chiton, or semitransparent material of silk or linen; cloth used in garments made by the mistress and daughters of the house and by the maid servants; all-over patterns on cloth, painted, dyed, or embroidered; sometimes, painted or gold-decorated borders embroidered or woven into garment; narrow gold plates and pliable wire worked into material; fret borders, and all-over patterns of sprigs, flowers, and leaves, woven into woolen or crinkled linen cloth; forms of domesticated animals and wild beasts also used in designs which were copied from the Persian weaver who in turn had taken the idea from India; later, transparent linen woven in olive oil; coarse woolen and hemp; some furs worn, skin of lion, leopard, and goat.

9. **Make-up:** great care used in being well groomed; manicure, perfume.

E. WOMEN (*Homeric or Archaic, 1200-510* B.C.)

1. **Garments:**
    Outer upper and outer lower: short or long *peplos*, forerunner of chiton, 1200-600 B.C.; long chiton; Doric chiton, 550 B.C.-A.D. 100, girded or ungirded, narrow at first; natural waist line; chiton sometimes ornamented with scrolls and dots; double girded chiton worn by Spartan woman; Ionic chiton, 600 B.C.-A.D. 200; crinkled Ionic chiton, more transparent than Doric type; sometimes, Doric chiton worn over Ionic chiton; kolpos; apotygma.
    Under: strophion; undertunic.
    Cloaks and overgarments: elaborately draped himation; chlamys, sometimes twisted and worn as girdle; *diplax; diploidon;* skin of leopard or other animal worn by huntress.

2. **Hair:** stiffly waved on forehead, giving effect of scalloped edge; side ringlets and coronet of stiff curls on forehead, with hair hanging down back and over shoulder in snake-like curls, often held in place by fillet.

3. **Headdress:** sometimes unadorned; fillet or wreath worn around head; fillet narrow at first, later becoming wider; miter worn by lady of rank; tiara; diadem; *ampyx; ceryphalos; bandeau;* stephane; petasus worn as protection from sun; Phrygian cap; veil or small chlamys draped over the head; flame-colored, semitransparent veil held in place by gold fillet, worn by bride; himation worn pulled up over the head, as a head or face covering; head covered for mourning

and for performing sacrifices; veil worn with peplos; gold ribbon or string of pearls wrapped around head several times.

4. **Footwear:** often barefoot; shoes, when worn, usually the most costly article of feminine dress; low open-work shoe; wooden or leather sole with thongs worn in earliest times; strip covering toes, used later; decorated or soft sandal; high-heeled sandal occasionally used to increase height.

5. **Accessories:** mirror and vanity case; courtesan distinguishable by hand-mirror; long-handled fan of leaves or feathers, carried by slave; fan showing Egyptian, Assyrian, or Persian influence, later of linen or silk, always with a long handle; parasol of linen or silk, smaller than those used by the Assyrian and the Persian, also used over sacrifice, and chariot; girdle of beautiful and intricate metal work; ornamental hairpins of gold or carved ivory; *stiletto* to hold hair in place.

6. **Jewelry:** yellow gold, worked in beautiful and intricate designs; good taste used in wearing jewelry; pearl or amber necklace; gold, silver, or bronze bracelet, shaped like a snake; plain or jeweled ring; pendant earrings; engraving on semiprecious stones, such as onyx, and jasper; stones not often set in jewelry until the following period; stickpin fastening chiton in early times, later, fibula.

7. **Typical Colors:** refer to *D. 7.*
8. **Typical Materials:** refer to *D. 8.*
9. **Make-up:** white lead; false hair dyed different colors, including gold and silver; a salve used to soften and clean the skin; rouge of vegetable dye and red lead; oils and powders, perfume.

F. MEN (*Hellenic, 510-336* B.C.)

1. Garments:

    Outer upper and outer lower: short chiton worn by all classes, fastened over left arm or pinned at intervals down the arm; sometimes part covering upper arm, sewed or buttoned; long chiton worn by elderly man, charioteer and man participating in a religious sacrifice; kolobus with long close-fitting sleeve, very fashionable; long sleeve showing Persian influence considered barbaric by some people. Refer to *D. 1.*
    Cloaks and overgarments: refer to *D. 1.*

2. **Hair:** fairly short hair fashionable, after 5th century B.C.; sometimes resembled a short bob; hair bound with fillet; short hair for athlete; whiskers worn by young man; small patch of hair on each cheek, resembling sideburns, 5th century B.C. by young man.

3. **Headdress:** refer to *D. 3.*
4. **Footwear:** refer to *D. 4.*

56

1. Bandeau   2. Himation   3. Splendone   4. Sakkos   5. Nimbus
6. Chlamys   7. Sandal   8. Cothurnus   9. Peplos, Veil   10. Boot

5. **Accessories:** refer to *D. 5.*
6. **Jewelry:** usually limited to 1 engraved seal ring. Refer to *D. 6.*
7. **Typical Colors:** refer to *D. 7.*
8. **Typical Materials:** cotton and silk not common, velvet and felt introduced from India and the Far East, 4th century B.C.; fine wool and linen used by higher class; crinkled linen for chiton, 430 B.C.; flax woven in oil to give glossy effect, finer and thinner cloth sometimes woven in the shape of the garment, 5th century B.C.
9. **Make-up:** refer to *D. 9.*

G. WOMEN (*Hellenic, 510-336* B.C.)

1. **Garments:** -
   Outer upper and outer lower: girdle worn over hip in this period. Refer to *E. 1.*
   Under: strophion; sometimes tunic of Ionic character worn as undertunic.
   Cloaks and overgarments: entire body often enveloped by the himation. Refer to *E. 1.*
2. **Hair:** side ringlets discarded; lowest forehead possible considered beautiful, high forehead denoting old age; hair usually worn high after the Persian wars; hair confined by band around head, upper portion falling out in curls at back; *psyche knot.*
3. **Headdress:** scarf; fillet; *splendone; sakkos; nimbus;* veil of rich filmy fabrics of various colors; gold band, or ribbon wound around head; sometimes, kerchief folded with wide part beneath the knot and points tied over the forehead.
4. **Footwear:** refer to *E. 4.*
5. **Accessories:** refer to *E. 5.*
6. **Jewelry:** jewels and gems not in general use; strings of pearls wound several times around head. Refer to *E. 6.*
7. **Typical Colors:** rose with a gold girdle for bride; refer to *D. 7.*
8. **Typical Materials:** refer to *D. 8.*
9. **Make-up:** refer to *E. 9.*

H. MEN (*Hellenistic, 336-146* B.C.)

1. **Garments:**
   Outer upper and outer lower: combination of Doric and Ionic dress. Refer to *D. 1.* and *F. 1.*
   Cloaks and overgarments: refer to *D. 1.*
2. **Hair:** fairly short and wavy; later, long hair and beard worn by old man, philosopher, high official and professional man; short hair popular, long hair considered effeminate by young man in latter part of period; fashion of shaving the face introduced by Alexander

the Great; beard and mustache still worn by philosopher and general.

3. **Headdress:** gold crown by king, purple scarf, draped white veil, and petasus with purple and white scarf worn by king, red petasus, by military man of rank; pilos; Phrygian cap sometimes worn; skull-cap of felt, beneath helmet; *cap with brim;* fold of himation or chlamys sometimes used as head covering.
4. **Footwear:** refer to *D. 4.*
5. **Accessories:** gold scepter and sword, set with precious stones. Refer to *D. 5.*
6. **Jewelry:** precious stones including diamond, ruby, topaz, emerald, carbuncle, pearl, onyx, opal; earring on one ear only, worn by fashionable youth. Refer to *D. 6.*
7. **Typical Colors:** refer to *D. 7.*
8. **Typical Materials:** fabrics as in former periods; lavish use of figured cloth; later, plain and finer fabrics; silk more transparent, sometimes woven with gold threads; leather, linen, or wool; caste shown by various methods of draping; new conquests brought rich fabrics from other countries, especially beautiful silk.
9. **Make-up:** refer to *D. 9.*

I. WOMEN (*Helenistic, 336-146* B.C.)
   1. **Garments:**
      Outer upper and outer lower: girdle high under arm; combination of Doric and Ionic chitons, separate long sleeve added. Refer to *E. 1.*
      Under: refer to *G. 1.*
      Cloaks and overgarments: refer to *E. 1.*
   2. **Hair:** close to head, waved off forehead, with knot at back or braids in funnel or cornucopia fashion; hair hanging loosely with wreath or fillet worn by young girl; curls tied at crown of head by maiden; hair parted in center and arranged in a psyche or classic knot by married woman; hair held in place by stiletto, also twisted or braided and covered with a *caul;* sometimes fastened with double or triple bands of ribbon.
   3. **Headdress:** *caul,* diadem.
   4. **Footwear:** sometimes claws or muzzle of animal falling from top of boot; shoe or half-boot sometimes lined with fur. Refer to *E. 4.*
   5. **Accessories:** refer to *E. 5.*
   6. **Jewelry:** filigree; cameo, *intaglio;* stones set in jewelry. Refer to *E. 6.*
   7. **Typical Colors:** refer to *D. 7.*
   8. **Typical Materials:** refer to *D. 8.*
   9. **Make-up:** hair dyed saffron or red. Refer to *E. 9.*

SIGNIFICANT MOTIFS

The *acanthus, anthemion,* honeysuckle, scroll, *guilloche,* egg and dart, bead and reel, laurel, waterleaf, ivy, medallion; designs in the motif of man, animal, or bird, rosette, key or fret, *dentil,* wave, and *meander.*

INFLUENCES ON LATER COSTUMES

Motifs of this period often used in decorations of later years; hair styles and garments of this time later adopted by the Romans and by the French at the time of the French Revolution; influence shown in hair arrangement, 1820; draped skirt, 1880 and drapery used after 2nd World War showed the Grecian influence; modern corset adapted from triple bands worn by Grecian woman; modern safety pin similar to the fibula; tunic and drapery in evening and day dress, 1908 showed Grecian influence; cowl neckline of present day influenced by drapery of the Grecian chiton; neckline showing soft folds, 1931; general lines of dress and draping, hairdress, bloused bodice, and pleated sleeve, 1935 and 1940's; influence of Ionic chiton, 1938; net to confine the hair used in the Roman Period, Middle Ages, 1860, and 20th century.

BOOKS OF REFERENCE

(See also GENERAL BIBLIOGRAPHY, p. 433)

Abrahams, Ethel B., *Greek Dress* (London, J. Murray, 1908)

Allen, J. T., *Stage Antiquities of the Greeks and Romans and Their Influence* (New York, Longmans, Green and Co., 1927)

Curtis, C. D., *Sardis,* Vol. XIII, *Jewelry and Gold Work* (Rome, Syndacato Italiano Artigrafich, 1925)

Gall, Rob, *Wandtafein zur Veranschaulichung des Lebens der Grieschen und Römer* (Vienna and Leipzig, A. P. Witwe and Sohn, 1913)

Hope, Thomas, *Costumes of the Ancients* (London, Henry G. Bohn, 1841)

Horn, Rudolf, *Stehende Weibliche Gewandstatuen in der Hellenistischen Plastik* (München, F. Bruckmann, 1931)

Houston, Mary Galway, *Ancient Greek, Roman and Byzantine Costume,* Vol. 2 (London, A. and C. Black, Ltd., 1931)

McClees, Helen, *The Daily Life of the Greeks and Romans* (New York, The Metropolitan Museum of Art, 1928)

Norris, Herbert, *Costume and Fashion,* Vol. 1 (New York, E. P. Dutton and Co., 1925)

Perrot and Chipiez, *History of Art in Primitive Greece* (London, Chapman and Hall, Ltd., 1894)

GLOSSARY

Acanthus—prickly herb-like plant used as a decoration.
Ampyx—metal diadem or snood resembling a cap worn on the back or front of head and ending in a tie or band.
Anthemion—plant with radiating petals used as a decoration.
Apotygma—folded upper portion of the chiton.
Bandeau—band of ribbon or metal which held the hair in place. *Pl. VII, 1.*
Boot—type of shoe. Refer to *Pl. VII, 10.*
Buskin—kind of boot worn upon the stage by an actor of tragedy.
Cap with Brim—cap with narrow brim. Refer to *Pl. VI, 2.*
Cape—refer to *Chaps. 2, 3.*
Carabitina—sandal with separate large toe, worn by peasant.
Caul—net which held the hair in place at the back. *Pl. VI, 1.*
Ceryphalos—bandage-shaped fillet which fitted snugly around the head. *Pl. VI, 9.*
Chiton—form of linen, cotton, or woolen tunic which may have been of Asiatic origin. The Doric chiton had an overfold and fastened on the shoulder. At first, it was held at the side with brooches and later was sewed at the side to just below the armpit. The Ionic chiton of the woman had no overfold, although occasionally a false overfold was added. This garment was girded in various ways and had a full sleeve fastening at intervals on outer side of arm, sometimes sleeve was formed by cutting out the sides of the garment. The Dorian, who was a soldier and practical man, expressed himself by simplicity of dress, whereas, the costume of the Ionian was distinguished by graceful folds. *Pl. VI, 6, 7.*
Chlamys—garment, oblong in shape, resembling the himation, but much smaller, used by a woman traveler, horseman, and foot soldier. *Pl. VII, 6.*
Cothurnus—thick-soled, high-laced boot worn by tragic actor. *Pl. VII, 8.*
Dentil—one of a series of close-fitting, tooth-like scallops.
Diadem—refer to *Chap. 3.*
Diplax—outdoor garment similar to chlamys, worn by a woman.
Diploidon—square or oblong piece of fabric doubled so that the folded edge was upward and draped under the left arm and fastened on the opposite shoulder.
Ephebi—military cloak resembling the chlamys. *Pl. VI, 8.*
Fibula—brooch worn to fasten garment at shoulder; originally made from the fibula or small bone of the leg of an animal.
Fillet—refer to *Chap. 2. Pl. VI, 5.*
Guilloche—decoration made by interlacing curved lines.
Himation—voluminous rectangular woolen or linen shawl or mantle, 12 to 15 feet long, worn alone or over a chiton, usually white, with an all-over pattern or decoration on the border. The draping of this garment designated the interests and culture of the wearer. The himation often served as a head-covering and cloak. It was considered very proper to wear the himation in such a way as to envelop the left arm, but very bad manners to envelop the right arm. *Pl. VII, 2.*
Intaglio—figure depressed below the surface of the material.
Kolobus—1-piece shirt-like garment worn by a man. It opened at the side for the arm instead of along the upper edge, as in the chiton. The kolobus with long fitted sleeve was considered fashionable; it may have been woven in one piece with an opening for the arm and the head.
Kolpos—overfold or bloused part at the waistline of the chiton.
Mantle—refer to *Chaps. 2, 3.*

Meander—deep wavy line.

Miter—woman's woolen headdress, wider at the top than at headband, enveloping hair at back. Refer to *Chap. 3.*

Nimbus—linen headband ornamented with gold embroidery. *Pl. VII, 5.*

Peplos—earliest form of chiton usually worn by a woman in the Homeric Period, consisted of a rectangular woolen cloth, often heavily embroidered, with overfold extending to waist, and fastened on the shoulder with a large pin. The peplos of Athena is shown with a 2nd girdle tied on top of the overfold. *Pl. VII, 9.*

Petasus—broad-brimmed, low, round-crowned or slightly-pointed hat, woven from grass or palm leaves, or made of felt; worn as a protection from the sun. *Pl. VI, 2.*

Phrygian Cap—refer to *Chap. 3. Pl. VI, 3.*

Pilos—conical hat worn by a peasant or a fisherman. *Pl. VI, 4.*

Psyche Knot—a hair arrangement; twisted roll worn vertically on back of head.

Sakkos—covering the head almost completely. *Pl. VII, 4.*

Sandal—footwear consisting of felt, matting, leather, cork or wooden sole with thongs tied over the foot; usually a strap fastened to the sole between the big and next toe. Refer to *Chaps. 1, 2, 3. Pl. VI, 8; Pl. VII, 7.*

Scepter—ornamental staff used by king.

Splendone—headband of ornamented cloth or leather, with widest part in front, the narrow ends tied in the back. *Pl. VII, 3.*

Stephane—brilliantly decorated, inverted crescent, with wider part standing up in front; worn as a head ornament.

Stiletto—a narrow pointed stick or rod, used as a hairpin.

Strophion—type of corset made of linen, wool or soft skin; consisting of shoulder straps and 3 supporting bands, 1 for the bust, 1 for the waist, and 1 for the hip; also used as a foundation for the chiton.

Tiara—refer to *Chap. 3.*

Tunic—loose fitted dress; sometimes worn as an undergarment. Refer to *Chaps. 2, 3.*

Veil—refer to *Chap. 3. Pl. VII, 9.*

Rome

CHRONOLOGY

THE KINGDOM (753-509 B.C.): Rome founded by Romulus, 753 B.C. (According to a professor in Sweden, recent excavations in the Roman Forum have shown evidence that Rome was founded about 575 B.C. by Numa Pompelius.)

THE REPUBLIC (509-31 B.C.): Twelve tablets of law, the basis of all Roman law drawn up by 450 B.C. First Macedonian War, 205 B.C. After Fourth Macedonian War, 148 B.C., Macedonia a Roman province. Parchment discovered about 200 B.C. First library in Rome about 200 B.C. Astronomy important as a science about 200 B.C. Orations of Cicero, 60 B.C. First invasion into Britain, 54 B.C. Second invasion, 53 B.C. Conquest of Gaul by Julius Caesar, 58-51 B.C. Caesar, consul for 5 years, tribune for life, 46 B.C. Latin dictionary compiled by Varro. Anthony and Cleopatra defeated at Actium, 31 B.C. Geographical knowledge and commerce extending as far as Central Asia about 30 B.C. Boundaries of Rome extended until they included Mediterranean basin and western Europe. Great interest in learning.

THE EMPIRE (31 B.C.-A.D. 476): Caesar Octavian, the first emperor, 31 B.C.-A.D. 14, received the title of Augustus in 27 B.C. Pantheon built, 27 B.C., rebuilt, A.D. 123. Dances introduced on Roman stage 22 B.C. Ara Pacis built in time of Augustus, about 9 B.C. Surrender of Britains in A.D. 51. Beginning of the persecution of the Christians by Nero, A.D. 64. Destruction of Pompeii and Herculaneum by eruption of Mt. Vesuvius, A.D. 79. Arch of Titus, A.D. 81. Trajan's column, A.D. 113. Building of road, ditches and stone wall in North Britain by Emperor Hadrian, A.D. 122. End of prosperity in Rome, A.D. 180. Fall of Western Roman Empire, A.D. 476.

CHAPTER 5

Rome

HISTORY

Rome was becoming influential, but was still borrowing ideas in art as well as in costume from the Greeks. The latter continued to exert a widespread cultural influence on the world. Greece had been the Fashion Center for some time and held her lead in this field until the 5th century A.D.

Economic prosperity and successful military expeditions were important factors in building up the power of the Roman Empire. Rome, located on the bank of the Tiber, was originally a small city state but eventually the boundaries of the Empire extended to include western Europe and the countries around the Mediterranean. By the reign of Trajan she was the great power of the civilized world except for the Far East.

During the kingdom of Rome, there were two groups of citizens, the patricians, who were the aristocrats and claimed to be descendants of the original founders of Latium, and the plebeians, the lower class of laborers and yeomen. An assembly of the people elected the king, the candidates being selected from only a few eligible families. Under the rule of Tarquinius Superbus, the patricians revolted in 509 B.C. and created the Republic with a conservative constitution..Executive power was given to two annually-elected consuls who appointed a dictator whose office was for only six months. The First Triumvirate consisting of three ambitious men, namely, Pompey, Crassus and Julius Caesar, was organized in 60 B.C. The latter became absolute monarch of the Roman state from July, 46 B.C. to his assassination in March, 44 B.C.

After his victorious achievement at Actium in 31 B.C., Octavian became the first emperor and on January 17, 27 B.C., was honored by the senate which bestowed on him the title Augustus or the "Reverend One," a term applied to succeeding emperors.

The collapse of the Roman Empire in A.D. 476 brought about a change in the entire Western Civilization since the Teutonic conquer-

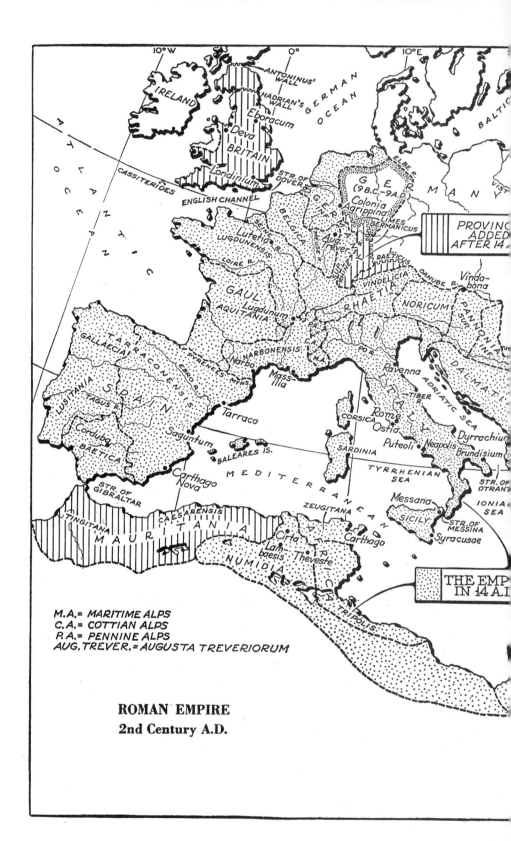

M.A. = MARITIME ALPS
C.A. = COTTIAN ALPS
P.A. = PENNINE ALPS
AUG. TREVER. = AUGUSTA TREVERIORUM

ROMAN EMPIRE
2nd Century A.D.

TEMPORARY
CONQUESTS

30°E   40°E   50°E   60°E

50°N

S A R M A T I A

VOLGA R.

DNIESTER R.

Olbia

DNIEPER R.

DON R.

SEA
OF AZOV

CASPIAN SEA

40°N

Chersonesus

CAUCASUS   MTNS.

ACIA

BLACK   SEA

Tomi

DANUBE R.

MOESIA INF.

Sinope

Trapezus

ARMENIA
MINOR

ARMENIA
(114–117 A.D.)

THRACE

Hadrianopolis

Byzantium

Heraclea

PONTUS

MEDIA
ATROPATENE

hessalonica

BITHYNIA

Ancyra

GA

Sophene   Amida

ASSYRIA

REGNUM

MYSIA

PHRYGIA

CAPPADOCIA

COMMA-
IGENE

Edessa   Nisibis

AEGEAN

LYDIA

Ephesus

LYCAONIA

CILICIA

Carrhae
OSROENE

PARTHORUM

Athens

CARIA   PISIDA

ME

Corinth

LYCIA

Antiochia   SYRIA

(116–1

Ctesiphon

RHODES

PAM-
PHYLIA

EUPHRATES R.

MIA

TIGRIS R.

SEA

CYPRUS
Damascus

Palmyra

30°N

CRETE

PALESTINE

PERSIAN
GULF

SEA

Hierosolyma
(Jerusalem)

ene

MARICA

Alex-
andria

ARABIA
PETRAEA

NAICA

Memphis

A R A B I A

E   G   Y   P   T

NILE R.

RED   SEA

Thebae

Syene   Berenice

500 MILES   TRM

ors were barbarians and incapable of continuing the Roman adminis-
trative system in the old empire or in their kingdom. There was likewise an almost complete eclipse of culture and a lack of interest in
literature and art in the early Middle Ages that followed this period.

The Roman Republic lasted for centuries and from her own highly
developed civilization, she left us important legacies. Her engineering
accomplishments have been handed down to us in magnificent roads
and aqueducts; the vault and dome in architecture; and her contribution in government, law, language, and customs is inestimable. We still
observe laws that have come to us from Roman jurisprudence.

The public baths, where much time was spent by Roman men, who
followed a standard of perfect grooming, were magnificent and an
important feature of every great city. They were decorated in marble
and mosaic, as were all other public buildings.

The *toga* was the national costume for men. Cloth was made to
the size necessary for the garment, which eliminated cutting. Some
garments were designed especially as offerings to the gods. It is very
difficult to distinguish the costume of the Roman from that of the
Greek during the early Republican Period. The typical Roman dress
had the armhole at the side whereas the Grecian costume had the opening along the upper edge of the fabric. In general the classical ideal
in costume was to enhance the body. Gradually European and Oriental
influence entered into the costume and the classic Roman dress became
extinct.

The fine sense of perfect equilibrium, which characterized the Grecian people was not found in the Romans. The latter affected pomp and
ostentation in everything, causing certain edicts to be made in regard
to clothes. A sumptuary law, passed by the Roman Senate about the
beginning of the Christian Era, prohibited the use of silk for a man's
garment because it was considered material appropriate only for a
woman. Emperor Aurelian forbade men to wear red, yellow, green, or
white shoes, these colors being reserved for women.

Various costumes and accessories have often developed to detract
from a ruler's disfigurement. The men usually wore the hair long, but
it is said that Julius Caesar adopted the wearing of the laurel wreath
to conceal his baldness. The portraits in sculpture of the rulers of this
time give us an excellent idea of the costume, since they portray the
rulers as men and not as gods as had been done in previous periods.
The sculptured portrait of the Roman woman is said to be made with
adjustable wigs in order that the hairdress could be kept in fashion.

CHAPTER 5: HISTORY

In the early years of the Republic, the Roman woman lived a dependent existence, with no legal status and no right to citizenship; she could neither act as a witness nor make a contract. She was not permitted to ride in a carriage within a limit of one mile from Rome, except to go to certain festivals. The sumptuary law of 215 B.C., established by Numa, forbidding a woman the use of more than one ounce of gold, brought so much protest from the Roman women that they formed a system of picketing the houses of leading citizens who supported the law. This aggressive act on the part of the women helped to bring more independence for them in the later years of Roman rule. In the time of the Republic the Roman was required to marry and after the marriage, lived in the house of his parents. Later, in the Empire Period there was no pride in having a family; family cares were regarded as an interference to the enjoyment of life; marriage was put aside. Since the population had decreased greatly because of the wars, Julius Caesar offered rewards of land to the fathers of large families. Augustus extended special privileges to a woman with three children; and four children released a freedwoman from bondage. In the earlier years of the Empire a woman had social freedom; she moved freely in the public thoroughfares with unveiled face, studied literature and philosophy, was permitted to defend her own case in court. She could be divorced by her husband, although she could not divorce him. She dined with her husband and his friends. When wealth and luxury came to Rome, the father felt it his duty to leave a dowry to his daughter which was sufficient to support her and made her more independent. Marriage became a contract that existed as long as both parties agreed.

While a woman took care of household duties, including the drawing and carrying of water, the preparation of food, directing the slave women in spinning and weaving, as well as the preliminary steps in the preparation of the thread, such as cleaning and spinning, the master of the house, or a trusted person of the household, attended to the marketing and took care of external transactions.

Gainful occupations of men included the cultivation of grain, brewing, woodworking, pottery making, quarrying, mining, and gold and silver smithing. Because of the expansion of Rome over the Mediterranean area, seafaring was also an important activity.

DRESS

A. *Sources of information:* wall paintings, frescoes in Pompeii, portraits, sculpture, figures on Ara Pacis, Arch of Trajan, other monuments, sarcophagi, mosaics, pottery, medals, literature.

B. MEN (*The Republic, 509-31* B.C.)
    1. Garments:
        Outer upper and outer lower: simple *tunica* or *tunic* in early times, sleeveless, or with half-sleeve, usually girded, low neckline, short length; *tunica palmata* with all-over embroidery; *tunica manicata.*
        Under: subligaculum; *tunica interior* worn under toga, after 300 B.C.
        Cloaks and overgarments: long toga; *toga pura, cinctus gabinus, toga trabea; toga pulla, toga candida, toga praetexta, toga virilis, toga picta, toga umbo; sinus, umbo.*

C. MEN (*The Empire, 31* B.C.-A.D. *476*)
    1. Garments:
        Outer upper: colobium; *tunica talaris* worn with toga umbo; clavus; *angustus clavus* on tunica, 2nd century A.D. *latus clavus;* decoration a matter of class distinction; development of long sleeve; tunica gathered at neck, end of 2nd century A.D.; *dalmatica,* a little longer than knee length, at first worn by dandy, the latter also imitated Teutonic dress of long trousers and fur tunic; *segmentum* in one color or more; *alb* or *albe.*
        Outer lower: bracco of Teutonic invader, worn by Roman dandy, 4th and 5th centuries A.D.
        Under: subligaculum; tunica interior, *camisia* or *subucula, colobium.*
        Cloaks and overgarments: paludamentum; pallium; abolla; laena; paenula with *capuchon; lacerna; birrus; cuculla; sagum;* chlamys; stiff jacket worn by herald; toga same, until after A.D. 100, then narrower until only a narrow band remained, becoming a pallium, then a stole; toga retained for ceremonials, after 2nd century A.D.
    2. Hair: short, stiff curls on forehead and nape of neck, after 3rd century A.D.; hair and beard well groomed; hair brushed forward from crown of head in Empire Period; *capillamentum;* long hair worn by young boy; hair left uncut at time of national calamity, grief, or misfortune; beard worn by elderly man, a custom not in general use because it was a Greek fashion; men smooth-shaven, 2nd-3rd century B.C.; clipped beard and mustache during the time of Hadrian, first part of 2nd century A.D.; side whiskers, 3rd century A.D.; the style of being clean-shaven started by the Emperor Constantine, 4th century A.D.

3. **Headdress:** ribbon or fillet; hat of leather or plaited straw worn by hunter and sailor; *cucullus* for rustic and fisherman; petasus; toga sometimes thrown over the head; laurel wreath and long ribbon for victor, later, laurel wreath of gold; wreath of olive branches worn by citizen at birth of son; garland of flowers at wedding and festival; *corona radiata* mark of divinity; crown and coronet for emperor or king; crown awarded for military, naval, civil, or artistic achievement.

4. **Footwear:** position in society sometimes shown by type of shoe; *calceus*, fine leather, handsomely painted, worn by wealthy; *calceus patricius*, elaborate sandal with sole studded with precious stones used by Emperor Nero to show his importance; *calceus senatorius*, sometimes with gold crest at top; shoe of senator cut higher than those of lower rank; high boot and shoe; *udo; cothurnus; crepida;* buskin; heavy hob-nailed sandal by soldier; *solea* worn in the house, and by slave; not considered good form to go barefoot indoors.

5. **Accessories:** *mappa; sudarium; orarium; fasces;* glove for boxing, eating food, driving or gardening; walking stick; umbrella of leather for rain; parasol of palm leaves, later, of silk.

6. **Jewelry:** Greek influence in design; restraint in use and type of jewelry at first, ostentatious, later; fibula; signet ring of iron used in earlier part of period; rings later worn on several joints of fingers; gold ring set with precious stones or engraved with portrait of friend or historical event, used for sealing documents, for state and military honors; gold, silver, bronze, and jeweled ornaments; bracelet worn by conquering general.

7. **Typical Colors:** until late Empire Period, white usually used for toga and tunica; purple ranging between scarlet, crimson, and deep violet, worn by upper class; special colors for special vocations: charioteer, blue-green, red, and white; philosopher, blue; theologist, black; doctor, green; astrologist, white; 1 color of somber hue, obligatory for peasant; officer, 2 colors; purple-edged toga for priest; purple silk toga, lined with gold, for victorious general; red shoe worn by patrician; natural color for dalmatica, later, bright colors, decorated profusely; red, yellow, white, or green shoe, forbidden for man by Emperor Aurelian, because used by woman; additional colors, including scarlet, violet, marigold, crocus yellow, rust, sea green, blue and green.

8. **Typical Materials:** similar to Greek but more delicate; fine linen and wool used for highest rank, in the previous period, silk little known before 1st century; silk embroidered with pure gold thread after the middle of the 1st century; fur and felt in Empire Period;

cotton little known until after Eastern conquests; earlier fabrics either woven in pattern or with embroidered design, later, with borders or bands of figures; woolen toga; linen, cotton or woolen dalmatica; woolen, linen or semisilk tunica; soft linen tunica interior; leather shoe, goat's hair for leg covering; coarse material for lowest rank.

9. **Make-up:** hairdressing and manicuring; teeth well cared for, toothpicks; beauty patches; public bath included places for exercise, rare perfume, oils and unguents, the latter used several times a day; curling tongs.

D. WOMEN (*The Republic and Empire, 509* B.C.-A.D. *476*)
1. **Garments:**

    Outer upper and outer lower: long stola; low neckline; sleeved tunica or tunica talaris; closer-fitting garment; stola discontinued after dalmatica appeared; dalmatica usually unbelted, ankle or longer, worn over tunica interior, 3rd century A.D.; in 4th century A.D. dalmatica narrow at top and worn with belt; several tunicas of various lengths; rather high-waisted tunica with single girdle popular, cut-out sleeve used; *institia;* extremely lavish dress later. *Under:* camisia, tunica interior.

    Cloaks and overgarments: toga, in early times, later worn only as a sign of disgrace; *palla;* paenula; veil worn with dalmatica.

2. **Hair:** in Republican Period, similar to that of the Grecian woman, parted in center with coil at back of neck; sometimes high, braided coil at back; hair also parted and waved, ears covered with back hair braided or coiled around crown of head, 4th century A.D.; puff of hair with stiff curls or frizzed in front; elaborate hairdress, Republic and early Empire; hair never flowing; sometimes cluster of curls escaping from top of small cap.

3. **Headdress:** ornaments worn in hair; stephane; wreath and *kerchief;* diadem of gold filigree; cap of gold net bound with solid gold band; double bandeau; heavy, twisted, gold circlet; *palliolum;* veil draped over head and shoulder, also used as a ritual accessory; petasus; cucullus.

4. **Footwear:** boot; footwear of thinner and more colorful and costlier leather than that for man, often ornamented with jewels and embroidery; sometimes tied with narrow bands of colored silk; sandal and solea worn indoors, and by slave; calceus worn out-of-doors; woman of high social position never seen on street wearing sandal.

5. **Accessories:** belt or girdle showing rank; perfume balls of amber and rock crystal; fan, one type with feathers; colorful parasol; hairpins of ivory, often elaborate pin in coil of hair; manicuring set;

1. Toga 2. Palla 3. Sudarium 4. Institia 5. Sandal

mirror of polished brass, silver or other metal; needles and work box; gold, silver or quill toothpick.

6. **Jewelry:** at first restraint in use of jewelry, later very ostentatious, resulting from conquests in the Orient; fibula in Republican Period, later a long brooch; snake bracelet; many bracelets, one above the other, often made of iron, copper or ivory; rings of gold and silver as well as baser metal, set with precious stones, pearl, emerald, ruby, diamond; wedding ring; jeweled earrings; gold and costly jewels used in hair ornaments; precious jewels on dress and footwear; yellow gold enameled or inlaid with bright colors.

7. **Typical Colors:** white stola, sometimes with yellow border; white and flame used as bridal colors; white or green shoe. Refer to C. 7.

8. **Typical Materials:** wool used for stola at first, later, silk or linen; linen palla or veil; thin leather shoe. Refer to C. 8.

9. **Make-up:** pomade taken over from barbaric invaders; eye make-up; face paint or rouge; powder of corn or pea flour and barley meal; patches on face and neck; mask of breadcrumbs soaked in milk or narcissus bulbs and honey spread on linen, kept on face over night; depilatory for excess hair; private baths for women, many baths taken in a day; milk used for bath, oils after the bath; hair oils; teeth well cared for, pumice-stone preparation used for cleaning the teeth; special care of fingers and nails; hair dyed red or color of saffron, sometimes destroyed hair; much false hair used, red or blonde, taken from head of northern barbarian woman; hair stylist employed in villa of well-to-do woman.

SIGNIFICANT MOTIFS

Significant motifs of the Roman Period followed the Grecian ornamentations. Egyptian and Oriental designs were added later. Special decorations included conventional floral, geometric, human and animal motifs. Realistic scenes and Christian symbols were used in the later years of this period.

INFLUENCES ON LATER COSTUMES

Roman influence shown in drapery and jewelry, 1840 and early part of 1900; sandal, 1940-52; flame-tipped emblem on Minerva's armor as a design on an evening cape used by a famous designer, late 1940's.

BOOKS OF REFERENCE

(See also GENERAL BIBLIOGRAPHY, p. 433)

Allen, J. T., *Stage Antiquities of the Greeks and Romans and Their Influence* (New York, Longmans, Green and Co., 1927)

1. Sagum   2. Cuculla   3. Cinctus Gabinus   4. Abolla
5. Paludamentum   6. Toga Umbo

Gall, Rob, *Wandtafein zur Veranschaulichung des Lebens der Grieschen und Römer* (Vienna and Leipzig, A. P. Witwe and Sohn, 1913)

Hope, Thomas, *Costumes of the Ancients* (London, Henry G. Bohn, 1841)

Houston, Mary Galway, *Ancient, Greek, Roman and Byzantine Costume*, Vol. 2 (London, A. and C. Black, Ltd., 1931)

McClees, Helen, *The Daily Life of the Greeks and Romans* (New York, The Metropolitan Museum of Art, 1928)

Norris, Herbert, *Costume and Fashion*, Vol. 1 (New York, E. P. Dutton and Co., 1925)

Saunders, Catherine, *Costume in Roman Comedy* (New York, Columbia University Press, 1909)

Wilson, Lillian M., *The Roman Toga* (Baltimore, The Johns Hopkins Press, 1924)

——, *The Clothing of the Ancient Romans* (Baltimore, The Johns Hopkins Press, 1938)

GLOSSARY

Abolla—red, rectangular, military cloak, resembling chlamys of soldier worn at beginning of Empire Period; made of fine linen, later, of silk. *Pl. IX, 4.*

Alb or Albe—shirt or white linen garment reaching to heel; worn under dalmatica.

Angustus Clavus—purple or red stripes about 1¼ inches wide, worn in front and back on dalmatica, tunica and stola, considered a badge of the upper class until the end of the 1st century.

Birrus—cape-like garment with a hood of fairly thick fabric; worn in winter by nobility.

Bracco—loose-fitting leg covering.

Buskin—refer to *Chap. 4.*

Calceus—most important type of shoe worn by citizen; consisted of a sole the shape of the foot, with straps fastened to the upper part and laced around the ankle; at first a brown leather boot.

Calceus Patricius—strapped shoe of red leather with a high sole, laced with hooks and decorated with a crescent-shaped buckle, worn by nobleman.

Calceus Senatorius—black leather shoe having 4 straps and no buckle, worn by senator.

Camisia—undergarment worn by man which resembled the tunica interior.

Capillamentum—wig of false hair.

Capuchon—hood, attached to a cloak called paenula.

Chlamys—shawl, similar in shape to himation, worn over chiton as a military cloak. Refer to *Chap. 4.*

Cinctus Gabinus—garment drawn over head and girded, worn on solemn occasions. *Pl. IX, 3.*

Circlet—refer to *Chap. 2.*

Clavus—scarlet and purple stripe worn on the tunica, showing class distinction, used until the 3rd century; band of embroidery used in 3rd and 4th centuries.

Colobium—similar to the Greek kolobus and made of wool or linen; although important as a man's garment, 300-100 B.C., by the 5th century, insignificant.

Corona Radiata—headdress of divinity representing rays of the sun.

CHAPTER 5: GLOSSARY

Cothurnus—refer to *Chap. 4.*

Crepida—type of sandal laced across the arch with the heel and sides of the foot enclosed in leather or fabric.

Cuculla—cape-like garment, similar to a poncho, used for traveling, and as a protection from the weather. *Pl. IX, 2.*

Cucullus—hood attached to a paenula, sometimes worn without cloak.

Dalmatica—loose garment with flowing sleeve open partly at the sides, and having clavi as decoration; worn over tunica interior, 3rd century. This dress was copied from a Dalmatian costume, hence its name.

Diadem—refer to *Chaps. 3, 4.*

Fasces—bundle of rods enclosing an axe, used by magistrate as a symbol of power.

Fibula—refer to *Chap. 4.*

Fillet—refer to *Chaps. 2, 4.*

Institia—flounce or narrow border around bottom of dress, distinguished an honorable matron. *Pl. VIII, 4.*

Kerchief—cloth used as covering for the head, or as an ornament.

Lacerna—summer wrap of brilliant or dull, fine woolen fabric, sometimes with hood fastened at right shoulder with fibula; worn by nobility; resembled chlamys except for rounded corners.

Laena—oblong, woolen cloak, similar to Grecian chlamys, sometimes thrown over head for protection.

Latus Clavus—stripes about 3 inches wide, decoration of dalmatica and tunica; similar to angustus clavus.

Mappa—large piece of cloth used to give signals for games, or used as table napkin. In late Republican times the mappa was supplied by the owner of the house, but in days of the Empire, guests brought their own mappas.

Orarium—large napkin which the servants used to clean dishes.

Paenula—short dark-colored semicircular woolen cloak with hood, adopted by peasant class; worn by both woman and man when traveling.

Palla—shawl-like garment, resembling the Greek himation, worn by woman; fastened with fibula on left breast; often thrown over head. *Pl. VIII, 2.*

Palliolum—beautiful veil, sometimes held in place by a wreath, worn by woman.

Pallium—himation of the Greeks; rectangular mantle worn by man; superseded toga, by 2nd century; state dress and vestment of Pope, middle of 5th to end of 9th century.

Paludamentum—long military cloak, usually purple or dark in color, sometimes white or scarlet; worn over armor or tunic; used in place of toga picta, after seat of government was transferred to Constantinople; corners of this cape were cut off in such a way as to make upper part smaller than lower, ankle length in 5th century. *Pl. IX, 5.*

Patch—an item of make-up appearing from time to time throughout history.

Petasus—refer to *Chap. 4.*

Pomade—perfumed ointment.

Sagum—practical, dark or red, thick woolen cloak, resembling paludamentum; pinned at right shoulder; worn by citizen in wartime. *Pl. IX, 1.*

Sandal—refer to *Chaps. 1, 2, 3, 4. Pl. VIII, 5.*

Segmentum—decoration worn on sleeve of tunic or dalmatica; embroidered.

Sinus—upper edge of toga draped to form deeply curved fold falling at right hip; sometimes worn over head during sacrificial ceremony.

Solea—informal type of sandal.

Stephane—headdress similar to stephane worn by Greek. Refer to *Chap. 4.*

Stola—long tunic, usually of woolen material, resembling Greek chiton, except that armhole was located at side instead of at top. In later periods several stolas of

different lengths and colors were worn. In the 2nd century, the neck opening of the Ionic stola was finished with a narrow band.

Stole—embroidered band or scarf used as part of ecclesiastical vestment of priest; said to be developed from the orarium which had become similar to the pallium.

Subligaculum—loin cloth worn under toga. In the Empire Period an elaborately embroidered type was often worn by slave, gladiator, actor, and dancer.

Subucula—undergarment or tunica interior.

Sudarium—handkerchief, often embroidered with silk or gold, attached to pastoral staff in 8th century, later used as handkerchief; also worn around neck, in sinus of toga, or carried in the hand. *Pl. VIII, 3.*

Toga—garment of natural-colored wool worn by Roman citizen; later of silk, worn by aristocrat. In earlier periods, it was small and semicircular, later, elliptical, measuring about 18 feet by 7 feet, with decoration on curved edge. The draping of this garment was very important and often signified the rank of the wearer. *Pl. VIII, 1.*

Toga Candida—toga worn by candidate for office, similar to toga pura, but very white.

Toga Picta—official robe of emperor; purple toga of fine woolen fabric, worn over purple tunica palmata, and embroidered or painted with conventional figures; originally worn by victorious general, later by emperor. In the 1st century B.C., it was made of silk. In the 2nd century, it was worn by consul, and during the Empire Period, was considered the correct costume of the court.

Toga Praetexta—at first worn by patrician boy to age of sixteen, and by king; later, in Republican Period, by some officials and priests. The straight edge had a wide purple border. The sinus was draped over the head during sacrificial ceremony.

Toga Pulla—dark, somber-colored or black toga worn for mourning.

Toga Pura—national costume for men; from the 3rd century B.C., a woolen toga denoted enfranchisement of the person wearing the garment, not worn by peasant, foreigner or outlawed subject; after 2nd century A.D., worn usually in the home.

Toga Trabea—purple-bordered toga of white and red stripes worn only as badge of distinction on ceremonial occasions; border followed straight edge. Purple and white were reserved for king, purple and scarlet for augur.

Toga Umbo—regular toga with a red or purple band; worn with arm in umbo. *Pl. IX, 6.*

Toga Virilus—pure white toga worn by youth of 14 to 16 years.

Tunic or Tunica—garment of various lengths, usually several of different colors, worn at the same time. The woolen tunica reached to calf or ankle. The natural-colored or white, woolen garment was worn girded, similar to Greek chiton. This tunica was knee length or a little longer, but shorter in back, and was worn slipped off right shoulder by laborer. Refer to *Chaps. 2, 3, 4.*

Tunica Interior—tunic or chemise worn next to skin.

Tunica Manicata—tunica with sleeve to wrist.

Tunica Palmata—purple and gold embroidered, ceremonial tunica; reached to ankle; worn with toga picta on triumphal occasions. Later, this garment with sleeve became the magnificent costume of the Byzantine Court.

Tunica Talaris—the long-sleeved, long-girded tunica worn by woman and elderly man.

Udo—covering for the foot resembling our present day houseslipper.

Umbo—pouch or fold formed by draping upper left part of toga to envelop right hand; abandoned in 1st century.

Veil—short or long rectangular piece of light wool, silk, linen or cotton, often fringed and ornamented with gold; draped over head and shoulder. Refer to *Chaps. 3, 4.*

Byzantium

CHRONOLOGY

Byzantium founded *c. 658* B.C. Reduced by Pausanias, *479* B.C.

Constantine the Great, A.D. *323-337*, sole ruler A.D. *324*, Constantinople, capital of Roman Empire, A.D. *330*. Empire divided at his death among his three sons.

Division of Roman Empire, A.D. *364*, Valentinian elected Emperor of Western Empire, his brother, Valens became Emperor of Eastern Empire.

Theodosius the Great, A.D. *379-395*. Constantinople, capital of Eastern or Grecian Empire; Rome capital of Western Empire. Public schools established. Theodosius made ruler of the East and later became ruler of entire Empire, A.D. *394-395*. After his death *395*, division of Roman Empire between his two sons, Honorius received the Western and Arcadius the Eastern half.

Fall of the Western Empire, A.D. *476*.

Justinian the Great, A.D. *527-565*, reunited the Empire. Great patron of the arts. Legislation compiled in the *Novellae,* A.D. *529*, giving Roman law much prestige, publication of *Codex Justinianus,* A.D. *529*. Building of Santa Sophia, A.D. *532-537*.

Division of Early Christian Church in A.D. *729*. Eastern portion in Constantinople known as Greek Orthodox Church.

Iconoclastic Controversy, A.D. *726, 741, 753*.

Irene, First Empress, A.D. *797-802*.

Coronation of Charlemagne, Western Empire, A.D. *800*, not recognized by Eastern Empire until A.D. *803*. Peace with the Emperor of the Eastern Empire, the latter retaining southern Italy, Venice, and Dalmatia.

University of Constantinople opened about A.D. *850*.

Final separation of the Roman Church, *1054*.

CHAPTER 6

Byzantium

HISTORY

The influence of Byzantine culture spread far and wide—to all the important cities of Italy—to the Merovingians and Carlovingians of Western Europe—as far north as Russia and as far south as North Africa. From the 5th to the 12th centuries Byzantium became the most important power of the period and a center of culture, including fashions.

The colony of Byzantium was founded in 658 B.C. by a small band of immigrants who left Megara, a port on the Isthmus of Corinth, and landed on the promontory dividing Asia from Europe. They established primitive fortifications, built reed huts.

Constantine the Great, realizing that the site of Byzantium was important as a connecting link between Western and Eastern civilizations, founded a city there in A.D. 330 and named it "New Rome," the capital of the Roman Empire. Later, it was given his name and the two names—Byzantium and Constantinople—were used interchangeably. Before the time of Constantine, the Christian religion was for slaves, hermits, and humble folk; under his reign it became a religion for conquerors, courtiers, and soldiers.

After the death of Theodosius the Great in A.D. 395 the Roman Empire was divided into the Eastern and the Western Empires. Constantinople became the capital of the East Roman or the Byzantine Empire, known also as the Greek Empire and the Eastern Empire. For ten and a half centuries the Byzantine Empire existed, and during a long time it was the most important center of commerce and civilization in the world. Caravans of vast wealth from northern and eastern Asia converged on Constantinople, bearing goods to be traded with Western Europe. In turn, these same caravans carried back Byzantine works of art, and other products of much interest and value to the Asiatic people. Shipping on the Mediterranean was largely controlled by the Byzantines.

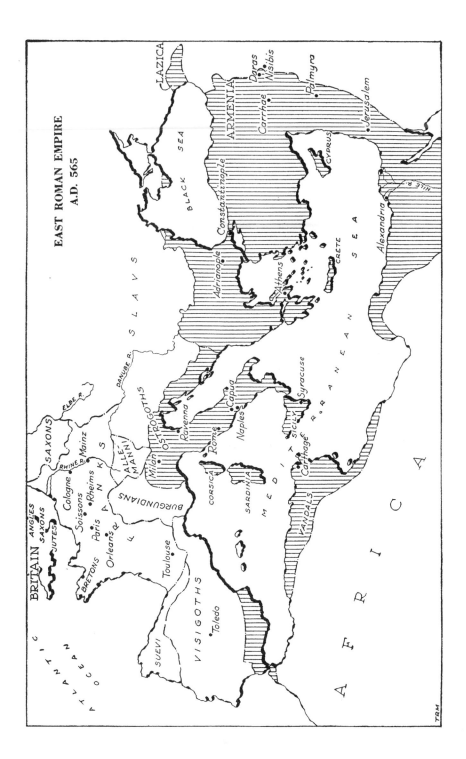

EAST ROMAN EMPIRE
A.D. 565

CHAPTER 6: HISTORY

The Classic Greek art had influenced the new or Christian art, as the latter was known. With the fall of the Western Roman Empire in A.D. 476, the influence of Classic art or Greek and Greco-Roman art, came to an end. Oriental influence in Constantinople became more and more important, until it superseded Western dominance. The simplicity of the old Roman dress gave way to the gay coloring, fringes, tassels, and jewels of the East. The idea in dress in this era was to conceal and obscure the body.

Emperor Justinian of the Eastern Empire, who was greatly influenced by his wife Theodora, did much to encourage the manufacture of silk fabrics. Excellent examples of the costumes worn by the Emperor and the Empress Theodora may be found in the mosaics in the church of St. Vitale in Ravenna. While costume showed elaborate display of jewels in the 6th century, it retained a more or less simple and dignified line. Emperor Justinian also was a great builder and patron of the arts. His important architectural achievement was the building of Santa Sophia, Church of the Holy Mission, dedicated on Christmas morning, A.D. 537. He is also known for collecting and codifying the Roman law, which forms the basis of modern law. The year A.D. 540 of his reign marked a high point of Byzantine power; after his death there was a decline of the Empire for several centuries.

When Constantine became emperor he abolished the penalties for celibacy and childlessness inaugurated during Roman times. Large families were not encouraged.

The women were respected and exerted power in politics. That they rose to a high position politically is shown by Empress Pulcheria, who ruled with her brother Theodosius, II, and Empress Theodora, the wife of Justinian, whose courage in refusing to leave when the rebels attacked the palace, during the great Niké insurrection of A.D. 532, saved her husband's crown. She acquired great influence over her husband and is cited as acting with great cruelty in her exercise of power. The Byzantine woman considered the interests of the entire household before those of her own. She was swayed emotionally rather than intellectually and her success was on the domestic rather than the social side of life. The seclusion of the woman of the East outside court circles was indicative of the protective care of her husband. In a number of cases this seclusion resulted in lack of freedom.

Craftsmen executed exquisite enameling and mosaics as well as beautiful objects in gold and silver. In A.D. 551 the eggs of silkworms were smuggled into Constantinople from China by two Persian monks who concealed them in a palmer stave, and eventually the chief occupation of the Byzantines was the manufacture of silk. Fresco painting was also known at this time.

DRESS

A. *Sources of information:* mosaics of San Vitale and Ravenna, sarcophagi, frescoes, sculpture, manuscripts, carved ivory, fragments of textiles still in existence.

B. MEN
1. **Garments:**
   Outer upper: sleeve and garment cut in one; sleeved dalmatica belted below waistline or about hip, at first, worn over tunica, high neckline with slit down front, length to below knee or to instep; segmentum; colobium; tunica talaris and tunica palmata, extending halfway between knee and ankle, for consul; tunica with decoration at neckline for middle class, 5th and 6th centuries; short tunic for courtier; latus clavus; angustus clavus; shorter tunica with jeweled embroidery at neck and hem, 10th and 11th centuries; simple tunic buttoned at neck and belted, for middle class.
   Outer lower: hosa; bracco or braies sometimes cross-gartered; close-fitting hose also often cross-gartered; *drawers* or *trousers* worn, 6th century A.D.
   Under: chemise.
   Cloak and overgarments: toga worn by consul until 6th century; toga picta; paludamentum; *tablion;* semicircular cloak fastened in front after 9th century; abolla; *chasuble;* pallium draped in various ways, 10th, 11th, and 12th centuries; cape or *cope* fastened at shoulder with large brooch, used for formal wear.
2. **Hair:** similar to that worn by man during Empire Period of Rome, cut medium-short and brushed away from crown of head, or in a bob with bang on forehead, the hair at the back often long and turned under; beard rare before 9th century; neatly trimmed beard and moustache after 9th century; *tonsure.*
3. **Headdress:** petasus; cucullus; Phrygian cap; *cowl* of monk's gown; fillet or gold circlet; diadem of double strand of pearls and a jewel, 5th-8th century; then low metal circlet which became taller and more ornate, developing into crown with ropes of pearls hanging

1. Bracco 2. Cowl on Monk's Gown 3. Dalmatica 4. Angustus Clavus
5. Circlet 6. Abolla 7. Bracco or Braies 8. Slipper

over each ear; imperial crown about 5 inches high, adorned with inset jewels and pendant pearls, worn by Justinian.

4. **Footwear:** openwork red boot, or sandal with buckle at ankle, 5th century; *slipper* introduced with toe pointed or following shape of foot; real shoe of soft fabric or leather, and heelless, taking place of sandal in 6th century; boot worn by consul; hose and shoe with ankle strap worn by courtiers, also toeless boot; hose and shoe, or bare foot, for lower classes, 7th-9th century; tall, red leather boot, 10th-12th century; gradual adoption of painted and embroidered shoe; *pedule*.

5. **Accessories:** sudarium; *reliquary;* stole; *lorum;* mappa used by consul; *orb* and scepter carried by emperor; scepter with imperial eagle carried by consul; knife; glove of fur, or leather trimmed with fur and gold embroidery, for nobleman; less ornate, for working class; *pouch* or wallet; waist belt of gold filigree with medallion of metal, or jeweled leather.

6. **Jewelry:** heavy jeweled collar; earrings; finger rings; brooch to hold cloak; filigree decoration; Greco-Roman influence until 4th century; later, Oriental styles; gold; emerald, sapphire, ruby, diamond, and pearls; mosaic, and enamel.

7. **Typical Colors:** black, gray, white, brown, green, blue, red, plum, violet, and royal purple; gold and purple very important in 10th century, royal purple reserved for Emperor and his subjects, not permitted to be taken out of Byzantium; dalmatica, sometimes of red on gold background, with jeweled border at neckline, sleeve, and hem; colored, circular decoration at top of each sleeve; colored shoes with embroidery of silk, gold, and jewels; white pedule by lower class.

8. **Typical Materials:** cloth of silk, *taffeta, sarcenet, damask,* brocatelle, lampos, velvet, tapestry, and brocade; cloth with embroidery; linen, wool, and cotton also used; no limit to extravagance, A.D. 350-700; often stripes of pure gold woven throughout fabric; complex weaving of stylized patterns.

9. **Make-up:** apparently none.

C. **WOMEN**

  1. **Garments:**

  Outer upper and outer lower: stola 5th-9th century, with high, round or low neckline, and tight, long sleeve; sleeve and body of dress cut in one, fitted and unbelted, or girded above or at normal waistline; variation of chiton, length to floor; angustus clavus, and latus clavus; dalmatica held by sash, 7th, 8th, and 9th centuries; tunica worn under dalmatica; sometimes 1 or more stolas, worn with knee-length palla, both held in place by girdle; sleeveless over-

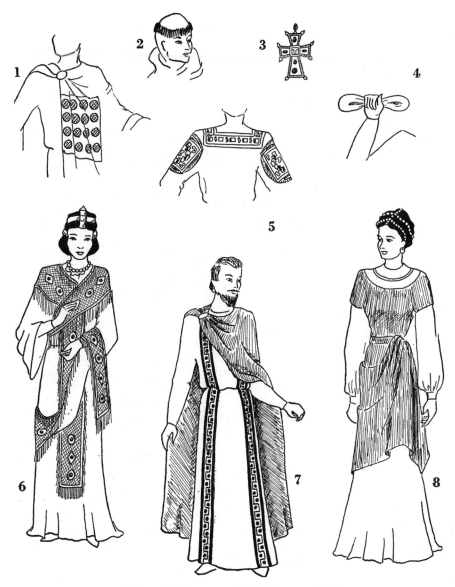

1. Tablion   2. Tonsure   3. Reliquary   4. Mappa
5. Segmentum   6. Lorum   7. Latus Clavus   8. Chemise

garment reaching to knee, and girded with jeweled belt, 10th and 11th centuries, also shorter, wide-sleeved tunic over close-sleeved, white undertunic; ungirded, fitted dalmatica over stola, 5th and 6th centuries worn by lower classes; tunic girded at waist by lower class, 7th, 8th, and 9th centuries.

Under: high-necked, long-sleeved chemise often visible beneath tunic, or white stola.

Cloaks and overgarments: palla; small scarf; rectangular shawl; cape or chasuble; semicircular cloak fastened on right shoulder, worn by the Empresses of 5th and 6th centuries; semicircular cloak held in front by brooch, 7th, 8th, and 9th centuries; hooded cloak.

2. **Hair:** hairdress resembling that of Roman woman of 4th century, worn in 6th century; hair often covered by turban; 2 long braids, with an extra lock braided closely behind the ear; metal ornaments and pearls as decoration at close of 10th century; braids sometimes brought up over outside of caul and fastened with jeweled band at forehead; rolled pompadour, sometimes frizzed, neck and ears exposed.

3. **Headdress:** Oriental type of headdress, a circular roll over skull cap, at end of 4th century; large rectangular veil; veil hung from jeweled band around head, 6th century; hair concealed by turban; later, turban with color according to caste, sometimes with diadem; veil secured by fillet, 7th-9th century; Chinese influence in hats, 10th-11th century; hair ornaments Oriental in style; triangular-shaped gold net or white veil restrained hair at back; white cap worn by lower class.

4. **Footwear:** footwear similar to that worn by man; slipper, transition between sandal and shoe, 5th century; red shoe worn by woman of high rank; real shoe worn in place of sandal, 6th century; low-cut shoe with strap over ankle.

5. **Accessories:** sash over dalmatica; sudarium carried in left hand; girdle made of cord, gold plates, or jeweled leather; lorum; reliquary carried as charm; stiletto-like hairpin with ivory or metal head, resembling those of the Greek.

6. **Jewelry:** workmanship showing Greco-Roman influence until end of 4th century; yellow gold; engraved ring of bronze, silver or gold; inscription or monogram used on ring for engagement and marriage; charm ring; intaglio and cameo; large elaborate pendant earrings; fibula; pearl, emerald, sapphire, ruby, diamond, mosaic work in bracelet; broad jeweled collar with pearls and precious stones, showing Egyptian influence, worn over tunic and mantle; gold dalmatica often decorated with square plaques of gold filigree

1. Cucullus   2. Clavus   3. Pedules   4. Petasus
5. Phrygian Cap   6. Pallium   7. Paludementum   8. Stola

set with pearls, rubies, and emeralds; girdle of enameled plaques or circlets.

7. **Typical Colors:** gold and emerald ornamentation for stola; white tunic. Refer to *B. 7*.

8. **Typical Materials:** Refer to *B. 8*.

9. **Make-up:** apparently none.

SIGNIFICANT MOTIFS

Acanthus and palmetto foliage; Christian emblems including the crown, the vine, the dove, the conventional animal form, geometric and abstract designs, and an intricate pattern of the scroll, leaf flower, and fruit.

INFLUENCES ON LATER COSTUMES

Rich fabrics used later in the Renaissance period; hood, 1640; tiara, 1890; evening wrap and hood, 20th century; monk-like dress, 1938 and '39; costume jewelry and belt, 1940's; hairdress, 1940's; modern cut and sewn garments often following Byzantine styles; coat with hood, 1948.

BOOKS OF REFERENCE

(See also GENERAL BIBLIOGRAPHY, p. 433)

Houston, Mary Galway, *Ancient Greek, Roman and Byzantine Costume,* Vol. 2 (London, A. and C. Black, Ltd., 1931)

Norris, Herbert, *Costume and Fashion,* Vol. 1 (New York, E. P. Dutton and Co., 1925)

GLOSSARY

Abolla—refer to *Chap. 5. Pl. X, 6.*

Angustus Clavus—refer to *Chap. 5. Pl. X, 4.*

Bracco or Braies—the former, a loose-fitting leg covering or hose; the latter, usually close-fitting, with or without cross-gartering. Refer to *Chap. 5. Pl. X, 1, 7.*

Cape—refer to *Chaps. 2, 3, 4.*

Chasuble—round or oval in shape, with a hole for the head; used also as an ecclesiastical garment. *Pl. XIII, 4.*

Chemise—undergarment with long sleeve that showed beneath sleeve of outer garment. *Pl. XI, 8.*

Chiton—revival of Greek costume. Refer to *Chap. 4. Pl. XIII, 3.*

Circlet—refer to *Chaps. 2, 5. Pl. X, 5.*

Clavus—extended to below the breast. Refer to *Chap. 5. Pl. XII, 2.*

Collar—refer to *Chap. 2. Pl. XIII, 5.*

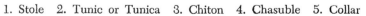

1. Stole   2. Tunic or Tunica   3. Chiton   4. Chasuble   5. Collar

Colobium—refer to *Chap. 5.*

Cope—half circular, formal cape—from Latin word *capa.*

Cowl—the hood of a monk's gown attached to the back of the collar and pulled over the head if desired. *Pl. X, 2.*

Cucullus—refer to *Chap. 5. Pl. XII, 1.*

Dalmatica—refer to *Chap. 5. Pl. X, 3.*

Damask—silk or linen cloth with a figured satin weave, named from the city of Damascus where it was first manufactured.

Diadem—refer to *Chaps. 3, 4, 5.*

Drawers or Trousers—leg-covering resembling national costume worn by the Medes, Persians, Parthians, and Phrygians.

Fibula—refer to *Chaps. 4, 5.*

Fillet—refer to *Chaps. 2, 4, 5.*

Hosa—hose or covering for the leg.

Intaglio—refer to *Chap. 4.*

Latus Clavus—refer to *Chap. 5. Pl. XI, 7.*

Lorum—long, narrow scarf originating from pallium, worn with Byzantine court costume 8th-12th century. *Pl. XI, 6.*

Mappa—refer to *Chap. 5. Pl. XI, 4.*

Orb—celestial sphere often surmounted by a cross, carried by Emperor and Empress.

Palla—refer to *Chap. 5.*

Pallium—refer to *Chap. 5. Pl. XII, 6.*

Paludamentum—the imperial mantle of rich material, often of purple silk embroidered in gold, or gold and jewels. Refer to *Chap. 5. Pl. XII, 7.*

Pedule—short hose usually turned down at knee. *Pl. XII, 3.*

Petasus—refer to *Chaps. 4, 5. Pl. XII, 4.*

Phrygian Cap—refer to *Chaps. 3, 4. Pl. XII, 5.*

Pouch—bag attached to belt.

Reliquary—pendant of gold or enamel containing a relic. *Pl. XI, 3.*

Sandal—refer to *Chaps. 1, 2, 3, 4, 5.*

Sarcenet—fine thin silk cloth originating in the Orient; named from Saracen.

Scepter—ornamented staff or baton used at first by the consul at games; after the 7th century, used as a symbol of royalty. Refer to *Chap. 4.*

Segmentum—refer to *Chap. 5. Pl. XI, 5.*

Slipper—low shoe fastened with a strap. *Pl. X, 8.*

Stola—revival of the Roman stola. Refer to *Chap. 5. Pl. XII, 8.*

Stole—refer to *Chap. 5. Pl. XIII, 1.*

Sudarium—refer to *Chap. 5.*

Tablion—the very elaborate oblong decoration embroidered in red and gold on the back and front of the imperial paludamentum. Purple mantle of Emperor Theodosius had gold tablion; white mantle of high official had purple tablion. *Pl. XI, 1.*

Taffeta—stiff silk cloth used as lining of rich mantle, possibly as early as the 4th century.

Toga—refer to *Chap. 5.*

Toga Picta—less wide than the one worn during the Roman period. Refer to *Chap. 5.*

Tonsure—manner of shaving the head as a mark of ecclesiastic order and *Pl. XI, 2.*

Trousers—refer to *Drawers.*

Tunic or Tunica—resembled dalmatica later in period, with exception of sleeve which fitted closely at wrist in the tunica. Refer to *Chaps. 2, 3, 4, 5. Pl. XIII, 2.*

Tunica Palmata—refer to *Chap. 5.*

Tunica Talaris—refer to *Chap. 5.*

Veil—refer to *Chaps. 3, 4, 5.*

The Middle Ages

PART I

5th-10th Century

CHRONOLOGY

GALLO-ROMAN PERIOD (51 B.C.-A.D. 428): Roman conquest of western Europe to the invasions of the Franks.

FRANK-MEROVINGIAN KINGDOM (486-750): inaugurated by Clovis (d. 511). Conversion to Christianity of Clovis, 496. Frankish lands divided after death of Clovis, 511; four capitals established: Metz, Orleans, Paris, Soissons. Saracens defeated by Charles Martel at Battle of Tours. Schools and monasteries flourished under Franks. Pepin conquered Franks and became King, 751. After his death, land divided between Pepin's two sons, Carloman and Charlemagne.

CARLOVINGIAN DYNASTY (751-986): Charlemagne became King, 768, later consolidated Franco-Germany, crowned Emperor of the Western Roman Empire, 800. Verdun Treaty divided Carlovingian Empire, 843.

ANGLO-SAXON KINGDOMS (9th century-1066): End of Roman occupation of Britain, c. 428. Conquest of Britain by various barbaric tribes, 450-613. Seven Anglo-Saxon kingdoms established which continued until the Norman Conquest. Scots and Picts united under one king, 844. Reign of Alfred the Great, King of the West Saxons, 871-901. Progress in national Education. Revision of laws. Foundation of British Navy. Invasion by William the Conqueror of Normandy, 1066.

FRANCE: Duchy of Normandy established by Rollo, 912. Capetian Dynasty (987-1328) founded by Hugh Capet, 987-996.

Art of paper making introduced by Arabs into Spain, c. 712, Arabic numerals, 980.

CHAPTER 7

The Middle Ages

PART I

5th-10th Century

HISTORY

The conquest of Gaul by Julius Caesar and the Roman occupation which followed had affected the civilization and culture of the Gallic men and women to such an extent that they followed the fashions in dress of the important families of the conquerors for eight centuries. Among the Roman customs which have lasted to the present time is that of frequent bathing—some families used the sunken bathtub, others the metal bowl and washstand.

Due to pressure of population, the Teutons who lived north of the Roman Empire, were driven to expand their territories, and later they divided into many tribes, the most important being the Franks, Saxons, and Jutes.

The Franks, one of the most important and advanced of the Teutonic peoples, both in culture and civilization, conquered and settled in Gaul in the 5th century. Many Franks migrated into Britain. Those who remained in their native territory established four states, which later became the kingdom of Charlemagne.

The Franks of Gaul lost many of their Teutonic characteristics. The first to be crowned their king in 428, was Clodian the Long-Haired. His younger brother, who was named Merovee or Merwig, later became King of the Salian Franks with the capital at Tournay. The latter dynasty which was called Merovingian, lasted three centuries, and was extended widely by Merwig's grandson, Clovis, from 481 to 511. It became known as the Kingdom of the Franks.

The descendants of Clovis were weak, puppet kings and were annihilated by Pepin in 751. The latter brought about the union of the Frankish kingdom. Upon the death of Pepin, in 768, his son, Charlemagne took the eastern part of the empire and another son Carloman received the western part. After the death of the latter in 771, Charlemagne took over the entire empire and became the first King of the Carlovingian Dynasty, which continued until 987.

At Christmas time in 800, Charlemagne was crowned by Pope Leo and proclaimed Emperor of the Romans. During his reign the popes of Rome and the churchmen of the West were brought into closer touch with each other. His coronation was not recognized by the Eastern Empire until 803. Under Charlemagne, there was an advancement in culture and a development in commerce.

Louis the Pious who followed was not the great leader that Charlemagne had been. His sons quarreled over their shares of the empire. These quarrels eventually ended in a civil war in which the two younger brothers united in a campaign against the elder brother and defeated him. The Treaty of Verdun that followed, in 843, divided the empire as follows: Lothaire, King of the Central Frankish lands, or Italy; Louis the German, King of the East Franks; Charles the Bald, King of the West Franks, or France. The final separation of Germany, France, and Italy came in 887.

Later, Henry, duke of Saxony, was chosen King of Germany and established the Saxon dynasty, becoming Henry I. Usually the kings of this dynasty protected the clergy and supported the work of the church and missionary activities. At this time, monks were permitted to move freely from one place to another and to circulate ideas. Libraries were established and the learning of the Carlovingian period was preserved and advanced. Germans went to Italy, Spain, and France to study.

The third or Capetian Dynasty of France was founded by Hugh Capet in 987. The crown of the West Franks had passed back and forth between the counts of France and the Carlovingians for one hundred years. The French royal family became very important and greatly influenced the history of Europe. During this dynasty, there were many changes in the life of the people. A decided advancement occurred in literature, music, and art.

The Angles, Saxons, and sea-roving Jutes invaded Britain in the 5th century and succeeded in firmly establishing themselves there. The Angles and the others were originally Teutonic but were known as Saxons to the native Celtic population. After Alfred the Great, King of the West Saxons, subdued the Angles, the people of his kingdom became known as Anglo-Saxons. The Britons, who had absorbed much

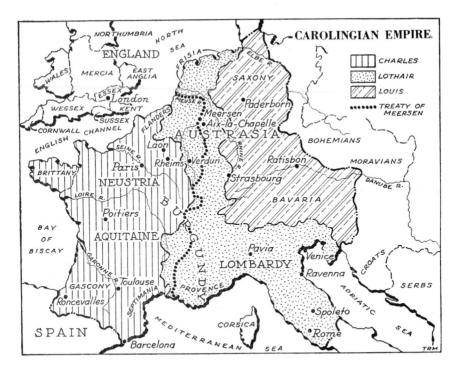

of Roman culture during the three hundred years of occupation, considered these Teutonic peoples barbaric. Actually civilization in Britain was retarded greatly by the coming of the invaders. Although this period was known as the Dark Ages, there was an advancement in learning evident during the reign of King Alfred, 871 to 901. The latter was an intellectual force and one of the greatest of English kings.

The Vikings from the Scandinavian peninsula in their long ships also raided the coasts of western Europe. By the 9th century they had established themselves in the British Isles and France. Wherever they settled they adopted the customs of the people of the country and many of their descendants were outstanding leaders later in religion, art, government, and learning.

Ever since the 8th century the Spaniards had been at war with their Moorish conquerors. Some Christians found refuge in the northern mountains of Asturia and managed to retain their freedom, but it was not until 1492 that the Moors were finally driven from Spanish soil. The occupancy of Spain by the Moslems for such a long period left an indelible imprint on the people and their culture, particularly architecture.

In the monasteries literature of all kinds was produced, fostered, and preserved by the monks who, being maintained by the Church, had both time and inclination for study. This situation continued to be true throughout the Dark Ages and was the chief means by which classical learning was transmitted to later periods. Prominent men of the period were the Venerable Bede (673-755) in England; Babanus Maurus (d. 858) in Germany whose writings were voluminous; and Notker, the German, who composed music in a monastery in Switzerland in the 9th century. The Christian Church during this period was growing in strength and numbers, although it was not until later that the physical symbols of its dominance of medieval life, the great cathedrals, were built.

Paralleling the growth of the Roman Church was the development of feudalism, a type of society in all European countries which divided society into three classes: the nobles who owned most of the land and were the leaders in war, the clergy, and the serfs who made up most of the population and performed the labor. The serf in the feudal system was required to work on the land of the lord of his manor a certain number of days a week and to plow a certain amount of ground. Additional work was required such as repairing buildings, cutting trees, and gathering fruit. On days that he did not work for his master he was permitted to cultivate his own small patch on land on the overlord's estate. In some cases rents were also paid by the serf, and artisans paid their way by special work—for instance a metal worker would contribute lances for the army.

Among the Anglo-Saxon people the father of the family was absolute master and had the power to dispose of his children as he wished; he frequently sold his daughters in marriage and his sons into slavery. By the 10th century customs had changed to the point that a girl could refuse her father's choice of a husband. The wedding ceremony of the time was no more than a bargain of sale that was pledged by clasping hands while a few words of love and affection were said by the woman and a promise of protection and care given by the man. In later years, the ring ceremony was introduced. If certain qualities in the wife were promised by her father which she did not possess, the bridegroom could return her to her parents and receive the money he had paid for her. As time progressed woman's position, in general, improved. She acquired the legal right to inherit her husband's property; this amount was forfeited if she married within a year. After the 10th century, a privilege granted to woman was permission to sit at the dining table with her husband and his friends. The special duties of the wife of the serf included spinning, weaving, and making a garment each year for the chief manor.

The Teuton woman wove the material and made garments for her husband and her family. Later, she was employed to direct the work of the slaves in industry where vestments of wool and linen, and bands for the leg were manufactured. The daughters of Charlemagne worked with women of all classes under good working conditions. After the age of Charlemagne, the workrooms for the women became very debased and ill-kept and the character of the women who worked there changed to a very low type.

The man of this period worked also as shoemaker, carpenter, silver- and goldsmith, fisherman, swordmaker, or soapmaker. The Teuton excelled as a craftsman and also was noted for his work as carpenter and shoemaker. After the 8th century, instructors from France taught him the craft of glass-blowing which enabled him to produce window glass and utensils.

Roman influence in dress continued in western Europe until the beginning of the 6th century, after which time the Byzantine influence gradually became dominant. Byzantine manufacturers brought the elegance of their costume to the people of the West, but due to transportation difficulties, this magnificent costume took a long time in reaching Europe; sometimes twenty-five to thirty years elapsed before a costume from the East was finally introduced. From time to time an official returned from Rome after some months of travel, bringing with him the latest styles. In the 7th century, one of the bishops brought examples of Byzantine art, crafts, illuminated manuscripts, ivory carving, and goldsmith work which had an influence in the early English period. During the time of Charlemagne edicts against luxury in dress were made, but to no avail, and the costume continued to be as extravagant as that worn by the kings of Constantinople.

DRESS

A. *Sources of information:* ancient chronicles, coins, and sculpture.

B. MEN (*Gallo-Roman 51* B.C.-A.D. *428*)
1. Garments:
    Outer upper: low neckline, knee-length tunica, embroidered around the lower edge and sleeve; sleeve sometimes long.
    Outer under: bracco cross-gartered with studded strap.
    Under: colobium or *sherte*.
    Cloaks and overgarments: rectangular cloak fastened with fibula.
2. Hair: short bob.
3. Headdress: helmet.
4. Footwear: sandal with sole, and strap joining a band around the ankle, resembling Roman sandal; shoe with pointed toe.
5. Accessories: gilded sword; bronze spear; baldrick; sudarium.
6. Jewelry: brooch, fibula.
7. Typical Colors: usually bright, scarlet, violet, yellow, purple, and green-blue.
8. Typical Materials: coarse fabrics, such as felt, in garment of first part of period; camelot, or coarse cloth of camel's hair, later with silk warp, followed by transparent fabric; silk for mantle, gilded leather, rich brocade as well as less costly worn by nobility; later, rich fabrics from the East; linen and wool worn by lower classes.
9. Make-up: apparently none.

C. WOMEN (*Gallo-Roman, 51* B.C.-A.D. *428*)
1. Garments:
    Outer upper and outer lower: tunic similar to stola, fairly low neck, gathered at waist by girdle, short- or long-waisted, according to fashion, length to foot; many tunics worn; overtunic, elbow-length sleeve, undertunic with long sleeve.
    Under: close-fitting boneless waist.
    Cloaks and overgarments: mantle resembling Roman palla, often fastening in front with a brooch.
2. Hair: long braids bound up at back of head.
3. Headdress: sometimes garland and fillet; Phrygian cap; turban-like cap; white linen draped over head and held by circlet.
4. Footwear: shoe or sandal of soft material, sometimes long, pointed, turned-up toe, no heel, cork sole; boot for walking.
5. Accessories: mirror of polished metal; parasol; gold or silver net containing crystal and amber balls which were carried in the hands, the crystal one to cool the hands, the amber one to give forth a fragrant odor.

1. Sagum   2. Wantus   3. Bracco or Braies   4. Fibula
5. Mantle   6. Sudarium   7. Tunic or Tunica   8. Dalmatica

6. **Jewelry:** luxurious; beautiful filigree necklace; disks of gold, inlaid with enamel or colored paste; many pearls; rings, bracelets, and earrings set with stones such as emerald, amethyst, and sapphire.
7. **Typical Colors:** refer to B. 7.
8. **Typical Materials:** gold tissue or heavy fabric for mantle; white linen square for head; linen, cotton or silk tunic. Refer to B. 8.
9. **Make-up:** cosmetics similar to those used by the Roman woman; eyelid stained; hair dyed auburn or lightened with bleach.

D. **MEN** (*Teuton 200* B.C.-A.D. *768*)
1. **Garments:**
   Outer upper: nude in early part of period; tunic of 2 pieces of skin, length above knee; short linen or woolen tunic, 5th century, short sleeve.
   Outer lower: type of bracco used in 2nd century, cross gartering in 5th century.
   Cloaks and overgarments: animal skin worn over shoulder.
2. **Hair:** fairly long and flowing to shoulder; beard and mustache, 5th century.
3. **Headdress:** helmet with horns; also feathers, 5th century.
4. **Footwear:** piece of skin bound to bare foot, fastened with thong.
5. **Accessories:** spear with iron point; shield; baldrick.
6. **Jewelry:** beautiful jewelry by skilled metal worker, both gold and bronze; polished pebbles; amber beads after 5th century.
7. **Typical Colors:** bright colors including red, yellow, blue, green, and purple.
8. **Typical Materials:** animal skin, furs; spun hemp; tunic of leather also worn in 5th century; linen and woolen fabric used later.
9. **Make-up:** apparently none.

E. **WOMEN** (*Teuton 200* B.C.-A.D. *768*)
1. **Garments:**
   Outer upper and outer lower: 2 long pieces of skin or fabric; tunica similar to Roman dress, sometimes with sleeve, worn later; tunic girded at waist; 2 tunics worn after 5th century.
   Cloaks or overgarments: semicircular mantle; mantle of fur after 5th century.
2. **Hair:** flowing to shoulder; parted and wound around the head, later.
3. **Headdress:** veil worn sometimes; hair held in place by colored band.
4. **Footwear:** soft shoe.
5. **Accessories:** belt or girdle of leather, metal ornament, chain extending from belt with keys, scissors, and knives attached.
6. **Jewelry:** large fibula, brooch, bracelet, necklace resembling *dog collar*.

CHAPTER 7: DRESS

7. **Typical Colors:** refer to *D. 7.*
8. **Typical Materials:** refer to *D. 8.*
9. **Make-up:** apparently none.

F. MEN (*Frank-Merovingian* A.D. *486-750*)

1. **Garments:**
   Outer upper: tight-fitting, low neckline tunic with short sleeve, length above knee; tunica palmata of Byzantium adopted during 6th, 7th, and 8th centuries; tunica with short sleeve worn also by lower classes.
   Outer lower: bracco tied at knee; pedule cross-gartered from ankle upward, worn by nobility; bare knee, and coarse, white, woolen pedule, cross-gartered with leather bands, by lower classes; linen or leather cross-gartered with straps of hide, worn by lowest class.
   Cloaks and overgarments: at first, short overtunic of fur, later, worn by freeman and serf; sagum; *amusse.*

2. **Hair:** back of head shaved, knot on top, ends hanging down over each cheek in some tribes; mustache, no beard; hair braided with ends rolled up and fastened by rings, worn by lower classes.

3. **Headdress:** Byzantine-like crown worn by king; helmet worn by nobleman; warrior often bareheaded; hood used by lower class.

4. **Footwear:** shoe of undressed leather worn by nobility; laced, ankle-length boot; Byzantine influence in open-toe shoe; pedule; shoe of untanned hide by lower class.

5. **Accessories:** belt and buckle, set with precious stones, and golden studs; small sword used by nobility; *francisque, scramasaxe;* baldrick, or belt with bronze buckle, pouch containing knife for eating, comb, steel and firestone, used by lower classes; pouch made of skin worn by warrior; *wantus* ornamented with gold and jewels, with fur on inside or outside.

6. **Jewelry:** gold for wealthy class, bronze for others; bracelet on right arm; bracelet and necklace showing Byzantine influence; necklace sometimes of colored glass beads; earrings; richly chased and inlaid buckle; metal plates as ornaments on jacket of skin.

7. **Typical Colors:** brilliant colors including red and scarlet, symbolic colors, white for purity, red for love of God, green for youth, gold for virtue, blue for sanctification, violet for humility, and purple for dignity.

8. **Typical Materials:** hide, leather, and fur; felt garments, also coarse cloth worn earlier; later, cloth of camel's hair with silk warp; linen cloth, sometimes with warp and woof of linen and wool; also silk; soft material worn by nobility; striped tunic or plain material with bright borders.

9. **Make-up:** tattooing on arm and leg as late as 789 for both nobleman and man of lower class.

G. WOMEN (*Frank-Merovingian* A.D. *486-750*)
1. **Garments:**
   Outer upper and outer lower: dalmatica with clavus; long flowing tunica or *gown*, often 2 tunicas worn, low neckline.
   Cloaks and overgarments: semicircular mantle woven with gold pattern in circles, also narrow mantle; *manteau.*
2. **Hair:** short hair prohibited; extremely long braid intertwined with ribbons and flowers, often extending to knee.
3. **Headdress:** drapery held in place by jeweled band; veil attached to hair by ornamental pin, worn by nobility.
4. **Footwear:** soft shoe to ankle.
5. **Accessories:** belt or girdle with intricately designed buckle, also belt of leather studded with gold, and belt of plaques of gold; fur mitten.
6. **Jewelry:** lavish use of jewelry; at first clumsy workmanship, later, work compared favorably with work of artisans of Byzantium; crowns; heavy, jeweled brooch; enamel work; bracelet, necklace, and rings with many jewels.
7. **Typical Colors:** refer to *F. 7.*
8. **Typical Materials:** refer to *F. 8.*
9. **Make-up:** hair curled with curling tongs.

H. MEN (*Carlovingian* A.D. *751-986*)
1. **Garments:**
   Outer upper: outertunic sometimes edged with border of colored silk or silver, long sleeve wide at armhole, and narrow at wrist, worn as everyday costume by Charlemagne, and by the people; tunic bloused over belt; very luxurious state dress, with much gold; dalmatica symbolizing protection of the Church, worn by Charlemagne.
   Outer lower: linen bracco cross-gartered with thongs of leather to knee.
   Under: linen undertunic.
   Cloaks and overgarments: short semicircular cape introduced, fastening on right shoulder with ornament; short jacket of marten or otter skin, with clasp on right shoulder, revived by Charlemagne; paludamentum and lorum worn with imperial robe.
2. **Hair:** about chin length; beard; mustache sometimes.
3. **Headdress:** round cap of cloth with embroidered headband, ornament on raised part in front; crown.

4. **Footwear:** shoe of leather or cloth; jeweled, scarlet slipper, worn by Charlemagne.
5. **Accessories:** walking stick; scepter and orb; stole, jeweled backs of glove distinguished higher ecclesiastical; classes in the state and the church.
6. **Jewelry:** collar of gold set with stones.
7. **Typical Colors:** white, scarlet or red, green, green-blue, blue, violet, purple, and gold.
8. **Typical Materials:** linen; elaborate silk fabric and brocaded gold; jacket of otter skin or marten.
9. **Make-up:** perfume.

I. **WOMEN** (*Carlovingian* A.D. *751-986*)
1. **Garments:**
   Outer upper and outer lower: tunic with low neckline, full sleeve; belt above hip, wide band of embroidery at neckline and lower edge of tunic; mourning costume resembled nun's dress of present day.
   Under: undertunic of different color from outertunic.
   Cloaks and overgarments: shawl and mantle.
2. **Hair:** long braids intertwined with ribbons and gold braid, extending below the waist; hair concealed by square of white linen in 8th century.
3. **Headdress:** gold crown or diadem; exquisitely embroidered veil or square of white linen used over head and shoulder, hiding the hair.
4. **Footwear:** soft shoe, sometimes colored.
5. **Accessories:** walking stick ornamented with bird or flower; rich girdle of gold or silver, with pendant ends extending down the front.
6. **Jewelry:** gold bracelets and necklaces of beautiful workmanship.
7. **Typical Colors:** yellow shoe decorated with gold. Refer to *H. 7.* for additional colors.
8. **Typical Materials:** gold and other rich fabric from the East; wide bands of embroidery at neck and hem of sleeve; precious stones set in embroidery; delicate, transparent fabric; mantle and veil interwoven with gold thread.
9. **Make-up:** no doubt face was painted.

J. **MEN** (*Anglo-Saxon* A.D. *9th century-1066*)
1. **Garments:**
   Outer upper: very full, skirted tunic or *kirtle* with decorated opening at neck, usually long sleeve, waist belted or effect of belt, worn by nobility; sometimes long tunic; 2 or 3 tunics, outer one ornate, worn by lower classes; *lorica*.

Outer lower: hosa or hose and *socca* combined; bracco.

Under: undertunic; sherte or colobium.

Cloaks and overgarments: semicircular, square, or oblong mantle; *poell.*

2. **Hair:** sometimes long and flowing, sometimes fringe on forehead; shape of beard varied.

3. **Headdress:** helmet; pointed cap similar to the Phrygian cap.

4. **Footwear:** cloth or leather boot or shoe, pointed or following line of foot, cut in a V-shape at the sides; boot buttoning at side or fastening with a strap or thong.

5. **Accessories:** sword, and shield.

6. **Jewelry:** bracelet showing Danish influence; necklace of gold chain and twisted wire, sometimes with jewels, worn by nobleman; necklace of terra cotta beads, and colored ornaments worn by lower classes.

7. **Typical Colors:** gilded leather, yellow, indigo, red-orange, red, purple, and green-blue.

8. **Typical Materials:** linen; elaborate silk fabric and brocaded gold; otter skin or marten.

9. **Make-up:** apparently none.

K. **WOMEN** (*Anglo-Saxon* A.D. *9th century-1066*)

1. **Garments:**

Outer upper and outer lower: undertunic and outertunic girded, laced or buttoned at neck, moderately wide sleeve or a little longer; undertunic very long; overtunic sometimes rather short, with horizontal bands but with long sleeve; gown made shorter by pulling up at sides, sometimes left ungirded.

Under: camise or chemise.

Cloaks and overgarments: mantle.

2. **Hair:** flowing hair bound by a band worn by young girl; at first, cut short after marriage to show servitude to husband, later this custom discontinued; long hair worn by woman in privacy of home; worn low on nape of neck, usually concealed by veil.

3. **Headdress:** square of transparent fabric, diadem of gold and jewels worn over veil; circular veil worn in 9th century; jeweled band resting over drapery on head; jeweled band worn over flowing hair by young girl; social position indicated by quality of band, gold with precious stones, highest rank, gold band for next class, silver next, and cotton for lowest class.

4. **Footwear:** soft cloth or leather shoe following shape of foot; sometimes barefoot.

5. **Accessories:** belt with buckle of bronze, silver, gold, or enamel; buttons.

6. **Jewelry:** native craftsman showed foreign influence; skilled goldsmith; necklace of amber or garnet; pear-shaped earrings of crystal, amethyst, pearl, or garnet, also small earrings; rings; beautiful hairpins; jewelry set with precious stones; cross, circular pendant on necklace; enamel work first copied from foreign samples, 10th century.
7. **Typical Colors:** gilded leather, yellow, indigo, red-orange, red, purple, and green-blue.
8. **Typical Materials:** linen, silk, and wool; gold embroidery.
9. **Make-up:** blue powder used in hair; hair curled; cheeks painted.

SIGNIFICANT MOTIFS

Designs with intertwining animals, birds, lizards, and snakes; narrow ribbons which were interlaced and knotted, spiral interlacing; diagonal and angular lines, circles, squares, *quatrefoils* and dots were evident. Conventional animal motifs, circles, squares, and scenes or figures from the gospel used by the Anglo-Saxon. Designs of grotesque animals taken from myths of the Norseman, by the Teutons; later decorations include scenes and figures from the Gospel and Christian symbols including the cross, vine, dove, lamb, square, and circle.

INFLUENCES ON LATER COSTUMES

The quatrefoil design of this time was used also in designs, *c.* 1610; other influences shown in train of dress, 19th and early 20th centuries; long-waisted dress, 1940; costume jewelry and metal girdle, 1940; jumper-like dress, 1940's; sideless tunic of some garments, 1948; page-boy bob, 1940's; Merovingian styles shown in 1920's.

BOOKS OF REFERENCE

(See also BOOKS OF REFERENCE, Parts II and III, *Middle Ages,* pp. 129, 147, and GENERAL BIBLIOGRAPHY, p. 433)

Addison, Julia de Wolf, *Arts and Crafts in the Middle Ages* (London, George Bell and Sons, 1908)
Arnold, Wilhelm, *Deutsche Geschichte* (Gotha, Perthes, 1881-83)
Besant, Sir Walter, *Early London: Prehistoric, Roman, Saxon and Norman* · (A. and C. Black, Ltd., 1908)
Blum, André, *Histoire du Costume en France* (Paris, Hachette, 1924)
Brett, E. J., *A Pictorial and Descriptive Record of the Origin and Development of Arms and Armor* (London, Sampson, Low, Marston and Co., Ltd., 1894)

Brooke, Iris, *English Costume of the Early Middle Ages: The Tenth to Thirteenth Century* (London, A. and C. Black, Ltd., 1936)

Calthrop, Dion Clayton, *English Costume* (London, A. and C. Black, Ltd., 1937)

Français e L'Époque Carlovingienne à la Renaissance, 6 vols. (Paris, Gründ et Maquet, 1854-75?)

Hartley, Dorothy, *Mediaeval Costume and Life* (New York, Charles Scribner's Sons, 1931)

Hefner-Alteneck, Jakob Heinrich von, *Costumes du Moyen Age Chrétien* (Darmstadt, Guillaume Beyerle, 1840-1854)

Hill, Georgianna, *History of English Dress* (London, R. Bentley and Sons, 1893)

Lacroix, P., *Manners, Customs, and Dress during the Middle Ages and during the Renaissance Period* (London, Bicker and Son, n.d.)

Mead, William Edward, *The English Medieval Feast* (Boston, Houghton Mifflin Co., 1931)

Meyrich, S. R. and Smith, C. H., *Costume of the Original Inhabitants of the British Islands and Adjacent Coasts of the Baltic* (London, T. M'Lean, 1821)

Norris, Herbert, *Costume and Fashion,* Vol. II (New York, E. P. Dutton, Inc., 1925-38)

Parducci, Amos, *Costumi, Ornati, Studi sugli Insegnamenti di Cortigiania Medievali* (Bologna, N. Zanichelli, 1928)

Parmentier, A., *Album Historique,* Vol. I-II (Paris, A. Colin, 1907-10)

Power, Eileen, *Medieval People* (London, Methuen and Co., Ltd., 1925)

Reynitzsch, Wilhelm, *Uber Truhten und Truhtensteine, Barden, und Hardenlieder, Feste, Schmäuse und Gerichte des Teutschen* (Gotha, Ettinger, 1802)

Shaw, Henry, *Dresses and Decoration of the Middle Ages,* 2 vols. (London, W. Pickering, 1843)

GLOSSARY

Amusse—hood with a small cape, worn by monk and nobility.

Baldrick—refer to *Chaps. 1, 3.*

Bracco or Braies—refer to *Chaps. 5, 6. Pl. XIV, 3.*

Button—disk sewn on garment.

Camise or Chemise—shirt or undergarment worn by man and woman. Refer to *Camisia Chap. 5.*

Chemise—refer to *Camise.*

Circlet—refer to *Chaps. 2, 5, 6.*

Clavus—refer to *Chaps. 5, 6.*

Colobium or Sherte—type of shirt with or without sleeve, called "sherte" in Anglo-Saxon. Refer to *Chaps. 5, 6.*

CHAPTER 7: GLOSSARY

Dalmatica—refer to *Chaps. 5, 6. Pl. XIV, 8.*

Diadem—refer to *Chaps. 3, 4, 5, 6.*

Dog Collar—refer to *Chap. 3.*

Fibula—refer to *Chaps. 4, 5, 6. Pl. XIV, 4.*

Fillet—refer to *Chaps. 2, 4, 5, 6.*

Francisque—axe worn in belt or carried in right hand by handle, or by loop attached to handle.

Gown—"gunn," Anglo-Saxon, and "gwn," Welsh, similar to tunic, also known as stola.

Hosa or Hose—close-fitting leg covering, sometimes separate hose fastened to the belt, or to the drawstring of the drawers. Refer to *Chap. 6.*

Kirtle—Anglo-Saxon for tunic.

Lorica—tunic or cuirass, sometimes made of leather and scales of guilded bronze; extended a little below the waist.

Lorum—refer to *Chap. 6.*

Manteau—cloak or mantle.

Mantle—semicircular or rectangular cape or cloak fastened with ornamental brooch. Refer to *Chaps. 2, 3. Pl. XIV, 5.*

Orb—refer to *Chap. 6.*

Palla—refer to *Chaps. 5, 6.*

Paludamentum—refer to *Chaps. 5, 6.*

Pedule—refer to *Chap. 6.*

Phrygian Cap—refer to *Chaps. 3, 4, 6.*

Poell—semicircular cloak similar to the paludamentum or sagum.

Pouch—refer to *Chap. 6.*

Quatrefoil—design having 4 lobes.

Sagum—refer to *Chap. 5. Pl. XIV, 1.*

Sandal—refer to *Chaps. 1, 2, 3, 4, 5, 6.*

Scepter—refer to *Chaps. 4, 6.*

Scramasaxe—large knife or dagger which hung from waist belt.

Sherte—refer to *Colobium.*

Socca or Soque—similar to pedule.

Stola—refer to *Chaps. 5, 6.*

Stole—refer to *Chaps. 5, 6.*

Sudarium—refer to *Chaps. 5, 6. Pl. XIV, 6.*

Tunic or Tunica—garment which sometimes consisted of 2 pieces of woolen material sewed together at the side and shoulder, leaving space for the head and arm, known also as tunic in Anglo-Saxon, and cotte in French. This garment was of various lengths, fabrics, and fashion. Refer to *Chaps. 2, 3, 4, 5, 6. Pl. XIV, 7.*

Veil—refer to *Chaps. 3, 4, 5, 6.*

Wantus—finely dressed kid mitten lined with fur, and decorated with jewels, sometimes with fur on outside and warm material on inside. *Pl. XIV, 2.*

The Middle Ages

PART II

11th-13th Century

CHRONOLOGY

11TH CENTURY: Danish supremacy over England, *1016-42*.
Canute recognized as King of England, *1017*.
William the Conqueror defeated Harold, King of England, in the Battle
    of Hastings, *1066;* became first Norman ruler.
Granting of letter of franchise to cities and towns by Louis VI of France.

12TH CENTURY: Silk manufacture in Sicily, *1146*.
Charter granted in Germany to first guild of tailors, *1153*.
Time of the Crusades, *1095-1270*, seven different crusades. Stimulation of
    commercial activity.
Building of Notre Dame Cathedral, Paris, *1163-1214*.
Building of Leaning Tower of Pisa, *1174-1350*.
Paris streets paved, *1184*.

13TH CENTURY: Chimneys introduced in England, *1200*.
Troubadours in France, *1137*, in England, *1200-1300*.
Cambridge University founded, *1210*.
Magna Charta granted to the Barons by King John of England, *1215*.
Cathedral of Amiens built, *1220-88*.
Gunpowder first used by Chinese, *1234*.
Compass used by Swedes, *1250*.
First regular Parliament in England, *1265*.
Marco Polo of Venice began his travels through Asia, *1271-95*.
Florence Academy of Fine Arts founded, *1272*.
Annexing of Wales to England, *1284*.
Church at height of spiritual power.
Italy became important as a cultural center for artists and poets.

CHAPTER 8

The Middle Ages

PART II

11th-13th Century

HISTORY

A new civilization was developing in western Europe in the middle of the 11th century. Christianity had spread throughout the North and East. There was a revival in education and in the economic life. International commerce again became important. However, due to the dangers of pirates and privateers, merchants did not go alone on voyages but went in caravans for protection. As trade expanded, maritime insurance developed that has resulted in our present-day insurance.

By the 13th century, strong national states were coming to the fore in France and England. At the beginning of the 13th century, England was ruled by kings who were absolute monarchs but by the end of the century the control of the government was practically under the class of barons. Although the English empire had included half of France at the beginning of the century, by the end of this century, she was reduced to England, Wales, and Gascony. Under Edward I, influences which were to result in the limited constitutional monarchy were evident. On the other hand, France became very powerful, with a centralized government and a king who was the strongest monarch in Europe.

The Crusades had a great influence on the life and costume of the people. These were a series of militant religious expeditions to the East between 1096 and 1270 to recover the Holy Land from the Mohammedans. The capture of Constantinople in 1204 brought about an increase in the power of the West.

Orders of knighthood developed into an elaborate affair in the 12th century, requiring the highest of Christian standards and physical excellence. A boy's training for knighthood began at the age of seven;

at fourteen he became an esquire, serving in that capacity until twenty-one when he was eligible to become a knight. When he left to fight, his lady presented him with a personal object, a sleeve, a scarf, or a chemise. This token was woven with silk and gold thread with strands of her own hair.

People at this time lived under the feudal system, which required that the man or serf who labored on the lands of a master or overlord had to render him military service when necessary. Gradually the vassals under the overlords had others to serve them, and when the feudal estates gave way to the towns, the original owners lost their power as overlords. With the growth of towns there emerged the middle class or bourgeoisie, chiefly merchants and traders. In time this group became very powerful, economically and politically.

Life in the towns was intellectual and religious, with the church the center of activity. The market place served as an important center of social activity. In the 12th century there was a great revival of learning and many cathedrals and universities were founded. Invention was stimulated, and as early as 1212 fire and sanitary laws were enforced.

An important innovation of the Middle Ages was the guild system during the early part of the 12th century. Guilds or unions were composed of both artisans and laborers. The merchant or trade guilds became very powerful and were connected with the governing groups of the town. The craft guild regulated prices and wages, and managed benefit and insurance societies; by the 13th century they had made such progress as to require special training of the craftsmen. Gowns distinguished the various craftsmen.

Romanesque Art, a combination and application in architecture of the Classic and the Byzantine tradition, flourished in France and Germany in the 11th century. This style which developed new characteristics in England was termed Norman. The conquest of William the Conqueror in 1066 brought about a great change in British culture. As soon as he established himself as King of England, he engaged architects from Normandy, France, and Italy and began building churches and cathedrals. A great change occurred also in dress; the influence of the Byzantine costume was superseded by that of the Norman.

Formerly, in the Anglo-Saxon period in England, sculpture had been applied mainly to the decoration of memorial slabs, and to architectural detail in scroll-work and conventional foliage. In the second

114

part of the 11th century, sculpture became more general in use, especially in ornamentation of fonts, and reliefs over church doors; figures frequently showed the costume of the time.

In the early part of the 12th century, sepulchral effigies were used in France. Later, they were introduced into England. These figures illustrate clearly the costume of the period.

The costume was also shown in outline in illustrated manuscripts that appeared as early as the 9th century. By the end of the Middle Ages, the illumination of manuscripts had become not only popular but a recognized art, representing many costumes of the period.

Beautifully woven tapestries were in evidence throughout this period. Sometimes they were used to divide a large chamber into numerous smaller quarters. They were also used to keep off drafts of air in the stone buildings. A famous tapestry showing scenes of the conquest of England was woven in the early part of the Middle Ages for the wall of the nave of the cathedral at Bayeux. The English figures depicted are in typical Norman costumes, because Queen Mathilda and her ladies who wove the tapestry assumed that English dress was the same as that of the conquerors.

The science of heraldry had its beginning in the 12th century. Crests and armorial bearings appeared on many garments and became hereditary as family identification. A red cross was worn on the bosom of an ordinary Crusader's robe; a red Maltese cross on the left shoulder of a Knight Templar's white mantle; and personal emblems were as that of the conquerors.

The family crest was worn on top of the helmet. The crest wreath or twisted material worn around the helmet was adopted in the third quarter of the 14th century. The badge or emblem which decorated the costume of both men and women was first worn on the surcot or shield. From the middle of the 13th century a husband's coat-of-arms was worn on the right side of his shield, and that of his wife's family on the left side.

Caps worn by the nuns of today are relics of the time when it was customary to wear the wimple and the veil. The expression "widow's veil" originated from the custom of widows taking the vows and becoming nuns.

During the time of Henry III, the costume in England had simple and graceful lines, but was made of very elaborate fabric. Sumptuary laws were unable to check the extravagance. The following reign of

Edward I was marked by a general simplicity in dress; the King set the example by dressing in an unpretentious manner.

There was a language or etiquette for the use of the glove: a staff with a glove attached was given by the king to his messenger: a glove accompanied the transferal of property, and even up to the 19th century a glove signified a challenge if thrown at the foot of another person. In the 12th century, after the introduction of fingers into gloves the lower classes were permitted to wear mittens or fingerless gloves. There were also rules on the use and wearing of a mantle to convey different meanings; a nobleman would give his mantle to the messenger who bore him good news, and to the poet or troubadour who entertained him.

Byzantine modes influenced the costume of the French and of the Anglo-Saxon in England until the Crusaders captured Constantinople. After that time, costume in Western Europe became more original, the people of each country adopted a costume, resembling that of other countries, but with distinctive characteristics.

Two important institutions, feudalism and chivalry had a great influence on the life of the medieval woman. Respect for woman during the Age of Chivalry was connected with nobility of birth, youth, and physical beauty and in the 12th century the position of woman was raised among the aristocracy. The principles of chivalry later changed to matters of show and ostentation; extravagance and rashness of conduct became popular. In the Age of Chivalry, a woman dared not counsel her husband; if she were so forward as to give advice, he had the right to strike her on the face. Generally she had little freedom although she was permitted to mingle with the guests at a banquet which she attended with her husband. Her religious instruction was given by the nuns; she studied Latin and was skilled in embroidery and sewing, often supervising her servants in these activities. She also occupied herself in repairing armor, baking, brewing, and the making of medicines from herbs. Among other activities in which she excelled, were reciting stories of romance, horsemanship, and hawking. Although knowing little of the science of medicine, when necessary, she could set a broken arm or dress a wounded knight. The woman in poor financial circumstances helped her husband in his crafts of farming, dairying, and stock raising. The only forms of labor in which she did not participate were ploughing and threshing. There were spinsters, tailors, innkeepers, butchers, brewers, ironmongers, netmakers, and woolcombers among the women of the time.

DRESS

A. *Sources of information:* Bayeux Tapestry, frescoes, ceramics, sculptured figures on various cathedrals, small carvings in wood, stone, stained glass, paintings, jewelry, medals.

B. MEN (*c. 1066-1150*)
1. Garments:
    Outer upper: long or knee-length tunic, *cote* or *cotte*, embroidered border on neckline, wide or tight-fitting, long sleeve; length of garment, resulted in the wearer using slow and dignified movements; tunic longer, end of 11th century, girded or ungirded at waist; ankle-length dalmatica, sometimes with border at wrist or hem; worn as state garment of king; cotte or tunic worn by lower classes.
    Outer lower: chausses; bracco or braies, very tight at latter part of the period, by 1150 short braies, an undergarment.
    Under: sherte; 2 or 3 undertunics, additional wool or silk undertunic with elbow-length sleeve; *jube* or *jupe.*
    Cloaks and overgarments: pallium with embroidered or woven pattern; embroidered semicircular or rectangular mantle or manteau with gold border, fastening in front or on right shoulder; short, knee-length, circular Persian mantle; amusse; *surcot;* paenula.
2. Hair: custom of shaving back of head, with remainder of hair brushed forward, initiated by William I of Normandy; sometimes, hair worn moderately short without shaving back of head; forehead shaved or with hair plucked, about 1110; long hair to shoulder, a style copied from the English, worn later; mustache; smooth shaven.
3. Headdress: *coif; liripipe; liripium;* crown, by king.
4. Footwear: boot halfway to knee; buskin; pointed shoe worn in latter part of period; shoe of many styles, sometimes embroidered band at top and down instep; moccasin; sandal; knitted hose extending over braies; pedule, socca; *garter* with fringed edge.
5. Accessories: elaborate belt worn by king, simple *girdle* by others; walking stick.
6. Jewelry: extravagant jewelry unknown; rings; brooch, mantle fastening.
7. Typical Colors: white, dark purple, red, or yellow tunic; vermilion mantle embroidered in gold; sometimes, gray or blue mantle; black shoe, scarlet first worn by pirate; blue and green also used in garment.
8. Typical Materials: embroidery with jewels, on royal gown, rich fabric for undergown; silk or wool tunic and dalmatica; embroidery

or colored stitching on neckband and cuff; linen sherte; leather or felt hose; leather, cloth, or silk shoe, ornamented with gold, and jewels, silk shoe worn as part of ecclesiastical or state costume; leather, cloth, or costly fur trimming and lining; additional fabrics including *diaper, fustian,* homespun, knitted, *passemente.*

9. **Make-up:** apparently none.

C. WOMEN (*1066-c. 1150*)

1. **Garments:**

   Outer upper: tunic with tight or loose bodice, girded; long sleeve widening from elbow to wrist; *bliaut,* laced on one or both sides; round neckline, belt at waistline or hip, *corsage;* cotte with tight or loose sleeve, open or closed in front; long cotte for peasant woman.
   Outer lower: skirt very long and full, falling in trailing folds.
   Under: camisa or camise, *smock* with colored stitching at neck and wrist; jube or jupe.
   Cloaks and overgarments: semicircular mantle.

2. **Hair:** sometimes hair braided with ribbons; later worn close to head by married woman; false hair; loose hair for young girls.

3. **Headdress:** coverchief; gold embroidered veil, for wealthy; rectangular veil, sometimes extremely long in back; circlet often worn over veil; circlet, or *chaplet* holding loose hair in place.

4. **Footwear:** soft shoe buttoning up the front.

5. **Accessories:** girdle of silk cord, cut leather, linked metal disks, gold or silver cord, or colored wool, with metal ornaments set with enamel and jewels; button and cord loop used as fastening.

6. **Jewelry:** ornaments seldom worn on head; rings; bracelets; brooch.

7. **Typical Colors:** refer to *B. 7.*

8. **Typical Materials:** linen chemise; linen, cambric, *cainsil* or *chainsil,* or gauze coverchief. Refer to *B. 8.*

9. **Make-up:** apparently none.

D. MEN (*c. 1150-1200*)

1. **Garments:**

   Outer upper: rich apparel of king copied by people and clergy; dalmatica; several undertunics, at first extending almost to ankle, tight sleeve; alb; bliaut; length of garment and sleeve exaggerated, by the middle of the century; garment caught up in front, and looped through girdle; cotte; *surcot; supertunic;* long tunic or cotte with circular or straight skirt, and with colored stitching, or band on edge of tunic, cuff, and open neckline, girded or ungirded, worn by lower classes; *particolored* cotte of coarse material worn by lowest class.
   Outer lower: chausses, long, tight-fitting hose or hosa worn by well-

1. Chaplet   2. Crispine or Crespinette   3. Veil   4. Caul   5. Corse
6. Particolored   7. Almoner, Aulmonier or Aumonièré   8. Surcot

dressed man; braies with or without cross-gartering, by lower classes; sometimes, tied at knee and cross-gartered; full knee-length breeches worn by lower classes; cross-gartered loose hose and leather boot worn by peasant.

Under: linen chemise showing at neck and wrist, extending below the hip or knee, and slit up the side; short braies by upper class; jube; sherte worn by middle class, coarse linen sherte, by lower class.

Cloaks and overgarments: surcot; long mantle lined with contrasting color fastened on right shoulder or in front; *rheno; capa; cagoule* worn by lower classes.

2. **Hair:** extremely long hair over forehead, prohibited by law; hair curled with curling tongs; sometimes worn in neat roll around head; long hair the exception, about the middle of the century; fairly long hair, waved and curled, sometimes to shoulder, late in the century; side hair sometimes braided and tied up in the back in a rather complicated fashion; beard pointed, sometimes making connection with the mustache, 2-pointed beard; clean shaven by close of 12th century; waved and curled, worn by young man.

3. **Headdress:** wide, black, felt hat, with flat crown and with strings tied under chin; soft hat with button on top; Phrygian cap; round-crowned hat with upstanding fur brim; funnel shaped hood with hole for face; hooded cape used at first, by lower classes, later fashionable among nobility, amusse; brimmed hat worn by lower classes, circlet of metal; chaplet; wreath for festive occasion.

4. **Footwear:** boot or shoe fastened with button on outer side of ankle; pedule, at first, following shape of foot, then very pointed, by 1140, later less pointed; sole fastened to braies, taking place of shoe.

5. **Accessories:** exquisite girdle, superstition regarding jewels in girdle —good fortune, honor, prestige, or victory attained if correct jewels were worn; fur and leather glove with separate fingers; spur; waist belt with sword; leather *gypsire* or pouch; reliquary; heavy cloth or leather glove and knife worn through belt by working class; cross on breast of Crusader; shield trimmed with fur.

6. **Jewelry:** ornaments of gold, and silver; brooch fastening neck of cyclas.

7. **Typical Colors:** white, crimson, or purple, for mantle; red, gold, or ermine trimming; particolored garments; colors of the spectrum with many shades of blue, brown, green, and gray; gray and yellow stripes.

8. **Typical Materials:** heavy fabric used at first, thin fabric, later; crinkled, crimped, or gauffered to appear like accordion pleated; silk bliaut; wool, felt, cotton, fur, or knitted cap; leather shoe and hose;

1. Cagoule 2. Clog 3. Cote, Cotte or Cotta 4. Girdle
5. Dalmatic or Dalmatica 6. Rheno 7. Chasuble

linen legging or stocking; rich fabrics worn by wealthy class; fur-lined silk mantle, fastened across front with jeweled ornament and cord, for winter; light weight silk garments for summer; robe woven of gold and studded with gems; decorated border at neckline, edge of sleeve, and hem of mantle, and tunic.

9. **Make-up:** apparently none.

E. **WOMEN** (*c. 1150-1200*)
  1. **Garments:**
    Outer upper: particolored bliaut, neckline lower than that of pre-ceding period; girded or ungirded; laced corsage, or wide girdle over bliaut, sometimes extending from below bust to hip; very long sleeve of overgown widening at forearm, or with opening at elbow, the lower part hanging as a tube; semifitted, or *dolman-like sleeve,* tight at wrist; detachable sleeve; side-seams of gown worn open to hip; man's gown of extreme length, trailing more in back than in front, copied by the daring woman; sleeve and even veil knotted by extremist; costume at end of period resembling that of 11th century, with loose, normal waist, and skirt of graceful folds; girdle or sash used, or if ungirded, bodice tighter and laced in back; costume clinging closely to line of figure, sleeve to just below elbow worn also by lower classes.
    Outer lower: skirt becoming fuller and longer; accordion pleating.
    Under: camisia gathered or smocked at neckline, fastened with but-ton or cord; *guimpe;* detachable sleeve, sometime bestowed as love-token to lady's knight; *corset; corse;* long braies of cloth showing through open side seams of long robe worn by daring woman.
    Cloaks and overgarments: mantle, fastened on right shoulder with jeweled brooch, draped over right arm by nobility; sometimes with large jeweled ring on right side of mantle, through which part of opposite side was drawn; cloak fastened by cord or fine chain which extended from an eyelet on one side, to eyelet on other side; hooded, semicircular cape; rectangular shawl.
  2. **Hair:** parted in middle, arranged close to the head, with coil at back; hair worn loose and flowing in privacy of home; sometimes, in 2 long braids, each plaited of 3 tresses of hair, later, of 2 tresses and a ribbon; false hair, and silk casing, used to make hair appear longer; braids wound around head, in latter part of period, held in place by a fillet.
  3. **Headdress:** Phrygian cap: funnel-shaped hood; circular veil or very long scarf; crown worn over veil; *barbe, barbette,* chin strap of gauze; veil topped by crown, introduced by Eleanor of Aquitaine; *wimple; head-rail;* coverchief; *gorget;* veil, symbol of authority of

1. Cyclas   2. Wimple and Veil   3. Barbette   4. Chaperone

husband who alone had right to see her unveiled; veil draped over head, and tied on right or left side, worn by lower classes.

4. **Footwear:** heelless soft shoe following shape of foot; shoe sometimes pointed; stocking gartered at knee.

5. **Accessories:** gypsire; glove, long-buttoned, and scented; sometimes adorned with jewels; sometimes ring worn on outside of glove.

6. **Jewelry:** brooch worn at neckline of dress; jeweled metallic plaque used as cloak fastening; exquisite girdle; double girdle with tasseled ends in front; bracelets; rings; chain; imitation and precious jewels.

7. **Typical Colors:** sometimes, brown shoe with red spots, and red lining. Refer to *D. 7.*

8. **Typical Materials:** wimple of silk or linen; white linen worn by nuns; crinkled material gave effect of pleating. Refer to *D. 8.*

9. **Make-up:** apparently none.

F. **MEN** (*c. 1200-1270*)

1. Garments:

Outer upper and outer lower: cotte reaching to below the knee; dress, calf- or ankle-length, worn by leisure class; sleeve and tunic usually cut in 1 piece; sleeve seams emphasized with braid, in Spain; long tunic caught up in waist-belt, worn by the king; sleeve tight below elbow; tunic, ankle-length with small, stand-up collar and tight sleeve worn by lower classes.

Under: chemise showing at neckline and wrist, short, and slit down front or back; camisia and drawers often worn by working man; shorter braies with longer outer hose by upper class.

Cloaks and overgarments: chape, after 1250; cape; semicircular mantle fastened on right shoulder with brooch in form of *fleur-de-lis,* worn by Louis IX of France; cape sometimes fastened in front, cord with jeweled clasps as fastening, flat braid used by Spanish; long mantle cut from quarter circle of fabric, and tucked into belt on left side, later, mantle length, to hip only; *cyclas; peliçon* with pocket slits; *gardcorp* with hood; surcot sometimes with sleeve; cape; cuculla; *cointise* or *quintise; dagges* and scallops; lower sleeve left unbuttoned, after 1250, developing into *tippet;* semicircular cape with or without capuchon.

2. **Hair:** bobbed to level of chin, and brushed away from crown; bang; face clean shaven, in first part of period, later, with beard and mustache.

3. **Headdress:** red velvet cap with upstanding fur brim, sometimes worn over a coif tied at the chin; cap with button on top; hood attached to short cape; fleur-de-lis used on crown of Louis IX; circlet of metal or band of linked pieces; wreath of fresh flowers for gala occasions.

1. Wimple 2. Ramshorn 3. Gardcorp **4. Coif** 5. Mantle 6. Mantle

4. **Footwear:** simple shoe and slipper, also highly ornamented; pointed shoe stuffed with tow; sole sometimes fastened to hose.

5. **Accessories:** scepter; baldrick or *bandolier;* leather pouch; knife worn through loop of pouch or gypsire; leather belt studded with jewels; rich patterned belts by Spanish; glove sometimes decorated with jewels; lap dog carried by nobleman; badge or emblem.

6. **Jewelry:** brooch and hat ornament set with jewels.

7. **Typical Colors:** olive-green mantle; crimson mantle edged with fur, lined with white; blue satin tunic; band on tunic sometimes same color as tunic; deep red, velvet hat; brown leather boot; red and white striped hose; white glove.

8. **Typical Materials:** velvet, and fur-lined mantle worn by wealthy; brocaded cyclas, lined with silk; wool, leather, or straw cross-gartering; cotton, knitted yarn, beaver, or felt hat.

9. **Make-up:** apparently none.

G. WOMEN (*c. 1200-1270*)

1. **Garments:**

    Outer upper and outer lower: tunic and outergarment of surcot often appear as one garment; costume of simple and graceful lines; long, loose gown, girded at waist, long front opening, turned back to form revers; cotte with round neck opening, slit down the front, and fastened with lacing or brooch; long tight sleeve, or full dolman-like sleeve, buttoned or sewed from elbow to wrist; girdle sloping downward to a point, holding fullness of skirt in pleats toward the front, after 1250; long gown, with sleeve tight from elbow to wrist, worn by lower classes.

    Under: chemise or camise with long sleeve, and high neckline; corset to reduce waistline, and to raise breasts.

    Cloaks and overgarments: long mantle trailing on ground worn by married woman, and young girl of noble birth, fastening in front with brooch; cyclas, train added for lady of the nobility; surcot with tight armhole, about 1250, sleeveless or sleeved, sometimes with tight sleeve left open from elbow to wrist, usually unbelted; surcot with decorative underarm lacing, in Spain; peliçon or loose robe with pocket slit on each side; gardcorp with hood, separate or attached.

2. **Hair:** parted in center, and plaited; braids worn around head; hair in bun at back, covered with colored net, after 1250; *ramshorn;* sometimes, with curls on forehead; false hair; loose hair for young girl.

3. **Headdress:** usually unadorned; coif; brimless hat with chin strap; high hats of patterned fabric with chin strap, by Spanish; gorget; coverchief; barbette; wimple; veil over the head, with elaborate

crown, or silver or gold chaplet with decoration of stylized flowers; braid on each side enclosed in crispine; *coffer headdress.*

4. Footwear: soft shoe, more pointed than in previous century, with tip of toe embroidered; hose, gartered with fancy buckles.

5. Accessories: *almoner, aulmonier* or *aumonière;* buttons; elaborate belt; gold and jewels used on sword and purse; glove with jeweled back; woolen mittens worn by the lowest class.

6. Jewelry: jeweled collar; pendant; jeweled brooch; emblem of owner or feudal overlord used on jewelry.

7. Typical Colors: brilliant colored cyclas woven in pattern of gold, worn by Queen Eleanor. Refer to *F. 7.*

8. Typical Materials: luxurious fabrics; block-printing used to decorate fabrics. Refer to *F. 8.*

9. Make-up: apparently none.

H. MEN (*c. 1270-1300*)

1. Garments:

    Outer upper: ankle-length tunic or robe, and dalmatica worn by king; long cotte worn by upper class.

    Outer lower: chausses worn by well-dressed man; braies.

    Under: undertunic, sherte and underdrawers worn by peasant; washable chemise.

    Cloaks and overgarments: gardcorp with or without hood; surcot; cyclas; *ganache;* mantle fastened on right shoulder with brooch; supertunic; peliçon; chasuble.

2. Hair: bobbed to lobe of ear; sometimes with deep bang, parted off across top of head, and rolled under; hair sometimes shaved above forehead, and at back of neck; tonsured head for clergy.

3. Headdress: crown; circlet of metal; band of linked pieces set with jewels or enamel; chaplet of metallic and jeweled flowers or of feathers or flowers worn on hat; chaperone, liripipe; coif.

4. Footwear: strong cloth boot; pedule.

5. Accessories: decorated gold and jeweled sword or dagger hilt; elaborate belt; gypsire; orb; scepter; stole worn across chest, by king.

6. Jewelry: brooch.

7. Typical Colors: purple or scarlet robe; scarlet gown; gray peliçon; white head covering; particolored garment, striped fabric, white and brown, yellow and blue, and scarlet and yellow; black tunic; olive-green mantle; black beaver hat; red hat; gray-blue, or slate-colored hose, hose of creamy tint, often dyed with saffron; dark colors of many shades worn by middle class.

8. Typical Materials: velvet, damask and satin commonly used by nobility; silk, or linen for gown; fur lining and trimming for cloak and

mantle; plaited straw, leather, felt or beaver hat; camelot, a soft fabric of wool or silk, cotton, dimity, cambric, linen, *linsey-woolsey,* wool, cashmere; furs of ermine, squirrel, miniver, or marten for cloak; Persian silk, famous in Europe, 13th century; rich cloth of fine wool, heavy silk or cloth of gold for surcot; canvas or fustian for blouse, used by working class; straw or cloth strip for cross-gartering, and knitted or sewn woolen hose, used by lowest class.

9. **Make-up:** apparently none.

I. WOMEN (*c. 1270-1300*)

1. **Garment:**

    Outer upper and outer lower: extremely long gown or cotte, sometimes with a train; wide *bateau neckline,* long tight sleeve, cut in one with body of cotte occasionally; overrobe with elbow-length sleeve; sleeve sometimes dolman-like, and tight from elbow to wrist; very high girdle or girdle just below waist, not as highly ornamented as in 12th century; cotte often ungirded, after 1300.

    Under: chemise, corset.

    Cloaks and overgarments: semicircular mantle worn by married woman and girl of nobility, fastened in front with large circular brooch; cyclas often with train and high round neckline, *c.* 1250; chape with capuchon; gardcorp with or without hood; surcot with open sides.

2. **Hair:** parted in middle, with 2 braids wrapped around head, 1st half of 13th century; ramshorn hairdress; very long braids, ribbons wound into hair; hair curled over forehead; also curled and plaited behind ears; bun worn at back of head; false hair worn; hair flowing over shoulder, wreath of fresh flowers, for young married woman and girl.

3. **Headdress:** crown; coverchief; wimple, with veil draped over head; sometimes 2 veils with gold crown; barbette; coif in form of pill box, and gorget over ramshorn headdress; gorget and wimple worn by widow and older woman; caul, *crispine* or *crespinette;* chaperone; small *bonnet;* capuchon; brimmed hat; gold, hat ornament of fine workmanship; headband; headdress, showing Oriental influence with vertical cylindrical casing on each side of face; turban worn by Spanish woman.

4. **Footwear:** followed shape of foot; black cloth or leather boot; *clog;* hose.

5. **Accessories:** buttons; devotional book with gold cover; very elaborate girdle with shears and sewing kit, dangling from belt, or included in a pouch, which hung from belt.

6. **Jewelry:** craft of goldsmith and jeweler of high perfection; brooch set with precious stone.

CHAPTER 8: DRESS

7. **Typical Colors:** refer to *H. 7.*

8. **Typical Materials:** refer to *H. 8.*

9. **Make-up:** face painted; natural hair dyed and bleached, saffron preferred; perfume used; wimple perfumed.

SIGNIFICANT MOTIFS

Bird, animal, floral and foliage designs, decorations of crosses, crowns and intricately woven patterns were used. Stripes which had been used in costume since primitive times, and plaids were also in vogue. Elaborate decorations characterized the German costume.

INFLUENCES ON LATER COSTUMES

The veil and wimple influenced the headdress, 1938, '40's, and '50's; particolored garments, 1930's, '47, and '48; fitted garment and sleeve of all periods had origin in the garments of this period; tight-fitting, long-waisted dress with full skirt, 1940's and '50's.

BOOKS OF REFERENCE

(See also BOOKS OF REFERENCE, Parts I and III, *Middle Ages,* pp. 107, 147, and GENERAL BIBLIOGRAPHY, p. 433)

Barfield, T., *Longmans Historical Illustrations* (New York, Longmans, Green and Co., 1910-14)

Belloc, Hilaire, *The Book of the Bayeux Tapestry* (New York, G. P. Putnam's Sons, 1914)

Bonnard, Camille, *Costume Historiques de XIIIe, XIVe et XVe Siècles* (Paris, Goupil et Vibert, editors, 1845)

Brooke, Iris, *English Costume of the Early Middle Ages: The Tenth to Thirteenth Century* (London, A. and C. Black, Ltd., 1936)

Giafferi, Paul Louis de, *L'Histoire au-Costume Feminin Français: Les Modes de Môyen Age, 1037-1461* (Paris, Editions Nilsson, 1922-23)

Goddard, Eunice R., *Women's Costume in French Texts of the Eleventh and Twelfth Centuries* (Baltimore, Maryland, The Johns Hopkins Press, 1927)

Hodgetts, J. Frederick, *The English in the Middle Ages: From the Norman Usurpation to the Days of the Stuarts* (London, Whiting and Co., 1885)

Houston, Mary Galway, *Medieval Costume in England and France: The Thirteenth, Fourteenth, and Fifteenth Centuries* (London, A. and C. Black, Ltd., 1939)

Norris, Herbert, *Costume and Fashion,* Vol. II (New York, E. P. Dutton, Inc., 1925-38)

ARTISTS FOR COSTUME REFERENCE

Duccio, di Buoninsegna (1255-1319)   Martini, Simone (1283?-1344/5)
Giotto di Bondone (1266/7-1336/7)

GLOSSARY

Accordion Pleating—refer to *Chap. 2.*

Alb or Albe—refer to *Chap. 5.*

Almoner, Aulmonier or Aumoniere—silk or leather pocket or purse of beautiful workmanship, attached to girdle. *Pl. XV, 7.*

Amusse—refer to *Chap. 7.*

Badge or Emblem—an early personal distinction worn on sleeve, or embroidered on robe, developed into armorial insignia. Refer to *Chap. 2.*

Baldrick or Bandolier—refer to *Chaps. 1, 3, 7.*

Barbe—piece of linen, often pleated, worn over or under chin especially by widow or other person in mourning.

Barbette—chin strap of linen. *Pl. XVII, 3.*

Bateau Neckline—boat-shaped neckline.

Belt—jewel-studded band worn by king. *Pl. XV, 1, 4.*

Bliaut—garment worn by man and woman, originated about 1130 in the East, brought to Europe and England from the first crusade, worn by upper class, 1130-50, consisted of a corset-like bodice with long, wide, decorated or embroidered sleeve, low curved waistline attached to gathered or pleated skirt, laced, buttoned, or hooked in back. The low slit, ornamented neckline of the bliaut displayed the embroidered neckband of the sherte. A fitted garment with armholes appeared for the first time in history in the bliaut.

Bracco or Braies—refer to *Chaps. 5, 6, 7.*

Buskin—refer to *Chaps. 4, 5.*

Button—solid dome-shaped top, with eye at base, used as trimming, beginning of Middle Ages; used as fastening, with buttonholes, middle of the 13th century. Refer to *Chap. 7.*

Cagoule—semicircular cape of cloth or fur, with hood, worn by peasant. *Pl. XVI, 1.*

Cainsil or Chainsil—fine lightweight or heavy linen cloth, of simple weave.

Camise or Camisia—refer to *Chaps. 5, 7.*

Capa or Cape—short cloak similar to paenula with attached hood, worn by man and woman. Refer to *Chaps. 2, 3, 4, 6.*

Capuchon—hood usually attached to cape. Refer to *Chap. 5.*

Caul—close-fitting gold hair net, worn by lady of distinction. Refer to *Chap. 4. Pl. XV, 4.*

Chape—similar to mantle, sometimes slit at sides, with cape-like or long, loose sleeve.

Chaperone—cape with hood ending in a point. The point of the hood later became so long that it resembled a tube called liripipe and was wound around the head in a variety of ways. *Pl. XVII, 4.*

Chaplet—headband of gold or silver filigree, set with jewels; or of fresh flowers or leaves. *Pl. XV, 1.*

Chasuble—refer to *Chap. 6. Pl. XVI, 7.*

Chausses—leg-covering of cloth, shaped and sewed.

Chemise—long undergarment having long tight sleeves and skirt showing from beneath

130

CHAPTER 8: GLOSSARY

the overdress; later the words camise and chemise are used interchangeably. Refer to *Chaps. 6, 7.*

Circlet—refer to *Chaps. 2, 5, 6, 7.*

Clog—wooden sole fastened to shoe. *Pl. XVI, 2.*

Coffer Headdress—box-like headdress, worn usually with hair braided at each side.

Coif—close-fitting cap of silk, linen, or cotton, tied under the chin, also pill box type of cap. Circlet or band of jewels was worn over coif by royalty. *Pl. XVIII, 4.*

Cointise or Quintise—cut-out decoration of the cyclas, also name applied to garment so decorated.

Corsage—tight-fitting sleeveless jacket resembling a corset, worn over bliaut.

Corse—tight-fitting jupe of leather or metal, laced up the front, and worn under tunic; similar to corsage. *Pl. XV, 5.*

Corset—inner laced bodice of leather, stiffened with wood or metal strips, worn under bliaut. Refer to *Strophium, Chap. 4.*

Cote, Cotte or Cotta—short or long tunic, with sleeve cut in one piece with body of garment. The cote reached to the calf of the leg or to the instep, 13th century. *Pl. XVI, 3.*

Crispine or Crespinette—headdress of gold net and pearls. Refer to *Caul. Pl. XV, 2.*

Cyclas—overgarment, cut from a single piece of cloth, with a hole in the center for the head, sometimes lined with fur or silk. The word is derived from Cyclades, where it was manufactured. *Pl. XVII, 1.*

Dagges—lower border of tunic adorned by deep-cut pendant scallops, or tabs.

Dalmatic or Dalmatica—refer to *Chaps. 5, 6, 7. Pl. XVI, 5.*

Diaper—silk, linen, or cotton cloth of one color, woven in ornamental pattern.

Dolman-like Sleeve—large cape-like sleeve.

Emblem—distinguishing symbol worn by Crusader. The use of emblems developed into heraldry. Refer to *Badge.*

Fillet—refer to *Chaps. 2, 4, 5, 6, 7.*

Fleur-de-lis—design with lily or iris, used as the royal insignia of monarchial France.

Fustian—kind of cloth with linen warp and cotton woof.

Ganache—surcot or robe worn for extra warmth.

Gardcorp—similar to cyclas, with sleeves added. *Pl. XVIII, 3.*

Garter—piece of material which confined hose to knee, sometimes with hose rolled down over it.

Girdle—type of waistband or belt which encircled the hips. *Pl. XVI, 4.*

Gorget—wimple worn over ramshorn headdress without additional headcovering; always put under neckline of gown.

Gown—refer to *Chap. 7.*

Guimpe—chemisette worn with a low-necked dress.

Gypsire—pouch; bag for alms which was also called almoner.

Head-rail—colorful rectangular veil, worn draped over head and shoulder from left to right, passed around neck, and tied under chin.

Hosa or Hose—refer to *Chaps. 6, 7.*

Jube or Jupe—undergarment or shirt, sometimes fur-lined, worn by both man and woman.

Linsey-Woolsey—homespun cloth of linen warp and woolen woof.

Liripipe—long tube-like point or tippet of the hood.

Liripium—hood with pointed top.

Manteau—refer to *Chap. 7.*

Mantle—refer to *Chaps. 2, 3, 7. Pl. XVIII, 5, 6.*

Moccasin—refer to *Chaps. 1, 3.*

Orb—refer to *Chaps. 6, 7.*

Paenula—refer to *Chap. 5.*

Pallium—refer to *Chaps. 5, 6.*

Particolored—2-colored garment, usually with 1 side embroidered. *Pl. XV, 6.*

Passemente—gold, silver, and colored braid.

Pedule—refer to *Chaps. 6, 7.*

Peliçon—originally a Persian coat, which was a short, light-weight jacket, worn by woman, later, a long, loose, beltless robe of heavy fabric, and with pocket slits. Although it was not, at first, lined with fur, the name was applied later to fur-lined garments.

Phrygian Cap—refer to *Chaps. 3, 4, 6, 7.*

Pouch—refer to *Chaps. 6, 7.*

Quintise—refer to *Cointise.*

Ramshorn—hair twisted and wound over each ear, resembling a ram's horn. *Pl. XVIII, 2.*

Reliquary—refer to *Chap. 6.*

Rheno—cloak without a hood. *Pl. XVI, 6.*

Robe—long tunic or gown; this word later referred to coronation and parliamentary garments. Refer to *Chap. 2.*

Sandal—refer to *Chaps. 1, 2, 3, 4, 5, 6, 7.*

Scepter—refer to *Chaps. 4, 6, 7.*

Sherte—straight knee-length garment with slits at back, front, and sides; resembling the modern shirt. Refer to *Chap. 7.*

Smock—innermost garment worn by woman; made of very fine linen.

Socca—refer to *Chap. 7.*

Stole—refer to *Chaps. 5, 6, 7.*

Supertunic—overgarment.

Surcot or surcoat—garment formerly worn over armor by Crusader as a protection from the sun. The surcot or overgarment, at first, was seamless or seamed, sleeveless or with wide or close-fitting sleeve, belted or unbelted, and of a length which varied from knee to ankle. In the middle of the 13th century, sleeve of the surcot was sometimes left unbuttoned and dangling, giving rise to the tippet. The surcot was made of silk, woolen, or gold cloth, and after 1300, had 2 slits or pockets on each side. *Pl. XV, 8.*

Tippet—band sewed around elbow of sleeve with end hanging as a streamer.

Tonsured Head—refer to *Tonsure, Chap. 6.*

Tunic—refer to *Chaps. 2, 3, 4, 5, 6, 7.*

Veil—refer to *Chaps. 3, 4, 5, 6, 7. Pl. XV, 3; Pl. XVII, 2.*

Wimple—fine, silk or linen, loose neck covering worn by Anglo-Saxon woman, consisting of a piece of material brought under the chin and pinned at the top of the head; used with another piece of cloth which extended over the top of the head from the forehead, and hung down the back as a veil. *Pl. XVII, 2; Pl. XVIII, 1.*

The Middle Ages

PART III

14th-15th Century

CHRONOLOGY

14TH CENTURY: Mirrors of glass in Venice, *c. 1300*.
Beginning of the Hundred Years' War between England and France, *1337-1453*.
Order of the Garter founded in England, *1347*.
First Bible in English, Wycliffe, *1320-84*.
Needle-making industry established in Nürnberg, *1370*
Gold wire used first in *1380*.
Revolt of peasants in England, *1381*.
University of Heidelberg founded, *1386*.

15TH CENTURY: Portuguese voyages of discovery, *1415-60*, encouraged by Prince Henry of Portugal.
Siege of Orleans by Joan of Arc, *1429*. Joan of Arc burned at Rouen, *1431*.
Florence, Italy, a great power under the Medici, *1434-64*.
Printing press with movable type invented by Johannes Gutenberg of Mainz, press established, *1448*. Bible printed at Mainz, *1450-55*, first book printed with movable type.
Paved streets in London, *1453*.
Bartholomeu Diaz, Portuguese, circled the Cape of Good Hope, *1487*.
First voyage of Columbus, *August 3, 1492-March 15, 1493;* landed at the Bahama Islands, October 12, *1492*.
Conquest of Granada by Ferdinand of Aragon, *1492*. Moors vanquished.
Invasion of Italy by Charles VIII of France, *1494*.
Voyage of John Cabot along southern coast of Newfoundland, *1497*.
Switzerland, an independent republic, *1499*.

CHAPTER 9

The Middle Ages

PART III

14th-15th Century

HISTORY

Despite the Hundred Years' War between France and England in the midst of these centuries it was an era of prosperity and luxurious living, at least for the upper classes. The arts and architecture flourished, commerce grew rapidly, and wealth increased. This period saw the end of the feudal system as a new merchant class emerged and laborers lived from wages instead of off the land. Because of the increase in trade, towns with municipal buildings and guild halls developed all over Europe and life in general became much easier. Domestic comforts were initiated—fireplaces and wooden bathtubs, to mention a few.

It was a period of many radical changes in all aspects of living. As gunpowder was perfected it revolutionized methods of warfare; the invention of printing in the 15th century was one of the most important milestones in the history of civilization; the voyages of discovery opened a whole new world. The Moors were driven from Spain, the Medici made Italy a glorious capital of the arts, nationalism grew in France and England after the Hundred Years' War. Universities were founded and there was a revival of the study of Roman law and classical literature. Vernacular literature developed in all countries. Early reformers like John Wycliffe of England and John Huss in Bohemia struck the first sparks of the Protestant Revolt.

The growth of wealth during this time was reflected in the costumes. In contrast to the simple and elegant styles of the 13th century, 14th-century dress was ostentatious and exaggerated. France became the leader in fashion although the styles of each country affected others to some degree. French dolls in the latest modes were sent as a gift to the Queen of England toward the end of the 14th century and fashion leaders of Venice imported them also to follow the trend in styles. The family coat-of-arms of the nobility was embroidered on all garments and accessories for identification and display. Some English women had elegant gowns that were brought back as spoils from other countries especially France. In England sumptuary laws were passed not only to restrain some of this extravagance but in order to prevent the importation of foreign-made cloths. An English law of 1355 made the costume of the prostitute distinctive; fur was prohibited, the costume had to be worn with the wrong side outward, and only striped hoods were permitted. A later law of 1363 prohibited persons under the rank of knight or those not possessing a specified amount of land from wearing anything made of gold or silver, silk or embroidered cloth. The woman of the lower class was not allowed to wear a veil or kerchief of silk, only those made of yarn thread. Sumptuary laws continued to be passed, although costumes seem to increase rather than decrease in absurdity.

A source for costume data of the latter part of the 14th and early 15th centuries is the beautifully illustrated manuscript, *Très Riches Heures* which was made by French artists for the Duke of Berry.

Costumes became more extreme after the first quarter of the 15th century. The headdress, called the *hennin*, varied according to the rank of the wearer; the higher the headdress the higher the nobility, until it grew to almost four feet in 1428. This caused much consternation, and churchmen especially preached against this atrocity but to no avail. It was not abandoned in England until 1470, although it had been discontinued elsewhere. Another absurdity was the *cotehardie* which became so long that the wearer developed a peculiar kind of walk. A law regarding the *poulaine* (long pointed shoe) decreed that the length of the point for common people could be six inches; for the middle class one foot; and for princes two feet. The state and ceremonial costume reached its greatest splendor in the first quarter of the 15th century. In passing it is interesting to note that many orders of knighthood were founded in this period, notably the Order of the Garter, so named after the Countess of Salisbury who lost her garter while dancing at a feast being given by King Edward III. The tactful king picked it up saying that he would advance the garter to such a high position the nobles would henceforth consider it an honor to wear it. Dress continued to be extravagant until the end of the

15th century. The upper part of the body was emphasized; hats were very large, gowns trailed, sleeves dragged. A decree issued in England in 1464 prohibited the use of gold cloth, purple silk, and sable by anyone who had a title below that of baron.

During the Middle Ages more attention was given to the education of a boy than to a girl. In order to keep property within a family or to settle a family feud, infants were often betrothed before they were out of the cradle. An indication of how low an opinion was held of women in general is shown in the action of weavers at Kingston-upon-Hull who in 1490 prohibited a woman from weaving certain types of cloth. Nevertheless a few energetic women distinguished themselves as lecturers and in law.

The most important industrial development in England was the weaving of wool. In France the making of tapestries reached a high perfection. One of the most interesting series of this period was "The Apocalypse," begun in 1376 and made for Louis of Anjou. Great progress was made in both England and France in gold- and silver-smithing and in the making of jewelry.

DRESS

A. *Sources of information:* seals, manuscripts, miniature statues of wood, stone, and ivory, stained glass, memorial brasses, paintings, *Book of Hours,* Flemish and Burgundian tapestries.

B. MEN (*14th Century*)
   1. Garments:
      Outer upper: gown; cote; knee-length, long-waisted, skirted cote-hardie, often with very extreme sleeve, sometimes long and tight with circular flair over hand; long-skirted cotehardie worn by un-fashionable man, latter part of 14th century, short one to hip or above, worn by fashionable man; sleeve tied on *paltock; pourpoint* developed from paltock; pourpoint stuffed with padding, after middle of century; *mahoîtres; bellows sleeve;* tippet looped back and attached to sleeve at elbow, *castellated,* dagged, or *foliated;* garment sometimes with very high collar; *aglet, aiglet, point* or *poynt, herlot* or *latchet,* robe with family badge or emblem, personal motto, and initials of the gentleman's lady used as decorations.
      Outer lower: fitted, woolen hose or chausses extending entire length

of leg; hose sometimes with crotch and foot, or strap under foot; hose sometimes padded; particolored or pied hose; aiglet or point, herlot or latchet; bare leg or cross-gartered hose for peasant.

Under: very short or thigh-length chemise; sleeved or sleeveless jube or jupe worn between chemise and cotehardie; very short underdrawers, or braies.

Cloaks and overgarments: gardcorp, first of period; long or full, normal-waisted *houpeland* or *houppelande,* latter part of period, often worn with hood; mantle fastened on right shoulder, or circular cloak with a number of ornamental fastenings over chest and with openings for head and arms; chape with capuchon; cyclas; ganache; *courtepy* or *jaquette; patte* or *paw;* peliçon; surcot still worn; *sideless gown.*

2. **Hair:** bob with straight bang across forehead; closely cropped hair, end of century; curled hair often worn by young man; neatly clipped beard, often trimmed in 1 or 2 points; turned-up mustache; sometimes clean-shaven; long beard worn by older man, 2nd half of century.

3. **Headdress:** capuchon having lower edge scalloped; headband or chaplet; cap of fur or felt; stiff hat with broad brim; hat trimmed with knots of silk or metallic ribbon; hat sometimes worn on top of chaperone or coif; liripipe; hat with visor-like brim, formed by rolling up the sides.

4. **Footwear:** sole fastened to bottom of foot of hose, worn as shoes; close-fitting, black *boot;* shoe exaggerated, 1350; shoe very highly decorated or simple in design; greatest length of toe of shoe reached, latter part of century; *crackow* or poulaine sometimes fastened with gold chain to garter at knee; tip of shoe stiffened with some kind of material; length of shoe distinguished class; round-toed shoe worn later; high boot with turned-down top; buskin.

5. **Accessories:** glove, sword, dagger or *misericorde;* pouch, gypsire or *escarcelle,* worn with dagger on *girdle; anelace; baselard; knapsack* on baldrick or bandolier worn by traveler, *penner* or box worn by messenger in similar way; reliquary; elaborate girdle with pendant; *pomander;* buttons; badge or emblem.

6. **Jewelry:** cross; 2 or 3 rings worn by wealthy man; necklace; bells and trinkets dangling from gentleman's belt; collar or flat necklace used as special emblem.

7. **Typical Colors:** particolored or pied, including white and blue, white and black, scarlet or red and black for robe, and hose; deep royal blue popular; green coat and hood; blue hood and mantle; red cap; striped hat; white purse and cotte; purple or light-blue gown designating a doctor of physics; black robe, canon; brown occasionally

1. Castellated, Dagged or Foliated 2. Pouch 3. Gardcorp
4. Sideless Gown 5. Pourpoint

worn for mourning; black cloak; black boot; black hat; contrasting color for lining of gown.

8. **Typical Materials:** silk scarf attached to hat; felt, velvet, or beaver hat; white linen coif, black velvet for older man; gold cloth mantle; taffeta lining; silk, satin, damask, velvet, and velvet brocade weaves for doublet and gown; also wool and silk gown; linen braies or drawers; woolen hose and chausses; silk hose rarely used; silk or leather shoe, beautiful fur; embroidered cloak, sometimes with precious stones; sheep skin also used; cloth of gold for man of rank lower than a knight prohibited at various times through sumptuary laws.

9. **Make-up:** apparently none.

C. WOMEN (*14th Century*)

1. **Garments:**

   Outer upper: close-fitting tunic; increase in heraldic blazoning; *plastron;* bateau neckline, after 1340, lower neckline, 2nd half of century; sleeve extending to knuckles, sometimes buttoned from elbow to wrist, with short cuff; long pendant sleeve out of style, last of century; narrow belt; cote or cotte; cotehardie; bodice and skirt separate, middle of century, usually back lacing before 1350, front lacing later.

   Outer lower: skirt; long train attached to belt by chain or *tussoire.*

   Under: chemise or *robe-linge* showing through slashes; petticoat or petticotte; corset with skirt attached.

   Cloaks and overgarments: mantle; *gueules;* chape with capuchon; cloak with train, first quarter of century; sleeveless surcot with fur trimming; sideless gown.

2. **Hair:** much attention spent on hair, golden or fair hair preferred; hair worn loose by unmarried woman; plaits in intricate styles worn around head by married woman, sometimes 4 braids, 2 on each side of head; braids encased in silk; roll on each side of head, ramshorn hairdress usually covered; hair pushed simply into cases, 1 at each side of head; in general, square or cylindrical shape given to head by hairdress, 1350, rounder, toward end of century.

3. **Headdress:** coif; caul of gold net; fillet; pearls across forehead; jeweled circlet or *coronet;* chaplet; cylinder of gold fretwork ornamented with precious stones on each side of head; *roundel* or *turban; tricorne hat;* wimple still worn at first of century; gorget tucked under neckline, used without veil; barbe; barbette; veil at end of century; *kerchief; reticulation.*

4. **Footwear:** soft shoe at first; shoe resembling that worn by man, lengthened, *c.* 1340; stocking, scarlet hose by lower classes.

5. **Accessories:** buttons used on tight-fitting gown; elaborate girdle; keys,

1. Liripipe   2. Escarcelle   3. Girdle   4. Crispine or Crespinette
5. Patten   6. Bellows Sleeve   7. Clog   8. Cape, Crackow or Poulaine
9. Aglet   10. Badge or Emblem   11. Poulaine

shears, sewing kit, and beautiful prayer book, Book of Hours, all dangling from belt; rosary; flag-shaped fan; parasol; glove, sometimes carried or placed in girdle; jeweled gauntlet; mitten; purse; pomander; baldrick or bandolier; reliquary.

6. **Jewelry:** 2 or 3 finger rings worn by wealthy woman, 2nd half of 14th century; beautiful ornaments set with jewels worn at top of sleeve on shoulder; garment embroidered with jewels; necklace in latter part of century, large neck chain with drop, collar or wide flat necklace extending from one shoulder to the other, middle of 14th century; earrings and bracelets not popular; pectoral; perpendicular band of jewels worn down center of plastron.

7. **Typical Colors:** black embroidery on head kerchief and shoe. Refer to *B. 7.*

8. **Typical Materials:** cloth of gold, silver, shot taffeta, and velvet used for wedding robes of Isabel of France; dress, petticoat and mantle embroidered with coats of arms of the wearer's family as well as that of her husband's family, velvet and silk tunic and cloak embroidered with gold and colored silk thread; mantle sometimes of fur. Refer to *B. 8.*

9. **Make-up:** hair often bleached yellow; hair sometimes shaved above forehead emphasizing its height; eyebrows plucked.

D. MEN (*15th Century*)

1. Garments:

Outer upper: great extravagance in dress; tunic or gown reaching to knee, worn in place of cotehardie, 1440-50, later, very short; fullness of garment in folds or pleats in back and front; cotehardie continued to be worn by court jester; pourpoint became *doublet* or *doblet,* by 1450; pourpoint or paltock worn under surcot, *c.* 1450; *jerkin;* long, unbelted gown; high collar opening in front, attached to short-skirted doublet; inner doublet to waist only worn for warmth; padding increased throughout costume; dagged, castellated, foliated; sleeve full at elbow; bellows sleeve introduced; short and round sleeve; *poky sleeve,* middle of 15th century; sleeve began to widen at top, toward end of 15th century, *leg-of-mutton sleeve;* tippet; robe embroidered with conservative family badge or initials of lady-fair.

Outer lower: trunk hose; hose and breeches replaced longer gown and robe; hose extending full length of leg, fastened to upper garment or doublet by points, often with strap fitted around foot; particolored.

Under: long-sleeved full chemise extending almost to thigh; jupe; drawers or braies similar to trunks worn by present-day acrobat.

142

1. Wimple   2. Atours   3. Reticulation   4. Chaplet
5. Jube or Jupe   6. Caul   7. Reliquary   8. Poulaine
9. Reliquary   10. Capuchon   11. Peliçon   12. Mantle

Cloaks and overgarments: very long houpeland with high collar, huge sleeve, belt at normal or low waistline, or unbelted, fur-trimmed, skirt sometimes slit to knee; later, sleeve lined with contrasting color; *jupon;* long robe with fairly close sleeve, and long padded folds meeting at center front and flaring slightly to hem, hook and eye on under pleat, served as fastening; hooded cape, with square of fabric worn like Roman toga; *journade;* peliçon; cape or mantle fastened on right shoulder with brooch, or fastened in center by king; short fur cape worn with royal mantle.

2. **Hair:** short or cropped, shaven halfway up back of head; hair usually straight, cut close in front of ears; with roll or bang on forehead, until middle of century; clean shaven, or beard cut in 1 or 2 points; mustache.

3. **Headdress:** beaver hat with feathers; tall hat, brimless or with narrow or wide brim; headband, sometimes, chaplet jeweled or with real flowers; close hood or capuchon; chaperone with extremely long liripipe; chaperone discontinued near end of century, liripipe still worn attached to hat; coif of white linen worn underneath hat; *bonnet;* black velvet coif worn by older man, coif later used as night cap; *bag-cap;* hat with trimming of fur, brooch, medal, or feathers.

4. **Footwear:** poulaine or crackow tip stiffened with material; by 1450, shoe with natural line, *solleret;* heelless; duckbill-toed, normal-shaped shoe, by middle of 15th century; soft boot to calf of leg, for outdoor wear, lacing on inner or outer side of leg; wooden chopine, *clog,* or *patten;* spurs, latter part of 15th century, worn indoors.

5. **Accessories:** girdle, escarcelle, pouch suspended from belt at waist or from additional hip-belt; misericorde; knife and spoon carried in wallet; walking stick of beautiful wood with ornamental top; baldrick or bandolier; pomander; small buttons on sleeve; large buttons or metal plaques sewed on various parts of garment; garters; kid or fabric glove, important for gentleman; *mitten* worn by peasant.

6. **Jewelry:** many rings; seal ring on thumb, chain often indicating position of person, circular pendant bearing coat of arms of guild or town.

7. **Typical Colors:** rich colors, brighter in 15th century; occasionally, crimson for entire costume; light blue robe; yellow robe and tunic; sometimes an all-white costume; purple hood, black robe; blue and white, or red and white, in particolored costume; dull-green, brown, dark blue-gray, dull orange-red, violet and other colors; painted or gilded shoe.

8. **Typical Materials:** felt or beaver hat; ostrich plume on hat; gown of gold, silver, silk or satin cloth with gold embroidery and pearls;

1. Jube or Jupe   2. Cotehardie   3. Cote, Cotte or Cotta   4. Jube or Jupe

damask or satin lining for king's mantle; fur hood and trimming; white cambric camisia; canvas, cotton, camel's hair, jersey, serge, flannel; brocade or silk mantle; painted or gilded leather, cloth, felt, or velvet shoe; kid, chamois or fabric glove; wool used by peasant.

9. **Make-up:** apparently none.

E. WOMEN (*15th Century*)

1. **Garments:**

   Outer upper: underdress close-fitting to hip early in period, worn with surcot; very long overdress; *kyrtle;* houpeland or robe, ungirded or with wide girdle, high under breasts, with extremely full sleeve; sleeve with large cuff coming down over knuckles, 2nd decade of century; gown with tubular sleeve having vertical or horizontal opening at elbow, round neckline, in first quarter of century, with sailor-like collar or small turnover collar; low neckline and bare shoulder, after 1450, V-shaped neckline and tight sleeve later; gown usually with wide shawl collar, and wide revers; low V-neck sometimes exposed breasts; plastron; high neckline worn by older woman; gown rather tight-fitting, and with long waist for young girl.

   Outer lower: skirt separate from bodice by end of century; very long, held up by tussoire or tucked in belt in front; long train with elegant lining.

   Under: sleeved camisia; corset-like garment similar to cote of former period; garter; night garment, if worn, consisting of camisia or sherte.

   Cloaks and overgarments: semicircular cape; *sideless gown;* chaperone or hooded circular cloak; gueules.

2. **Hair:** worn loose by girl or unmarried woman; crown worn by queen; ramshorn hairdress; braids looped up at temples, giving square effect; 2 braids around head; roll; forehead heightened by plucking the hair, wisp of hair on center of forehead showed below hennin.

3. **Headdress:** *cornet, little hennin, atours, escoffion;* very high headdress, until 1440; hennin covered with 2 rectangular veils, 1450; *butterfly headdress;* close-fitting cap; horned crescent or heart-shaped headdress; hennin disappeared in latter part of century; turban, turban roll, roundel; wimple, gorget, or barbette worn by older unmarried woman; caul, crispine or crespinette of gold; gold band; reticulation; brimless hat or cap with tall crown and with half-veil over face; mannish hat; chaperone hood, sometimes with liripipe.

4. **Footwear:** long, pointed shoe not as exaggerated as that worn by man; ankle boot or shoe worn, 1410-30, variety of types, 1450-70;

the long toe disappearing, *c.* 1460, the wide toe in style, solleret; patten, *galoche*, or clog with leather top.

5. **Accessories:** glove very important for lady; half-gloves or mitts; peacock fan; bag with draw-string; elaborate girdle with jeweled clasp; baldrick or bandolier; aiglet; pomander; jeweled prayer book.

6. **Jewelry:** resembled that of 14th century but more extravagant; antique types; fingers laden with rings, 2 or 3 on each finger, on all joints; many gold chains; jeweled rosary attached to finger ring or around waist; band of jewels on each shoulder.

7. **Typical Colors:** white veil, green and gold girdle; violet undertunic, black shoes; fur dyed green or red. Refer to *D. 7.*

8. **Typical Materials:** sheer lawn and batiste for wimple and veil; chiffon, crepe, or gauze for scarf and veil; velvet popular; ermine for nobility; marten, sheep, lamb, astrakhan. Refer to *D. 8.*

9. **Make-up:** eyebrows plucked to faint lines or entirely removed.

SIGNIFICANT MOTIFS

All-over patterns included the square, lozenge, star, circle and diagonal and horizontal stripes. At first the lord wore the badge of his master, but by the latter part of the 14th century he had his own particular badge. The personal badge or monogram was often an all-over pattern instead of the large heraldic blazonry.

INFLUENCES ON LATER COSTUMES

College cap or mortar board of today developed from skull cap, 14th century; college commencement gown from gown of Middle Ages; tricorne hat, 18th century and early 1900's; leg-of-mutton sleeve in Renaissance, 1814, '33, '37, '92, 1932 and '48; bobbed hair, 1926-52; page-boy bob, 1940's; bang, 1892, early 20th century, and 1948-52; plunging neckline, 1949-52.

BOOKS OF REFERENCE

(See also BOOKS OF REFERENCE, Parts I and II, *Middle Ages*, pp. 107, 129, and GENERAL BIBLIOGRAPHY, p. 433)

Barfield, T., *Longmans Historical Illustrations* (New York, Longmans, Green and Co., 1909-10)

Bonnard, Camille, *Costume Historiques de XIIIe, XIVe et XVe Siècles* (Paris, Goupil et Vibert, 1845)

THE MIDDLE AGES: PART III

Brooke, Iris, *English Costume of the Later Middle Ages* (London, A. and C. Black, Ltd., 1935)

Carey, William Paulet, *Critical Description of the Procession of Chaucer's Pilgrims to Canterbury, Painted by Thomas Stothard* (London, Cadell and Davies, 1808)

Giaferri, Paul Louis de, *L'Histoire au Costume Feminin Français: Les Modes du Môyen Age, 1037-1461* (Paris, Editions Nilsson, 1922-23)

Hope, W. H. St. John, *Heraldry for Craftsmen and Designers* (London, J. Hogg, 1913)

Houston, Mary Galway, *Medieval Costume in England and France: The Thirteenth, Fourteenth, and Fifteenth Centuries* (London, A. and C. Black, Ltd., 1939)

Norris, Herbert, *Costume and Fashion*, Vol. II (New York, E. P. Dutton, Inc., 1925-38)

Weiss, Hermann, *Kostümkunde: Geschichte der Tracht und des Geräths, Vol. III, vom 14 Jahrhundert bis auf die Gegenwart* (Stuttgart, Ebner and Seubert, 1872)

ARTISTS FOR COSTUME REFERENCE

Antonello da Messina (1422/30-79)
Baldovinetti, Alessio (1425-99)
Barbari, Jacopo de (1440/50-1511/15)
Bartolommeo, Fra (1472-1517)
Bellini, Gentile (1426/30-1507)
Boltraffio, Giovanni Antonio (1467-1516)
Botticelli, Sandro (1444/7-1510)
Bouts, Dirk (1410/20-75)
Burgkmair, Hans (Elder) (1473-1531)
Carpaccio, Vittore (1450/5-1520/26)
Castagno, Andrea del (1390-1457)
Costa, Lorenzo (Elder) (1460-1535)
Cranach, Lucas (Elder) (1472-1553)
Cristus Petrus (Pieter Christophsen) (1400?-72/3)
Crivelli, Carlo (1430/5-93)
Desiderio da Settigano (1428-64)
Duccio di Buoninsegna (1255-1319)
Dürer, Albrecht (1471-1528)
Eych, Hobert van (1366-1426)
Fiorenzo di Lorenzo (1440/5-1522/5)
Gentile da Fabriano (1360/70-1427/50)
Ghirlandajo, Domenico Bigordi (1449-94)
Giorgione, Georgio (1477/8-1510/1)

Giotto di Bondone (1266/7-1336/7)
Giovanni di Paola (1403?-82)
Goes, Hugo van der (1440-1482)
Gozzoli, Benozzo (1420/4-98)
Holbein, Hans (Elder) (1460/70-1524)
Leonardo da Vinci (1452-1519)
Lippi Fra Filippo (1406-69)
Lochner, Stephen (1410-51)
Lorenzetti, Ambrogio (1323-1348)
Lotto, Lorenzo (1480?-1554/6)
Mabuse, Jan Gosseart van (1462/70-1533/41)
Mantegna, Andrea (1431-1506)
Martini, Simone (1283-1344/5)
Massaccio, Tommaso Guidi (1401/2-1428/9)
Massys (Matsys) Quentin (1460/6-1530)
Melozzo da Forli (1438?-94)
Memling, Hans (1430-94)
Perugino, Pietro Vannucci (1445-1523)
Piero, Della Francesca (1416/20-92)
Pinturicchio, Bernardino (1454-1513)
Pollajuola, Piero (1443-96)
Predis, Giovanni Ambrogio de (1455-1522)

CHAPTER 9: GLOSSARY

Raphael, Sanzio (1483-1520)

Robbia, Andrea della (1435-1525)

Rosselli, Cosimo (1438/39-1507)

Signorelli, Lucca (1441/4-1523)

Spinello di Luca (1330/3-1410)

Uccello, Paolo di Dono (1396/7-1475)

Verrochio, Andrea del (1435-88)

Vivarini, Antonio da Murano (1400-1470?)

Weyden, Roger can der (1399/1400-1464)

Zeitbloom, Bartholmaus (1450?-1518/21)

GLOSSARY

Aglet, Aiglet, Point or Poynt—metal tag or point used to fasten pieces of plate armor, or various parts of other garments as sleeve and paltock. *Pl. XX, 9.*

Anelace—long knife often carried in sheath which hung from girdle.

Atours—padded headdress which resembled two horns. *Pl. XXI, 2.*

Badge or Emblem—refer to *Chaps. 2, 8. Pl. XX, 10.*

Bag-cap—cloth or velvet, brimless hat with fur band or ornament which resembled a turban.

Baldrick or Bandolier—refer to *Chaps. 1, 3, 7, 8.*

Barbe—refer to *Chap. 8.*

Barbette—refer to *Chap. 8.*

Baselard—very large sword worn on the left side.

Bateau Neckline—refer to *Chap. 8.*

Bellows Sleeve—gathered sleeve having cuff and long vertical slit through which the hand could pass. *Pl. XX, 6.*

Bonnet—small hat with crown pleated into a headband.

Book of Hours—book used for private devotions, divided into sections: one contained a calendar and another, the hours of meditation of the Virgin, hence the name *Book of Hours.*

Boot—foot covering which extended to the ankle.

Buskin—refer to *Chaps. 4, 5, 8.*

Butterfly Headdress—semitransparent linen, draped and wired to resemble a butterfly and worn over the tall headdress.

Camise, Camisia or Sherte—refer to *Chaps. 5, 7, 8.*

Cape—refer to *Chaps. 2, 3, 4, 6, 8.*

Capuchon—refer to *Chaps. 5, 8. Pl. XX, 8; Pl. XXI, 10.*

Castellated, Dagged or Foliated—deep scallops at hem or other edges of garment. Refer to *Dagges, Chap. 8. Pl. XIX, 1.*

Caul—refer to *Chaps. 4, 8. Pl. XXI, 6.*

Chape—refer to *Chap. 8.*

Chaperone—refer to *Chap. 8.*

Chaplet—refer to *Chap. 8. Pl. XXI, 4.*

Chausses—refer to *Chap. 8.*

Chemise—shirt-like garment. Refer to *Chaps. 6, 7, 8.*

Chopine, Clog or Patten—wooden-soled platform attached to shoe worn as a protection from the mud.

Circlet—refer to *Chaps. 2, 5, 6, 7, 8.*

Clog—wooden platform with strap fastening over instep. Refer to *Chopine* and to *Chap. 8. Pl. XX, 7.*

Coif—refer to *Chap. 8.*

Cornet or Hennin—steeple headdress which usually covered the hair, except for a small curved lock in the center of the forehead.

Coronet—an ornamental circlet worn around the head.

Corset—fitted garment worn over chemise, back-lacing until 1350, front lacing later. This garment was attached to a skirt. Refer to *Chap. 8.*

Cote, Cotte or Cotta—refer to *Chap. 8. Pl. XXII, 3.*

Cotehardie—shaped garment, tight-fitting around shoulder, waist and hip, when worn by woman; close-fitting to waist with circular skirt, when worn by man. The woman's garment had sleeves of different lengths, was laced up the front or back, and had a slit at each side which opened into a pocket. It is said to have been introduced by Anne, wife of Richard II. *Pl. XXII, 2.*

Courtepy or Jaquette—very short overgarment or cotehardie often particolored or embroidered with gems. It usually had a high collar.

Crackow or Poulaine—long-tipped hose and shoe introduced during the reign of Richard II, and named after the city of Crackow in Poland; length of toe became so long that it had to be tied to the knee. Refer to *Pl. XX, 8.*

Crispine or Crespinette—refer to *Chap. 8. Pl. XX, 4.*

Cyclas—refer to *Chap. 8.*

Dagged—refer to *Castellated.*

Doublet or Doblet—short jacket or variety of pourpoint, sleeved or sleeveless; worn under tight-fitting pourpoint. When used as an outer garment it was padded and had a short skirt.

Duckbilled-toed—shoe with blunt or square toe worn *c.* 1483 in England.

Emblem—refer to *Badge.*

Escarelle—pouch or purse attached to waist or hip-belt into which a knife was often inserted. *Pl. XX, 2.*

Escoffion—wired headdress of fine lawn about a yard wide, resembling 2 horns.

Fillet—refer to *Chaps. 2, 4, 5, 6, 7, 8.*

Foliated—refer to *Castellated.*

Galoche—wooden platform with an ornamental strap fastening, and the base beneath the heel and ball of the foot, elevated to varying heights. Refer to *Chopine.*

Ganache—refer to *Chap. 8.*

Gardcorp—refer to *Chap. 8. Pl. XIX, 3.*

Girdle—ornamental belt encircling hips. Refer to *Chap. 8. Pl. XX, 3.*

Gorget—refer to *Chap. 8.*

Gueules—small fur-lined shoulder cape with lower corners of cape turned back in front. It was attached to the peliçon.

Gypsire—refer to *Chap. 8.*

Hennin—refer to *Cornet.*

Herlot or Latchet—string used to tie the hose to the paltock, or sleeve in armhole of paltock.

Hose—leg-covering with all-over design worn during this period. Refer to *Hosa, Chaps. 6, 7, 8.*

Houpeland or Houppelande—loose and comfortable dress, introduced during the reign of Charles VI, which became very fashionable during the time of Richard II. One style worn by man had long flowing sleeves, a long fitted waist, floor-length or longer skirt slit to above the knee; another style was knee-length and had a high standing collar. Planché says this garment was probably introduced from Spain. An extremely exaggerated style was called "Bastard." The woman's gown of this period had a short waist, full skirt, and long, flaring sleeves.

Jaquette—refer to *Courtepy.*

Jerkin—short velvet or leather jacket.

CHAPTER 9: GLOSSARY

Jornade or Journade—short circular garment which at first had large full sleeves, and later, long, slit sleeves. It was often worn for riding.

Jube or Jupe—refer to *Chap. 8. Pl. XXI, 5; Pl. XXII, 1, 4.*

Jupon—overgarment having armorial blazonry, worn over armor in the 14th century; jupon referred to petticoat, similar civil garment called cotehardie.

Kerchief—scarf worn over head, formerly called the coverchief. A kerchief was often given by a lady to a knight, who wore it on his arm.

Knapsack—case of canvas or leather carried on the back.

Kyrtle—dress which evolved from the cotehardie about 1480. It was close-fitting at shoulder, waist and hip, and had a full skirt. The neckline, edged with fur, velvet or brocade, was very low in front, on shoulders, and in back. Refer to *Kirtle, Chap. 7.*

Latchet—refer to *Herlot.*

Leg-of-mutton Sleeve—very wide at shoulder, tapering down to wrist.

Liripipe—tail of the hood of the chaperone, which became 6 feet or more in length, tucked in belt, or wrapped around neck. Later, it was twisted around the head in turban-like fashion. Refer to *Chap. 8. Pl. XX, 1.*

Little Hennin—headdress shaped like a truncated cone.

Mahoîtres—name given to shoulder padding of gown and jacket.

Mantle—refer to *Chaps. 2, 3, 7, 8. Pl. XXI, 12.*

Misericorde—dagger, worn on the right side.

Mitten—same as modern mitten, made of heavy hide or fabric.

Paltock—short jacket to which undersleeve and hose were attached, later called pourpoint.

Particolored or Pied—garment with each side of a different color. Refer to *Chap. 8.*

Patten—iron support worn under shoe. Refer to *Chopine. Pl. XX, 5.*

Patte or Paw—earliest form of lapel that resembled a narrow collar and tabs, worn on the ganache.

Pectoral—large breast brooch. Refer to *Chap. 2.*

Peliçon—fur-lined garment. Refer to *Chap. 8. Pl. XXI, 11.*

Penner—container for pen and ink-horn, often attached to girdle.

Petticoat or Petticotte—at first a little coat; later skirt of the cotte, which was worn as a separate garment.

Pied—refer to *Particolored.*

Plastron—type of garment which later became the stomacher. It was sometimes of fur, and was worn as a decoration of the costume.

Point or Poynt—refer to *Aglet.*

Poky Sleeve—bag-like sleeve in which objects were carried.

Pomander—ball or hollow ornament often made of filigree, containing sponge of perfume, suspended from necklace, or attached to girdle.

Pouch—refer to *Chaps. 6, 7, 8. Pl. XIX, 2.*

Poulaine—refer to *Crackow. Pl. XX, 11; Pl. XXI, 8.*

Pourpoint—short jacket with tight sleeve buttoned from elbow to wrist, worn under the cotehardie, formerly known as paltock. *Pl. XIX, 5.*

Ramshorn Hairdress—refer to *Chap. 8.*

Reliquary—refer to *Chaps. 6, 8. Pl. XXI, 7, 9.*

Reticulation—decorative netting which confined the hair at either side of the face. *Pl. XXI, 3.*

Robe—refer to *Chaps. 2, 8.*

Robe-linge—linen chemise.

Roundel or Turban—headdress made of a thick roll of material, sometimes with a piece of cloth hanging down on one side.

Sherte—refer to *Camise.*

Sideless Gown—gown resembling a narrow poncho. *Pl. XIX, 4.*

Solleret—shoe with rounded toe.

Surcot—refer to *Chap. 8.*

Tippet—refer to *Chap. 8.*

Tricorne-hat—3-cornered hat.

Trunk Hose—upper hose or leg garment which extended from waist to knee.

Tunic—short, knee-length garment. Refer to *Chaps. 2, 3, 4, 5, 6, 7, 8.*

Turban—refer to *Roundel.*

Tussoire—chain and clasp which hung from the girdle and held up one side of the long skirt.

Veil—refer to *Chaps. 3, 4, 5, 6, 7, 8.*

Wimple—refer to *Chap. 8. Pl. XXI, 1.*

16th Century

CHRONOLOGY

Ponce de Leon explored Florida, *1512*.

Balboa crossed the Isthmus of Panama to the Pacific, *1513*.

France invaded by Henry VIII of England and Emperor Maximilian of Germany, *1513*.

Commercial relations between Portugal and China, *1516*.

Martin Luther makes first protest against Catholicism, *1517*.

Conquest of Mexico by Cortez, *1519-21*.

Magellan expedition, the first to circumnavigate the globe, *1519-21*.

First war of Charles V with Francis I, *1521-26*.

Portuguese began colonization of Brazil, *1530*.

Spinning wheel invented in Germany, *1530*.

Conquest of Peru by Pizarro, *1532-34*.

De Soto discovered the Mississippi, *1541*.

Beginning of needle-making industry in England, *1545*.

First coffee house opened in Constantinople, *1554*.

Wars of the Huguenots, *1562-98*.

Sir Francis Drake, first Englishman to circumnavigate the globe, *1577-83*.

First English colony in Newfoundland, founded by Gilbert, *1583*.

Expedition to Virginia by Sir Walter Raleigh, *1583;* Virginia Dare, first child of English parentage, born in North America, *1587*.

Defeat of the Spanish Armada by the English, *1588*.

Knitting machine invented by William Lee, an Englishman, *1589*.

Political rights equal to those of the Catholics given to the Huguenots by the Edict of Nantes, *1598*.

CHAPTER 10

16th Century

HISTORY

Historians differ as to the beginning and span of the Renaissance but it is agreed that the revival of interest in learning reached its zenith by the 16th century in Italy. The 16th century was important as an age of expansion as well as of development in the arts and sciences. This outline is concerned with the effect of the Renaissance on costume, and the historical periods are considered in relationship to it.

Italy had become the center of culture in the 14th and 15th centuries but the discovery of America in 1492 changed the trade of Spain, France, and England from the east to the west and thus brought about the ruin of the Italian mercantile states. Italy became disorganized in 1492 after the death of Lorenzo Medici, who had prevented the breaking out of dissension among the various princes. In the same year the Spanish, German, and French armies invaded Italy and met with little resistance because of the lack of co-operative effort among the petty states. In 1530 Charles I of Spain entered Italy and was crowned Emperor. The Spanish domination of Italy continued until the 18th century.

The dominant influence in Spanish art until the 15th century was Saracen because the Moors had been in power in Spain for 800 years. At that time Spain was divided into the small states—Asturia, Leon, Aragon and Castile—but the last became so powerful that it absorbed the others. The Moors were driven out of Spain in 1492, during the reign of Ferdinand and Isabella. Portugal, which had been part of Spain since 1140, became a Spanish dominion in 1580 and obtained her independence in 1664.

During the 16th century Spain became one of the greatest powers in Europe. Charles I, son of Ferdinand and Isabella, succeeded his father as King of Spain; he inherited the Netherlands, and on the death of Maximilian, was proclaimed Emperor of Germany in 1519.

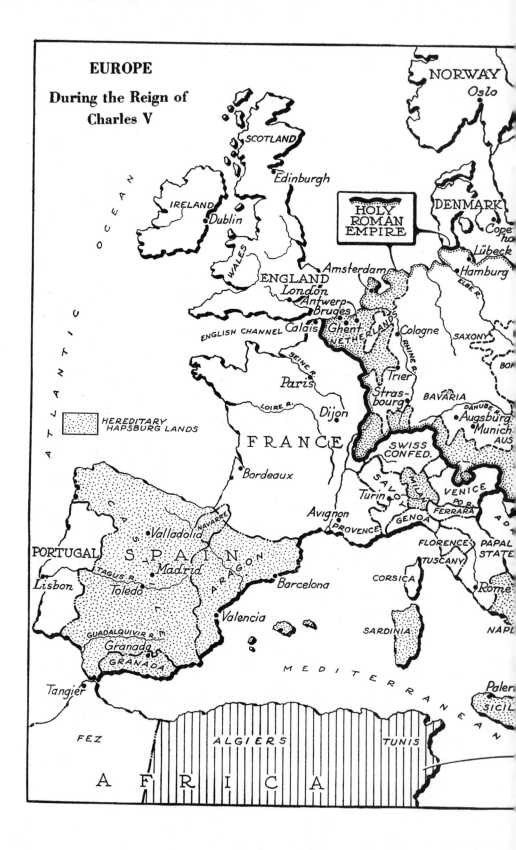

EUROPE

During the Reign of
Charles V

NORWAY
Oslo

SCOTLAND

Edinburgh

DENMARK

*Cope
ha*

IRELAND

Dublin

HOLY
ROMAN
EMPIRE

Lübeck

Hamburg

WALES

Amsterdam

ELBE R.

ENGLAND
London
Antwerp
Bruges

ENGLISH CHANNEL Calais

Ghent
NETHERLAND

Cologne

SAXONY

RHINE R.

BO

SEINE R.

Paris

Trier

Strasbourg

BAVARIA

LOIRE R.

Dijon

DANUBE R.
Augsburg
Munich
AUS

HEREDITARY
HAPSBURG LANDS

FRANCE

SWISS
CONFED.

Bordeaux

SAVOY
Turin

MIL

VENICE
PO R.

FERRARA

AVIGNON
PROVENCE

GENOA

AD

Valladolid

NAVARRE

PORTUGAL

SPAIN

ARAGON

FLORENCE
TUSCANY

PAPAL
STATE

Madrid

TAGUS R.

CORSICA

Rome

Lisbon

Toledo

Barcelona

Valencia

GUADALQUIVIR R.

Granada
GRANADA

SARDINIA

NAPL

Tangier

MEDITERRANEAN

Paler

SICIL

FEZ

ALGIERS

TUNIS

AFRICA

ATLANTIC OCEAN

He became known as Charles V. Due to heavy taxation levied to support a vast war with other countries, the populace was impoverished and the empire lasted less than two hundred years.

The first ten years of the reign of Francis I (1515-47) were occupied with foreign wars. The king was very ambitious and wished to make France the most powerful European power. Religious difficulties disturbed much of this period, ending in the Edict of Nantes in 1598, signed by Henry IV. This was the first document to grant religious toleration. After this edict, Henry IV started his plan of expansion and of destroying the power of the House of Hapsburg. He laid the groundwork for an expedition but when his plans were discovered, he was stabbed to death in 1610.

At the same time that Francis I was reigning in France, and Charles I was receiving acclaim as the great Emperor Charles V, Henry VIII of England was proving himself a typical exponent of the Renaissance. England continued to rise in importance, and the middle of the 16th century marked the beginning of her supremacy in Europe. By the end of the century, she was mistress of the seas, and wide exploration was continued in all parts of the world. The Renaissance in England also produced a golden age of literature.

During the reign of Queen Elizabeth, England became more prosperous than it had been for many years. At the ascension of the Queen, the Treasury was bankrupt and the credit of the country was low. With the extension of trade and manufacture, a new industrial period began and wages and prices became higher. The population drifted to the towns early in the 16th century, resulting in the formation of a middle class which shared in the general prosperity and exerted power formerly wielded by the feudal nobility. By the end of the 16th century, social conditions were affected by religious conflicts. The first poor law, passed by Parliament in 1563, regulated the conditions of apprenticeship and labor.

The trends in these countries, Italy, Spain, France, and England, affected the costume of the day, and the period of each country's influence coincided with the time when that country exerted its greatest power in Europe.

Italian fashions prevailed in the early years of the century. There was a gracefulness and lack of stiffness in the Italian modes. The man of Italy did not resort to padding in the costume as did the Spaniard. The woman likewise preferred the soft lines created by drapery to the stiffness of the Spanish dress. Instead of the *farthingale*, she wore many petticoats, used lacing, not to minimize the waistline but to elevate the bust, which was left practically uncovered by the women of Rome, Venice, Florence, Piza, or Ferrara. The woman of the Spanish dominions wore a higher neckline.

The Spanish influence extended into the field of costume as well as in politics. There was a stiffness and formality in the garments worn by the Spanish man and woman. The farthingale is an excellent example of the rigidity and stiffness that prevailed in the costume of that country. The style of coat varied according to rank; short, silk or velvet coats were worn by the upper class, long cloth coats, by the middle class, and a coarse covering was used by the country person.

After Francis I ascended the throne, attention was focused on clothes. The King became a leader of fashion and introduced a number of styles. Internal disturbances during the reign of Henry II held the attention of France and for a time this country exerted scarcely any influence in fashion.

The costume of the French woman in the early part of the 16th century, revealed the Spanish influence, but with less stiffness and rigidity. The low neckline of the French costume was retained but a neckerchief was worn to suggest the modesty of the wearer. The costume and accessories worn by the French queen on state occasions were extravagant and elegant; one gown was decorated with 32,000 pearls and 3,000 diamonds. Because of the bulk and weight of the skirt, ladies developed an awkward type of walking. Edicts issued in France against excess in dress resulted in a costume lovely in its simplicity, no longer overloaded with trimming.

The English costume had dignity and elegance. The Spanish cape was used on the tight-fitting doublet. The peplum of the doublet showed the Italian influence. Stockings which were pulled over the breeches had been used in England since the 15th century but they did not appear on the Continent until the 16th century. Later the Englishman adopted the Venetian style of breeches which were full at the top and padded so they would stand out from the wearer's body. The costume of this period may be seen on the conventional playing cards of today.

Slashing, puffing, and the use of leather characterized the German costume of the 16th century. At first the close-fitting garments were made more comfortable by making slits at various places in it to relieve the strain. Necessity is often the mother of invention and so it is with many innovations in costume. The slits which had been used because of necessity now became part of the design of the costume and were adopted in other parts of the garment as a colorful decoration since the lining showed through the slits of the outside garment. The mercenary soldiers in Germany started the custom of excessive slashing.

In England during the preceding centuries, a boy was given harsh treatment to harden him to reality. In the 16th century it was believed that the child should remain sheltered, under the supervision of his mother until he reached the age of seven and that he should develop physically, by living out-of-doors as much as possible.

The girl of this age had an appreciation of music and art, and was taught tapestry and embroidery. She studied Latin and equally difficult subjects under men teachers. One author has said that at seven, a girl was expected to maintain a conversation and by thirteen to have become efficient in her studies, and to be ready to marry. Some girls, however, waited until the age of twenty years before accepting the responsibility of the home.

The grandeur of the castle of the Middle Ages gave way to the manor house. Life became easier, and more comfortable, the habits and manners of men more genteel. With the rise of the middle class, more importance was placed on wealth and an effort was made to imitate and excel in elegance and finery.

The life of the well-to-do woman became easier. A woman was respected as the companion to man. Although she did not experience the freedom of the woman of the present day, she was a co-partner in the revival of learning and enjoyed new opportunities for intellectual and artistic development. The woman of France traveled widely for the time and delighted in the works of Boccaccio, one of the favorite authors of the day. On the other hand the female pauper was forced to enter domestic service or be imprisoned.

. During the time of Queen Elizabeth, the lady of rank kept an elaborate notebook which was handed down from one generation to another. This book contained recipes for cooking and elaborate formulas for perfume.

The names of many famous painters, sculptors, architects, authors, scientists, and explorers have come down to us. There were also merchants, agriculturists, and artisans in the minor arts and crafts, who worked in wood, stone, iron, and stained glass.

DRESS

A. Sources of information: literature, sculpture, paintings, manuscripts, coins, medals, garments and their accessories which are extant.

B. MEN (1500-9)

1. Garments:

    Outer upper: doublet with laced opening in front or back, worn by French and Italians, until 1510, often skirtless with square, deep V or U neckline and with chemise showing under doublet or *stomacher;* jerkin with elbow-length or longer sleeve worn over doublet; sleeve sewed or laced into armscye; aglet, aiglet, point or poynt; sometimes full sleeve, tight at wrist with *panes* or bands above elbow, puffed at shoulder and elbow; *epaulette; shoulder wing; mancheron;* lapel facings of jerkin formed broad collar; knee-length or hip-length skirt; slashing continued, from *c.* 1470 to middle of 17th century, at first in sleeve only, later in entire garment.

    Outer lower: striped and particolored hose, tights laced to doublet; herlot or latchet; point; *slops; codpiece;* garter below knee.

    Under: white or colored linen, or silk chemise with large, full sleeve gathered into ruffle or band; drawers.

    Cloaks and overgarments: gown worn indoors as well as out-of-doors, often with fur collar; knee-length mantle; semicircular cape or cloak.

    Neckwear and wristwear: large *ruff* developed from *fraise* or tiny frill worn at base of throat and tied with cord.

2. **Hair:** bobbed hair, with bang over forehead, worn by fashionable young man, later short hair; still shorter hair worn by older man; usually clean shaven; sometimes short beard, turned-down mustache.

3. **Headdress:** hat low and rather flat; hat resembling petasus still worn by traveler; turned-up brim; drooping ostrich tips, or jewels used as ornamentation; white linen coif sometimes worn under hat or cap, black velvet used later; *balzo;* red *nightcap.*

4. **Footwear:** round-toed shoe; square or duckbilled-toe shoe; heel developed from slipper with platform sole consisting of several soles placed on top of one another; shoe with high front, or latchets tied over instep; stocking.

5. **Accessories:** baldrick; sword seldom used with regular costume; badge; dagger with sheath, hilt set with gems; cane with knob; beautifully embroidered gloves usually carried, gauntlet glove; pouch; metal belt or sash; cane and tall stick; badge or emblem.

6. Jewelry: very fashionable; hat and sleeve brooches, slashing of glove revealing rings; rings on all fingers, even on thumb and 1st joint of fingers; *chain;* jeweled pins used to hold slashes together at intervals.

7. Typical Colors: particolored hose in first of period; gold, black, and white, rich shades of red, blue, and wine; elegant black costume worn by Venetian man; red or blue tunic; scarlet, apple-green, or blue stocking; red, violet, or yellow shoe; red, blue, black, or gold embroidery on ruffle of chemise; red, blue, purple, green, or yellow colored starch used.

8. Typical Materials: rich heavy fabrics including velvet, taffeta, brocade, satin, and damask weaves; metallic cloth, gold or black lace; silk, wool, linen and cotton; poplin or camelot used for coat; fur-lined coat; fur or felt cap; leather boot; leather, velvet, heavy silk, or satin shoe; velvet and silk trimming on breeches; hose of silk or woolen fabric cut and sewed, in early part of period, knitted hose or stocking later in century; velvet cap or hood; feathers on cap; changeable taffeta, satin or linen shirt; lace, linen, or linen edged with lace, for ruff.

9. Make-up: perfume.

C. WOMEN (*1500-9*)

1. Garments:

Outer upper: gown with *bodice* worn in Italy, low neck revealing most of breasts; square, round or V-shaped neckline; broad *neck-whisk* or whisk-like collar; sleeve plain and close-fitting, later, wide and long, tied at armscye, with shoulder puff; sleeve puffed to elbow, and tight-fitting at forearm; sleeve turned back, forming huge bell; undersleeve; mancheron; sleeve rather tight in armscye, used in the Netherlands; sleeve full above elbow, narrow at wrist in Italy; both long and short-waisted bodices worn in all countries; pointed waistline, becoming higher, until 1525; fur or embroidered borders; Spanish influence shown in *basquine.*

Outer lower: pleated skirt at first, then bell-shaped skirt on hoops; Spanish influence shown in stiffness of costume; length of skirt usually to the floor; skirt closed in front; long train carried in hand by a band, or caught up in back by points or brooch.

Under: chemise of fine linen, showing at top of gown and through slashings; smock; *shakefold;* garter.

Cloaks and overgarments: hooded cape; long mantle, sometimes with collar, tied across breast with tasseled cords; small shoulder cape.

2. Hair: parted in center, rather flat coiffure with braid at back; flowing hair with wreath or diadem for bride or girl; more hair shown below

1

2

3

4

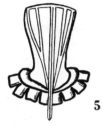

5

6

7

8

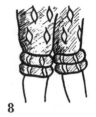

9

10

11

12

13

14

1. Architectural Headdress   2. Chemise   3. Coif   4. Balzo   5. Corset
6. Ruff   7. Ear String   8. Canions   9. Peascod Belly
10. Pantaloons   11. Haute-de-chausses   12. Busk-point   13. Panes   14. Slashing

headdress by Italian woman than by woman from the northern countries; hair displayed about face in France and Flanders; more informal hairdress usually worn by French woman; hair worn pinned up under headdress in England.

3. **Headdress:** extreme headdress disappearing; nun-like hood with long lappet on each side, fold hanging at back, or sometimes pinned up at the ears; *architectural headdress* of English origin practically concealing the hair, known as diamond, kennel, arched, gable, crescent, or horseshoe-shaped hood; cap of velvet usually joined to kennel at back and sometimes additional piece of fabric added to top of kennel; transparent veil, caul, crispine or crespinette or cap of net embroidered with gold and pearls draped over head; round roll or toque of gilded leather and copper foil, showing Italian influence; elaborate white linen headdress worn by German woman; *calotte; barret; bonnet* worn by Flemish woman; influence of Italian and Flemish styles shown in French costume; nightcap.

4. **Footwear:** shoe resembling that worn by man; thick-soled chopine, clog or pattern; hose sometimes red.

5. **Accessories:** *cordelière,* pouch with needle case, and scissors, Book of Hours or rosary hung from girdle; dagger; marten skin.

6. **Jewelry:** many pearls used on all parts of garment; rings visible through slits in glove; brooch; jewel at center of forehead, hung on ribbon worn around the head; short and long necklaces, several often worn at the same time; cross worn on chain; girdle of gold plaques or gold braid.

7. **Typical Colors:** crimson gown worn by princesses. Refer to *B. 7.*

8. **Typical Materials:** cloth of gold, silver taffeta embroidered in gold; sable and marten; cotton chemise, occasionally silk, often embroidered. Refer to *B. 8.*

9. **Make-up:** perfume.

D. MEN (*1510-49*)

1. **Garments:**

   Outer upper: doublet usually with low or broad neckline, square, until 1530; skirtless doublet, until 1530; puffs; slashings; *piccadil;* doublet and jerkin wrapped over in front; jerkin with sleeve puffed to elbow, or to wrist; much *slashing,* 1520-35 with colored linings showing through short puff, or sleeve with circular shoulder, and high neckline, 1533; sleeve of doublet tied in armscye, or sewed tight at wrist; jerkin worn over doublet, with vertical folds reaching to knee, and with or without sleeve, until 1530, high-waisted, until 1540; stiff folds of skirt of jerkin disappearing, after 1540; collar with deep revers, 1540, jerkin sleeve larger than that of

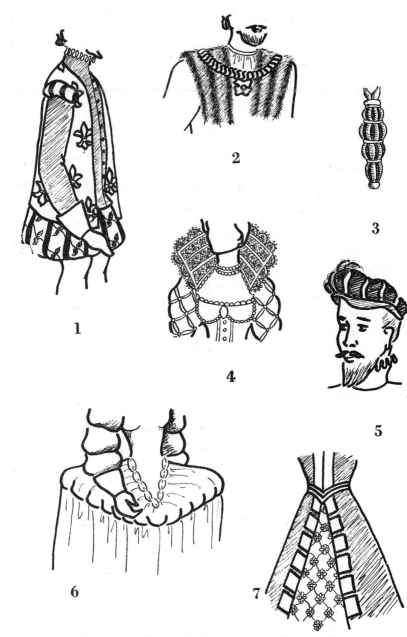

1. Jerkin 2. Chain 3. Aglet, Aiglet, Point or Poynt
4. Neck-whisk 5. Hat with Narrow Brim 6. Stomacher 7. Overgown

doublet, and of different lengths; hanging sleeve or mancheron under doublet, resembling vest.

Outer lower: upper-stock, haut-de-chausses or *breeches,* much slashing, 1520-35, showing fabric of another color beneath; panes; *lower-stock, netherstock, bas-de-chausses* or stocking sometimes striped but not slashed; codpiece; garter sometimes jeweled, worn above or below knee, more often below, garter of the Order worn by Garter Knights in latter part of 16th century; cross gartering.

Under: shirt with ruffle at neck and wrist, slashes in doublet revealing linen; shirt higher at neckline, after 1525; drawers.

Cloaks and overgarments: long or short gown, becoming more square at shoulders, broad collar; petti-cotte; cloak or cape seldom worn.

Neckwear and wristwear: collar higher, with small, tiny frill or fraise, *c.* 1525; *band* sometimes embroidered, tied with cords or *band-strings;* turnover collar worn after 1525; also elaborate ruff.

2. **Hair:** often bobbed, until 1520; short hair in vogue, after 1520; short beard worn, 1520; long beard, 1540; mustache.

3. **Headdress:** flat bonnet; small hat with ostrich tips instead of plumes; wide brim, after 1530; barret; coif and undercap not fashionable at end of period; red nightcap.

4. **Footwear:** at first very wide with square toe; shoes with jewels; toe of shoe narrower and rounded, by 1540, with ankle strap, or slashed across instep; boot usually worn by traveler and hunter; galoche.

5. **Accessories:** light dress sword with cruciform hilt worn with civilian attire; *knuckle bow,* after 1520; dagger; *watch* with hour hand only; glove often carried; elaborate pouch at girdle; cane; jeweled points and slashes.

6. **Jewelry:** rings on all fingers and thumb, visible through glove; neckchain, sometimes several; hat and sleeve brooches; drop earrings.

7. **Typical Colors:** cloth or silk hose with gold or silver thread. Refer to B. 7.

8. **Typical Materials:** refer to *B. 8.*

9. **Make-up:** perfume popular, individual recipe for special fragrance often used by man of nobility.

E. WOMEN (*1510-49*)

1. **Garments:**

Outer upper: bodice with square neckline, sometimes of different color from skirt; large bell-like or close-fitting sleeve, after 1510, wide bell-like sleeve turned back at lower edge; low neckline arched upward, after 1530; gown with standing collar, 1540; round neckline preferred by Italian woman; sleeve puffed at top, both in France and Italy; sleeve full at elbow, but tight above and below,

1. Partlet or Tucker 2. Bodice 3. Rebato, Underpropper or Supportasso
4. Panes 5. Architectural Headdress
6. Skirt with Farthingale or Verdingale 7. Steeple-crown Hat
8. Epaulette 9. Bodice 10. Petticoat 11. Gown

worn in England, Germany, and the Netherlands; puff at top of sleeve disappearing, rows of loops or iron rings used on sleeve at shoulder; cap sleeve; sleeve of different color from gown, sometimes several pairs for each gown; hanging sleeve or mancheron; very tight corsage, or corset laced at front or back; pointed waistline, high or low.

Outer lower: wide funnel-shaped skirt, very long, divided overskirt showing elaborate petticoat; very long skirt worn by fashionable lady; train disappearing from skirt, *c.* 1530.

Under: chemise showing at neckline, as standing collar or frill, and in puffs at lower arm beneath fairly wide undersleeve; shakefold; petticoat; corset.

Cloaks and overgarments: hooded gown; small shoulder cape.
2. **Hair:** parted in center, with gable-hood; in 2 rolls across top of head; often frizzed at temples, *c.* 1530; long flowing hair worn by young girl.
3. **Headdress:** similar to previous period, *pyramidal, pedimental, angular;* sometimes flat bonnet with full gathered crown worn in Germany, Italy, and Spain; caul, crispine or crespinette; nightcap.
4. **Footwear:** resembling man's shoe.
5. **Accessories:** small mirror hung on chain or cordelière attached to girdle; marten skin hanging by chain from handsome girdle when not used around the neck; wire hairpins; lawn or costly lace apron worn by wealthy bourgeois.
6. **Jewelry:** lavish use of jewelry; many pearls scattered over apparel; several necklaces worn, sometimes of different lengths; rings visible through glove; single jewel on ribbon at middle of forehead; jeweled girdle.
7. **Typical Colors:** blue, purple, gold, crimson, peach. Refer to *B. 7.*
8. **Typical Materials:** dress sometimes ornamented with diamonds; silk, satin, velvet, wool. Refer to *B. 8.*
9. **Make-up:** dry perfume placed in small silk bag, carried in pocket or placed with clothes; cosmetics.

F. **MEN** (*1550-99*)
1. **Garments:**
    Outer upper: Spanish influence shown in stiffness of English, French, and Dutch costume; high neckline; tight, long-waisted corset-like doublet; *busk,* 1580; *goose-belly* or *peascod-belly;* doublet often skirtless, until 1590; shoulder roll, epaulette or wing, 1580; sleeve tight, until *c.* 1580; sleeve with *bombast,* wide at shoulder, tapering to wrist; doublet sometimes sleeveless or having detachable sleeve fastened with points under epaulette; doublet worn with or without jerkin; jerkin with or without skirt, longer jerkin, some-

times covering trunk hose, sleeved or sleeveless, leg-of-mutton sleeve; hanging sleeve or mancheron; leather jerkin worn by soldier; much slashing, pleating, and gathering; less elaborate in England by time of James I.

Outer lower: slops; short trunk hose or *French round hose*, with bombast of horsehair or bran or wool; *canions* below trunk hose to knee; *Venetians* with stockings rolled over them, *c.* 1580; particolored hose discontinued; pockets introduced in trunk hose, latter part of century; *breeches* round or somewhat bell-shaped, panes, slashed; sometimes breeches loose at knee; codpiece less fashionable, out of style, *c.* 1570, practically obsolete, by 1590; buttoned slit introduced; pantaloons; slops; very short breeches, 1585-1610; cross-garter at knee; garter with large bow at side of knee.

Under: embroidered shirt resembling that of preceding period; large-full-sleeved blouse gathered on yoke or shirred into neckband; corset similar to that worn by woman during the reign of Henry III; drawers.

Cloaks and overgarments: short Spanish cape with half erect collar, often with hanging cowl; long stiff cape; sedate long gown often with fur collar worn by scholar, professional man, citizen, and official; also short gown; *mandilion.*

Neckwear and wristwear: some wore fraise; elaborate ruff; huge cartwheel ruff, 1580; strings fastening ruff or band at front; ruffled cuff on wrist; *falling ruff,* at close of period; wider ruff with band fastening under collar; falling band; falling collar and turned-back cuff.

2. **Hair:** very short, pompadour in front, 1570-90; close curls, 1580's, rather long, 1590's; pointed beard; small mustache with natural lines, until 1570, later brushed upward; face sometimes smooth-shaven.

3. **Headdress:** chaperone; flat cap distinguished professional, city, or elderly man, after 1565; broad *sombrero*, small plume and jewel, after 1580; *hat with narrow brim* and gathered crown, 1590-1605; elderly man with coif beneath headdress, coif tied under chin; nightcap.

4. **Footwear:** heelless thick-soled shoe, until 1600; bow over instep, after 1570; shoe slashed in front; boot with edge of fur, sometimes extending to calf of leg; *pantoffle,* 1570-75; shoe with rounded toe, cut high over instep, fastened with ribbon or thong, later adorned with *shoe rose* or rosette; tight-fitting boot, with cuff that turned upward; shoe of light color; cloth stocking still worn; knitted stocking pulled over knee; cross-gartering; clocks of silk and metallic embroidery on hose, several pairs of silk hose worn for warmth; boot hose to protect stocking.

5. **Accessories:** *ear string;* sometimes rose tucked in hair behind ear by extremist; *loup* or *mask; rapier* or sword hanging from girdle or belt; braided decoration, time of Edward VI; exquisite workmanship shown by accessories, time of Elizabeth; baldrick with bow on right shoulder and sash; belt serving also as pocket for gloves; handkerchief with lace edge; purse; spectacles with rim of bone, wood, lead, or copper worn in England, 1589, gold-rimmed spectacles in Spain.

6. **Jewelry:** earring in one ear; rings on all fingers; jeweled pendant; neck-chain or collar; diamonds and rubies set in jewelry.

7. **Typical Colors:** black costume worn by Venetian man. Refer to B. 7.

8. **Typical Materials:** silk shirts mentioned in 1582. Refer to B. 8.

9. **Make-up:** night mask of oil and pomade on face and hands; paint and patch, from *c.* 1580; eyebrow and mustache plucked to form thin line.

G. WOMEN (*1550-99*)

1. **Garments:**

Outer upper: elaborate bodice sometimes similar to man's doublet; skirt and upper gown of different fabrics; low neckline with frill of chemisette showing, until 1570; very low neck, 1575, almost entire breast often exposed, after 1575; cartwheel ruff sometimes worn with low neckline; bell sleeve, until 1560; leg-of-mutton sleeve held by many ribbons; wristband turned back forming cuff with ruff; padded sleeve narrowing at wrist; hanging sleeve or mancheron; shoulder roll, wing or puff; bodice with long, wasp waist, ending in a pronounced downward peak in front, 1550, the peak increasing, until 1603; stomacher; busk; *busk-point; fers.*

Outer lower: bell-shaped skirt introduced in Spain, *c.* 1550, skirt of *overgown* separating in front, showing skirt of undergown; huge flounce extending outward with radiating pleats on padded hip, 1590.

Under: chemise rarely showed except at neck and wrist, 1550; chemisette often left open in front, 1570; farthingale or *verdingale* introduced in Spain, *c.* 1550; stiffened petticoat holding outerskirt in place, used concurrently in Italy; cartwheel verdingale with French-inspired, thick hip-bolster, the drum-like wire structure covered by a pleated ruffle, worn in France, 1570; corset of pierced steel, wood, cane, and whalebone introduced by Catherine de' Medici; *partlet* or *tucker;* narrow jeweled garter.

Cloaks and overgarments: long, close or loose-fitting gown, often with open-hanging sleeve, with yoke, and small or large collar; sometimes overgown omitted; mandilion; short or long cape, with or without armholes, fur or fur-lined; sleeveless jacket; silk scarf with gold or silver fringe.

Neckwear and wristwear: ruff of fine linen, gradually becoming fan-shaped, by 1550, enormous ruff, after 1555, ruff left open at neck, until 1570, fan-shape more common, 1575, neck-whisk or wired upright collar, after 1580; piccadil; white, blue, purple, green, and yellow-colored starch used; *partlet* or *tucker; piccadil, rebato, underpropper* or *supportasso.*

2. **Hair:** definite coiffure developed about middle of century; hair parted in center and puffed at each side; high coiffure influenced by style worn by Catherine de' Medici; short-haired wig; 80 wigs owned by Queen Elizabeth; long loose curls worn by Italian woman; hair arranged higher on head later; hair usually worn covered by most women, until 1560, then displayed from under headdress; wired and arranged in bun or *chignon* at back, 1570; hairdress high, until end of period; pearls worn in hair, after 1570.

3. **Headdress:** turban headdress by Italian women, first part of century; French hood, an arched cap of linen similar to cap of Mary Queen of Scots, called *Mary Stuart Cap,* worn in France and England; tall hat with feathers; narrow or wide brim with fairly high crown; balzo; barret; calotte; *steeple-crown* or *sugarloaf hat;* caul; nightcap.

4. **Footwear:** resembling footwear of man; ornamented with pearls; narrow and pointed, *c.* 1560; high heel; high heel pantoffle; chopine, clog or patten, 1575-1600; silk stockings worn by Queen Elizabeth, 1560; clocked hose embroidered in light or metallic thread.

5. **Accessories:** lace-edged handkerchief; flag-shaped fan; fan of ostrich or peacock feathers and gold or silver handle; folding fan later; silk or gauze veil; sometimes broad ribbon across chest; articles such as keys, needle case, rosary or small mirror hung from chain, cordelière, or ribbon worn around waist; watch, pomander or fan dangled from jeweled girdle; perfumed, elaborately embroidered and scented glove; mask or loup worn to preserve the complexion; comb; elaborate walking stick; apron; wire hairpin; sunshade parasol, 1578; small and elaborate muff decorated with lace and jewels.

6. **Jewelry:** more pearls than in preceding century; magnificent jewels, diamonds, rubies; jeweled necklace and bracelet; chain; brooches pinned everywhere; finger rings; pear-shaped pearl earrings; hair jewels, pearls worn in hair, after 1570; metallic ornaments across chest.

7. **Typical Colors:** refer to *B. 7.*

8. **Typical Materials:** refer to *B. 8.*

9. **Make-up:** Queen Elizabeth painted face, neck, and breasts; white lead and vermilion used, last half of century, supposed to have

171

been introduced by Catherine de' Medici; perfume; patch; hair dye; belladonna used by Venetian woman to dilate the pupil and brighten the eye.

SIGNIFICANT MOTIFS

Interlaced designs, conventional and pendant flowers, shells, fruit and leaf form, pineapple, rose, and pomegranate.

INFLUENCES ON LATER COSTUMES

Wide pannier or hoop reappeared, 1711 and 19th century; cut of the English riding coat, c. 1771; stiffened and pointed bodice, 1814, '51, and '90; tam-o'-shanter, 1890; bell-shaped skirt and cape, early 20th century and 1948; high collar and ruff, 1800, '51, '90's, and 1940's; Juliet cap worn after release of the movie *Romeo and Juliet*. Corset of this time influenced costume in all succeeding centuries. Other influences, 20th century: Elizabethan toque; heart-shaped hat of the Medici and locket in the form of a book; beret, similar to the barret of this time; wide shoulders again popular, 1940's; epaulette on shoulder reappeared, 1904, '17, '30's, and '40's; several pairs of sleeves for one gown, 1950's.

BOOKS OF REFERENCE

(See also GENERAL BIBLIOGRAPHY, p. 433)

Brooke, Iris, *English Costume in the Age of Elizabeth* (London, A. and C. Black, Ltd., 1933)

Christensen, Sigrid Flamand, *Die Mannlich Kleidung in der Süddentichen Renaissance* (Berlin, Deutscher Kunstverlag, 1934)

Hall, Hubert, *Society in the Elizabethan Age* (London, S. Sonnenschein, Lowrey and Co., 1852)

Kelly, Francis M., and Schwabe, Randolph, *Historic Costume, 1490-1790* (London, B. T. Batsford, 1925)

——, *Shakespearean Costume for Stage and Screen* (Los Angeles, W. E. Baker Co., 1938)

Lacroix, P., *Manners, Customs and Dress during the Middle Ages and during the Renaissance Period* (London, Bickers and Son, n.d.)

Laver, James, *Costume of the Western World, 1485-1558* (New York, Harper & Bros., 1951)

Linthicum, Marie Channing, *Costume in the Drama of Shakespeare and His Contemporaries* (Oxford, The Clarendon Press, 1936)

Morse, H. K., *Elizabethan Pageantry* (New York, Studio Publications, 1934)

Norris, Herbert, *Costume and Fashion*, Vol. III (London, J. M. Dent and Sons, 1938)

CHAPTER 10: GLOSSARY

ARTISTS FOR COSTUME REFERENCE

Aldegrever, Heinrich (1502-58)
Baldung, Hans (Grien) (1484-1545)
Barbari, Jacopa de (1440/50-1511/15)
Bartolommeo, Fra (1472-1517)
Bellini, Gentile (1426/30-1507)
Bles, Henri Met de (Civetta) 1480-1550)
Boltraffio, Giovanni Antonio (1487-1516)
Bordone, Paris Paschalinus (1500-70)
Botticelli, Alessandro (1444/7-1510)
Bronzino, Angelo (Agnolo) (1502/3-1572)
Bruegel, Pieter (Elder) 1525-69)
Bruyn, Bartholomaeus (Elder) (1493-1553/6)
Burgkmair, Hans (Elder) (1473-1531)
Caravaggio, Michel Angelo (1560/5-1609)
Carpaccio, Vittore (1450/5-1522/6)
Clouet, François (1505/10-1572)
Clouet, Jean (1486-1546)
Coello, Alonzo Sanchez (1515-90)
Costa, Lorenzo (Elder) (1460-1535)
Cranach, Lucas (Elder) (1472-1553)
Credi, Lorenzo di (1456/9-1537)
Dürer, Albrecht (1471-1528)
Gheeraerts, Marcus (Elder) (1516-90)
Giorgione, Giorgio (1477/8-1510)
Greco, El (Domenico Theotocopuli) (1545/8-1614)
Holbein, Hans (Elder) (1460/70-1524)
Holbein, Hans (Ygr.) (1497/8-1543)
Lorenzo, Fiorenzo di (1440/5-1522/5)

Lucas van Leyden (Jacobsz) (1494?-1533)
Luini, Bernardino (1465/75-1531/3)
Mantegna, Andrea (1431-1506)
Mabuse, Jan Gosseart van (1462/70-1533/41)
Massys (Matsys) Jan H. (1509/11-75/80)
Massys (Matsys) Quentin (1460/6-1530)
Miereveld, Michel van (1567-1641)
Moro (Mor) Antonio (1512/9-75/7)
Moroni, Giovanni Battista (1510/25-78)
Mostaert, Jan (1475-1555/6)
Orley, Bernard (Barend) van (1485/93-1542)
Pantoja de la Cruz, Juan (1551-1608/9)
Pencz, George (1500-50)
Perugino, Pietro Vannucci (1446-1523)
Pourbus, Frans (Elder) (1545-81)
Pourbus, Frans (Ygr.) 1568/70-1622)
Predis, Giovanni Ambrogio de (1455-1522)
Raphael, Sanzio (1483-1520)
Robbia, Andrea della (1435-1525)
Rosselli Cosimo (1438/9-1507)
Rubens, Peter Paul (1577-1640)
Sarto, Andrea del (1486/7-1531)
Scorel, Jan van (1475-1562)
Teniers, David (Elder) (1582-1640)
Tintoretto, Jacopo (1512/18-94)
Titian, (Tiziano) Vecelli (1477/89-1576)
Veronese, Bonifazio (1490/1-1540)
Zeitbloon, Bartholomaus (1450?-1518/21)

GLOSSARY

Aglet, Aiglet, Point or Poynt—refer to *Chap. 9. Pl. XXIV, 3.*
Architectural Headdress—stiff type of headdress resembling a diamond, kennel, arch, gable, crescent, or horseshoe. *Pl. XXIII, 1; Pl. XXV, 5.*
Badge—refer to *Chaps. 2, 8, 9.*
Baldrick—refer to *Chaps. 1, 3, 7, 8, 9.*
Balzo—headdress consisting of high round roll of gilded leather or copper foil, worn in Italy. *Pl. XXIII, 4.*
Band—turnover collar, which succeeded the ruff.
Band-string—1 of the laces or strings which tied the neck band in front.
Barret—flat Spanish cap of gorgeous material which was slashed, puffed, and embroidered.
Bas-de-chausses—hose which showed below the haut-de-chausses.
Basquine—boned bodice resembling a corset.

Bodice—tight-fitting garment, extending to the waist. *Pl. XXV, 2, 9.*

Bombast—stuffing of wool, flax, or hair.

Bonnet—refer to *Chap. 9.*

Book of Hours—refer to *Chap. 9.*

Boot—high leather footwear used for walking or riding. Refer to *Chap. 9.*

Breeches—male attire formerly known as hose, upper-stock, and slops. The word breeches for this type of garment was used first toward the end of the 16th century.

Busk—rigid piece of wood set in fake front or stomacher, which gave straight-line effect.

Busk-point—tag or tip of lacing which fastened the end of the busk. *Pl. XXIII, 12.*

Calotte—cap or coif, usually of expensive material, over which the barret was worn. This name also given to small black cap worn by Roman clergy.

Canions—tight knee breeches or tubular secion of hose from trunk hose to below knee, c. 1570. *Pl. XXIII, 8.*

Cape—refer to *Chaps. 2, 3, 4, 6, 8, 9.*

Caul, Crispine or Crespinette—refer to *Chaps. 4, 8, 9.*

Chain—heavy chain worn by man as decoration across the chest; neckline which often signified the Order to which a man belonged. *Pl. XXIV, 2.*

Chaperone—refer to *Chaps. 8, 9.*

Chemise—refer to *Chaps. 6, 7, 8, 9. Pl. XXIII, 2.*

Chignon—mass or knot of hair worn on back of head.

Chopine, Clog or Patten—wooden or cork sole fastened over instep of shoe. Refer to *Chap. 9.*

Clog—refer to *Chopine,* and to *Chaps. 8, 9.*

Codpiece—flap-like appendage at front of man's breeches made of similar material as the jerkin or upper hose and fastened with ties or buckles.

Coif—refer to *Chaps. 8, 9. Pl. XXIII, 3.*

Cordelière—long chain usually of gold which hung from the girdle.

Corset—tight-fitting bodice, also called whale-bone or petty-coat badge with whale-bone. Refer to *Chaps. 8, 9. Pl. XXIII, 5.*

Crespinette—refer to *Caul.*

Crispine—refer to *Caul.*

Diadem—refer to *Chaps. 3, 4, 5, 6.*

Doublet—short close-fitting jacket with sleeve sometimes detachable and fastened at armhole by means of points; possible forerunner of vest. Refer to *Chap. 9.*

Duckbilled-toe Shoe—refer to *Chap. 9.*

Ear String—black string worn through pierced left ear during latter part of period of Queen Elizabeth. *Pl. XXIII, 7.*

Epaulette—shoulder ornament. *Pl. XXV, 8.*

Falling Band or Falling Collar—flat collar.

Falling Ruff—unstarched ruff falling loosely around neck.

Farthingale or Verdingale—petticoat with a contrivance or hoop of iron, wood, bone, or cane which distended the outerskirt, known at first as shakefold, also named verdingale. In later centuries a similar contrivance was called a crinoline, hoop, pannier, or bustle. *Pl. XXV, 6.*

Fers—metal buttons used by woman of rank, worn as decoration on costume.

Fraise—small ruff which edged the standing collar. It is said that Henry II of France adopted this neckline to conceal a scar.

French Round Hose—short, round trunk hose.

Galoche—refer to *Chap. 9.*

Goose Belly or Peascod Belly—padded doublet having the shape of a peascod.

Gown—indoor or outdoor garment with large fur collar. It was long or short, open in

CHAPTER 10: GLOSSARY

front and often had a pleated yoke in front and back, shoulder puff, wing, short or hanging long sleeve, or sleeveless. Refer to *Chaps. 7, 8. Pl. XXV, 11.*

Hat with Narrow Brim—small hat with crown gathered to a narrow brim, ostrich tips on the side. *Pl. XXIV, 5.*

Haut-de-chausses—breeches or hose which covered lower part of trunk as well as the upper part of legs. *Pl. XXIII, 11.*

Herlot or Latchet—refer to *Chap. 9.*

Hose—refer to *Chaps. 6, 7, 8, 9.*

Jerkin or Jacket—outergarment often of leather which had shoulder puff or wing, sometimes hanging sleeve; sleeved or sleeveless and worn over the doublet. When sleeves were used they were often made of the same fabric as the doublet. The jerkin was very short or to knee length and had formal pleats, frequently made of 2 kinds of fabric arranged in stripes. Refer to *Chap. 9. Pl. XXIV, 1.*

Knuckle Bow—curved guard on dagger extending from hilt to pommel.

Lappet—fabric hanging at back or sides of headdress. Refer to *Chap. 2.*

Latchet—refer to *Herlot.*

Leg-of-mutton Sleeve—refer to *Chap. 9.*

Loup or Mask—mask used as protection from sunburn and to give an atmosphere of mystery. It was called loup (wolf) because it frightened children.

Lower-stock—silk or woolen cloth stocking, showing below upper-stock. Refer to *bas-de-chausses.*

Mancheron—false, hanging sleeve.

Mandilion—wide jacket or jerkin with hanging sleeve, often open under arms, usually worn by soldier.

Mantle—refer to *Chaps. 3, 7, 8, 9.*

Mary Stuart Cap—small cap, heart-shaped in front, and draped bag-like in the back, concealing hair.

Mask—refer to *Loup* and to *Chap. 1.*

Neck-whisk—standing fan-shaped, wired collar. *Pl. XXIV, 4.*

Netherstock—refer to *Lower-stock.*

Nightcap—cap worn when sleeping.

Overgown—outergarment worn over underdress. *Pl. XXIV, 7.*

Panes—loose vertical bands used on various parts of a garment. *Pl. XXIII, 13; Pl. XXV, 4.*

Pantaloons—knee-length, bloused trousers. Refer to *Chap. 3. Pl. XXIII, 10.*

Pantoffle—mule or slipper with cork sole worn as a protection for the shoe.

Particolored—costume or any part of garment having different colors on either side. Refer to *Chaps. 8, 9.*

Partlet or Tucker—linen, covering the neck and shoulder and displayed above the low neckline, worn 1560-75. *Pl. XXV, 1.*

Patch—small piece of black velvet stuck on the face; real vogue for patches does not begin until the next period. Refer to *Chap. 5.*

Patten—refer to *Chopine.*

Peascod Belly—refer to *Goose Belly. Pl. XXIII, 9.*

Petasus—refer to *Chaps. 4, 5, 6.*

Petticoat—name of underskirt used without a bodice. Refer to *Chap. 9. Pl. XXV, 10.*

Petti-cotte—short coat.

Piccadil—tabbed finish on the edge of garment; this name also applied to a kind of collar support or underprop made of tabs.

Point or Pount—refer to *Aglet.*

Pouch—large bag often carried with shoulder strap, similar to modern type of shoulder bag. Refer to *Chaps. 6, 7, 8, 9.*

Pyramidal, Pedimental or Angular—headdress worn by woman during time of Henry VII and Henry VIII; names describe shapes of headdress.

Rapier—straight sword, having 2-edged narrow blade.

Rebato, Underpropper or Supportasso—support of cardboard, wire, or wood which held ruff in place. *Pl. XXV, 3.*

Round Hose—refer to *Trunk Hose, Chap. 9.*

Ruff—circular collar formed of radiating vertical pleats, said to have been introduced by Catherine de' Medici. *Pl. XXIII, 6.*

Shakefold—stiffened pad on wire frame, an early type of farthingale. The name was given to this part of the garment since it swayed back and forth as the wearer moved.

Shoe Rose—puffs of ribbon worn as decoration on shoe.

Shoulder Wing—projecting decoration on each shoulder.

Slashing—slit in garment, through which lining or undergarment showed. *Pl. XXIII, 14.*

Slops—large, unpadded breeches which extended to the knees.

Smock—woman's undergarment similar to chemise. Refer to *Chap. 8.*

Sombrero—Spanish word for hat.

Steeple-crown or Sugarloaf Hat—hat with a very tapering high crown. *Pl. XXV, 7.*

Stomacher—false front or ornamental covering on front of bodice. *Pl. XXIV, 6.*

Sugarloaf Hat—refer to *Steeple-crown.*

Supportasso—refer to *Rebato.*

Toque—round hat or cap. Refer to *Chap. 2.*

Trunk Hose—refer to *Chap. 9.*

Tucker—refer to *Partlet.*

Underpropper—refer to *Rebato.*

Upper-stock—refer to *Haut-de-chausses.*

Veil—refer to *Chaps. 3, 4, 5, 6, 7, 8, 9.*

Venetians—padded knee-breeches, tied or fastened below the knee.

Verdingale—refer to *Farthingale.*

Watch—small watch made to hang on hook attached to the dress or on chain around the neck; made by Peter Henlein, Nürnberg, 1511.

17th Century

PART I

1600-42

CHRONOLOGY

Union of Scotland and England through James VI of Scotland, who became James I of England and Ireland, *1603*.

French settlement in Acadia, Nova Scotia, *1604*.

First permanent settlement by the English, in North America, at Jamestown, Virginia, *1607*.

Mention of table forks for first time in Italy, *1608*.

Holland became independent, *1609*.

Hudson Bay explored by Henry Hudson, *1610-11*.

Completion of the translation of the King James version of the Bible in *1611*, after seven years' work by scholars.

Thirty Years' War that involved most of the nations of Continental Europe, *1618-48*.

First Negro slaves at Jamestown, Virginia, *1619*.

Arrival of Pilgrims of Mayflower at Cape Cod, *1620*.

Settlement of Plymouth, *Massachusetts, 1620*.

First weekly newspaper in England, *1622*.

Settlement of Maine, *1625*.

French settlements in West Indies, *1625-64*.

Manhattan purchased from Indians for the equivalent of $24.00 in *1626*. Settlement named New Amsterdam.

Maryland settled, *1634;* Connecticut, *1635;* Delaware, *1638*.

Founding of French Academy, by Cardinal Richelieu, *1635*.

Roger Williams organized democratic government in Providence, Rhode Island, *1635*.

Harvard College began, *1636*, named Harvard University, *1639*.

First printing press in the British Colonies of North America, established in Harvard University, *1639*.

Independence of Portugal, *1640*.

Civil War in England, *1642*.

CHAPTER 11

17th Century

PART I

1600-42

Henry IV of France had been a great king, and had much influence on the reconstruction of the country after the religious strife of the preceding period. He was followed by Louis XIII, a very weak king. Marie de Medici, mother of Louis, Anne of Austria, his wife, and a leader of fashion, and Cardinal Richelieu figured prominently in the history of France at this time.

England was experiencing a political struggle between King and Parliament. The impasse reached an acute phase before the death of James I, and culminated in a civil war during the reign of Charles I. This struggle resulted in the important document known as the Petition of Rights, which gave everyone the right of due process of law.

The Thirty Years' War from 1618-48 occupied most of the period. It was a religious and political war and had a calamitous effect on Germany by giving greater importance to the small principalities. The literature and art of the country was also eclipsed by the conflict. After a period of great enterprise Spain had become a secondary power.

The New World suddenly became very important. It was a haven for those who were searching for religious freedom; and a source of revenue for those who remained at home. It was also a place to which the undesirable could be banished. Spain sent adventurers to find gold and priests to gain religious converts. Explorers from France went to the North and to the West of North America. Immigrants from Holland and England settled along the Atlantic Seaboard.

Many of our records of costume of this period come from the portraits of Van Dyck, Rembrandt, Hals, and Rubens. In a number of these paintings, every detail of dress and accessory can be studied. A dearth of artists in England caused Henry VIII in the preceding period to send to Germany for Holbein and for Charles I of this period to obtain the services of Van Dyck from Flanders so that they might portray English life. These artists, however, painted in a manner characteristic of their own countries.

Despite the common expression "There is nothing new under the sun," people often wonder how and why various unusual styles come about. Those words could not have been uttered in the time of Louis XIII of France, when there were many innovations in costumes. Patches on the face, at first, thought to be a cure for headache were retained because they gave an illusion of adding luster to the eyes and accented the fairness of the skin. Another innovation was the muff dog, an important accessory.

Until 1620, the Spanish influence was reflected in the graceful and elegant costume which continued in France, due to the marriage of Louis XIII to Anne of Austria, and replaced Italian styles which had been introduced by Catherine de' Medici and Marguerite de Valois. In France everyone except princes and nobles, was prohibited the wearing of precious stones. Edicts were issued by Cardinal Richelieu, in 1628, against the extravagant use of lace and gold. This sumptuary law and the scarcity of these materials were important factors in the trend toward a simplicity and beauty of dress.

On the other hand, in England the artist Van Dyck was painting the cavalier type, reflecting such extravagances of the period in male costume as the satin doublet, breeches fastened by ribbon rosettes or buttons, ribbon sashes, long curling locks, and even a pearl in the left ear. As has happened at various times in history, the costume of the man appeared much more elegant than that of the woman. The latter had discontinued the wearing of the farthingale, and other artificial devices which changed the natural figure. In fact, all stiffening except the corset was discarded and with the raised waistline and falling collar, the silhouette became very different. Patches, which had been in fashion during the reign of Charles I, were prohibited by the Puritans.

Due to the boarding schools, especially in England, education for women increased. This training was chiefly domestic and superficial for it was still considered unnecessary for a girl to study the same subjects that were included in a boy's educational program.

During this time, the woman of the English aristocracy busied herself with household duties, and affairs pertaining to estates and

180

government. The relationship between husband and wife was one of partnership during the first years of the 17th century. Later, the position of woman became less important due to the perfection of organizations for trade purposes which made the man independent of his wife and family.

The duties of the housewife of the middle class included caring of the home, spinning flax and wool, brewing, dairy work, care of poultry and pigs, production of vegetables and fruit, and a certain amount of nursing and doctoring. In addition to all this, a woman sometimes did industrial labor or followed a professional life. The domestic work of the house fell on the unmarried girl under the supervision of the housewife.

The occupations which occupied the men included the production of wool for manufacturing; spinning, dyeing, milling, and all work pertaining to the production of cloth. Farming continued to have great importance; the family usually took care of producing the food as well as the necessities consumed in the home. Thomas Baird (sometimes spelled Beard) the first shoemaker in the United States arrived on the second voyage of the *Mayflower* in 1629. Shoemakers were itinerant cobblers, traveled from one place to another, remaining with one family while making shoes for the entire household. The cobbler might be called upon to cut hair, pull teeth, and work at other odd jobs that needed attention.

As capital was accumulated by manufacturers and merchants, the destruction of the medieval guilds gradually came about.

DRESS

A. *Sources of information:* literature, paintings, sculpture, coins, medals, garments and accessories which are still extant.

B. MEN
   1. Garments:
      Outer upper: styles of previous period continue until 1610; waist-length underdoublet, similar to *waistcoat* of later period, 1610-20; shoulder wing; sleeve sometimes tight, often detachable and tied with ribbon having metal tip, full to the elbow, gradually becoming smaller from elbow to wrist; puffs and panes from shoulder to elbow after 1600, vertical slashing early in century, often on upper sleeve only, later with slash from armscye to cuff; slashing un-

popular at close of period; fine cambric of shirt showed through the slash; wide cuff or pleated wrist ruff; sleeve sometimes turned back to form cuff; corset-like doublet padded toward lower part of front, pointed waistline; waist becoming shorter and not so stiff, 1630-40, skirt of doublet longer; many buttons for ornamental purposes; lower part of doublet left open; waist and skirt or *peplum,* sometimes cut in 1 piece, the peplum with overlapping front panels; doublet shorter, after 1640; sleeveless jerkin or *buff coat* used for utilitarian and military purposes, sometimes laced up the sides and front; armor worn as ornament along with elaborate laces and velvet.

Outer lower: trunk hose discarded, except for page, *c.* 1620; breeches or slops extending to just below knee, fastened to doublet with tapes or ribbons with metal tags or points, 1625-30; rows of ribbon bows with points, or wide ribbon garter with large bow or rosette at the side; breeches wide at top and narrow at bottom, extending to about 6 inches below knee, 1625-30, breeches close-fitting, usually confined at knee, and left unbuttoned at side above kneeband, showing linen lining or extending to knee with band and frill of lace, after 1630.

Under: shirt or blouse gathered on yoke or to neckband, with full sleeve and cuff, showing at collar, cuff, and through slash of doublet; very short or long drawers; black night-clothes for mourning.

Cloaks and overgarments: short or long semicircular cape, with or without collar, falling in softer lines than in preceding period; coat with no collar or falling collar; long gown for statesman, clergyman, or scholar; *cassock;* lining at coat sometimes matched doublet; cloak often matched breeches; hip-length cape with fur lining, worn attached at one shoulder.

Neckwear and wristwear: small ruff worn only by conservative man; small neck-whisk and falling ruff used through 1620; falling band or falling collar, after 1625, plain or lace-edged; lace collar with *Van Dyck edge,* covering shoulder, 1630, band smaller, after 1640, band strings tasseled; white cuff, funnel shaped at first; pleated wrist-ruff.

2. **Hair:** short hair worn with ruff by older men; brushed straight back without a part at first; hair to shoulders, *c.* 1600; very long, after 1630, often in waves, straight bang or curls across forehead; *love-lock* sometimes with ribbon, worn on left side, square cut on right side; pointed or *Van Dyck beard,* 1620; *imperial,* 1630; beard not worn, after 1640, except by elderly man; mustache trained upward or brushed out toward each side, very small mustache later in period.

3. **Headdress:** barret in beginning of period; hat with high crown and

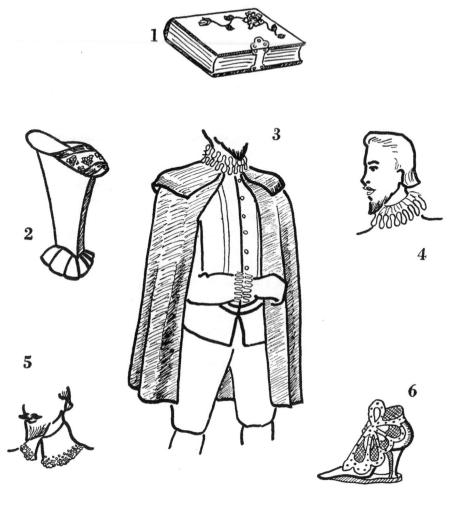

1. Book of Hours   2. Chopine   3. Cape
4. Ruff   5. Band   6. Clog   7. Shoe Rose

183

broad brim with jewel on right side, until 1603; hat with soft brim often turned up at side or front; broad, trimmed sombrero with 3 plumes curling around crown, *chapeau-bras,* until 1640; hat with moderate crown; high, tapering crown with narrow brim, having band and buckle, after 1645, often worn by Puritan in England, elaborate jeweled band worn by others; hat worn indoors, until 1685; nightcap.

4. **Footwear:** shoe with round toe, until 1625, then square; long vamp, moderately high, red heel, high tongue, and side pieces fastened by latchet, leather, or ribbon; later square-toed shoe; latchet covered with shoe rose at first, later with large ribbon bow; loose-fitting boot; shorter boot with *bucket top,* after 1625, top turned down, showing broad lace fold or *canon* of boot hose; extravagant boot top, after 1625; spurs worn by all men with *quatrefoil* decoration, worn indoors; yarn stocking for everyday wear, silk for dress occasion; knitted stocking; long wide-topped leather gaiter with foot worn between stocking and shoe or boot; several pairs of hose worn at one time; chopine, clog, or patten, pantoffle.

5. **Accessories:** watch, second hand invented early in century; broad military sash tied in bow; baldrick, from 1621; embroidered, red sword-belt; long sword; dagger discarded; badge showing *Order* of courtier; walking stick; soft bag purse or pouch; handkerchief; gauntlet or other type of glove; purse hung from belt; buttons used as trimming at first; loup or mask: muff carried later in period.

6. **Jewelry:** earrings worn only by sailor and pirate; rings; brooch; studs.

7. **Typical Colors:** gold lace; scarlet, apple-green, or blue for silk stocking; violet or red for shoe, deep blue, wine, red, green, gray, and orange for costumes used by French; blue, violet, green, gray, and orange worn by Italians; blue and red, by Germans and Dutch; very rich colors, gold and silver, preferred by Spanish; dark-colored or black hats; wide range of colors, black and gold worn by English; additional colors including light tones of blue, green, rose, and gray.

8. **Typical Materials:** silk, jeweled doublet; thinner fabric used than in the previous period, fine and heavy, bleached linen, for collar and cuff; heavy cotton for suit and lining; silk stocking; silk trimming; beaver hat; also velvet, brocade, taffeta, satin, damask, sarcenet, batiste, Holland cloth, poplin, fustian, buckram, flannel, lawn, gauze, jersey, linsey-woolsey, russet, and many other fabrics; feathers; expensive fur for muff; muff of cat or dog skin for middle class.

9. **Make-up:** paint; patch in the 1640's; curling iron used; perfume.

184

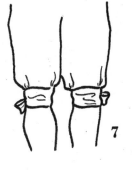

1. Patch 2. Band Strings 3. Falling Ruff 4. Falling Band or Falling Collar
5. Van Dyck Beard 6. Loup 7. Slops 8. Bucket Top Boot
9. Apron 10. Clog 11. Pantoffle

C. WOMEN

1. **Garments:**

   Outer upper: styles of previous period continued until 1610; shoulder wing on earlier dress; square low neckline of last period continued until 1630's, high neckline in back, later, very wide on shoulder; often low neckline with draped collar, showing bust; large collar of fine lace, or linen and lace extended low on shoulder; sleeve with small slashes and puffs, 1603; sleeve shorter 1620, reached to elbow, by 1640, long sleeve worn by some, sleeve divided by ribbon into 2 paned puffs; not as full after 1630; cuff loose, after 1640; upper sleeve decorated with buttons, fastened at armscye and cuff, white or colored under-sleeve showing through slash; double ruffle on cuff; narrow silk band at front of waist; peak at waist increased, until 1603, curved from each side to points; wasp waist and long pointed stomacher, until 1630, round, pointed stomacher or stomacher of undergown concealed by short-waisted overgown; decorated stomacher; overlapping tabs on bodice; soft ribbon sash tied at side or front; galant.

   Outer lower: ankle-length skirt, 1610-20; bell-shaped; size of farthingale changed the size of the skirt; skirt falling to floor, after 1620, in simple folds, fullness toward back; skirt often open, displaying petticoat, until 1630; skirt seldom open in front, by middle of century; floor-length skirt; very long skirt looped up when walking.

   Under: corset of laths about 2 inches wide, held together by tapes passing over and under them, worn by Spanish lady; chemise showing above blouse and with cuff beneath lace of sleeve of bodice; farthingale smaller, 1615, discontinued, 1620, except in Spain; petticoat showed when skirt was left open.

   Cloaks and overgarments: circular cape until 1645; high-waisted cloak with full sleeve; cape with capuchon; jacket.

2. **Hair:** hair pad disappearing, *c.* 1620; short hair introduced by Anne of Austria; bang over forehead; corkscrew curls or frizzed at temples or bunches of curls over ears and hanging around face; flat coiled knot at back; lovelock; bows and pearls worn at sides.

3. **Headdress:** custom of going without head covering introduced by Catherine de' Medici; hood, 1640; Mary Stuart cap; cap sometimes with plumes; low barret, small hat or cap emphasizing the short curls; hat resembling that worn by man, with close-fitting, high, feathered crown; large-brimmed hat, *c.* 1640; nightcap.

4. **Footwear:** similar to shoe worn by man; elaborate shoe ornamented with pearls and large shoe rose or ribbon latchet; high tongue; very high heel, first worn to increase height, sometimes red; chopine,

clog; silk stocking, worn by wealthy, knitted yarn stocking, by lower class.

5. **Accessories**: beautiful buttons, some of diamonds and other precious stones, also ivory, bone, wood, and paste buttons rivaling the precious stones; watch; handkerchief; wide comb with pearls around the arch; long glove worn with short sleeve, after 1640; small to moderate-sized muff of luxurious fabric, lap dog carried in muff; frilled apron; loup or mask worn during entire century, unseemly for lady to appear unmasked, at first confined to eyes only, later covered entire chin and held in place by button resting between teeth; scissors, fan, needle case and keys hanging from girdle; also Book of Hours, beautiful fans mounted in wood; gold, silver, and mother-of-pearl, also exquisite one made of lace, rigid or folding fan; patch box; mirror.

6. **Jewelry**: worn at first with extravagance, with more discrimination, after 1630; chain; brooch; rings; large choker; pearl or gold beads; long necklace of pearls held in front by a brooch, sometimes only a simple string of pearls worn by court lady; several bracelets worn with short sleeve, bracelet sometimes made of double strand of pearls or of jeweled bangles of gold; long pear-shaped earrings, worn less with side curls.

7. **Typical Colors**: crimson gown; black hood and white veil worn by Italian woman; apple green, light blue, or red stocking; white collar and cuffs; rich deep Burgundy, purple, apple green, blue, and brown, favorite colors; for additional colors refer to *B. 7.*

8. **Typical Materials**: linen for apron, linen crash for jacket, petticoat, and under bodice; ribbon replacing lace in latter part of period; satin and light-weight brocades for gloves and shoes as well as the garment; gold lace, fringe, and rich fabric prohibited by Richelieu, 1638. Refer to *B. 8.*

9. **Make-up**: white paint; rouge; patch.

SIGNIFICANT MOTIFS

Diaper patterns, small floral sprigs, spiral designs.

INFLUENCES ON LATER COSTUMES

Patches were in vogue until the French Revolution, also in early 19th century; Van Dyck collar from Cavalier era used often in later periods, also lace-edged handkerchief; ostrich plumes fashionable in time of Marie Antoinette and early 20th century; small collar resembling the neck-whisk worn by women, 1948; hair styles with bang over forehead and knot at the back, late 1940's and '50's.

BOOKS OF REFERENCE

(See also GENERAL BIBLIOGRAPHY, p. 433)

Blum, André, *Histoire au Costume: Les Modes au XVIIe et au XVIIIe Siècle* (Paris, Hachette, 1928)

Brooke, Iris, *English Costume of the Seventeenth Century* (London, A. and C. Black, Ltd., 1924)

Earle, Alice Morse, *Two Centuries of Costume in America, 1620-1820,* 2 vols. (New York, The Macmillan Co., 1903)

Hippolyte, Roy, *La Vie, La Mode, et Le Costume au XVIIe Siècle, Époque Louis XIII* (Paris, E. Champion, 1924)

Jones, I., *Designs by Inigo Jones for Masques and Plays at Court* (Oxford, University Press, 1924)

Kelly, Francis M., and Schwab, Randolph, *Historic Costume, 1490-1790* (London, B. T. Batsford, 1925)

McClellan, Elizabeth, *Historic Dress in America, 1607-1800* (Philadelphia, G. W. Jacobs and Co., 1904)

McPharlin, Paul, *Life and Fashion in America, 1650-1900* (New York, Hastings House, 1946)

ARTISTS FOR COSTUME REFERENCE

Bol, Ferdinand (1616-80)
Caravaggio, Michel Angelo (1560/5-1609)
Champaigne, Philippe de (1602-74)
Cuyp, Aelbert (1620-91)
Greco, El (Domenico Theotocopuli) (1545/8-1614)
Hals, Frans (1580-1666)
Hooch, Pieter de (1629/32-77/83)
Jordaens, Jakob (1593-1678)
Kneller, Sir Godfrey (1646-1723)
Maes, Nicholaes (1632-93)
Mazo, Juan B. del (1606-67)
Metsu, Gabriel (1629-67)
Miereveld, Michael van (1567-1641)
Mytens, Daniel (Elder) (1590-1658)
Netscher, Casper (1639-84)

Poussin, Nicholas (1593/4-1665)
Ravesteyn, Jan Anthonisz van (1572-1657)
Rembrandt, van Rijn (1606-69)
Rigaud y Ros, Hyacinthe (1659-1743)
Rubens, Peter Paul (1577-1640)
Steen, Jan Havicksz (1626-79)
Sustermans, Justus (1597-1681)
Teniers, David (Elder) (1582-1649)
Teniers, David (Ygr.) (1610-90)
Ter Borch, Géraerd (1584-1662)
Tiepole, Giovanni Battista (1693/6-1770)
Van Dyck (Sir) Anthony (1599-1641)
Velasquez, Diego Rodriguez de Silva y (1509-1660)
Vermeer, Johannes (1632-75?)
Vos, Simon de (1603-76)

GLOSSARY

Apron—article of dress worn over the front of the skirt, utilitarian or decorative. Refer to *Chap. 2. Pl. XXVII, 9.*
Badge—refer to *Chaps. 2, 8, 9, 10.*

CHAPTER 11: GLOSSARY

Baldrick—refer to *Chaps. 1, 3, 7, 8, 9, 10.*

Band—refer to *Chap. 10. Pl. XXVI, 5.*

Band-strings—refer to *Chap. 10. Pl. XXVII, 2.*

Barret—refer to *Chap. 10.*

Bodice—refer to *Chap. 10.*

Book of Hours—refer to *Chaps 9, 10. Pl. XXVI, 1.*

Bucket Top Boot—wide-topped boot, sometimes turned in a broad cuff. *Pl. XXVII, 8.*

Buff coat—jacket of buffalo leather.

Canon—frill of lace extending above the boot, or at the knee of the breeches.

Cape—refer to *Chaps. 2, 3, 4, 6, 8, 9, 10. Pl. XXVI, 3.*

Capuchon—refer to *Chaps. 5, 8, 9.*

Cassock—long, close-fitting garment worn by clergy, collarless and with full turned-up sleeve.

Chapeau-bras—name given to hat carried under arm because the size of hairdress and wig prohibited the wearing of a hat.

Chemise—refer to *Chaps. 6, 7, 8, 9, 10.*

Chopine, Clog or Patten—refer to *Chaps. 9, 10. Pl. XXVI, 2*

Clog—refer to *Chopine,* and to *Chaps. 8, 9, 10. Pl. XXVI, 6; Pl. XXVII, 10.*

Corset—refer to *Chaps. 8, 9, 10.*

Doublet—refer to *Chaps. 9, 10.*

Falling Band or Falling Collar—elaborate lace collar, sometimes called Louis XIII collar. Refer to *Chap. 10. Pl. XXVII, 4.*

Falling Ruff—refer to *Chap. 10. Pl. XXVII, 3.*

Farthingale—refer to *Chap. 10.*

Galant—tie of ribbon used on sleeve, bodice, or skirt.

Imperial—small tuft or beard on chin.

Jerkin—refer to *Chaps. 9, 10.*

Latchet—refer to *Chaps. 9, 10.*

Loup or Mask—half-mask worn to cover the eyes, also known as domino. Refer to *Chap. 10. Pl. XXVII, 6.*

Lovelock—plait or curl of hair near left ear, and tied with a ribbon, worn by both man and woman.

Mary Stuart Cap—refer to *Chap. 10.*

Mask—covering for the face. Refer to *Loup* and to *Chap. 1.*

Neck-whisk—refer to *Chap. 10.*

Nightcap—refer to *Chap. 10.*

Order—chivalric organization to which men belonged.

Pantoffle—type of soft slipper. Refer to *Chap. 10. Pl. XXVII, 11.*

Patch—refer to *Chaps. 5, 10. Pl. XXVII, 1.*

Patten—refer to *Chopine.*

Peplum—short skirt of the bodice.

Petticoat—refer to *Chaps. 9, 10.*

Point—refer to *Aglet, Chaps. 9, 10.*

Pouch—refer to *Chaps. 6, 7, 8, 9, 10.*

Quatrefoil—design of 4 ornamental lobes used on spurs that were attached to shoes. Refer to *Chap. 7.*

Ruff—refer to *Chap. 10. Pl. XXVI, 4.*

Shoe Rose—refer to *Chap. 10. Pl. XXVI, 7.*

Shoulder Wing—refer to *Chap. 10.*

Slops—knee breeches. Refer to *Chap. 10. Pl. XXVII, 7.*

Sombrero—refer to *Chap. 10.*

Stomacher—refer to *Chap. 10.*

Trunk Hose—refer to *Chaps. 9, 10.*

Van Dyck Beard—small, pointed beard, shown in portraits by Van Dyck. *Pl. XXVII, 5.*

Van Dyck Edge—lace having edge as shown in Van Dyck's paintings.

Waistcoat—garment which developed from the Doublet.

17th Century

PART II

1643-1714

CHRONOLOGY

Battle of Rocroi marked end of supremacy of Spanish power, *1643.*

End of Thirty Years' War, *1648.* Treaty of Westphalia.

Settlement of South Carolina, *1659.*

Emperor Leopold of Germany, *1658-1705.* Various wars ensued.

Marriage of Louis XIV of France to Maria Theresa, daughter of Philip IV, *1659.*

Building of Versailles, *1661-87.*

Connecticut granted charter, *1662.* Charter of Rhode Island, *1663.* New Hampshire and Massachusetts, *1680.*

St. Paul's Cathedral in London destroyed by the Great Fire, *1666,* rebuilt, *1675-1710,* Sir Christopher Wren, architect.

LaSalle explored Great Lakes, *1679;* took possession of Mississippi for Louis XIV, *1682.*

Royal charter given to William Penn for Pennsylvania, *1681.*

First attempt to light London streets, *1684.*

Louis XIV revoked Edict of Nantes, *1685,* many people left country.

Defeat of English fleet by French, *1690.*

England, mistress of the seas, after victory of La Hogue, *1692.*

Charter of William and Mary College in Virginia, *1692.*

Bank of England established, *1694.*

London stock exchange founded, *1698.*

Yale College founded, *1701.*

Queen Anne's War, *1702-13.*

Excavation at Pompeii and Herculaneum, *1706.*

Union of England and Scotland with name of Great Britain, *1707.*

War of Spanish Succession, *1700-13,* Peace of Utrecht, *1713.*

CHAPTER 12

17th Century

PART II

1643-1714

HISTORY

Louis XIV of France was only five years of age when he ascended the throne, and during his minority the affairs of government were conducted by his mother, Anne of Austria, and Cardinal Mazarin, the Prime Minister. When Louis came of age he ushered in an era of unprecedented extravagance and splendor, and Paris very shortly became the fashion capital of the world. The elegance of the time was reflected not only in dress but in architecture. The magnificent palace of Versailles, designed especially for Louis XIV and filled with great works of art, excited the admiration and envy of the world. At the court and among the aristocracy, luxury was the last word, finding expression in lavish paintings, sculptured alabaster, gold stucco, elaborate carving, exquisite furnishings, and handsome examples of printing and binding.

But Louis XIV, called the "Sun King" because of the emblem of the sun and snake on all of his appointments, was blind to the increasing misery that his recklessness was bringing to the lower classes in France and indifferent to the ultimate effect of his ambitious schemes and irresponsible spending. He had little feeling for the rights of others, one of his ruthless acts being a revoking of the Edict of Nantes of 1598 which resulted in widespread persecution of the Protestants. Large numbers of these Huguenots were forced to flee from the country but France's loss was a gain for Holland and England as many of these people were skilled craftsmen and capable merchants.

This period, known as the "Grand Monarchy," lasted for seventy-two years and during it France ranked as the most important European power. Except for encouraging the economic reforms of his minister,

Jena Baptiste Colbert, which instituted a general industrial reorganization of the country, Louis' political activity consisted chiefly of making war on the other nations of Europe. Toward the end of his reign he became embroiled in the War of the Spanish Succession. This grew out of rival claims to the Spanish throne which Philip II in his will had left to Philip, duke of Anjou, the grandson of his sister who was Louis' wife. Emperor Leopold I of Austria also claimed the throne for his son Charles VI, and in this struggle to keep the balance of power the Grand Alliance (Austria, England, Holland, Brandenburg, and Savoy) leagued together to fight it out with France. The war lasted for thirteen years, resulting in victories for the Alliance, and by the Treaty of Utrecht (1713) France lost most of her colonial possessions—Newfoundland, Nova Scotia, and Hudson Bay—to England, although the French monarchy was allowed to remain intact.

During this time England also was dominated by autocratic rulers who attempted to govern without the consent of Parliament. The despotism of James I and Charles I brought about civil war from 1642 to 1649 and the Puritan regime of Oliver Cromwell. Stuart power was restored after the death of Cromwell in 1658 and Charles II ascended the English throne, ushering in the period of the Restoration which compared in its pursuit of pleasure and all the elegancies of living with the French court. Charles II was followed by James II, William and Mary, and Queen Anne. During the latter's reign England and Scotland were made one country, called Great Britain, by the Act of Union of 1707. By the end of this period Parliament had grown quite strong again and had greatly curbed royal power.

Under Charles I many Puritans fled from persecution to New England to begin life anew in America, leaving their indelible imprint on the national character. Charles II and his brother granted large grants along the Middle Atlantic seaboard and in the southern American colonies to friends who had supported the Stuart cause. New York was captured from the Dutch by the English in 1664. William Penn, the most idealistic of the colonizers, was given a charter for Pennsylvania, and Philadelphia, city of Brotherly Love, was founded in 1682. Local rule of the colonies varied considerably but was in general democratic. Frontier conditions still prevailed and the daily life of the colonists was pretty rugged. Agriculture was the chief occupation and household necessities were manufactured in the home, although toward the end of the period various industries began to develop.

CHAPTER 12: HISTORY

France as the arbiter of fashion set the styles for the rest of the world. Dress was extreme and ostentatious; the informal dress had a train which had to be carried by a lackey hired for this purpose. Men's garments were just as luxurious as women's; the king at one time purchased 1600 yards of lace for his personal use. Queens and royal mistresses had always influenced fashion but this was especially true during the reign of the Sun King. Among these were Louise de la Vallière, Mme de Montespan, Duchess de Fontanges, and Mme de Maintenon. The latter introduced a note of sobriety and simplicity into the French court, but before the close of the century the King showed a dislike for this sort of restraint, and lavish dress was again restored to favor. Women dressmakers were not known until after the reign of Louis XIV; costumes for women were fashioned by tailors. France excelled also in the manufacture of fine fabrics and furnishings, among which were the Gobelin tapestries, designed by court painters.

During Cromwell's time in England dress was very somber and dull but with the Restoration under Charles II extravagant styles were again in vogue. In America the colonists were too preoccupied with the struggle for existence to give much thought to fashion. It should be noted, however, that the simplicity of the Puritan costume was in many ways more artistic than any that had been known for centuries.

Although the popular view of woman's place in the world was a narrow one, authors were beginning to write in their behalf. The English essayists, Addison and Steele, argued for an improvement in women's position, and other books devoted to the subject first appeared in this period, among them: *The Lady's New Year's Gift: Advice to a Daughter* (1673); *L'Education des Filles* (1687), and *The Ladies Calling* (1673). In the colonies education for women met with more support after 1700.

In general, though, women were considered inferior and weaker in body and mind than men. It was felt that they should devote themselves to music, drawing, embroidery, and the making of sweetmeats. Some did study a little French and Italian and read the Bible, Milton, and history and geography, but it was believed that no matter how much a woman might read she could never attain the intellectual level of an ordinary schoolboy; some critics even suggested that learning a language might overload a woman's mind. So women stayed pretty close to home, dominated by their husbands, many of whom objected to their wives even having a small allowance of their own. Frequent appearance in public places was frowned upon and any participation in political activity out of the question. Nevertheless it was during the reign of Charles II in England that women were first permitted to act professionally on the stage.

The occupations of men continued to be in agriculture and industry. From 1600 to 1700 travel and an exchange of ideas brought about an advancement in scientific farming. Cloth manufactured in France was exported all over the world. The French government regulated the method of dyeing and the making of all fabrics; new kinds of cloth had to be endorsed by royal decree. The guilds in France were so powerful that frequently new inventions for the manufacture of materials were opposed. England had attained first place in European commerce and industry, but France held her own in products of artistic merit—tapestries, lace, silk, and furniture.

DRESS

A. *Sources of information:* paintings, sculpture, coins, medals, garments of the time which are still preserved, and literature.

B. **MEN**
  1. **Garments:**
   Outer upper: jerkin with long skirt, until 1650, collarless, turned-up sleeve; sleeveless type worn over sleeved garment; doublet; *bolero,* often buttoned from breast downward, showing shirt below, short sleeve extending to above or below elbow, with large cuff or flare; also sleeve with no cuff, but slit up forearm and with buttons on either side, used until the middle of the 17th century; longer form of embroidered doublet, 1660's; braid and buttons used profusely; first coat collarless because of *cravat* and *periwig;* sleeve with scarcely any fullness in armscye; sleeve lengthened, after 1675; huge cuff buttoned back on sleeve, *c.* 1694; sometimes sleeve with small cuff, also slit and buttoned at wrist; coat buttoned all the way down the front; lower button left unbuttoned until 1690; skirt of coat with outward flare, stiff inner lining, decoration or buttons on slit extending upward to either hip; shaped to waist, after 1675; slit at back and over each hip for convenience in riding after 1680, and for the sword, after 1690; buttons and buttonholes used; radiating pleats extending from the button on each side of coat, after 1675; pleat at side back of coat, 1690; pockets vertical, horizontal, or crescent-shaped; position of pockets varied, at first very low, later, higher; doublet discarded and waistcoat worn, after 1670; coat often

196

1. Cravat   2. Cassock   3. Falbala or Furbelow
4. Mantelet or Mantelette   5. Culotte

worn without waistcoat, until 1690; waistcoat at first extending below hip, thigh-length and collarless, *c.* 1670, and to the knee or below, 1670-1720; embroidered waistcoat almost as long as coat, 1680; waistcoat usually buttoned, until 1690's, fastened only at waist, after 1695; with or without sleeves; close sleeve of waistcoat sometimes visible under coat sleeve, bulky cuff of waistcoat sometimes false, often turned back over cuff of coat; jerkin replaced by cassock; jerkin worn by middle class.

Outer lower: large tubular breeches; very large rosette at knee; elaborate *petticoat breeches* or *Rhingraves,* 1655-70; breeches of moderate width, gartered at the knee, 1670; rather full breeches, 1685; plain, close-fitting breeches buckled at knee, 1690; *culottes* fastening below the knee; full breeches fastened at side with buttons or buckle, after 1690; garter with ribbon bow worn below knee, 1665-80.

Under: full white shirt, opening in front, with large sleeve, often gathered at neck either into band or with drawstring; shirt visible at waist, *c.* 1660; frill at wrist and elbow held by ribbon tie; short or long drawers.

Cloaks and overgarments: cape, used only for traveling, after 1670; loose overcoat later in period; *justaucorps; Roquelaure,* cassock.

Neckwear and wristwear: wide collar continued in first part of period, until 1660; collar became narrow with box pleat in front; cravat or neckcloth worn by military man early in period, in general use after 1640; first cravat held by bow; narrow black or colored ribbon tied in front over the 2 ends of the cravat, 1660; cravat consisting of strip of lace or lawn wrapped around neck with one end turned up over other end, 1670; *Geneva bands,* 1660-80; stiff, light or dark ribbon bow showing from under cravat, 1690-1700; *Steinkirk, c.* 1692, continued to be worn, until 1770, although not fashionable; plain neckcloth, *c.* 1700; lawn or lace ruffle at wrist.

2. **Hair:** parted in center; naturally curled or uncurled hair often extending to shoulder in early part of period; *periwig* or *full bottomed wig* of natural color, 1660, worn by fashionable man; few instances of powdered hair, before 1700; head shaved or hair cut very short to accommodate periwig; corkscrew curls hanging over breast and back, from 1670; sometimes tied in back, 1678, lovelock worn, until 1680; *peruke,* 1690-1700; curls pushed to back to accommodate wide bow at neck; smaller periwig, without exaggeration, after 1700; large wig brought about custom of combing hair in public; *Ramilie wig;* lovelock tied with ribbon; *catogan* or *club wig,* 1705, powdered white; clean shaven, 1655; beard seldom worn, some-

198

1. Canon or Cannon 2. Peruke 3. Bolero 4. Periwig 5. Lovelock

times very narrow mustache and tiny fleck centered below lower lip; beard and mustache unfashionable, after 1680.

3. **Headdress:** steeple crown hat, with bow in front, until 1660; low crown, with long and varicolored plumes, fashionable in first part of period; also wide, soft brim, cocked on 1 or 2 sides, worn by fashionable man; plain band and buckle worn by Puritan in England; tricorne hat, decorated with ribbon and plumes, by 1690, popular for more than one hundred years; braid and metal lace, after 1670; fringe-like decoration on brim in latter part of period; silver or gold cord hatband; fur cap with adjustable brim; *montero* used as riding hat or worn indoors; chapeau-bras; nightcap.

4. **Footwear:** boot out of style for general use, after 1660; buskin used with hunting costume; tabular *jackboot* most popular, after 1665; close-fitting boot with flaring top, until 1670; high leather legging or *spatterdash;* red heel still used on shoe, not on boot; to increase his height, Louis XIV ordered high cork heels made on his shoes, effect lost when courtiers copied this style; high heel shoe with outstanding tongue and with metal buckle, until 1680; long tongue discarded, after 1690; red lining of tongue shaped as a cupid's bow, turned over at top of shoe, 1690's; heavy or light-weight shoe with long, square toe, until 1690; shoe rose replaced by buckle or wired ribbon tie; bow of large loops on shoe worn by extremist, small bow worn by others; strap and buckle, only form of shoe fastening, after 1680; canon; boot hose worn with shoe, until 1680, sometimes with wide-spreading top showing over breeches and garters, 2 pairs sometimes worn; garter below knee, bunch of ribbon loops on outer or on both sides of garter band; stocking rolled over breeches, 1680-90, and held by buckled garter; clog.

5. **Accessories:** extravagant; sword knot on belt or below; knots of ribbon at various positions over entire costume according to mode, until 1680; shoulder-knot or looped cord on right shoulder, until 1700; sash often around hip, or wide sash wound over right shoulder and fastened under left arm, 1660's and '70's; badge of Order sometimes shown on broad ribbon, tied formally with short ends, in front over coat or vest, 1690; elaborate sword baldrick or shoulder belt out of fashion, after 1695, sword then hung on sling beneath waistcoat; plain glove, utilitarian glove usually only for soldier or horseman; large pillow-shaped muff of silk or other cloth hung on ribbon, 1668, *passe caille,* or chain around the neck; long or short *walking stick;* snuff box and lace handkerchief; pouch attached to belt disappearing with introduction of coat with pockets; paint box; *miser* or *stocking purse;* dress sword on sword belt at last of period; first eye glasses or spectacles, size increased with rank of wearer.

1. Petticoat Breeches   2. Steinkirk   3. Tricorne Hat
4. Walking Stick   5. Fontange Headdress   6. Steeple Crown Hat   7. Tricorne Hat

6. **Jewelry:** watch on chain, now worn as ornament at top of breeches.
7. **Typical Colors:** colors very rich and brilliant; gold and silver lace and brocade; sometimes 3 different colors and gold used in costume; black or purple suit; violet or white showing through slash in sleeve; buff, gray or scarlet coat; blue waistcoat embroidered and fringed with silver, breeches often of black velvet; light or white stocking; black or brown shoe; russet boot; black used generally for man's footwear, after 1670; brown leather with hunting costume; black or dark gray hat; colors in the French court somewhat subdued, after 1690, in England bright colors prevailing; sea-green uniform for footman.
8. **Typical Materials:** brocade; cotton and linen prints; block printing; pliant fabrics used; velvet suit with satin or silk showing through slash in sleeve; taffeta ribbon; much gold thread, and heavy embroidery; imitation of Venetian cut velvet; crepe; velvet and satin knee breeches; flannel or cotton trousers; lace handkerchief used because of general use of snuff; magnificent fabrics, 1662, gold and silver cloth used only by king and his court, feathered hat.
9. **Make-up:** face painted by courtier; patch; mustache curled with curling tongs.

C. WOMEN
1. Garments:

Outer upper: separate bodice and skirt; horizontal neckline across shoulder; folded kerchief sometimes used for modesty; low and wide drop shoulder or V-neckline over low-cut underdress, after 1690; sleeve at first slit up the front from wrist to elbow or above, revealing sleeve of chemise; sleeve to wrist, out of style, after 1660, and elbow sleeve worn, trimmed profusely with lace or ribbon; large open or fairly straight sleeve with fringe, lace, or ribbon, from 1670; *engageant;* shoulder roll or flap; full sleeve worn sometimes, until 1700; bodice short-waisted, not boned, during first of period; long stomacher of undergown showing beneath short-waisted overgown; waistline becoming slightly pointed, lowered, and exaggerated; tabs forming a peplum still used all around waist, or 1 or 2 in back; outerdress or robe of velvet or heavy silk, sometimes lined in contrasting color, closed at waist, 1660; very long pointed, wasp-like bodice fastened in front, and decorated with ribbon bows and embroidery or jeweled clips, or laced in back; later, point of bodice shorter; very good clothes worn by market woman and shopkeeper.

Outer lower: open-front skirt worn, 1650, dress closed in front when not wearing overgown; skirt looped up when walking, or carried over left arm; simpler dress cleared the ground; formal dress with panel train held up sometimes by ribbon; front of skirt caught up at intervals; small pleats on hip of skirt, 1655-75; satin petticoat often revealed beneath draping; elaborate apron became part of costume; much draping, after 1690, skirt draped to resemble a bustle, held back by brooch; *falbala* or *furbelow; pretintailles.*

Under: shift or chemise with lace border on shoulder; puffed chemise, sleeve showing below sleeve of bodice; corset short-waisted and less stiff; farthingale out of fashion, and many petticoats in its place, 1665; *bustle* after 1680; petticoat often with many ribbons, lace and festoons, often quilted, 1680-1710; train on petticoat; red woolen petticoat by middle class; hoop or *pannier* of whalebone, reed or whalebone used, *c.* 1711, at first, funnel-shaped, later increasing in width and flattened in back and front.

Cloaks and overgarments: cloak followed lines of gown; loose, fur-trimmed, knee-length, or shorter, velvet jacket; large shawl; *palatine; pelerine; mantelet* or *mantelette; night-rail;* cape with capuchon.

Neckwear and wristwear: large collar and cuff superceded by pleated ruching and lace; cravat; Steinkirk, 1690's; puffed sleeve of chemise extending below bodice sleeve; wide lace ruffle on short full and later longer tight sleeve.

Additional garments: manteau or *mantua,* 1675-1700; quilted gown worn as a *housecoat;* masculine influence shown in riding attire, coat, vest, cravat, and wig.

2. **Hair:** short curls over entire head; *bun* on back of head; wired-out side curls, 1660's; closer to face after 1670; coiffure *hurluberlu,* 1671; *taure;* braided lock, resembling lovelock of earlier period worn, 1670's; hair dressed high and away from forehead in 1 to 3 peaks, hair in ringlets on shoulder, 1690-1700; close hairdress, after 1700; coiffure *à la Maintenon.*

3. **Headdress:** large brimmed hat in first of period; small cap or hood, until 1690, by middle class; cap having frontpiece or round disk of cardboard or light wood covered with black silk extending forward in the center, worn by the Dutch bourgeoise; masculine hunting hat; tricorne; bunches or loops of ribbon worn on side of bun; *à la Fontanges, fontange, commode,* or *tower headdress,* 1690-1700, kerchief sometimes worn over this headdress; small lace or linen hat used, after 1710; head covered by shawl; nightcap.

4. **Footwear:** small shoe with very high, sharp-pointed, jeweled, diamond-studded heel; shoe of woman differing from that of man, after 1660; long square toe, *c.* 1665, later pointed; enameled buckle; ribbon bow; pantoffle or mule; buskin for hunting; patten, chopine, or high stilted clog that necessitated help for the wearer when walking.

5. **Accessories:** various types of aprons worn by everyone; knee-length or shorter apron worn by lady of the court, 1680-1700; elbow-length glove of fine leather worn with short sleeve; long mitten and glove, after 1690; glove with short cuff; broad scarf; beautiful, tall walking stick; fringed parasol; many ribbon trimmings, 1670-1700; small muff; fur neckpiece; mask; folding fan and ostrich fan came into use because tight corset caused difficulty in breathing; fan often painted by eminent artist; scented Spanish leather fan; elaborate handkerchief; beautiful tortoise shell and ivory box with mirror in lid of box, for patches; steel, brass, copper, or jet buttons, some decorated with flowers and figures in bone or ivory; miser or stocking purse.

6. **Jewelry:** watch on chain; dangling earrings worn even by peasant; pearl choker, in first of period, later, long necklace; jeweled brooches worn in different places on costume; hair decorated with strands of pearls and jewels.

7. **Typical Colors:** skirt and bodice sometimes of different colors; gray damask with silver, blue, brown, gray, or white apron; red petticoat. Refer to *B. 7.*

8. **Typical Materials:** transparent black dress worn over gown of gold brocade; velvet coat; lace puffs on undergarment; ribbon, chenille, pearls, flowers, and muslin for headdress à la Fontanges; lace mantilla; lace or silk mitten or glove; short red glove; silk stocking worn by upper class, woolen stocking for lower class; satin, brocade, or embroidered silk mule for house wear; fabric painted with exquisite flowers and figures, or embroidered; lace, silk and lace, or silk apron by gentlewoman, white linen or lace-edged lawn apron by bourgeoise; heavy cloth apron worn by peasant.

9. **Make-up:** patch in shape of circle, star or other form; English lady belonging to Tory party with patch on left cheek, of the Whig party, with patch on right cheek; paint, white lead, flour, rice, quicksilver and bismuth; face enamel used by elderly woman; highly scented perfume.

SIGNIFICANT MOTIFS

Stylized flowers, single sprays of flowers, various Renaissance patterns, rock and shell, acanthus-leaf designs, and pastoral, Biblical, and legendary pictures. In general, the designs were larger than in previous periods.

INFLUENCES ON LATER COSTUMES

Fontange-type headdress shown in high brimless hat, 1940's; apron, 1811, early 20th century, 1930's, '40's, '50's; quilted silk again used in later years;

transparent gown, *c.* 1947-52; lace and transparent fabric over heavier cloth, later periods and today.

BOOKS OF REFERENCE

(See Books of Reference, Part I, *17th Century* p. 188, and General Bibliography, p. 433)

ARTISTS FOR COSTUME REFERENCE
(See p. 188)

GLOSSARY

à la Fontanges, Fontange, Commode, or Tower Headdress—tall fan-like headdress of lace or lawn originated by Duchess de Fontanges. The term commode was used in England during the time of William III.

à la Maintenon—coiffure with hair parted in center, trimmed in graduated lengths, curled and fluffed; designed by Mme Martin, a hairdresser, and first worn by Mme de Maintenon.

Apron—refer to *Chaps. 2, 11.*

Baldrick—refer to *Chaps. 3, 7, 8, 9, 10, 11.*

Bodice—refer to *Chaps. 10, 11.*

Bolero—short jacket. *Pl. XXIX, 3.*

Boot—refer to *Chaps. 9, 10,* and to *Bucket Top Boot, Chap. 11.*

Bun—flat knot of hair worn on back of head.

Buskin—close-fitting boot to the calf of the leg of fine leather or fabric, with turnover top. Refer to *Chaps. 4, 5, 8, 9.*

Bustle—pad worn in the back to extend the contour of the skirt at the hip.

Canon or Cannon—refer to *Chap. 11. Pl. XXIX, 1.*

Capuchon—refer to *Chaps. 5, 8, 9, 11.*

Cassock—refer to *Chap. 11. Pl. XXVIII, 2.*

Catogan or Club Wig—wig having ends of hair turned under, sometimes known as cadogan; named in honor of 1st Earl Cadogan.

Chapeau-bras—refer to *Chap. 11.*

Chemise—refer to *Chaps. 6, 7, 8, 9, 10, 11.*

Chopine, Clog, or Patten—refer to *Chaps. 9, 10, 11.*

Clog—refer to *Chopine* and to *Chaps. 8, 9, 10, 11.*

Club—refer to *Catogan Wig.*

Commode—refer to *à la Fontanges.*

Corset—refer to *Chaps. 8, 9, 10, 11.*

Cravat—neckcloth or neckerchief popular in the latter part of 17th century. At first, the cravat was a piece of lawn, folded and wrapped around the neck, with colored or black ribbon tied over it to hold the 2 ends in place. Later, a more simple type of cravat was used, one end lapping over the other. *Pl. XXVIII, 1.*

Culotte—breeches tied below the knee and trimmed in braid. *Pl. XXVIII, 5.*

Doublet—refer to *Chaps. 9, 10, 11.*

Engageant—ruffle of lace falling below 3-quarter or elbow sleeve.

Falbala or Furbelow—deep, puckered silk or lace flounce of skirt. *Pl. XXVIII, 3.*

Farthingale—refer to *Chaps. 10, 11.*

Fontange Headdress—refer to *à la Fontanges. Pl. XXX, 5.*

Full-bottomed Wig—very large wig which extended over shoulder in front and back.

Geneva Bands—collar which consisted merely of 2 small tabs.

Housecoat—long coat worn in the house.

Hurluberlu—short curls over entire head; first worn by Mme. de Montespan, 1670.

Jackboot—large, heavy boot extending above the knee.

Jerkin—refer to *Chaps. 9, 10, 11.*

Justacorps—long coat with full skirt, buttoned down front, with sleeves often having turned back cuffs. This coat replaced the cassock, underwent various changes. .

Lovelock—refer to *Chap. 11. Pl. XXIX, 5.*

Manteau or Mantua—loose gown.

Mantelet or Mantelette—silk scarf or mantle, narrow in front, wide in back. *Pl. XXVIII, 4.*

Miser or Stocking Purse—purse of silk net with a slit in the middle, and a movable ring which kept the money at one end or the other.

Montero—round fur cap with turned up brim.

Nightcap—plain cap worn in bed. Refer to *Chaps. 10, 11.*

Night-rail—shoulder cape of muslin and lace which was an informal street wrap about 1670, at first worn as boudoir jacket.

Palatine—small shoulder cape introduced, c. 1671, by Princess Palatine (Princess Charlotte of Bavaria) to avoid appearing immodest by exposing the shoulders.

Pannier—framework forming a basket-like projection worn under each side of skirt.

Pantoffle or Mule—refer to *Chaps. 10, 11.*

Passe Caille—ribbon on which muff was hung.

Patch—small pieces of "court plaster," an adhesive on black silk which was so-called because of having been made for the ladies of the court. Refer to *Chaps. 5, 10, 11.*

Patten—wooden shoe with iron base, 1694. Refer to *Chopine.*

Pelerine—short shoulder cape, usually with long ends hanging down in front.

Peplum—refer to *Chap. 11.*

Periwig—wig introduced by the courtiers when Louis XIV was a child in admiration of his beautiful curls. Later, the king adopted the periwig in appreciation of the compliment paid him by the courtiers. *Pl. XXIX, 4.*

Peruke—wig with curls, and a peak on each side of the part. *Pl. XXIX, 2.*

Petticoat—refer to *Chaps. 9, 10, 11.*

Petticoat Breeches or Rhingraves—breeches which had several flounces and ribbons, first worn by Count of Salm who had the title of Rhingrave; one had a divided skirt, the other a wide kilt. *Pl. XXX, 1.*

Pretintailles—cut brocade flowers of various sizes used as trimming on dress.

Ramilie or Ramillie Wig—wig with puff at the side, and a braid in the back having bows at both upper and lower ends, worn by the Englishman in honor of the victory of the Duke of Marlborough on the battlefield of Ramillies, Belgium, 1706.

Roquelaure—large, full overcoat with cape; named after the Duke of Roquelaure.

Shift—chemise of fine linen, formerly called a smock.

Shoe Rose—refer to *Chaps. 10, 11.*

Spatterdash—high leather legging.

Steeple Crown Hat—refer to *Chap. 10. Pl. XXX, 6.*

Steinkirk—twisted cravat first worn by French officers dressing hurriedly for the Battle of Steinkirk, August, 1692. *Pl. XXX, 2.*

Stomacher—refer to *Chaps. 10, 11.*

Taure—hairdress resembling a bull's head, c. 1674.

Tricorne Hat—refer to *Chap. 9. Pl. XXX, 3, 7.*

Waistcoat—refer to *Chap. 11.*

Walking Stick—short or long stick often decorated with ribbon and tassel. *Pl. XXX, 4.*

18th Century

PART I

1715-73

CHRONOLOGY

France declared war on Spain, *1719*.

War between Spain and England, *1739*.

England's roads improved by Highway Act, *1741*.

India rubber used in Europe, *1744*.

Wool-carding machine invented by Lewis Paul, England, *1748*.

French and Indian Wars in America, *1755-63*.

Seven Years' War, land and naval battles between France and England, *1755-63*. Spain entered as an ally of France, *1762*. Treaty of Paris, *1763;* France ceded to England: Canada, Cape Breton Island, Grenada in the West Indies, and French possessions in Africa; France ceded Louisiana to Spain; Spain ceded Florida to England; England gave to Spain all conquests in Cuba and restored to France various islands and certain possessions in Africa and India.

Factory for making colored cotton prints established at Jouy-en-Josas, France, by Philippe Christophe Oberkampf, *1759*.

Pottery works of Wedgwood, *1760*.

Condensers, first step toward steam engine, invented by James Watt, Scotland, *1764*.

Stamp Act on legal documents, almanacs, and playing cards passed by England in *1765*.

American imports of tea, glass, paper, and dyestuffs taxed by England, *1767*.

Invention of modern steam engine by James Watt, Scotland, *1770*.

First spinning mill in England founded by Arkwright, *1771*.

Boston Tea Party, *1773*.

CHAPTER 13

18th Century

PART 1

1715-73

HISTORY

The extravagance and frivolity of Louis XIV's reign in France continued to an even greater degree into the regency of the Duke of Orleans and the later reign of Louis XV, adding further to the country's impoverishment. Gayety and triviality, sparkle and light-heartedness characterized Louis XV's court, and royal favorites—male and female—were a drain on the royal treasury. Étienne de Silhouette, Minister of Finance, tried to avoid his country's bankruptcy in 1759. Because of his program of public economy his name was linked to everything noticeably frugal—hence our word "silhouette," a black profile drawing of the human head which was substituted for the more expensive portrait. Plain coats without folds became the vogue and snuff boxes were without decoration.

The colonies in America were becoming more and more important and the colonists were beginning to enjoy a more settled life, free from the hardships of pioneer existence. Philadelphia, New York, and Boston became sophisticated centers of social life. Americans were also developing a sense of independence. A number of restricting acts against the colonies, passed by the British government caused constant irritation between the two countries during the years 1770-74. The first open act of defiance was the Boston Tea Party in 1773 when the colonists, disguised as Indians, went aboard British ships and dumped their cargo of tea into the harbor rather than pay the tax that the British were trying to collect on it.

There was marked friction and competition for colonial as well as maritime supremacy between France, Spain, and England. After her acquisition of India and the end of the Seven Years' War in 1763,

Great Britain became supreme and emerged stronger than ever as a naval power. Maria Theresa, daughter of Emperor Charles VI, became Queen of Austria and reigned from 1740 to 1780. A law forbade a woman to reign in Austria and Frederick II of Prussia claimed succession to the throne. He was crowned King in 1742 and a war ensued, 1740-48, which was known as the War of the Austrian Succession.

Art, the opera, and oratory enjoyed increased popularity in France, and in England the accumulation of wealth stimulated increased interest in artistic endeavors. In France elaborate and rather heavy designs in furniture and furnishings gave way to the delicate and rococo type of ornamentation. The Chinese influence was prevalent in fabrics and furniture. Fashion continued to be dictated by the French court under the direction of the favorites of Louis XV, the Duchess of Chateauroux, Mme de Pompadour and Mme du Barry, the latter two spending enormous sums on make-up. Mme de Pompadour was noted for the *pompadour headdress* and for the stripe pattern in dress fabric. Perfume, which had been discontinued because of Louis XIV's dislike for it, was again in favor and used to great excess. True then as today, a clever woman sought new and novel styles, but as soon as other women had adopted them, the leader of fashion dropped the mode for a more original one.

The farthingale, abandoned for a time, was renewed—probably as the result of a visit of Queen Anne of England to some small town in Germany where the device had never gone out of style. The panniers, as the farthingale was now called, reached the extreme width of six feet with a circumference of eighteen feet. As in other times, the press, clergy, authors, and others wrote and preached against the absurdity, but with little effect. It was not long before woman's interest turned to another extreme—to the small waist and elaborate shoe.

In England, little originality was shown in costume during the time of George I and George II. Styles were very uninteresting; the native designers copied the modes of the French and later the shoemaker, milliner, and dressmaker were brought over from France. Among those who followed the French modes was a group of dandies who founded the *Macaroni* Club in 1772, which accounts for the use of the word "macaroni" in the song "Yankee Doodle."

Admiration for Parisian innovations was obvious in 1755. After

210

the French *cabriolet* a light one-horse carriage was introduced, this design in miniature was embroidered on the man's waistcoat, painted on his socks, and even the woman wore the silk face patch cut to resemble the cabriolet. Since waistcoats became so elaborate that few could afford the expense of buying them, they were often rented for festive occasions. Innovations were also started in England; Jonas Hanway made it fashionable for an Englishman to carry an umbrella—until then it was carried only by the opposite sex.

A young girl of the middle class in Europe was sent to a convent at the age of eleven where she received religious instruction. She had lessons in dancing and music, attended the opera, concerts and the salon of painting. The decision regarding her marriage was left to the girl although, after her marriage, her husband was definitely the master. She was advised to be respectful to her husband, to study his humor, to overlook his mistakes, and to follow his suggestions. The qualities which a woman should possess were: sweetness of disposition and an ability to bear insult and injustice from her husband.

Due to the experiments in farming made by Jethro Tull (1674-1740), England became the most advanced agricultural nation in the world. Tull's book on *The Horseshoeing Husbandry* was published in 1733. He also invented a drill which sowed seeds at a certain depth, in rows. At about the same time, using scientific methods, Lord Townshend increased the value of one part of his estate from $900 to $4000. Sheep were raised for wool production, and cattle for milk and meat. Pottery and the making of furniture were also important industries.

By 1770 great changes began to transform the life of the time. The new industrial system brought about the capitalist and the workman. The factory with numerous workmen replaced the shop of the craftsman. The spinning jenny invented by James Hargreaves in 1767, was a great labor-saving device, although at first it was not accepted generally, and the steam engine invented by James Watt made a very important contribution to the industrial age.

DRESS

A. *Sources of information:* paintings, sculpture, coins, medals, garments of the time and literature.

B. MEN

1. Garments:

Outer upper: Macaroni; coat of the same style as in the previous period, until the 1750's; high neck, collarless at first, turn back collar, 1730's; coat having buttons, with or without buttonholes, down the front, worn partially or entirely unbuttoned; coat skirt to knee or below, not very wide, until 1720; later wide, flared skirt, stiffened with buckram, 1720-50; stiffened skirt seldom used after 1750; pockets almost to waist, after 1700, pocket flap large; front of coat sloping away at waist; long tailed coat often with pleats; at first, sleeve often shorter than to wrist, later, becoming longer; wide or narrow cuff, matching vest; cuff sometimes turned back on sleeve and fastened by several buttons, lace, and gold thread included in the decoration; cuff often omitted and sleeve buttoned vertically *c.* 1770; buttons retained later as decoration; smaller pocket flap; *coatee;* waistcoat extending almost to knee, or to within a few inches above hem of coat, until 1750; long waistcoat buttoned to neck or worn unbuttoned to waist, to display frill of shirt, usually with pockets.

Outer lower: breeches fairly full at top and fitted above knee, until 1750, sometimes with embroidered band; buckle and 3 to 5 buttons above knee, or very tight breeches with no knee fastenings, after 1770.

Under: very full shirt of heavy muslin, or of very fine cambric, and with a band or small turnover collar, full shirt-sleeve with wide ruffle; ruffle of cambric or lace showing beneath sleeve of coat; drawers.

Cloaks and overgarments: cape sometimes extending to knee, not in general use; *greatcoat;* Roquelaure; *justaucorps; Chesterfield.*

Neckwear and wristwear: cravat and Steinkirk worn, until 1720; folded *stock* fastening in back, after 1720; narrow black ribbon sometimes worn loosely over stock; *solitaire* or broad black ribbon tying *bag-wig* in back with a spreading bow, or the ends fastened by a bow in front of the neck, or with a buckle; solitaire tied under chin, until 1750; muslin *neckerchief* tied in bow by extremist or Macaroni; *jabot,* 1770.

Additional garments: full-length dressing gown with long rolling collar showing contrasting lining; velvet jacket with fur turnover collar.

2. Hair: much time and emphasis placed on arrangement of hair; gray or white powdered wig, also natural colored hair; full-bottomed wig declining, but still worn by older or professional man, after 1730; fashionable wig tied in a queue at back of neck, with side hair

1. Fichu   2. Patch   3. Polonaise   4. Cloak   5. Robe à la Française   6. Night-rail

usually covering or partly covering the ears; *pigeon wings; tie wig* or *tie periwig;* bag-wig or *crapaud; pigtail wig;* Ramilie wig; catogan or club wig; *toupet* with hair higher in front, after 1750; horizontal rolls; natural hair worn in various ways; powder frequently omitted from wig, after 1760; each profession distinguished by different wig; buckle and strap at back of neck holding wig in place; fringe of own hair showing at forehead or at back of neck; clean shaven.

3. **Headdress:** tricorne hat with gold or gilt braid on brim; usually symmetrically cocked, until 1770; wide-brimmed hat of previous century worn by Quaker and clergy; a little higher crown than preceding period, worn later; *cockade;* plume an occasional decoration for hat; turban; hat worn indoors; montero, nightcap.

4. **Footwear:** broad, square-toed shoe, until 1720, then long, rounded point; large and often jeweled buckle; tongue of shoe not so high after 1750, fairly high red heel for dress, lower heel about 1750; jackboot, similar type with boot top hollowed out at back of knee for riding; *gaiter,* first worn by soldier, and by civilian, after 1770; upper part turned down close to boot, c. 1770; spatterdash; boot hose of former period still worn and often visible above boot; dark silk stocking with clocks of gold or silver; light-colored clock on black; stocking usually rolled outside of breeches with garter concealed under rolled top, until 1750, sometimes stocking pulled up under breeches; sometimes cross-garter at knee in Elizabethan style; artificial calves to make legs shapely.

5. **Accessories:** light dress sword or rapier hanging from belt underneath waistcoat and protruding through slit in coat, gold or silver hilt; very long walking stick ornamented with amber or ivory knob, grotesque head or tasseled cord; large muff, until 1750; pipe; elaborate snuff box; handkerchief; nosegay; badge of Order pinned on left breast; glove, utilitarian; miser or stocking purse.

6. **Jewelry:** discrimination used in wearing jewelry; usually 1 ring only; pair of fob ribbons with very thick watches, one sometimes a dummy, chain dangling from watch in fob pocket, c. 1735.

7. **Typical Colors:** dark blue, burgundy, black, or brown coat; pink or scarlet hunting coat; light-colored waistcoat, sometimes same color as the coat, also made of cloth woven with floral design; black and light-colored breeches; white boot hose; light-colored stocking for dress; black shoe often with red heel; somber colors for working class.

8. **Typical Materials:** shirt of heavy muslin or fine cambric; velvet or satin breeches and coat; woolen greatcoat; silk stocking; woolen boot hose; India calico dressing gown; lace handkerchief.

9. **Make-up:** powdered hair; hair curlers, curling tongs used.

1. Petticoat   2. Apron   3. Contouche   4. Pompadour   5. Mob Cap   6. Cockade

C. WOMEN

1. Garments:

Outer upper: dress with bodice and skirt together; at first, neckline same as in previous period, being wide, open, round or square; open neck showing part of shoulder, after 1750, often edged with flower wreath, lace, ruffle, or other decoration; wider sleeve with cuff in earlier part of period; sleeve elbow-length or above, with puffs and lace ruffles, after 1740; engageant; tighter sleeve with turned back cuff, until 1750; sleeve caught up with loops or buttons, until 1750; sometimes cuff formed by turning back sleeve or sleeve of chemise; long sleeve seldom worn; bodice laced up front over a stomacher or false front in France, laced up the back in other countries; long V-pointed or U-curved bodice, often with exaggerated point; occasionally pointed in back; sometimes, few tabs forming peplum; *echelle.*

Outer lower: skirt open in front; gathered full at hip; flounces and ruches; both skirt and petticoat with side pocket slits concealed in gathers; skirt to the ground or over instep, until 1750; dancing dress to ankle.

Under: chemise usually with wrist.ruffle and tiny frill at neck, until 1760; stiff petticoat having whalebone strips from hip to hem or hoop resembling shape of bell, *c.* 1711, often showed through opening of skirt; wide farthingale called pannier; cupola-shaped, following the funnel-shaped farthingale; *considerations; paniers à guéridon; paniers à coudes;* the 2 panniers, 6 feet in width, 1725; flattened, 1740; panniers composed of 2 side-frames made of light weight materials; bustle, 1770; quilted petticoat in middle of century; many petticoats replaced farthingale, 1760; tight corset; handsome garter.

Cloaks and overgarments: cloak; scarf and hooded cape; furred *pelisse;* cape sometimes attached to garment for formal wear; English riding coat with collar; both masculine coat and waistcoat adopted for riding and hunting; saque or loose jacket with short sleeve; *caraco; à la polonaise; cardinal;* mantelet or mantelette; pelerine; Indian or cashmere shawl; night-rail.

Neckwear and wristwear: soft neck-ruff, *Elizabethan ruff;* deep lace ruffle at neck and at wrist; scarf, kerchief or *fichu* tucked in dress, covering exposed neck; shirred ribbon of white cotton tulle.

Additional garments: night gown; Du Barry costume; Watteau pleat dress, polonaise; circa or *contouche; robe à la français, sack-backed dress, c.* 1720-80.

2. Hair:
hair sometimes in ringlets to shoulder early in period; high headdress having bows, rolls, ribbons, feathers, and jewels; Pompa-

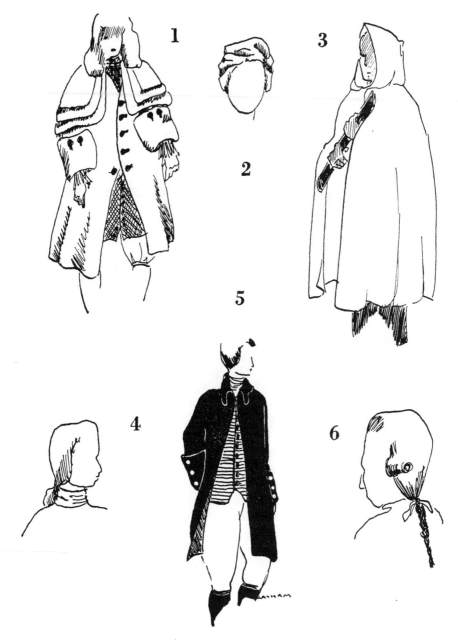

1. Greatcoat   2. Turban   3. Cardinal   4. Stock   5. Waistcoat   6. Pigtail Wig

dour hairdress, 1745-64; Roman influence after excavations in Pompeii, 1753; fairly close to the head, until 1760; curls at side and bun at back; sometimes locks or curls at back of neck with 1 or 2 curls hanging over shoulder, after 1760; powder used on hair for full dress and other occasions; hair dressed higher with pads of cotton, wool, or masses of false hair, due to influence of Mme du Barry after about 1770.

3. **Headdress:** headdress à la Fontanges, discarded; tricorne worn by Venetian lady; hood or *bagnolette;* low crowned, wide-brimmed hat of black beaver; *gypsy hat;* occasionally worn over cap, sometimes tied under chin with broad ribbons; cap worn with house dress and outside the home by widow and elderly woman; *dormeuse,* 1770; *mob cap* later became the dust cap; broad straw or milkmaid type of hat; extreme styles, 1770; capuchon, 1772; *calash,* 1770's and '80's; formal Pompadour headdress with artificial flowers, wreath or strings of pearls, 1745-69; nightcap.

4. **Footwear:** very tall Louis heel, often red or covered with the same material as the shoe; at first, long pointed toe; less pointed, after 1750; lower heel for formal wear, 1760; seldom, with high front and side latchets; ribbon tie or rosette; pantoffle or mule; galoche or galosh; clog fastened over instep and under arch.

5. **Accessories:** long glove or mit; small bunch of delicate artificial flowers or wreath worn in hair, flowers, on bodice; very small muff, 1720, later, large muff; cane; long-handled parasol sometimes carried over the lady by a little black boy; lace, and hand-painted silk parasol; lace-trimmed handkerchief; fan; beautiful buttons; expensive toothpick; pomander; *reticule;* miser or stocking purse; apron only an accessory, after 1720, almost touched the ground, 1744, seldom worn, after 1750; thimble case.

6. **Jewelry:** restraint in the wearing of jewelry; jeweled pin; earrings worn only by few; pear-drop earrings by some; cross of gold filigree; watch sometimes attached to long neck chain at belt, also watch with fob; any accessory might be set with gems; ring on chain around the neck; elaborate magic or talisman ring.

7. **Typical Colors:** absurd names for colors included: "Canary's Tail," "Newly-Arrived People," "Burnt Opera House" (a kind of flame color); yellow dress; black petticoat; rose cape; blue scarf; crimson, orange apron; silver dress; pink shoe; gray cap; gold lace; green jacket; brown or violet coat; other colors included pastel colors, pale green, pink, lavender, and brilliant colored flowers on black background.

8. **Typical Materials:** satin, taffeta, cotton, or linen for dress; *Jouy prints;* printed India calico for house dress; hand-painted or embroidered

1. Fichu   2. Polonaise   3. Engageant   4. Calash

silk; silk gauze scarf; fine, yellow **straw hat** worn by fashionable woman; straw, rush, or even soft bark used by peasant; soft silk, taffeta, or woolen hood; lace and linen **cap worn** with housedress; silk or kid glove, lace and embroidered kid mitten; satin, or brocade with gold decoration for shoe; gayly flowered Pompadour taffeta popular.

9. **Make-up:** first appearance of scented powder, made of starch, used on hair and face, discontinued, after 1760; white paint still in use; skin often plastered with paste; soap not in general use; placing of court plaster patch on face meaningful; mask; perfume.

SIGNIFICANT MOTIFS

The bow and loops of ribbon, arrow, garland, urn, dove, lyre, burning torch, and an allover pattern of circles and dots were used. After the Pompeian excavations of 1755, a delicate floral pattern was popular. In general, designs were smaller than during the preceding period and a definite Chinese influence was evident in decoration.

INFLUENCES ON LATER COSTUMES

Drapery, 1850's; tricorne hat, 1930's; pompadour, 1888, '90's, and 20th century; apron, 1948; watch fob, 1890, 1915-20, and 1949.

BOOKS OF REFERENCE

(See also GENERAL BIBLIOGRAPHY, p. 433)

Ashton, James, *Old Times: A Picture of Social Life at the End of the 18th Century* (New York, Scirnber's and Welford, 1885)

Blum, André, *Histoire du Costume: Les Modes au XVIIe et au XVIIIe Siècle* (Paris, Hachette, 1928)

Boehn, Max von, *Modes and Manners*, Vol. IV, *18th Century* (London, George C. Harrap, Ltd., 1935)

Brooke, Iris, and Laver, James, *English Costume of the Eighteenth Century* (London, A. and C. Black, Ltd., 1931)

Calthrop, Dion Clayton, *English Costume from William I to George IV* (London, A. and C. Black, Ltd., 1937)

Earle, Alice Morse, *Costume of Colonial Times* (New York, Charles Scribner's Sons, 1894)

Grand-Carteret, John, *Les Elegances de la Toilette: Robes, Chapeaux, Coiffures de Style, 1780-1825* (Paris, A. Michel, 1911)

Kelly, Francis M., and Schwabe, Randolph, *Historic Costume, 1490-1790* (London, B. T. Batsford, Ltd., 1925)

CHAPTER 13: REFERENCE

Langdale, Émile, *Rose Bertin: The Creator of Fashion at the Court of Marie Antoinette* (New York, Charles Scribner's Sons, 1913)

Lefferts, C. M., *Uniforms of the American, British Armies in the War of the American Revolution* (New York, New York Historical Society, 1926)

McClellan, Elizabeth, *Historic Dress in America, 1607-1800* (Philadelphia, G. W. Jacobs and Co., 1904)

———, *History of American Costume, 1607-1870* (New York, Tudor Publishing Co., 1942)

McPharlin, Paul, *Life and Fashion in America, 1650-1900* (New York, Hastings House, 1946)

Murphy, Michelle, *Two Centuries of French Costume: An Album of Mannequin Dolls* (New York, Charles Scribner's Sons, 1950)

Tondouze, Gustave, *Le Roy Soliel* (Paris, Bolvin, 1908)

Young, Agnes Brooks, *Recurring Cycles of Fashion, 1760-1937* (New York, Harper and Bros., 1937)

ARTISTS FOR COSTUME REFERENCE

Boucher, François (1703-70)
Chardin, Jean Baptiste Simeon (1699-1779)
Copley, John Singleton (1737-1815)
Cosway, Richard (1740-1841)
David, Jacques Louis (1748-1825)
Fragonard, Jean Honoré (1732-1806)
Gainsborough, Thomas (1727-88)
Gérard, François Pascal (1770-1837)
Goya, Francisco José de (1746-1828)
Greuze, Jean Baptiste (1725/6-1805)
Gros, Antoine Jean (1771-1835)
Hogarth, William (1697-1764)
Hoppner, John (1758-1810)
Kneller, Godfrey (1646-1723)
Lancret, Nicolas (1690-1743)

Largillière Nicolas de (1656-1746)
La Tour, Maurice Quentin de (1704-88)
Lawrence, (Sir) Thomas (1769-1830)
Pater, Jean Baptiste Joseph (1695-1736)
Prud'hon, Pierre (1758-1823)
Raeburn, (Sir) Henry (1756-1823)
Ramsay, Allan (1713-84)
Reynolds, (Sir) Joshua (1723-92)
Rigaud y Ros, Hyacinthe (1659-1743)
Romney, George (1734-1802)
Stuart, Gilbert (1755-1828)
Tiepoli, Giovanni Bautista (1693/6-1770)
Trumbull, John (1756-1843)
Vigee-Lebrun, Marie Louise Elizabeth (1755-1842)
Watteau, Jean Antoine (1684-1721)

GLOSSARY

à la Fontanges—refer to *Chap. 12.*

à la Polonaise—name given to cape which resembled the polonaise dress.

Apron—length of cloth, hemmed, usually ornamented, gathered into waist band, having long, wide ornamented strings of same fabric, almost touching floor, 1774. Refer to *Chaps. 2, 11, 12. Pl. XXXII, 2.*

Badge—refer to *Chaps. 2, 8, 9, 10, 11.*

Bagnolette—hood wired away from the face.

Bag-wig or Crapaud—wig having bag in back which held the loose ends of the hair, tied at nape of neck with bow.

Bodice—tight-fitting corset-shaped waist. Refer to *Chaps. 10, 11, 12.*

Bun—refer to *Chap. 12.*

Cabriolet—a light 1-horse carriage with 2 seats, and often with a calash; a cab.

Calash—a large hood with hinged hoops which raised and lowered like the top of a gig or calash. It was often of silk or transparent fabric. *Pl. XXXIV, 4.*

Capuchon—refer to *Chaps. 5, 8, 9, 11, 12.*

Caraco—woman's close-fitting jacket, having a full skirt falling gracefully over the panniered gown.

Cardinal—cloak with hood made throughout of scarlet cloth, worn in the early part of the 18th century. It resembled the mozetta worn by cardinals, originally of scarlet cloth. *Pl. XXXIII, 3.*

Catogan or Club Wig—refer to *Chap. 12.*

Chemise—refer to *Chaps. 6, 7, 8, 9, 10, 11, 12.*

Chesterfield—single-breasted, fly-front coat with notched lapel and velvet collar; first worn by Philip Dormer Stanhope, 4th Earl of Chesterfield.

Circa or Contouche—overdress hanging from the shoulder and resembling a long, loose coat; fashionable in 1715.

Cloak—outergarment following form of figure. *Pl. XXXI, 4.*

Clog—revived by Mme de Pompadour. Refer to *Chaps. 8, 9, 10, 11, 12.*

Club—refer to *Catogan.*

Coatee—small coat in fashion in 1757.

Cockade—bow or knot of ribbon on one side of hat or cap, worn as an ornament, or as a national party distinction. *Pl. XXXII, 6.*

Considerations—small panniers.

Contouche—refer to *Circa. Pl. XXXII, 3.*

Corset—refer to *Chaps. 8, 9, 10, 11, 12.*

Crapaud—refer to *Bag-wig.*

Cravat—refer to *Chap. 12.*

Dormeuse—fancy nightcap with ruffles and bows, which framed the face.

Du Barry Costume—typical style of the time of Louis XV, having a fitted bodice with low décolletage, frilled neckline, ruffled sleeve extending to the elbow; full, long skirt.

Echelle—ladder-like decoration of ribbon bows, braid, or lace extending across the opening of the bodice.

Elizabethan Ruff—refer to *Ruff, Chaps. 10, 11.*

Engageant—refer to *Chap. 12. Pl. XXXIV, 3.*

Farthingale—series of hoops of graduating sizes, attached to each other by ribbons or strings, with frame of metal hinged so that hoops could be lifted. Refer to *Chaps. 10, 11, 12.*

Fichu—light-weight, 3-cornered scarf or shawl worn about shoulders and tied in knot in front with ends hanging or tucked in blouse. *Pl. XXXI, 1; Pl. XXXIV, 1.*

Full-bottomed Wig—refer to *Chap. 12.*

Gaiter—covering for ankle or instep, sometimes extending to knee.

Galoche or Galosh—protective overshoe, worn in wet weather. Refer to *Chaps. 9, 10.*

Greatcoat—overcoat with double or triple shoulder cape. *Pl. XXXIII, 1.*

Gypsy Hat—large leghorn straw hat, sometimes worn over cap.

Jabot—neckwear knotted at back of neck and worn with pin at throat; double frill running down front.

CHAPTER 13: GLOSSARY

Jackboot—refer to *Chap. 12.*

Jouy Prints—printed cambric manufactured in Jouy, France, 1759.

Justaucorps—close-fitting, long-skirted coat.

Macaroni—member of a London club who dressed in the extreme fashion of the times. His costume consisted of a bobtailed coat and wig a foot high, topped by a small tricorne hat.

Mantelet or Mantelette—refer to *Chap. 12.*

Miser or Stocking Purse—refer to *Chap. 12.*

Mob Cap—cap gathered with a ruffle around lower edge; later used as a dust cap. *Pl. XXXII, 5.*

Montero—refer to *Chap. 12.*

Neckerchief—neck cloth of gauze or other material.

Nightcap—refer to *Chaps. 10, 11, 12.*

Night Gown—a loose robe, originally an underdress, used for sleeping, and also worn as a dressing gown.

Night-rail—refer to *Chap. 12. Pl. XXXI, 6.*

Paniers à Coudes—very wide type of panniers on which the elbows could rest.

Paniers à Guéridon—panniers made of large hoops fastened together with tape.

Pannier—refer to *Chap. 12.*

Pantoffle or Mule—half slipper similar to those worn at the present time. Refer to *Chaps. 10, 11, 12.*

Patch—refer to *Chaps. 5, 10, 11, 12. Pl. XXXI, 2.*

Pelerine—refer to *Chap. 12.*

Pelisse—knee-length fur cape having a broad collar or hood.

Peplum—refer to *Chaps. 11, 12.*

Petticoat—refer to *Chaps. 9, 10, 11, 12. Pl. XXXII, 1.*

Pigeon Wings—bunches of hair curled carelessly over each ear.

Pigtail Wig—wig with black hair wound with a ribbon, and with the ends free or folded under. *Pl. XXXIII, 6.*

Polonaise—dress with close-fitting body, and full skirt looped up to form 3 vertical panels and festoons; worn over a separate skirt during the late 18th century. This costume was named after the Polish national costume. Term also given to a cape which was drawn back like a polonaise dress. *Pl. XXXI, 3; Pl. XXXIV, 2.*

Pomander—refer to *Chap. 9.*

Pompadour Hairdress—hair combed back from the forehead with a few curls displayed at the side or back, named after Mme de Pompadour. *Pl. XXXII, 4.*

Ramilie or Ramillie Wig—refer to *Chap. 12.*

Reticule—small bag carried by woman.

Robe à la français—sack-like garment with train, and with Watteau pleat in back. *Pl. XXXI, 5.*

Roquelaure—refer to *Chap. 12.*

Sack-backed Dress—dress having loose back with pleats or folds which extended from shoulders to waistline or lower.

Solitaire—wide, black ribbon worn around neck and attached to tie of the wig.

Spatterdash—refer to *Chap. 12.*

Steinkirk—refer to *Chap. 12.*

Stock—close-fitting, wide neckcloth. *Pl. XXXIII, 4.*

Stocking Purse—refer to *Miser Purse.*

Tie Wig or Tie Periwig—wig tied in the back with a ribbon.

Toupet—another name for wig.

Tricorne Hat—refer to *Chaps. 9, 12.*

Turban—refer to *Chap. 9. Pl. XXXIII, 2.*

Waistcoat—refer to *Chaps. 11, 12. Pl. XXXIII, 5.*

Watteau Pleat—box pleat sweeping down from shoulders to hem in the loose back of a gown, which however was fitted at front and sides; popular about 1745. Many of the paintings of Watteau (1684-1721) show a similar type of gown.

18th Century

PART II

1774-88

CHRONOLOGY

Revolutionary War in American colonies, 1775-83. Battles of Lexington and Concord, 1775. Declaration of Independence, July 4, 1776. Articles of Confederation of the United States of America, November 15, 1777, in effect, 1781. Surrender of British at Yorktown, 1781. Treaty of peace signed in Paris between England and the United States, September 3, 1783. Federal Constitution signed in the State House at Philadelphia, September 17, 1787.

Tailors' co-operative workshop organized, Birmingham, England, 1777.

Patent on first spinning jenny obtained by James Hargreaves, England, 1777. Samuel Compton combines previous spinning machines in his "mule," 1779.

Invention of steel pen, England, 1780.

Invention of balloon, a paper bag filled with hot air, by Jacques Étienne and Joseph Michel Montgolfier, Annonay, France, 1783. Hydrogen balloon of same year invented by the Robert brothers in Paris.

The Advertiser, first daily paper in America, issued in Philadelphia, 1784.

Immense debt contracted by France, 1783-87.

Steam engine used in cotton mills, England, 1785.

Assembly of Notables called at Versailles for reform of public finance, February 22, 1787.

Association for abolishment of slave trade formed by Quakers in England, 1787.

CHAPTER 14

18th Century

PART II

1774-88

HISTORY

There was a steady advance of the middle class in this period brought about by the rise of industry and the new social theories that evolved out of the 18th century. Philosophers, writers, scientists, awakened to the injustices of society at the time, devoted their talents chiefly to working for the abolishment of the prevailing order. In France the outstanding figure in this movement, which came to be known as The Enlightenment, was the brilliant, witty author Voltaire. Early in his life he had been a successful historian and dramatist, but as he became aware of the shocking inequalities of men in his own country he directed his writings to the cause of humanitarian reforms. The oppressive living conditions had grown worse for the French people, and while Louis XVI was an amiable man and a better one than Louis XIV, his lack of decision made him a helpless leader when the entire government was undisciplined and woefully corrupt and the populace reduced to a state of desperation. His wife, Marie Antoinette, had no more awareness of the crisis the country was reaching and when the starving people demanded more bread from the King she made her celebrated retort: "Let them eat cake!" Shortly thereafter discontent swelled into the great French Revolution and its subsequent years of deplorable bloodshed, but out of the upheaval mankind ultimately derived a new faith in the ideal of liberty and justice for all.

Much of the encouragement for revolution in France derived from America where the colonies had revolted against restricting acts on the part of the mother country, England. Slowly but steadily England had grown into a dominant world power, and although social reforms had been instituted there by a gradual process and democratic principles were incorporated in her laws, the government still tried to impose an oppressive and unjust control on colonial commerce and government. Several generations had passed since the first settlements along the Atlantic seaboard and Americans had come of age as a people in their own right. They refused to bow any longer to England, and guided by a group of sober but determined leaders they embarked on the Revolutionary War out of which they won complete independence after a long, often heartbreaking struggle. In this conflict, which lasted from 1775 to 1783, they were aided by military and naval help from France, a country which had every reason for revenge on England at the time. Frenchmen returning home from the war, notably Lafayette, were inspired by the victory that had been won in the colonies and devoted their efforts toward achieving a democracy in France.

Conditions in England and the rest of Europe were relatively calm by comparison with these two focal spots of revolution. On the Continent it was an era of enlightened despots: Frederick II of Prussia, Joseph II of Austria, Charles III of Spain, Gustavus III of Sweden, Catherine the Great of Russia. In their very different ways these distinguished rulers gave their countries strong governments, instituted social reforms, encouraged cultural advancement. In England the Industrial Revolution was making rapid progress due to the invention of many new machines, chiefly in textile manufacturing. The American colonists emerged from the Revolution a free and independent people whose new democratic form of government was to prove the most successful in the history of man.

France continued to be the leader in fashion through Marie Antoinette who sponsored many absurdities in dress, notably the high headdress. This artificial structure was decorated with all sorts of ornaments—flowers, cupids, birds, fruits, miniature gardens, landscapes, seascapes—and was so elaborate that it was worn for days without rearrangement. In 1774 the farthingale was reinstated to balance the top-heaviness of the structure. It is said that the style originated when one day in 1775 Marie Antoinette stuck peacock and ostrich feathers in her hair and Louis XVI admired the effect so greatly it very shortly became the vogue. When the Queen sent a portrait to her mother, Empress Maria Theresa of Austria, in the new headdress it was returned curtly with this message: "I received a portrait of an actress, not that of a queen: I am expecting the right one." At the Petit Trianon, a miniature farm on the grounds of the palace of Versailles, Marie Antoinette and the women of her court lead a make-believe existence, playing at being shepherdesses and milkmaids and dressing the part. All these frivolous activities of the Queen were reflected in the styles of the time. Every new play, any unique idea at Trianon brought about some new fashion. Tragically enough this irresponsible extravagance, which was true of the court in general, was to come to a bitter end at the guillotine not many years later.

The status of women in society and the middle class began to change in the 18th century as the Industrial Revolution brought about the new leisured lady. Education was more extensive and social life—card playing, dancing—much livelier as women were relieved of household tasks and the rearing of their children who were now put in the care of governesses and boarding schools. It was considered fashionable for a woman to cultivate delicate health as a sign of gentility.

DRESS

A. *Sources of information:* paintings, sculpture, coins, medals, garments of the time and literature.

B. MEN
   1. Garments:

      Outer upper: coat similar to English riding coat with stand-up collar; high-waisted, double-breasted, cutaway coat, with high standing collar, or with deep turnover, and pointed lapel, cut square across front at waistline, skirt of coat becoming merely sloping tails, after 1780; large collar, after 1780; embroidered dress coat still worn in France, often not meeting in front; wrist-length sleeve with lace or cambric ruffle showing below; sleeve with small turned-back cuff, 1780; cuff of sleeve omitted and sleeve buttoned perpendicularly at back, 1780; pocket high and pocket flap small, after 1770; buttons on everyday costume were functional, sometimes omitted on dress coat which was left slightly open in front; waistcoat shorter, and cut away, with front cut square at waist, or extending downward in 2 V-shaped points; sometimes double-breasted; sometimes with lapel; short vest; *le gilet; veston; veste;* Macaroni. *Outer lower:* tight, black velvet or satin breeches extending to below

229

kneecap, with an embroidered band, buttoned or buckled; ribbon often used on fastening; very tight breeches worn with short waist-coat.

Under: frilled shirt; drawers.

Cloaks and overgarments: cape; semicircular cape with hood; redingote; neat, double-breasted coat with standing collar and long skirt; *greatcoat.*

Neckwear and wristwear: solitaire; stock or jabot; also cravat or neckcloth for informal wear; cravat or muslin neckerchief tied in bow, after 1780; collar.

Additional garments: dressing gown.

2. **Hair:** many kinds of smaller wigs, until 1780; pigtail wig; bag-wig; powdered catogan or club wig, similar to that of George Washington, with 1 or 2 puffs on each side; hair or wig high in front, 1770's; wig having bushy hair on top and over ear, with curls at back of neck, after 1780; also, single curl-like roll over each ear; solitaire; unpowdered hair worn after 1780; own hair worn loose by some men but not fashionable to do so; clean-shaven.

3. **Headdress:** tricorne hat, one type higher in back than in front; cockade; *bicorne* hat, after 1780; hat with narrow stiff brim and tapering crown; broad-brimmed beaver hat; nightcap; montero; turban worn after wig was taken off; straw hat over cap worn by peasant.

4. **Footwear:** heel of shoe lower than in previous period, long vamp, shorter tongue, large elaborate buckle; close-fitting high boot; gaiter sometimes decorated with clock; gaiter worn also by country people and infantryman; garter; long silk stocking; long woolen hose visible above riding boot.

5. **Accessories:** sword for court function; cane with amber or ivory knob and tasseled cord, used instead of sword, after 1770; muff carried by some men; elaborate snuff box; handkerchief; nosegay; hair or *face cone.*

6. **Jewelry:** 1 or 2 rings, gold semiprecious stones set in gold watch-fob; 2 watches worn, 1 in each pocket on either side of breeches, 1 watch often a dummy.

7. **Typical Colors:** black, brown, burgundy, dark blue, bright red, light pink; plain dark suit, 1780; white or light-colored stocking.

8. **Typical Materials:** velvet, satin, or fine woolen fabric; broadcloth suit, after 1780; heavy silk stocking.

9. **Make-up:** patch, strong perfume, face heavily made up.

C. **WOMEN**

1. **Garments:**

   Outer upper: low-necked dress often with round or square neckline, until 1780; round, low neckline extending out over shoulder, after

1. Skirt with Pannier   2. Levite   3. Engageant
4. Redingote   5. Robe à la Française

1780; neckline high in back and low in front; bateau neckline with ruffle; wide frill falling over shoulder; ruffle or starched and pleated lace at neckline; fichu tucked into bodice or draped with slight V in back; fichu supported by whalebone strips placed in lining, or *liars, menteurs,* or *trompeurs;* engageant showing below tight short sleeve; bodice sometimes of fabric different from the skirt; round waist, after 1780, except for formal wear; striped sash often worn; long formal dress.

Outer lower: panniers diminished in size, after 1780, later worn only for court ceremony; drapery out of style; enlargement of skirt, puffed in back only, profusely trimmed with bows holding festoons in place, gold cords, and tassels; skirt draped by cord pulled through rings sewed to skirt; skirt to instep, ankle, or higher, before 1780; long formal dress, daytime dress to floor, 1780-90; outer garment open in front; train, even street dress with train.

Under: collapsible farthingale of iron ribs introduced by Marie Antoinette, 1774; corset; whalebone petticoat; ruffled chemise; petticoat very elaborate and quilted, 1750-80; pulled-back skirt showed rows of lace; skirt draped by invisible tape running through rings sewed to it; hip pad replaced farthingale; pocket in side-gathers of petticoat or jupon.

Cloaks and overgarments: jacket of various forms, caraco; mantelet, mantelette, or mantelot; cape with slit for arm or loose sleeve; hooded cape; redingote showing English influence; masculine type of coat and waistcoat; pelisse.

Neckwear and wristwear: mannish stock worn sometimes.

Additional garments: sacque or sack-backed dress; robe à la français; polonaise or overgrown, often fur-lined in front; shepherdess costume; *levite.*

2. Hair: extreme and large hairdress, after 1775, 1½-3 feet high, pomade holding hair in place; plumes worn in hair by Marie Antoinette; hair grayed with powder; natural-colored hair in latter part of period; hair remained set for 2 weeks or longer; roll of hair worn on top and at side; low and wide hairdress, after 1780; *pouf;* many different and absurd hairdresses, 1784-86, sometimes showing cardboard figures of men, women, and children; hairdress consisting of miniature landscape, windmill, seascape, garden, fruit basket, bird or cupid made of cardboard; 1 or several bunches of vegetables hooked into side curls; absurd names for hairdress mode or pouf, included "bitter complaint" and "stifled sigh"; doorways enlarged to accommodate woman with high hair arrangement; wig similar to that worn by man used when attending the theater because of complaint about the size of the absurd headdress; hairdress acad-

1. Gainsborough Hat   2. Catogan   3. Waistcoat   4. Calash   5. Jabot   6. Caraco

emies for teaching operators; style more natural, *c.* 1786; curl or curls on either side of neck; chignon or catogan at back of head; 1787; *hedgehog style.*

3. **Headdress:** cap worn indoors, after 1785; mob cap became large with lace frill and bow, 1780-90; bonnet-hat trimmed with bows of ribbon; calash, lowered by pulling a string, 1780; *Gainsborough hat* in England, after 1780; often very small hat tilted forward; gypsy hat often worn over a ruffled cap; plumed or feathered hat; turban; small hat for high coiffure; enormous hat worn, *c.* 1780 with ridiculous names such as "cradle of love" or "novice of Venus"; steeple-crown hat in England, with band and buckle, ruching or ribbon, and feathers; tricorne hat similar to that worn by man; absurd hairdress and headdress almost the same; nightcap.

4. **Footwear:** heavily embroidered shoes; long, narrow toe, very high heel set with jewels; type of heel studded with emeralds known as "come and see"; jeweled shoe buckle; slipper; Greek sandal; high, laced, kid riding boot; clog or patten.

5. **Accessories:** muff; elaborate hand-painted fan; wedding fan of Marie Antoinette decorated with diamonds and emeralds; bouquet in flat glass bottle, worn at waist; parasol with fairly short handle; shepherd's crook; tall walking stick; black velvet bands around throat and wrist; striped sash of gay colors; glove; scissors, sometimes attached to hook, at waist; elaborate apron sometimes short and full; cotton apron with bib worn by servant; reticule.

6. **Jewelry:** not so elaborate as in other centuries; fob sometimes showing over sash; jeweled ring; earrings worn by some; jewels, cameo in brooch and in bracelet; diamond necklace; hair ornament of circle or chain of diamonds; small gold beads; watch often attached to *chatelaine.*

7. **Typical Colors:** pastel colors often used for woman's costume; several colors in one ensemble: red kerchief, black coat and hat, vermilion sash, brownish-green gown, blue dress, white petticoat, white or blue or pink pelisse; straw-colored, apple-green or flame-colored gown.

8. **Typical Materials:** muslin, cambric or velvet gown; velvet or swansdown cape; woolen fabric; gauze fichu; gauze or tulle scarf; satin or brocade dress; lace and painted satin trimming; gold or silver net; satin or velvet court costume; calico from India; block-printed linen; fabric woven in checks, plaid, or stripes; soft, pliable fabrics replacing stiff, heavy ones; cretonne, lawn, dimity, muslin; quilted silk or satin; Pompadour silk, striped or flowered; feather, ribbon bow, ribbon; pastel-colored cambric from India and Persia, more popular than silk; silk or velvet suit; satin coat, lace lappets, flannel

CHAPTER 14: DRESS

jacket, woolen or damask petticoat, straw hat, net decoration, house-dress of chintz; canvas and dimity for peasant use.

9. **Make-up:** face, hands, made up heavily; patch discontinued; heavy perfume; pulverized, scented starch used as face powder, again in style, 1780.

SIGNIFICANT MOTIFS

The bow and arrow, garland, urn, dove, lyre, burning torch, and ribbon bow were used. Other designs universally used included the basket, Chinese and Japanese figures.

INFLUENCES ON LATER COSTUMES

The draped gown an influence on the designs of Worth, 1870; elaborately trimmed hats, 1916, similar to those of this period; watch attached to chatelaine, 1900's and '49; black velvet band again worn around throat and wrists, 1915 and '40's; pinafore used as child's dress, 20th century; high heel; platform shoe resembling patten, 1940's; gilet in sport and street costumes, 1948.

BOOKS OF REFERENCE

(See BOOKS OF REFERENCE, Part I, *18th Century,* p. 220, and
GENERAL BIBLIOGRAPHY, p. 433)

ARTISTS FOR COSTUME REFERENCE

(See p. 221)

GLOSSARY

Apron—refer to *Chaps. 2, 11, 12, 13.*
Bag-wig—refer to *Chap. 13.*
Bateau Neckline—refer to *Chaps. 8, 9.*
Bicorne Hat—hat turned up in back and front, forming points at either side.
Bodice—refer to *Chaps. 10, 11, 12, 13.*
Calash—refer to *Chap. 13. Pl. XXXVI, 4.*
Caraco—refer to *Chap. 13. Pl. XXXVI, 6.*
Catogan or Club Wig—refer to *Chaps. 12, 13. Pl. XXXVI, 2.*
Chatelaine—hook at waist to which scissors, needle-and-thimble case, and even watch were attached.
Chemise—refer to *Chaps. 6, 7, 8, 9, 10, 11, 12, 13.*
Chignon—refer to *Chap. 10.*
Clog or Patten—refer to *Chaps. 8, 9, 10, 11, 12, 13.*
Club Wig—refer to *Catogan.*

Cockade—rosette or similar ornament worn on side of hat; known as cocarde in France. Refer to *Chap. 13.*

Corset—refer to *Chaps. 8, 9, 10, 11, 12, 13.*

Cravat—refer to *Chaps. 12, 13.*

Engageant—deep, double ruffle or puffing of sheer fabric, lace, or of self-material at the elbow or wrist. Refer to *Chaps. 12, 13. Pl. XXXV, 3.*

Face Cone—cone placed over face when hair was powdered.

Farthingale—refer to *Chaps. 10, 11, 12, 13.*

Fichu—material, gathered or pleated, which filled the low-cut neck of the bodice. Refer to *Chap. 13.*

Gainsborough Hat—velvet, beaver, or straw hat having a low crown and broad brim, trimmed with feathers. *Pl. XXXVI, 1.*

Gaiter—refer to *Chap. 13.*

Greatcoat—refer to *Chap. 13.*

Gypsy Hat—refer to *Chap. 13.*

Hedgehog Style—frizzled and tangled hairdress.

Jabot—refer to *Chap. 13. Pl. XXXVI, 5.*

Jupon—undershirt. Refer to *Chap. 9.*

Le Gilet—copy of the English sleeveless waistcoat with a laced back of lining material which fitted the figure; also, the inner vest.

Levite—gown with undraped skirt, after 1780. *Pl. XXXV, 2.*

Liars, Menteurs or Trompeurs—wire which supported the fichu.

Macaroni—refer to *Macaroni, Chap. 13.*

Mantelet, Mantelette, or Mantelot—refer to *Chaps. 12, 13.*

Menteurs—refer to *Liars.*

Mob Cap—refer to *Chap. 13.*

Montero—refer to *Chaps. 12, 13.*

Neckerchief—refer to *Chap. 13.*

Nightcap—refer to *Chaps. 10, 11, 12, 13.*

Pannier—refer to *Chaps. 12, 13. Pl. XXXV, 1.*

Patch—refer to *Chaps. 5, 10, 11, 12, 13.*

Patten—refer to *Clog.*

Pelisse—refer to *Chap. 13.*

Petticoat—refer to *Chaps. 9, 10, 11, 12, 13.*

Pigtail Wig—refer to *Chap. 13.*

Polonaise—refer to *Chap. 13.*

Pouf—huge hairdress with ornaments which were attached to framework or gauze.

Redingote—long overcoat similar to English riding coat. *Pl. XXXV, 4.*

Reticule—refer to *Chap. 13.*

Robe à la Français—refer to *Chap. 13. Pl. XXXV, 5.*

Sack-backed Dress—refer to *Chap. 13.*

Solitaire—refer to *Chap. 13.*

Steeple-crown Hat—refer to *Chaps. 10, 12.*

Stock—refer to *Chap. 13.*

Tricorne Hat—3-cornered, velvet hat, at first with white feather showing above upturned brim, later with cockade of ribbon. Refer to *Chaps. 9, 12, 13.*

Trompeurs—refer to *Liars.*

Turban—refer to *Chaps. 9, 13.*

Vest—very short waistcoat.

Veste—waistcoat with sleeves, and skirt.

Veston—waistcoat with short skirt.

Waistcoat—refer to *Chaps. 11, 12, 13. Pl. XXXVI, 3.*

Transition Period

1789-1813

CHRONOLOGY

Fall of the Bastille and beginning of the French Revolution, *July 14, 1789.*

Feudal system abolished in France, *1789.*

France declared a Republic, *1792.*

The Prussians defeated by the French, *1792.*

Gas used for light in England, *1792.*

Execution of Louis XVI, *1793.*

Invention of cotton gin in *1794* by Eli Whitney, a native of Massachusetts.

Government known as the Directory established in France, *1795.*

Invention of lithography by Aloys Senefelder, *1796,* originally from Prague.

Seat of national government of the United States transferred from Philadelphia to Washington, *1800.*

Invention of Jacquard loom with device for weaving figured materials, Joseph Marie Jacquard, Lyons, France, *1801.*

Union of Great Britain with Ireland under the name of United Kingdom, *1801.*

Louisiana purchased from France by the United States for $15,000,000, *1803.*

Napoleon appointed Emperor of France, *1804.*

Continued successes by Napoleon, *1804-12.*

Navigation of steamship on the Hudson from New York to Albany by Fulton, *1807.*

Invention of arc light by Sir Humphrey Davy, England, *1809.*

First mill for weaving of silk cloth, Rodney and Horatio Hanks, United States, *1810.*

War of 1812 between United States and England.

First power-driven cotton mill in the world, Waltham, Massachusetts, *1813.*

CHAPTER 15

Transition Period

1789-1813

HISTORY

The crisis in France came to a head when popular demand forced the summoning of the national legislative body, in May, 1789. The attitude of the king and queen was one of boredom with the situation.

Matters grew steadily worse and in July, the populace revolted by storming the Bastille, releasing political as well as other prisoners. Within a month the aristocratic government had collapsed, and the French National Assembly, made up of the middle class and artisans, was called upon to create a new political system. Bloodshed and destruction followed, and in January, 1792, King Louis XVI was executed. Marie Antoinette met with a similar fate. Later under the rule of Robespierre a reign of terror was established during which thousands were put to death whose opinions differed from the party in power.

Before the end of 1792, France had armies on foreign soil in different countries. Gradually the wars which presumably were being fought for freedom were turned into wars of aggression. In these, the brilliant military successes of Napoleon Bonaparte, a young Corsican, were a prelude to his rise to power.

In 1795 the executive power was vested in a five-member Directory, but in 1799 it was replaced by a three-man Consulate, to which Napoleon was elected First Consul for a period of ten years. Within three years, however, he succeeded by a plebiscite in having himself named First Consul for life, with power to appoint a successor; two years later he assumed the title of Emperor of France.

Napoleon's successes continued to outshine his defeats for a while, but in 1814—after France was invaded by the Swedes, Germans, Austrians, Russians, British, and Spanish—he abdicated, and soon after Paris capitulated. The Bourbons, reigning house of France, now had an opportunity to return to Paris.

Across the Atlantic, the American Congress had a different task. Whereas the French were surrounded by aggressive neighbors, the Americans had only the British government as an antagonist. Furthermore, the French were in a state of bankruptcy, while the Americans had great undeveloped resources.

In the new country political parties appeared: the Republican (later known as Democratic) Party under the leadership of Jefferson, and the Federalist Party, under Hamilton. Relations between the United States and England had been very unsatisfactory since the Treaty of 1783. John Jay was sent to England with the result that Jay's Treaty was concluded. Louisiana had been retroceded to France in 1800, and three years later, Jefferson, who was then President of the United States, instructed the American minister to negotiate, with the help of Monroe who was also sent to France, for the purchase of this section of North America. Within these years the various offending actions of England, including her Orders in Council which had been issued earlier, and which violated international law, resulted in the War of 1812.

England became very important as a manufacturing nation during this period. In the United States, hand production existed until 1810 when the Industrial Revolution began in this country. The fishing industry became very important along the coast of New England. The fishing fleets from England helped to provide a market for flour and meat produced in the colonies; the United States in turn imported large quantities of manufactured goods. As time went on, the chief occupations in the United States included farming, mining, shipbuilding, and the manufacture of boots, shoes, hardware and textiles.

The political situation during the French Revolution was reflected perhaps more in the costume of the time than ever before. A man dared not appear in any type of material that suggested royalty, and from that time until recently, men have had to be content with costumes of somber tones. The political upheaval was reflected also in the costume of woman: the neckline was an extreme décolletage, the waistline raised to just below the breasts, and the skirt long, and narrow. Heelless thin shoes, pink tights, and the long silk stocking visible through the slit side of the dress, completed the costume. Hair was either arranged in short curls over the head or in the manner of Greek and Roman statues. Mme Vigée Lebrun revived the classic custom of having her guests served by beautiful youths. Pursuit of pleasure was almost an obsession and only those who had lost a relative by guillotine could attend the Bal des Victimes in Paris.

CHAPTER 15: HISTORY

The center of fashion for the man passed from Paris to London at the time of the French Revolution and the later wars of Napoleon. The English fashions were adopted by the women in France as well as England who wore the close-fitting jackets with large lapels and the club hairdress that was worn by the men. Beau Brummel, an Englishman, whose real name was George Bryan exerted a great influence on all men's styles from 1800 to 1812, and he was looked upon as the authority of fashionable attire. Commerce in France was interrupted during this entire period because the male population was called to serve in the army and since France was unable to clothe her own soldiers, England became the clothing workshop of the world.

More simplicity and restraint was shown in the costume of the Directory. However, there were still the followers of the indecent styles of the Revolution. Dress during the Consulate period remained the same, although extreme styles of the former periods were discarded. Sometimes a second tunic, colored and of a different texture, was worn over the first tunic. The Empire period was characterized by a more simple and beautiful costume. The Jacquard loom invented in 1801 brought about a variety of patterns in cloth. The Indian shawl, introduced after the Egyptian campaign of Napoleon, was followed by a French imitation and the *Paisley copy* from Scotland. The Empress Josephine was the only one permitted by Napoleon to wear the shawl imported from India.

In England and the United States a modest neckline, high waistline, and several petticoats worn under the dress, were in vogue. After 1800, the women of France and Germany wore a similar costume.

DRESS

A. *Sources of information:* costumes, paintings, illustrations, and literature.

B. **MEN** (*1789-94*)
1. Garments:
> *Outer upper:* coat cut square at waist, collar very high, large revers, single- or double-breasted; tight-fitting sleeve set plain into tight armhole; tail coat cut away abruptly in front, coat tail very long, sometimes below calf, tail sloping from waistline used for riding; skirted coat; short waistcoat or vest with longer trousers; *incroyable.*
> *Outer lower:* knee-breeches used for formal occasion; knitted breeches halfway between knee and ankle, 1791, extending to shoe,

1793; knee ribbon instead of buckle worn on riding breeches; 3 or more buttons at side of extremely tight breeches covering knee; very tight pantaloons, at first of knitted fabric covering knee, later extending to calf of leg; trousers influenced by English sailor; opening of pantaloons and breeches by slits, one at either side-front. *Under:* frilled shirt; tight corset; drawers.

Cloaks and overgarments: greatcoat or heavy, long, single or double-breasted overcoat with several capes; cape still worn by a few men; *Spencer.*

Neckwear and wristwear: white stock with or without black band, showing frill of shirt below; wide white or black cravat with bow in front, and fastened at back; lace fall, in place of cambric frill, worn by Napoleon; *Robespierre collar;* extremely high collar worn by extremist, stiff collar points standing up against lower cheeks.

2. **Hair:** at first, wig with queue in the back, bag-wig; powder used by some, natural hair in vogue due to tax on hair powder; then hair appeared unkempt; short or long, pompadour, parted in middle or on side, or short hair worn carelessly on each side, with queue or pigtail in back.

3. **Headdress:** tricorne hat not popular but worn by some; bicorne hat; cockade; also hat with narrow, slightly rolling brim, and with plain buckle on side of hat; nightcap.

4. **Footwear:** black kid pump with short vamp, tongue and plain buckle, flat or no heel, *c.* 1790; boot to middle of calf, short boot for civilian wear; boot worn both indoors and out-of-doors; white stocking with clock worn with knee breeches, silk for dress occasion; colored, striped hose worn by dandy; gaiter; garter.

5. **Accessories:** short bamboo cane; gnarled walking stick; scarf wrapped around neck several times; glove of delicate color, snuff box occasionally; dress sword with highly ornamented hilt; *quizzing glass;* handkerchief; miser or stocking purse.

6. **Jewelry:** stickpin for shirt frill; ring sometimes; single or pair of heavy gold watches, fob and fob-seal.

7. **Typical Colors:** stripes used, 1790's, somber colors; breeches often lighter than coat; blue, plum, bottle green, brown, or black coat; light colored, patterned, or waistcoat embroidered, made to order with color schemes of various motifs—insects, bullfights, and scenes.

8. **Typical Materials:** silk, satin, linen, or fine cashmere for waistcoat; satin, wool, or elastic knitted fabric for pantaloons; during the Revolution coarse material replaced the finer fabrics, woolen material becoming more popular for winter and cotton and linen for summer.

9. **Make-up:** none.

CHAPTER 15: DRESS

C. WOMEN (1789-94)

1. Garments:

Outer upper: at first, long, tight and pleated bodice, large fichu, long tight sleeve with ruching at wrist, or elbow sleeve with cuff; *merveilleuse;* later, bodice and skirt joined to form a 1-piece dress, extremely low neckline; puffed fichu smaller than that of preceding period; *chemise tucker;* very thin gown, with low neck, high waist-line, and full skirt; ruffled collar and V-neckline; also dress with high neckline, girdle below breast, no sleeve, or one consisting of a small puff, a strap, or resembling the Ionic Greek sleeve; sometimes very long sleeve.

Outer lower: at first, skirt fairly full all the way around and with ruching at hem; later, skirt tighter in front, with more fullness in back; often short in front, long in back; extremist with dress slit down side from hip, or surplus length of gown thrown over arm, or lifted to knee, when walking.

Under: small hoops over hips and bustle at back in first of period; corset or stays discarded; chemise, gathered at neck with draw-string; pink tights; opaque petticoat worn by English woman.

Cloaks and overgarments: coat with triple collar and wide cuffs with lace ruffles; redingote; mantle; *rotonde;* scarf, clothing inade-quate for protection from cold; close-fitting jacket with large lapels, resembling the English waistcoat.

Neckwear and wristwear: bouffant neckwear; fichu or gauze neck-·cloth which filled the extreme décolletage.

Additional garments: costume à la Constitution.

2. Hair:
combed up at back, and brought forward in wild locks, or worn longer in front, with clusters of ringlets, and cut close at the back; sometimes knot in back with ringlets at nape of neck; names of headdress reflected the times, *à la Titus* or *à la Victime;* braid or club worn.

3. Headdress:
hats of various styles but with high crown and small brim; hat-like helmet; beribboned crown; cap-bonnet; *cap à la Charlotte Corday;* lace bordered veil draped on bonnet or hat; Grecian influence; diadem of artificial flowers or laurel wreath; fillet, small tiara; nightcap.

4. Footwear:
flat-heeled, embroidered shoe with rounded toe; sandal, or ballet-like slipper; some women without foot-covering; ankle boot fur-lined and pointed worn in winter; flesh-colored stocking or bare leg.

5. Accessories:
cane; red parasol used, 1791; very small and adjustable parasol; large muff; 2-inch belt set with brilliants; small purse or reticule containing handkerchief, essence bottle, and fan; miser or

stocking purse; red necklace; red shawl; very small apron; long or short glove; walking stick; tricolor cockade obligatory.

6. **Jewelry:** rings on toes; golden circlet and arrow set with precious stones or rope of pearls for hair ornament; imitation of antique jewelry instead of using diamonds and precious stones; cameo, intaglio, coral, and mosaic; earrings; bracelets worn on bare arm; some of cut steel; plumes held by jeweled ornament; watch with fob; scarcely any ornaments after 1792.

7. **Typical Colors:** white costume with color in sash, and hair ribbon; delicate pastel color for cotton dress; white, black, pastel, or bright-colored sandal or slipper; white fabric embroidered with metallic thread; bright yellow, chartreuse, pink, and black and white striped material.

8. **Typical Materials:** during the Revolution, elaborate fabrics of silk, satin and wool replaced by prints from India, leather, and coarse cloth; very beautiful cotton fabrics; glazed paper parasol; embroidered, watered or striped silk, marten, sable or astrakhan muff, sometimes muff made of strips of shirred silk alternating with fur strips; satin, silk, or soft kid slipper.

9. **Make-up:** very little powder and rouge used; custom of wearing patch discontinued.

D. MEN (1795-98)

1. Garments:

Outer upper: coat with high, turnover coat collar with a deep notch on either side separating it from revers which were worn closed and buttoned, or left open; long, narrow sleeve, set in snug armscye, turned back cuff, later finished plain at wrist, fastening with 2 buttons; coat with long tail, cut away abruptly in front, or with square-cut front, large revers, at first single-breasted, later double-breasted, fastened with 2 to 7 buttons, pockets about at waistline; tailed coat single-breasted at first, later double-breasted, buttoning across front, or open to show shirt frill; double-breasted waistcoat sometimes left open, forming lapels which extended over the coat; standing collar on single-breasted waistcoat; waistcoat ended in an inverted V or 2 V-shaped points in front, worn with cutaway coat; the square fronted waistcoat extending to waistline or downward a little farther than front of coat; shallow pockets.

Outer lower: knee breeches covering the knee with 3 buttons at the side for formal dress; pantaloons, at first, calf-length, full length by end of century, worn for general use.

Under: frilled shirt showing between cravat and waistcoat; cambric ruffle of cuff sometimes extending below coat sleeve; drawers.

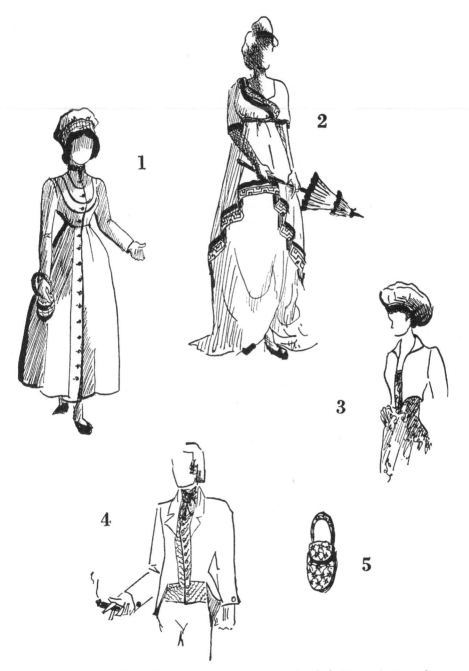

1. Pelisse   2. Tunic Dress   3. Spencer   4. Bobtailed Coat   5. Reticule

Cloak and overgarments: riding coat sloping gradually away from high waist; shorter, skirted coat, small cuff; greatcoat.

Neckwear and wristwear: huge, high neck cloth extending over chin worn by extremely fashionable man, stiff points of shirt collar often extended above neck cloth; white stock with black band outside and shirt frill showing below; lace instead of cambric frill for court.

2. **Hair:** refer to *B. 2.*
3. **Headdress:** black bicorne with feathers, cockade or other ornament; beaver hat; tall silk hat or *top hat* with narrow band at base of crown; nightcap.
4. **Footwear:** refer to *B. 4.*
5. **Accessories:** refer to *B. 5.*
6. **Jewelry:** watch with fob and seal. Refer to *B. 6.*
7. **Typical Colors:** refer to *B. 7.*
8. **Typical Materials:** refer to *B. 8.*
9. **Make-up:** none.

E. **WOMEN** (*1795-98*)
1. **Garments:**

Outer upper: merveilleuse continued; long chemise or tunic dress, small puffy fichu; ruffled collar with small puff sleeve, extremely short waist, bouffant skirt; dress often buttoned up the back; round, low neckline later.

Outer lower: long train, lifted and carried in front, or plainer skirt with sash.

Under: pink silk tights; corset or stays not worn; opaque undergarments worn in England.

Cloaks and overgarments: huge cravat kerchief and scarf folded several times about the neck above the bare chest; mantelette; mantle; red shawl; shawl with Persian design, Paisley shawl; spencer sometimes with long, plain sleeve, with turnover collar or ruff, fur-lined for winter; pelerine; fur-edged cape, silk cape.

2. **Hair:** à la Titus or à la Victime coiffure resembling hairdress on Greek and Roman sculpture; braids and close hairdress; style varied by use of wig; later, hair cut closely, with ringlets in front; various shades of hair; also high and elaborate hairdress.
3. **Headdress:** exaggerated poke bonnet with huge brim; large bonnet-shaped hat trimmed profusely with ribbons and feathers; cap à la Charlotte Corday; net used; laurel wreath; diadem; large and lacey mob cap worn in France; cap worn in house by conservative woman; feathers used in evening headdress or on hat, last of 18th century; nightcap.
4. **Footwear:** sandal; thin flat-soled shoe with round toe; ballet-like

slipper, having ribbon laced around ankle; low-sided shoe with tiny bow at tip.

5. **Accessories:** small parasol, 1798; utilitarian apron, sometimes embroidered; long glove; reticule. Refer to *C. 5.*

6. **Jewelry:** Grecian influence; delicate workmanship; cameo, intaglio, mosaic or coral; bracelets on arm; earrings; matching set of jewelry; gold and jeweled hair ornament.

7. **Typical Colors:** white or light-colored dress; white, tan, or colored glove to match dress; black lace shawl, sometimes bright colors embroidered on scarf; colored neckerchief often worn; black velvet, pink, scarlet, blue, purple, or white bonnet; white, delicate colors, or black for shoe.

8. **Typical Materials:** finer fabrics; shawl from India, or Paisley; velvet mantle, thin muslin, or gauze dress; satin, silk, or soft kid shoes.

9. **Make-up:** powder or a pulverized, scented starch.

F. MEN (*1799-1803*)

1. **Garments:**

Outer upper: British influence; coat definitely cutaway, after 1800, sloping from high center front to end of tail in back, tail to knee or a little longer; pleats topped with buttons in center back; square-front, tailed coat still worn; coat collar high, or worn open, forming wide revers; single-breasted *bobtailed coat;* more fullness in top of sleeve; cuff not popular, after 1800, sleeve plain at wrist, fastened with 2 buttons, sometimes buttons left unfastened; covered buttons, after 1802; shallow pocket with narrow flap, as high as waistline on each side; waistcoat varied in length, after 1800; square front waistcoat usually to waistline or a little below; inverted V or 2 V's with cutaway coat; double-breasted waistcoat sometimes buttoned to chin or left open with lapels extending over coat; single-breasted waistcoat usually with high standing collar.

Outer lower: full-length pantaloons very tight, 1800; breeches extending over knee worn for formal dress.

Under: frilled shirt; drawers.

Cloaks and overgarments: refer to *D. 1.*

Neckwear and wristwear: white band or collar points showing above cravat or stock; sometimes points of collar turned down over cravat; wide black or white stock, plain front and fastening in back, after 1800; sometimes cambric frill showed below cravat; wrist buttons of sleeve of coat often left unbuttoned to display white wristband or shirt sleeve.

2. **Hair:** style resembling portrait busts of Roman emperors with hair clipped in back and set in ringlets over crown or brushed over forehead and curled, *c.* 1800; style varying, with short pigtail, or

bag-wig at back, with short side locks; natural hair worn in careless fashion; hair powdered, by a few, until 1800; unparted or parted in middle, side hair curled; sideburns.

3. **Headdress:** top hat popular, after 1800, high crown becoming smaller at top of hat; crown of hat tapering less than in previous centuries; cocked hat or bicorne; tricorne hat and buckle on hat out of fashion, after 1800; low-crowned, wide-brimmed hat worn by conservative; nightcap.

4. **Footwear:** shoe similar to preceding period; heelless, black, short vamp pump, short tongue and plain buckle; short boot, then boot with turnover cuff, higher boot than in previous period, with band of lighter leather around top, after 1800; differentiation between right and left shoe; shoe polish replaced the mixture of lampblack, suet and tallow formerly used; gaiter.

5. **Accessories:** refer to *B. 5.*

6. **Jewelry:** refer to *B. 6.*

7. **Typical Colors:** more somber costume for men after the Revolution; gold embroidered or braided court costume; red military and hunting coats; waistcoat white or lighter in color than coat, with designs of dots, sprigs, checks, and stripes; pantaloons white, tan, or gray, frequently lighter in color than the coat; black and scarlet cloak; white stocking generally worn; dark brown stocking; black or occasionally light-colored hat; black boot with cuff facing and gold trimming.

8. **Typical Materials:** brushed beaver hat; patterned or embroidered fabric for waistcoat; velvet trimmed coats, silk and fine broadcloth coats; coarse, woolen coat worn by some. Refer to *B. 8.*

9. **Make-up:** None.

G. WOMEN (*1799-1803*)

1. **Garments:**

Outer upper: no great difference between costume of the French, German, English, and North American woman, after 1800; merveilleuse; woman more clothed than in previous period, breast and arm partly exposed; simple white dress; tunic or overdress, second dress of different color sometimes worn, long or short puff sleeve, neck frill or ruffle; neckerchief used with Greek styles, puffy fichu worn by conservative woman; high wrapped cravat often worn around neck, with low-neck dress; standing collar, showing military influence; inelegant bag-like gown, *c.* 1803.

Outer lower: tight-fitting skirt, after 1800; smooth-fitting in front, and gathered at back; with slight flair at bottom; gored, and then bell-shaped; shoulder train in first years; demi-train; dress shorter, ankle-length dress popular; tucks and lace, 1802; various lengths of skirt, 1803.

Under: cotton or linen chemise extending to knee; cotton, cambric or linen petticoat with bodice attached, small flounces on petticoat; drawers considered a man's garment, and not worn by many women.

Cloaks and overgarments: short jacket; long rectangular shawl; 3-quarter length, sleeveless coat with ruff collar; pelisse; spencer; *Spanish cloak; curricle cloak.*

2. **Hair:** combed up in bunch on top of head, or coiled at back, 1801; highly frizzed, or curled in front; à la Titus style no longer fashionable.

3. **Headdress:** high crown and small brim, with many plumes; beaver or straw hat; at first, fairly small headdress, then ugly lampshade hat and *cabriolet;* hood; bonnet; calash; hat with ostrich feathers; *conversation hat;* turban, 1800; Grecian tiara; mob cap; *biggin;* gypsy hat; veil or scarf tied on hat or bonnet; face veil of different lengths, 1800; wreath of flowers or feathers; ruching and lace used as trimming; nightcap.

4. **Footwear:** ankle boot, 1800; heelless slipper, very narrow, 1803; stocking with yellow clock.

5. **Accessories:** covered buttons, invented, *c.* 1802; reticule; glove; small adjustable parasol.

6. **Jewelry:** diamond, amber, coral or pearl necklace; gold bandeau, 1800.

7. **Typical Colors:** refer to *E. 7.*

8. **Typical Materials:** figured muslin dress; lace or silk evening dress; muslin, silk, lace, *sarcenet, kersey-mere* for dress; silk, satin, or cotton petticoat; cotton drawers; *shot silk* pelisse, 1800; black velvet cloak; silk neckerchief; velvet or satin spencer; lace shawl and dress, white swansdown muff and tippet; silk, net or leather glove; kid shoe; satin evening shoe; silk, velvet, beaver, straw or chip bonnet; ribbon or ruching, lace and ostrich plumes used as decoration on hat; *patent lace,* 1803.

9. **Make-up:** custom of the daily bath introduced by Napoleon; cleanliness emphasized, washstand introduced into every bedroom; pulverized scented starch used in first years of period.

H. MEN (*1804-13*)

1. **Garments:**

Outer upper: British influence continued; costume more simple; long-tailed coat with high turnover collar, rolled and separated from the narrow lapel with a notch, single-breasted at first, later double-breasted; also cut short and square in front; *swallow-tailed coat;*

249

cutaway coat sloping from a high point in front to below the knee in back, fastened in front with hook; bobtailed coat; coat with sleeve full at top and tight at wrist, 2 buttons at wrist, fastened or unfastened collar turned over with long roll; waistcoat similar to type worn in the Consulate period, varied in length, with cutaway blunt inverted V or 2 V's, single- or double-breasted, shallow pockets with narrow flap.

Outer lower: fairly tight pantaloons, at first; ankle-length, loose pantaloons, 1810; strap worn under foot for riding; small fob pockets at waist band on either side; tight knee breeches, with buttons at side, still worn for formal and court wear.

Under: plainer shirt than formerly, wrist ruffle for court costume; tight-fitting corset; drawers.

Cloak and overgarment: refer to *D. 1.*

Neckwear and wristwear: stock; long lace ruffle at wrist for court function; sometimes wristband showed beneath sleeve. Refer to *F. 1.*

2. **Hair:** refer to *F. 2.*
3. **Headdress:** refer to *F. 3.*
4. **Footwear:** refer to *F. 4.*
5. **Accessories:** quizzing glass; dress sword discontinued; walking stick used, some occasionally containing a sword; glove popular.
6. **Jewelry:** refer to *B. 6.*
7. **Typical Colors:** sky blue or green topcoat. Refer to *F. 7.*
8. **Typical Materials:** after 1800 finer materials again in vogue; nankeen twill, velveteen and corduroy used for trousers. Refer to *F. 8.*
9. **Make-up:** none.

I. **WOMEN** (*1804-13*)

1. **Garments:**

Outer upper: simple and beautiful *tunic dress; chemise frock;* bodice with very low neck in front but high in back; deep V in front with low neckline in back, 1805-6; street dress, low or high at neck; *lozenge front,* 1807; *cherusse; betsie;* moderately high back, by 1810; high ruff with high neckline; low neckline in back, 1813; sleeve with 2 thick rolls, short puff sleeve, very long sleeve, often extending to knuckle, full, long sleeve held at elbow by ribbon, series of puffs from shoulder to wrist, also *bishop sleeve,* 1810-11; *corset frock; waistcoat front;* girdle under breasts; Greek and Roman silhouette; ugly, bag-like gown or chemise dress continued; longer waist, by 1810-11, *stomacher front, cottage front,* wrap front, *casings;* lacing in front of morning dress, 1812.

Outer lower: skirt smooth across front with fullness in back; gored skirt and stiff bell-shaped model, 1813; dress shorter, reaching to ankle or calf of leg; formal dress still with train; overdress often worn; train attached to waist of court robe.

Under: white muslin underwear introduced by Empress Josephine; petticoat; vest and drawers, a 1-piece garment, 1807; footed drawers, 1813; long stays, 1810-11; tight lacing, 1811; short stays after 1811; sometimes a small bustle consisting of a roll or pad 3 inches wide, long roll used, after 1813; *pantalettes.*

Cloaks and overgarments: continuation of previous styles; fur boa; tippet; shawl; *Barouche coat,* short jacket at first; pelisse, spencer and redingote trimmed with braid; mantelette and shoulder cape toward end of period; *capote;* large silk scarf with colored border, *c.* 1809; *Wellington mantle;* mantle with small hood.

Additional garments: circassian wrapper; Roguelo dress; Andalusian casaque; canezou.

2. **Hair:** cut close to head, by 1808; Grecian influence; flat curls on top of head and forehead; braids; bead ornaments, worn in hair, 1809; hair in ringlets, 1809; knot on top of head and curls in front, by 1810; occasionally different colored wig worn over cropped hair; parted with curls at temples, 1812; parted and waved, flat at sides, by 1813.

3. **Headdress:** extremely long veil in 1804; round stiff crown with flaring brim about 1804; scoop brim similar to Quaker bonnet, *c.* 1807; extreme and ridiculous bonnet, by 1810; coal-scuttle style; cap-bonnet tied under chin; gauze scarf worn like a turban, sometimes adorned with feathers worn by young girl; artificial flowers, or wreath worn instead of hat; tiara; cap or *cornette; cottage bonnet,* 1812; *Victoria hat,* 1813; mob cap; variety of caps worn by older woman, but not by fashionable woman; fashionable woman not appearing twice with same bonnet; opera cap; gypsy hat; military influence shown in hat; *yeoman hat,* 1812; higher crown, by 1814; cap often worn under bonnet; wide brim with plumes and small puffed crown; veil with lace border draped over hat; nightcap.

4. **Footwear:** elaborate shoe, 1810; small flat wedged-shaped heel; shoe pointed at first, then rounded toe, by 1810, again pointed, by 1813; colored satin slipper for evening; leather slipper; fur-lined and pointed ankle boot; half-boot, until 1808; slight heel on walking boot, 1810; laced at back, 1812; ballet slipper and shoe copied from antique types; Greek sandal not worn, after 1813; white stocking with clocks; gaiter worn with calf-length dress.

5. **Accessories:** tiny parasol; blue umbrella, 1804; *pagoda parasol,* 1809; apron worn to some extent, 1811; Chinese fan for middle class, circular fan with opera glass in center carried by élite, folding wheel fan, larger fan, by 1810; fan stuck in girdle; artificial flowers;

small muff and tippet of swansdown or fur, 1812, tippet for day, only; waist buckle of steel or copper; fresh flowers ordered from Genoa and Nice; long, pastel-colored glove with short sleeve, white only, by 1812; bright-colored, short glove with long sleeve; handbag, reticule or small change purse; later detachable pocket instead of reticule; jeweled comb.

6. **Jewelry:** small necklace with flat stones or plates of gold; patriotic trinkets; jeweled and gold hair ornaments; locket; hoop earrings, 1810, earrings showing Grecian or Roman influence; bracelet; heavier jewelry; brooch; pearls in 1812; small tiara, coronet; matching sets of jewelry in vogue.

7. **Typical Colors:** black dress; white or pastel colors for tunic dress; white hat; scarlet or green bonnet; rich and strong colors for elaborate fabric, including Pompeian red, green, yellow, violet blue, and blue, used in redingote and spencer; white and brown fur; various colors for parasol.

8. **Typical Materials:** costly and luxuriant fabric; gown of gold tissue embroidered in large emeralds worn by Empress Josephine; kerseymere, *jaconet*, cambric lace, *bombazine*, or velvet dress; muslin dress; sarcenet tunic dress; satin spencer; tafetta or velvet with fur edge for mantelette; silk cape; light-colored wraps with white or brown fur; angora, and swansdown muff; lace scarf; much embroidery, 1812; fringe, spangles, crepe, and net for cap or bonnet, 1808; fur trimming on hat; patent lace; silk stocking.

9. **Make-up:** very little; pearl white powder; no rouge.

SIGNIFICANT MOTIFS

The expeditions of Napoleon influenced the motifs used in decoration: Egyptian, Grecian, and Roman designs, the Napoleonic crown, bee, and winged liberty figure. Other motifs of significance were: circle, dot, square, lozenge, the Persian palm, and naturalistic flowers. The delicate Grecian patterns were discarded for heavy Roman designs during the Empire period. The influence of the Renaissance was also shown in the designs used in 1810.

INFLUENCES ON LATER COSTUMES

Influence of Directory costume in bolero of 1952 and Empire dress, 1908 and '52; chemise dress revived, 1924-25; 2 rows of buttons on men's coats in later time originating from custom of buttoning back revers of coat uniform; cockade resembling that of French Revolution revived, 1925; childish haircut, 1940 and short haircut, 1952; coat with matching dress, 1948 and

'50's; turban made from scarf, 1940's and '50's resembled type worn in this period.

BOOKS OF REFERENCE

(See Books of Reference, Part I, *18th Century*, p. 220, Part I, *19th Century*, p. 268, and General Bibliography, p. 433)

ARTISTS FOR COSTUME REFERENCE

(See pp. 221, 269)

GLOSSARY

à la Titus or à la Victime—type of coiffure resembling a condemned person's locks before execution and required by those attending the Bal des Victimes. It was worn with a red shawl and red necklace.

Andalusian Casaque—tunic which fastened down the front with ribbons and sloped away to bend of knee in the back.

Apron—refer to *Chaps. 2, 11, 13, 14.*

Bag-wig—refer to *Chap. 13.*

Barouche Coat—tight-fitting 3-quarter length coat having full sleeve, fastened down the front with gold barrel-shaped snaps, and confined to waist with elastic girdle and buckle.

Betsie—ruff made of Brabant lace, named after Queen Elizabeth.

Bicorne Hat—plain or feather-trimmed hat, with brim pulled upward at front and back and held together at the sides; sometimes with cockade or ornament. Refer to *Chap. 14.*

Biggin—similar to the mob cap but larger and not tied.

Bishop Sleeve—wide, long sleeve gathered at cuff.

Bobtailed Coat—an informal short-tailed coat with narrow revers. *Pl. XXXVII, 4.*

Bombazine—fabric of silk and worsted having a twilled effect.

Bouffant Neckwear—gauze, linen, or lace used with extreme fullness giving pouter pigeon effect.

Bustle—refer to *Chap. 12.*

Cabriolet—huge hat with elaborate silk trimming.

Calash—refer to *Chaps. 13, 14.*

Canezou—bodice with high neckline and long sleeve.

Cap à la Charlotte Corday—soft cap, with frill framing the face, tied on by ribbon band. This cap was worn by Charlotte Corday who was guillotined during the French revolution.

Capote—coat with several capes known as greatcoat in England, type without capes or with cape resembling large revers known as redingote.

Casings—series of transverse pleatings in the front of the bodice or sleeve.

Chemise—refer to *Chaps. 6, 7, 8, 9, 10, 11, 12, 13, 14.*

Chemise Frock—dress which hung loosely from the shoulder.

Chemise Tucker—neckerchief worn to fill in the front of a low-cut bodice.

Cherusse—standing ruff of delicate lace worn by the women in England.

Circassian Wrapper—dress similar to night chemise with very low lace bodice, and with sleeve of lace and muslin in alternate stripes.

Club—hair pulled together in the back and turned under to resemble the club wig of the men. Refer to *Chaps. 12, 13, 14.*

Cockade—red, white, and blue cockade worn on hat in time of French Revolution. Refer to *Chaps. 13, 14.*

Conversation Hat—hat of muslin or sarcenet, decorated with a wreath of flowers which covered one ear.

Cornette—cone-shaped cap tied under chin.

Corset—refer to *Chaps. 8, 9, 10, 11, 12, 13, 14.*

Corset Frock—bodice laced across back like a corset, with 3 gores of white satin at front.

Costume à la Constitution—red, white, and blue striped or flowered dress of fine lawn or muslin worn with a vermilion sash and helmet-shaped cap.

Cottage Bonnet—close-fitting straw bonnet, with projecting sides.

Cottage Front—laced bodice.

Cravat—refer to *Chaps. 12, 13, 14.*

Curricle Cloak—half or 3-quarter length, shaped cloak with sloping sides, edges with fur or lace, 1801-6.

Diadem—refer to *Chaps. 3, 4, 6, 7.*

Fichu—refer to *Chaps. 13, 14.*

Fillet—refer to *Chaps. 2, 4, 5, 6, 7, 8, 9.*

Gaiter—refer to *Chaps. 13, 14.*

Greatcoat—refer to *Chaps. 13, 14.*

Gypsy Hat—refer to *Chaps. 13, 14.*

Incroyable—man who wore very extreme costume.

Jaconet—thin cotton material similar to nainsook.

Kersey-mere—kind of woolen cloth.

Lozenge Front—day dress with bodice having crossed strips of net or other material which formed a diamond pattern.

Mantelette—refer to *Chaps. 12, 13, 14.*

Mantle—refer to *Chaps. 2, 3, 7, 8, 9, 10.*

Merveilleuse—woman who wore very extreme clothes.

Miser or Stocking Purse—purse of knitted material. Refer to *Chaps. 12, 13.*

Mob Cap—cap of cambric or muslin sometimes tied beneath the chin. Refer to *Chaps. 13, 14.*

Neckerchief—scarf which was passed around the shoulders, across the front of the waist, and tied in the back. Refer to *Chaps. 13, 14.*

Nightcap—refer to *Chaps. 10, 11, 12, 13, 14.*

Pagoda Parasol—parasol shaped like a pagoda.

Paisley Copy—copy of Indian shawl, made in Paisley, Scotland.

Pantalettes—separate leg covering with ruffles and embroidery that extended below the hem of the dress.

Pantaloons—trousers. Refer to *Chaps. 3, 10.*

Patent Lace—lace made by machine.

Pelerine—refer to *Chaps. 12, 13.*

Pelisse—outdoor garment worn over dress, fastened or left unfastened down the front, its length varying from 3-quarter to ankle. It was lined in winter, and unlined in the summer. Refer to *Chaps. 13, 14. Pl. XXXVII, 1.*

Petticoat—refer to *Chaps. 9, 10, 11, 12, 13, 14.*

Pigtail Wig—refer to *Chaps. 13, 14.*

Quizzing Glass—glass for magnifying, carried by extremist.

CHAPTER 15: GLOSSARY

Redingote—refer to *Chap. 14.*

Reticule—bag carried because the dress was too thin to have a pocket in the seam. Refer to *Chaps. 13, 14. Pl. XXXVII, 5.*

Robespierre Collar—high turn-down coat collar worn with frilly jabot and stock tied in bow in front; worn by the French Statesman Robespierre, 1790.

Roguelo Dress—morning dress with loose back and bias front.

Rotonde—short cape of same material as dress.

Sarcenet—silk fabric, plain or twilled. Refer to *Chap. 6.*

Shot Silk—silk woven to produce changeable colors or figures.

Spanish Cloak—short cape or cloak which fastened on the shoulder.

Spencer—short jacket named for Lord Spencer. It had a turnover collar or ruff, and was lined with fur when worn in winter. At first, this jacket came to a little below the waist and was sleeveless, later it came to the waist and had sleeves. *Pl. XXXVII, 3.*

Stays—name often applied to corset.

Stock—refer to *Chaps. 13, 14.*

Stocking Purse—refer to *Miser Purse.*

Stomacher Front—front section of bodice which encircled the waist and was tied in back.

Swallow-tailed Coat—coat having tail that was forked and tapered.

Tiara—refer to *Chaps. 3, 4.*

Tippet—swansdown or fur neckpiece. Refer to *Chaps. 8, 9.*

Top Hat—hat of brushed beaver with high crown slightly tapering to top, and with slightly rolling brim.

Tricorne—refer to *Chaps. 9, 12, 13, 14.*

Tunic Dress—dress consisting of underdress and overtunic. *Pl. XXXVII, 2.*

Turban—refer to *Chaps. 9, 13, 14.*

Veil—refer to *Chaps. 3, 4, 5, 6, 7, 8, 9, 10.*

Vest—refer to *Chap. 14.*

Victoria Hat—made of straw with front brim turned upward, and with ostrich feather on left side.

Waistcoat—refer to *Chaps. 11, 12, 13, 14.*

Waistcoat Front—bodice which buttoned in front.

Wellington Mantle—garment which resembled a Spanish cloak of merino, lined with sarcenet.

Yeoman Hat—triangular hat turned up in front and ornamented at top with button and tasseled cord.

19th Century

PART I

1814-35

CHRONOLOGY

Construction of locomotive engine by George Stephenson, England, *1814.*

Napoleon abdicated throne, *April 11, 1814.*

Restoration of the Bourbons in France under Louis XVIII, *1814.*

Effort made by Napoleon to recover his throne, Hundred Days' rule *March 20, 1815—June 22, 1815.*

Napoleon defeated in the Battle of Waterloo, *June 18, 1815.*

Severe economic depression in England after Napoleonic Wars, *1815-20.*

Manufacture of silk trimmings, Philadelphia, *1815.*

Transatlantic ship service between New York and Liverpool, *1816.*

Second Factory Act passed in England in *1816.*

First steamboat, the *Savannah,* crossed the Atlantic from Savannah to Liverpool, *1819.*

Waterproof garments invented by Charles Mackintosh, an Englishman, *1823.*

Monroe Doctrine enunciated by President Monroe, *1823.*

New Harmony, Indiana, first of a number of communal towns in America, *1824.*

First steam railway operated between Stockton and Darlington, England, *September 27, 1825.*

Great Lakes and the Atlantic Ocean united by the opening of the Erie Canal, *1825.*

Manufacture of silk ribbon, Baltimore, *1829.*

Greece, an independent power, *1830.*

First practical electric telegraph by Samuel F. Morse, American, *1832.*

Factory Act for more adequate protection for workers in textile industries, England, *1833.*

Bill passed for abolishment of slavery in the British colonies, *1833.*

New Poor Law in England, *August 4, 1834.*

CHAPTER 16

19th Century

PART I

1814-35

HISTORY

After the Treaty of Paris, May 30, 1814, the Bourbons were restored to the throne. The new king, brother of Louis XVI, took the title of Louis XVIII, after learning of the death of his nephew, Louis XVII. But he was an inadequate ruler for France at such a critical time; the people began to wish for Napoleon again, and asked him to return from Elba. This too was a failure; he had been ruler of France for only a hundred days when defeat at the battle of Waterloo forced him to leave the country. He was exiled to the lonely tropical island of St. Helena, where he died in 1821.

The French Revolution and the bloodless "July Revolution" of 1830 —brought about by the five "July" ordinances, including rigid governmental control of the press—created a class of common people, who were to be definitely affected by the industrial age and the system of capitalism which it involved. During this period there was much liberal thinking, but there was friction between the liberalists who opposed class distinction and the conservatives who did not. The latter desired a monarchy, organized religion, and in general a more disciplined life. The entire period was one of struggle for the common man who was endeavoring to break away from and overcome the oppression which had been his lot. This feeling of unrest gave rise to new schools of thought; new ideas in the field of art were also developed.

The British Parliament passed the Great Reform Bill in 1832. The social welfare of the common man was of paramount interest: laws were passed protecting children up to nine years of age, and limiting their hours of labor; trade unions developed among the mass of workers: and labor began to agitate for the coming organized struggle to share in the economic and political life of the country.

On the other side of the Atlantic there was constant conflict between the Latin countries in America, and Spain and Portugal, which resulted in independence for the Spanish and Portuguese possessions in the first quarter of the 19th century. To prevent future intervention by Europeans operating in behalf of Ferdinand VII of Spain or others, the Monroe Doctrine was signed in the United States on December 2, 1823, by President Monroe.

The United States was witnessing a tremendous growth and the development of many comforts: gas lights, steam power, and the railway. But life was not easy, and it would be a few years before attention could be turned to anything as luxurious as fashion.

Labor-saving machines were imported from abroad or invented in the United States. The quantity of products manufactured increased as the cost of production was reduced, although the quality did not improve. France and England excelled in quality production. The Pennsylvania coal and iron mines brought large returns from investments. Western expansion in the United States continued and many people with an agricultural background moved westward as inducements became attractive in the new states. Railroads brought about specialization in various parts of the country, which resulted in the production of articles specific for each section.

Political influence showed in the costume of the United States as well as France. Feminine admirers of Napoleon wore violets in 1815, while the French Royalists took eighteen tucks in their skirts in honor of Louis XVIII. In a few years, aprons of calico imprinted with medallions of the head of Jackson were being worn by his adherents in one of our first Presidential campaigns.

In the first part of the century, the costume of the French woman still showed the Grecian influence: milady wore a cylinder-shaped dress that by 1830 took on the silhouette effect of a capital X. Women cultivated a delicate and pallid appearance in order to appear romantic and the years from 1827 to 1837 became known as the Romantic period in fashion. A healthy appearance was considered crude and materialistic.

The clinging picturesque modes of the Empire changed to the more somber and conservative styles in England. Although one author declares that the period around 1830 was the most beautiful of all, there are many who hold the opinion that the wide shoulderline, small waist, and wide hips creating an hour-glass figure was anything but artistic. *Godey's Lady's Book,* the first woman's magazine published in the United States appeared in 1830 and exerted a great influence on the costume and the customs of the time.

Frances Wright, a Scotchwoman, who came to the United States in 1826, was the first person to bring the question of enfranchisement for women before the public. Women were also beginning to take an active part in the philanthropic issues of the day. After freeing their slaves in 1828, Sarah and Angeline Grimké of South Carolina came north and gave many speeches which aroused public sentiment against slavery. Due to the interest, stimulated by these talks and lectures, the first Women's Anti-Slavery Convention was held in 1837 in New York.

At this time, it was not unusual for a girl in England to go around unchaperoned. In the preceding periods, it would have been impossible for her to have gone anywhere unattended. Although the English girl had greater freedom than girls of other countries, there was still a difference in the standard for the sexes. A woman who did not uphold high ideals met with greater condemnation than a male delinquent. Even the public whipping post where a woman was punished was continued until 1817.

DRESS

A. *Sources of information:* costumes of the period, photographs, paintings, illustrations, and literature.

B. MEN.
   1. Garments:
      Outer upper: lines of costume producing a womanish figure with sloping shoulder; collar of coat rolled high across back of neck, often velvet collar, notch of each side of collar formed revers; coat with very long leg-of-mutton sleeve, full at top, fitted from elbow down; sometimes set-on cuff; no ruffle; tight sleeve left unseamed short distance above wrist; small waist, at normal waistline; outspreading hip; cutaway coat replaced by one with square-cut skirt; tailed coat double-breasted or resembling one, with 2 rows of buttons; single-breasted *frock coat* with 2 rows of buttons, for sports wear and morning, often left open; riding coat, shorter and tighter across the front than the regular frock coat; coat tail and lapel sewed on in 1820; flaring coat tail with pleats in back; short coat also worn; sleeve sometimes fastened by 1 or 2 buttons sometimes with flare over hand; small cuff worn on short jacket or riding

coat, bobtailed coat for informal wear, sometimes with set-on cuff, especially worn by young boy; frock coat with flat collar of black velvet, or of same material as coat, until 1830; double-breasted waistcoat, 1820, single-breasted, about 1830; waistcoat sometimes with lacing at back, worn without corset; narrow collar on waistcoat, 1825; cut of waistcoat varied, usually of same length or a little longer than the coat in front; waistcoat with square front, slight dip, or with V-shaped points; waistcoat extended about an inch below front of evening coat or evening dress coat often worn open to display the waistcoat; sometimes inner waistcoat showed above outer waistcoat.

Outer lower: knee breeches for court function; ankle-length trousers, full at top, tight from knee downward and with open seam which fastened on side with 4 or 5 buttons, at first opposed by clergy; trousers loose by 1820, length above ankle; longer trousers with leather strap under foot, 1825; strap discontinued except for evening and horseback riding, 1830; with broader front closing flap, 1835; loose baggy pantaloons.

Under: shirt frill still worn by a few men; white shirt with pleated front; corset by fashionable man; drawers.

Cloaks and overgarments: cape for evening; greatcoat or cloak with overlapping cape for traveler, worn mostly by coachman, by 1830; full-skirted, double-breasted overcoat, vertical or diagonal slit-pockets.

Neckwear and wristwear: stock, cravat or neckcloth shaped with whalebone, extending high above the neck, plain in front, stiff points of collar often showing above cravat; neckcloth stiffened and extended over sides of cheeks, 1818; black cravat tied and puffed out; ends of white cravat tied in front in small bow, 1820, sometimes bow loops not visible; white neckcloth also knotted in front; white used for evening or daytime, black very popular for day; sometimes cravat folded over, worn with riding outfit; black cravat tied and worn loosely, filling space between collar and waistcoat, 1820-30; large bow, or white neckcloth tied in front; plaid cravat with sport clothes, 1828; *Bryon collar* unstarched; stiffened cravat with narrow, frilled shirt front, 1830; pleated shirt front worn by extremist, 1828.

Additional garments: dressing gown worn with loose-fitting pantaloons; *riding smalls;* smock worn by peasant.

2. **Hair:** cut fairly short; parted usually on one side and swirled; hair brushed forward at the sides; clean-shaven; sideburns occasionally; small mustache, by 1828.

3. **Headdress:** cap with visor, similar to that worn by jockey, used for

1. Falling Tucker   2. Bavaria Pelisse Robe
3. Pelerine   4. Riding Smalls   5. Apollo Knot

traveling; top hat with bell-shaped or high tapering crown very fashionable; high, brushed beaver hat, 1830-35; flatter crown, and broad brimmed hat for country people; stocking cap; nightcap.

4. **Footwear:** ankle-high shoe with low square heel and rather round toe, short tongue and latchet; shoe longer and narrower, 1830; short vamp slipper with low heel and small bow or buckle; black evening pump; short *Wellington boot; Hessian boot;* black boot to calf with turnover cuff; stocking; gaiter for country use, worn by fashionable man in early part of period, later used by peasant.

5. **Accessories:** walking stick with telescope or pedometer; field glass; quizzing glass; *boutonnière;* light-colored glove.

6. **Jewelry:** heavy seal ring; coral or gold shirt buttons worn in shirt front; diamond stick pin; watch, usually only 1 instead of 2 as in previous periods; fob with gold seal.

7. **Typical Colors:** cap matched coat; dark blue, green, or brown, double-breasted overcoat with black velvet collar; blue broadcloth cape with contrasting lining for evening; plum, chestnut-colored, or gray-brown coat; white, light shades of cream, tan, fawn, or buff pantaloons for daytime; light blue cravat for riding habit; gray or black for evening; white neckcloth for evening, black more popular than colors for daytime; white waistcoat for evening; light waistcoat; jonquil-yellow, golden brown, pale green, light blue, royal blue, gray-lilac, or figured waistcoat as well as white and black waistcoat for daytime; light-colored inner waistcoat; gray, white, tan, or black top hat; white, gray, or black silk stocking for evening; striped stocking sometimes for daytime; black shoe and boot.

8. **Typical Materials:** linen for suit; nankeen, cord, moleskin, wool or silk jersey, or kersey-mere for pantaloons; velvet collar or sable trimming on overcoat and tailed coat; broadcloth for coat; white *Marseilles* for evening; plaid and striped fabric; beaver, straw, or felt hat; cloth cap; white linen suit in warm climate; homespun woolens used by common people; chintz dressing gown.

9. **Make-up:** perfume.

C. WOMEN

1. Garments:

Outer upper: silhouette of figure: short waisted, bust and hip about the same size, early in the period; stomacher front or wrapped bodice, 1814; separate bodice and skirt, 1818; low neck for day and evening, square neck seldom worn; high neck, 1815, evening dress with low V in back and front; low neck sometimes with long-sleeved gown; short sleeve puffed at top, 1815-18; drop shoulder popular for daytime dress, 1820, much used until 1830; shoulder-line wider, 1829; sleeve full at shoulder, similar to leg-of-mutton or long and tubular sleeve; *Gabrielle sleeve,* 1820; scalloped trimming; sleeve with several graduated puffs to wrist, 1825; sleeve varied in size, some with as much fabric as required for skirt; *Marie sleeve; demi-gigot* or *gigot sleeve,* 1825; *Mameluke; imbecile;* or *Donna Maria sleeve,* 1827; ham-shaped sleeve; *beret sleeve,* 1829; leg-of-mutton sleeve, 1830; *amadis sleeve; Du Barry sleeve;* whalebone and crinoline used to support sleeve; *Montespan sleeve;* sleeve plain to elbow, then full, and tight again at wrist, 1832; large round sleeve, 1835; sleeve for evening extending about halfway down upper arm; very short waist, 1815; low or high waist, 1820; normal waistline, 1822; pointed or round bodice, after 1822; bodice usually attached to skirt, 1822; *Swiss belt* emphasizing long, slim waistline; back fastening, 1824; sash often replaced by band, 1826; smooth-fitted bodice covered by overdrapery; ruffle, bertha, or collar, and wide revers or *bretelles,* emphasizing wide shoulder and narrow waist.

Outer lower: full, gored skirts, tight around hip with fullness at back, 1815-19; wide skirt to ankle, 1828; calf-length dress by extremist, 1828-30; evening dress to ankle, 1825; dress longer, by 1837; trimming below knee, scalloped flounces, 1822; 1 or 2 flounces to knee level, making skirt appear wider, 1823; skirt wider with more gores, also *wadded hem,* 1824-28; pleating and fullness at waist, 1828; separate skirt suspended by shoulder straps; pocket holes in walking dress.

Under: quilted and heavily starched cotton petticoat attached to bodice with wide shoulder straps, sometimes of silk; *chemisette;* chemise with low square neck and short sleeve gathered at shoulder; drawers consisting of 2 separate pieces held together with narrow tape, 1820, not worn by many women, until 1830; white cambric pantalettes or pantaloons often trimmed in lace worn sometimes by young ladies in the United States and England, and by children in France; pair of large pockets attached to each other, tied around waist and under petticoat; bustle; *frisk;* nipped-in corset brought about change in silhouette; longer corset worn, 1825; stays and garter at first of India rubber.

Cloaks and overgarments: cashmere shawl worn, 1814; pelisse with casings and fastened with frogs; pelisse with triple cape, 1815; Wellington mantle, 1815; spencer, 1816-20; capote or greatcoat, 1816; redingote; mantelette; light gauze scarf for summer; pelerine or shoulder cape; small ruffled cape for evening; Paisley shawl, 1820; cloak without hood, 1823; pelisse with double cape, 1824; canezou; several short capes or fichu worn with low-necked dress, 1830; opera cloak an innovation; *mantilla,* 1835; cloak becoming known as a wrap; *frog fastening.*

Neckwear and wristwear: ruff worn, *c.* 1820, sometimes worn with open V-neck, after 1820; flat shoulder cape and narrow frill worn, 1827; fichu worn with conservative dress; *tucker* filled in extremely low neck; *falling tucker; sautoir;* falling collar; neck emphasized by bertha or ruffle, 1830; high-necked dress with fichu or turnover collar.

Additional garments: walking dress; riding habit; carriage dress; court dress; *pelisse robe; Bavaria pelisse robe;* tunic robe, 1820's; *round dress;* pantaloons for riding; nightgown with small collar, and long sleeve with cuff, 1825.

2. **Hair:** parted in center with cluster of curls, puffs, or loops on either side; ringlets at temples, braided in the back and arranged in a round knot, 1816; hair dressed high with curls covering each ear, 1818; natural ringlets or false curls worn; arranged loosely in front and falling low at each side, 1820; *Charles II hairdress,* 1821; large coiffure; puffs worn at sides instead of curls, 1820-30; back curls held high by comb and side curls falling irregularly around the face; *Apollo knot,* 1824, hair still worn high by a few; coiffure *à la chinoise,* latter part of 1830's; hairdress very extreme and absurd before the end of the period.

3. **Headdress:** ridiculous bonnet; *Angoulême bonnet,* 1814-17; English straw bonnet with green gauze veil, 1816-17; "zebra" or striped feathers, 1816; bonnet worn, until 1830, with low crown, 1819, and with high crown and deep open brim, 1825; cap sometimes worn under bonnet, 1819; *cottage bonnet; poke bonnet* with plumes and ribbon bows; brim of bonnet flaring upwards showing curls; chin ribbon; turban conforming to style of coiffure; hat with high crown accommodating high hairdress, 1815-30; *Bourbon hat; Victoria hat;* broad-brimmed hat with veil, *c.* 1820; *Valois hat,* 1822; many flowers, bows, quills, and plumes, bird of paradise and aigrette used as decoration, strings dangling from hat often left untied, 1822-23; toque, 1825; width of headdress huge and with excessive decoration, by 1830; cap sometimes worn under bonnet, 1819; cap worn with housedress by woman of all ages, made with decoration, colored lining, and long ribbon, 1830's, cap with frills and puffs worn indoors; pearls, plumes, flowers, and ribbons worn in hair, or tiara or turban worn for evening; nightcap.

4. **Footwear:** pointed toe, until 1820, then rounded, until 1830, square toe later, flat heel; heelless shoe tied around ankle, similar to ballet slipper, some with tiny bow at top, or embroidery; slipper; boot without heel, laced on inner side of ankle; half boot and shoe, 1830; shoe with strip of kid on instep; striped or colored stocking, ribbed

stocking with clock, silk stocking worn with silk dress, 1822; gaiter, 1824; clog.

5. **Accessories:** short sash tied in bow at back, with evening dress, 1815; bag; sachet; fan; walking stick; parasol with fringe and long handle, small parasol with long handle, after 1825; eyeglasses; large muff ornamented with bow; boa with the animal's tail at one end and head at the other; handkerchief carried in hand; elbow-length mitten or white glove with many buttons, for dinner and evening, white glove decorated on back with Lafayette's picture worn by an admirer attending ball given in honor of this hero, 1822, short kid glove for daytime; reticule with tassels, one style resembling modern purse with flap, another style with drawstring; chatelaine; tortoise shell or metal comb, 1830; *Glauvina pin;* buttons of wood or mother-of-pearl; copper or tin hook and eye; large bouquet carried, put in water glass while at dinner; bandbox containing cap and other trifles, carried to parties.

6. **Jewelry:** sentimental jewelry; cross, locket, or watch on long chain, latter pinned at belt; cameo brooch, earrings, and necklace in matched set; pair of bracelets worn over long sleeve or outside of long glove; armlet above elbow; jeweled comb, diadem, and pin; necklet; large pearl necklace, 1814, also pearls on small gold chain with diamond clasp; large earrings, 1817; drop earrings, 1822; many rings on all fingers.

7. **Typical Colors:** white, gray, pale yellow, pink, rose, lavender, lilac, blue, amber, or Indian red, for gown; color of spencer darker than dress; sometimes white or light bodice with dark skirt; colors very bright, 1825; skirt and bodice of different colors, 1827, bodice usually of darker color than skirt; bottle-green, olive green, pine green, or black for coat; bottle green, purple, or brown for half dress and outdoor wrap; lemon, orange, or cream-colored daytime glove, long white glove for evening; black shoe for dancing; absurd names given to colors, 1830, including "frightened mouse," "amorous toad," and "nitewater."

8. **Typical Materials:** satin, silk, taffeta, white cambric, muslin, striped gingham, or cashmere for dress, 1825; gauze worn over silk petticoat and bodice for party dress; thicker material in wide skirt, 1827-33; embroidered muslin canezou; chintz, calico, muslin, or bombazine housedress; cashmere or lace shawl; merino half dress; velvet, fur, muslin, or sarcenet cloak; cambric, cotton or linen petticoat; embroidered crepe; gold or silver gauze turban; silk with satin weave; straw, beaver, or plush bonnet with trimming of satin, pearls, or feathers; velvet coat, cape, spencer, pelisse, or mantelette; swans-

down tippet; gauze neckerchief; other fabrics including organdie, tarlatan, and linsey-woolsey; bombazine; India muslin; jaconet muslin; gossamer satin.

9. **Make-up:** powder and rouge used discriminately; hair dye, hair sometimes turned green after its use.

SIGNIFICANT MOTIFS

All-over patterns of floral or leaf designs, spiral, Persian motifs, stripes, and plaids. Grecian designs appeared after 1820.

INFLUENCES ON LATER COSTUMES

The low, wide neckline, drop shoulder, and silhouette, 1948; separate skirt suspended by shoulder straps, 20th century; clock on side of stocking, 1914, '20's, '40's, and '50-'52; transparent fabric worn over silk slip in later periods shows the influence of this period.

BOOKS OF REFERENCE

(See also GENERAL BIBLIOGRAPHY, p. 433)

Bell, Quentin, *On Human Finery* (New York, A. A. Wyn, Inc., 1949)

Blum, André, *Histoire du Costume: Les Modes au XIX Siècle* (Paris, Hachette, 1931)

Boehn, Max von, *Modes and Manners, 19th Century* (New York, E. P. Dutton and Co., 1927)

Brown, Margaret W., *The Dresses of the First Ladies of the White House* (Washington, D. C., Smithsonian Institution, 1952)

Cohn, David Lewis, *The Good Old Days: A History of American Morals and Manners As Seen Through the Sears Roebuck Catalogue,* 1905 (New York, Simon and Schuster, 1940)

Cunnington, C. Willett, *English Women's Clothing in the Nineteenth Century* (London, Faber and Faber, Ltd., 1937)

Earle, Alice Morse, *Two Centuries of Costume in America, 1620-1820,* Vols. 1 and 2 (New York, The Macmillan Co., 1903)

Glover, Mary Julian, and Kreps, Ruth Margaret, *Costume Design in the Gay Nineties* (New York, The House of Little Books, 1945)

Hall, Carrie A., *From Hoop Skirts to Nudity* (Caldwell, Ida., The Caxton Printers, 1938)

Hoes, Rose Gouverneur, *The Dresses of the Mistresses of the White House* (Washington, D. C., Historical Publishing Co., 1931)

Holden, Angus, *Elegant Modes in the Nineteenth Century from High Waist to Bustle* (New York, Greenberg, 1936)

CHAPTER 16: REFERENCE

Keezer, Mlle. R., *La Toilette Féminine et les Bibelots de l'Époque Romantique* (Paris, Éditions Nilsson, 1930)

Kerr, Rose Netzorq, *100 Years of Costumes in America* (New York, The Davis Press, Inc., 1951)

Laver, James, *Fashion and Fashion Plates, 1800-1900* (New York, Penguin Books, 1943)

———, *Taste and Fashion: From the French Revolution Until Today* (London, George C. Harrap and Co., Ltd., 1945)

———, *"Vulgar Society": The Romantic Career of James Tissot* (London, Constable and Co., 1936)

Laver, James, and Brooke, Iris, *English Costume of the Nineteenth Century* (New York, The Macmillan Co., 1925)

LeBlanc, H., *The Art of Tying the Cravat* (London, E. Wilson, 1828)

Lhuer, Victor, *Le Costume Breton de 1900 Jusqu'a Nos Jours* (Paris, Au Moulin de Pen Mur, 1943)

Mackey, Margaret Gilbert, and Sooy, Louise, *Early California Costume* (Stanford University, Calif., Stanford University Press, 1932)

Maigron, L., *Le Romantisme et la Mode* (Paris, H. Chamdion, 1911)

McClellan, ·Elizabeth, *Historic Dress in America, 1800-1870* (Philadelphia, G. W. Jacobs and Co., 1910)

Murphy, Michelle, *Two Centuries of French Costume: An Album of Mannequin Dolls* (New York, Charles Scribner's Sons, 1950)

Nineteenth Century Costume (Victoria and Albert Museum, London, H. M. Stationery Office, 1947)

Norris, Herbert, *Costume and Fashion*, Vol. VI (New York, E. P. Dutton, Inc., 1925-28)

Quennell, Peter, *Victorian Panorama: A Survey of Life and Fashion from Contemporary Photographs* (London, B. T. Batsford, Ltd., 1937)

Price, Julius M., *Dame Fashion, Paris-London* (New York, Charles Scribner's Sons, 1912)

Worth, Jean Philippe, *A Century of Fashion* (Boston, Little, Brown, and Co., 1928)

Young, Agnes Brooks, *Recurring Cycles of Fashion, 1760-1937* (New York, Harper and Bros., 1937)

ARTISTS FOR COSTUME REFERENCE

Alexander, John White (1856-1915)

Benson, Frank Weston (1862-   )

Bonnat Léon Joseph Florentin (1833/4-1922)

Bréton, Jules Adolphe Aime Louis (1827-1906)

Carolus-Duran, Charles Émile Auguste (1838-1917)

Cassatt, Mary (1855-1926)

Cézanne, Paul (1839-1906)

Chaplin, Charles Joshua (1825-91)

Chase, William Merritt (1849-1916)

Chassériau, Théodore (1819-56)

Copley, John Singleton (Elder) (1737-1815)

Corot, Jean Baptiste Camille (1796-1875)

Cosway, Richard (1740-1821)

Courbet, Gustave (1819-77)

Couture, Thomas (1815-79)

David, Jacques Louis (1748-1825)

Degas, Edgar Hilaire Germain (1834-1917)

Delacroix, Ferdinand Victor Eugène (1798-1863)

Duveneck, Frank (1848-1919)

Eakins, Thomas W. (1844-1916)

Fantin-Latour, Ignace Henri Jean Théodore (1836-1904)

Fortuny y Carbó, Mariano José Maria (1838-74)

Fragonard, Jean Honoré (1732-1806)

Fuller, George (1822-84)

Gerard, François Pascal Simon (1770-1837)

Gericault, Jean Louis André Théodore (1791-1824)

Glackens, William J. (1870-1936)

Goya, Francisco José de (1746-1828)

Greuse, Jean Baptiste (1725/6-1805)

Gros, Antoine Jean (1771-1835)

Hawthorne, Charles Webster (1872-1930)

Haydon, Benjamin R. (1786-1846)

Homer, Winslow (1836-1910)

Hoppner, John (1758-1810)

Hunt, William Morris (1824-79)

Ingres, Jean Auguste Dominique (1780-1867)

Jalabert, Charles François (1819-1901)

Lawrence, (Sir) Thomas (1769-1830)

Manet, Édouard (1832-83)

McEwen, Walter (1860-   )

Meissonier, Jean Louis Ernest (1815-91)

Millet, Jean (1814-75)

Morse, Samuel Finley Breeze (1791-1872)

Neagle, John (1796-1865)

Nittis, Giuseppe de (1845/6-84)

Opie, John (1761-1807)

Orchardson, (Sir) William Quiller (1832-1910)

Paxton, William McGregor (1869-   )

Prud'hon, Pierre (1758-1823)

Puvis de Chavannes, Pierre Cecile (1824-98)

Raeburn, (Sir) Henry (1756-1823)

Renoir, Pierre Auguste (1841-1919)

Romney, George (1734-1802)

Rossetti, Dante Gabriel (1828-82)

Rothermel, Peter Frederick (1817-95)

Sargent, John Singer (1856-1925)

Soutine, Haim (1894-   )

Stevens, Alfred Émile Léopold Victor (1828-1906)

Thayer, Abbott Handerson (1849-1921)

Tito, Ettore (1859-   )

Toulouse-Lautrec, Henri de (1864-1901)

Trumbull, John (1756-1843)

Watts, George Frederick (1817-1904)

Whistler, James Abbott McNeill (1834-1903)

Wilkie, (Sir) David (1785-1841)

Zorn, Anders Leonard (1860-1920)

GLOSSARY

Aigrette—refer to *Chap. 3.*

à la chinoise—coiffure which consisted of hair tightly pulled up from sides of head, with knot held in position by ornamental pins, or bows.

Amadis Sleeve—sleeve with tight short cuff at wrist.

Angoulême Bonnet—bonnet with a high crown, and tied at the side.

Apollo Knot—type of elaborate headdress worn for evening, 1824. It consisted of loops, often false and wired, and was decorated with a comb at top of head. *Pl. XXXVIII, 5.*

Bavaria Pelisse Robe—dress with 2 lines of trimming from shoulder to hem. *Pl. XXXVIII, 2.*

Beret Sleeve—sleeve formed from a very wide circle of fabric, resembling a beret headdress.

270

CHAPTER 16: GLOSSARY

Bobtailed Coat—refer to *Chap. 15.*

Bourbon Hat—blue satin hat trimmed with fleur-de-lis of pearls, worn to celebrate the return of the royal family to Paris.

Boutonnière—real flower, or small artificial nosegay usually worn in buttonhole of left lapel by man, or on left shoulder of dress by woman.

Bretelles—revers which together resembled a cape, and extended to waist in front and back.

Byron Collar—unstarched collar left open at the throat, and held together by a silk scarf carelessly tied.

Canezou—sleeveless guimpe or outer fichu-shaped garment often of transparent muslin worn over the bodice, 1824. Later it had the form of a jacket, and was made of delicate thin fabric, edged with lace or a buttonhole stitch. Refer to *Chap. 15.*

Capote—refer to *Chap. 15.*

Charles II Hairdress—hair arranged with 2 rows of curls and corkscrew ringlets at each side of forehead.

Chatelaine—small handbag in which various small articles were carried. Later, an ornamental clasp or brooch worn at the waist, with a chain for keys, etc. Refer to *Chap. 14.*

Chemise—refer to *Chaps. 6, 7, 8, 9, 10, 11, 12, 13, 14, 15.*

Chemisette—cambric, tulle, or muslin fabric worn to fill in very low-necked bodice; also sleeveless undergarment.

Clog—refer to *Chaps. 8, 9, 10, 11, 12, 13.*

Corset—refer to *Chaps. 8, 9, 10, 11, 13, 14, 15.*

Cottage Bonnet—small bonnet tied under chin.

Cravat—refer to *Chaps. 12, 13, 14, 15.*

Demi-gigot Sleeve—sleeve full at top, but tight from elbow to wrist.

Donna Maria—full sleeve puffed to below elbow, and then tighter to wrist.

du Barry Sleeve—sleeve with puff above and below elbow.

Falling Collar—collar with Van Dyck edge worn sometimes with ruff. Refer to *Chaps. 10, 11.*

Falling Tucker—fabric or edging extending down over front of low bodice. *Pl. XXXVIII, 1.*

Fichu—light-colored 3-cornered, cape-like scarf often of net, edged with lace. Refer to *Chaps. 13, 14, 15.*

Frisk—outside bustle.

Frock Coat—double-breasted coat having long skirt of equal length in front and back.

Frog Fastening—ornamental fastening with cord loop and suspended button.

Gabrielle Sleeve—sleeve which was full from shoulder to elbow, then fairly full to middle of forearm, ending in deep cuff with lace band.

Gaiter—refer to *Chap. 13, 14, 15.*

Gigot Sleeve—sleeve very full to below elbow, then tighter to wrist.

Glauvina Pin—pin with detachable head, used as hair ornament.

Greatcoat—refer to *Chaps. 13, 14, 15.*

Hessian Boot—rather tight-fitting high boot.

Imbecile—very full sleeve with longitudinal folds extending downward from elbow.

Jaconet—refer to *Chap. 15.*

Leg-of-mutton Sleeve—refer to *Chaps. 9, 10.*

Mameluke—sleeve full nearly to wrist.

Mantelette—muslin, silk, lace or fur scarf, wide at back and narrow in front, and worn around shoulder crossed in front, and if long tied underneath in back. Usually of a dark color, or black. Refer to *Chaps. 12, 13, 14, 15.*

Mantilla—Spanish veil worn draped over head.

Marie Sleeve—full sleeve tied at intervals and at wrist forming puffs.

Marseilles—heavy barred cotton fabric.

Montespan—sleeve with upper part full, a band at elbow and ruffle extending over part of forearm.

Nightcap—refer to *Chaps. 10, 11, 12, 13, 14, 15.*

Paisley Shawl—refer to *Paisley Copy, Chap. 15.*

Pantalettes—refer to *Chap. 15.*

Pantaloons—refer to *Chaps. 3, 10, 15.*

Pelerine—refer to *Chaps. 12, 13, 15. Pl. XXXVIII,* **3.**

Pelisse—refer to *Chaps. 13, 14, 15.*

Pelisse Robe—dress developed from the pelisse by wearing the latter garment closed.

Petticoat—refer to *Chaps. 9, 10, 11, 12, 13, 14, 15.*

Poke Bonnet—bonnet with brim projecting in front.

Quizzing Glass—refer to *Chap. 15.*

Redingote—refer to *Chaps. 14, 15.*

Reticule—refer to *Chaps. 13, 14, 15.*

Riding Smalls—riding pantaloons of light-colored doeskin or cloth, wide at the hip but tight from the knee down. *Pl. XXXVIII, 4.*

Round Dress—dress with plain high bodice, draped or with trimming forming a V-shape in front from shoulder to waist, skirt usually plain.

Sautoir—silk cravat worn to support ruff.

Spencer—type of jacket, 1816, darker than dress. In 1819 the spencer was high-necked with epaulette or mancheron on shoulder. Refer to *Chap. 15.*

Stock—refer to *Chaps. 13, 14, 15.*

Stomacher Front—refer to *Chap. 15.*

Swiss Belt—pointed girdle.

Tiara—refer to *Chaps. 3, 4, 15.*

Toque—brimless cap made of silk or velvet. Refer to *Chaps. 2, 10.*

Tucker—frilled material worn to fill in low square décolletage.

Turban—refer to *Chaps. 9, 13, 14, 15.*

Valois Hat—plush velvet or beaver hat with brim of equal width all around.

Veil—refer to *Chaps. 3, 4, 5, 6, 7, 8, 9, 10, 15.*

Victoria Hat—straw hat with brim turned up in front and lined with white satin.

Wadded Hem—hem with gathered strip applied over padding.

Waistcoat—refer to *Chaps. 11, 12, 13, 14, 15.*

Wellington Boot—boot worn with riding habit.

Wellington Mantle—refer to *Chap. 15.*

19th *Century*

PART II

1836-49

CHRONOLOGY

Texas declared its independence from Mexico, *1836*. Republic established.

Underground railroad organization, a secret method used by sympathetic northerners in conducting slaves from the South to the North, established in Ohio, *1837*.

Daquerre camera invented by Louis Jacques Mandé Daquerre, France, *1837*.

Panic of *1837* in United States, due to recklessness in expansion and speculation.

Invention of first real bicycle by Kirpatrick MacMillan of Dumfries, Scotland, *1839*.

Discovery of process of vulcanizing rubber discovered by American Charles Goodyear, *1839*.

Invention of first incandescent electric light, Sir William Grove, England, *1840*.

First law for the protection of workmen in France, *1841*.

First telegraph message transmitted over a line from Baltimore to Washington, by Samuel F. Morse, United States, *1844*.

Annexation of Texas to the United States, *1845*.

War between Mexico and the United States, *1845-48*. Mexican Cession— New Mexico, Arizona, and California. Mexico also gave up claims to Texas.

Discovery of gold in California, *1845*.

Patent for sewing machine obtained by Elias Howe of Spencer, Massachusetts, *1846*.

Woman's Rights Convention, first in history of world, Seneca Falls, New York, *July 19 and 20, 1848*.

Second Republic of France, *1848-52*.

19th Century

PART II

1836-49

HISTORY

Following the French Revolution, conscious women of the time looked to England for guidance in styles. Later Paris again became the center of fashion, luxury and pleasure, through the beautiful Empress Eugénie, wife of Napoleon III, who maintained a court of dazzling display.

Across the Channel, England was being ruled by the young Queen Victoria, who was eighteen years of age when she came to the throne in 1837. Three years later she married Prince Albert, nephew of Leopold I, her maternal uncle and King of Belgium.

The British and French made steady advancement in scientific knowledge. The Germans also showed great skill in this field. The mechanical revolution brought about disruptions in the social and economic life that led to continual strife and conflict in European countries. Many political leaders and their followers were banished from their countries and they naturally sought refuge, as emigrants, in the United States.

At this critical time the United States was expanding; California and New Mexico were granted statehood after the Mexican War and the treaty of 1848; gold was discovered in California and the following year many Americans went West to try their fortune. Products of labor increased due to new inventions in industry. The construction of 5,996 miles of railroad in the United States exerted a great influence on the economic development of the country, 1830-48. Improvements were being made; reforms were planned and undertaken. The American Emancipation Society for the abolishment of slavery was formed. Slavery and the divergence of the North and South were the important issues, although the tariff and financial problems occupied much time and thought.

The women of the United States began to show dissatisfaction with the inequality of woman, the subordinate position she was forced to occupy, and the inadequacy of the educational laws. In 1846, the women delegates from the United States attending the World's Anti-Slavery Convention in London were refused recognition since the men who were present were indignant that women would be permitted to attend the discussion of such an important issue. This action brought about such resentment among the women that after returning home they devoted themselves to the cause of woman's rights and organized the first Woman's Rights Convention held in the Wesleyan Methodist Church in Seneca Falls, in 1848. The declaration, prepared and published in the newspaper, followed the principles of the Declaration of Independence and incorporated in the statements included, practically all of the rights that women enjoy today. The women who were leaders in this movement, were members of the Society of Friends, an organization which has always resented discrimination toward any group. About 1836, a petition was circulated in Albany, New York, for a law to enable a married woman to hold property. Although this first attempt for equality met with no success, by 1848 the common law in New York was changed to permit a wife to own property.

One of the greatest inventions of this period was the sewing machine, patented in 1846 by Elias Howe, Jr.; five years later, Allen B. Wilson and Isaac M. Singer secured patents for a similar labor-saving device. These modern inventions became so popular that it became the style to have dresses made by machine; handmade dresses were looked upon as old-fashioned.

Various French fashion magazines brought Parisian styles to the United States. Mrs. Sarah Josepha Hale, associate editor of *Godey's Lady's Book* (founded by Louis Antoine Godey) in the United States, exerted an important influence on both the fashions and thought of the day in this country. Other women's magazines which helped to create an interest in the fashions of the time, were *The Union Magazine, Peterson's Magazine* and *Harper's Bazaar.*

Between 1836 and 1840, the costume became less exaggerated and more simplified. A definite type developed by 1849—that of a demure lady with hair parted in the middle, and with curls or puffs over the ears, tight smooth bodice, drooping shoulders, pointed waist, and a profusion of lace. The man continued to wear the nipped-in-waist and dressed in a seemingly more elegant style. The *antimacassar,* used on the backs of chairs was necessary because of the oils used by men on the hair.

DRESS

A. *Sources of information:* costumes, paintings, illustrations, and literature.

B. **MEN**

1. **Garments:**

Outer upper: feminine type of figure, styles resemble those of the latter part of last period; tail coat; frock coat; cutaway and sack coat; single- or double-breasted coat cut away from middle of chest, 1837; dropped shoulderline; collar of coat much lower, 1840's, flat or high lapel on sport coat; normal waistline, 1830, low waistline and small waist, 1840; sleeve fitted smoothly in armscye, sometimes buttoned at wrist; cuff or cuffless daytime coat, cuffless evening coat; double-breasted tail coat buttoned to about middle of chest, 1840; single-breasted frock coat, buttoned lower, 1830's and '40's, later fastened higher; tail coat with straight tails, 1841; full and pleated skirt of coat sometimes cut separately from body of coat; frock coat worn later for festive occasions, also costume for upper classes; pockets in tails of evening coat, in skirt and below waistline in frock coat; waistcoat cut high, double-breasted with tail day coat or sport coat, low oval neckline for formal coat, often rolled-over collar on waistcoat for both day and evening wear.

Outer lower: tight, slim effeminate effect, 1830-50; knee breeches practically discontinued; evening trousers rather tight and strapped under foot; trousers wide at hip and tight at foot; strap at foot not common toward end of period; front flap discarded for slit, 1840.

Under: stays worn by some men, not used at end of period, natural figure in style; pleated shirt front, white shirt often concealed by waistcoat and cravat; small ruffle on shirt front still worn, until 1850; stiff shirt cuff showed below coat sometimes, 1840's; drawers.

Cloaks and overgarments: cape out of style, except for evening; loose coat with cape sleeve and velvet collar also worn for evening; fitted top coat often with quilted lining.

Neckwear and wristwear: wide stock used generally, whale-boned for support at sides, and fastened with strap and buckle in back; sometimes plain in front, extending around neck, crossing in back, and tying in front with bow or knot; collar with upstanding or turn-down points, and cravat; bow worn with turndown collar, 1840, also wide tie; neckcloth still used by some men; colored cravat for sports.

2. **Hair:** bushy, curly locks showing from beneath hat brim, 1840; hair parted on side or in middle, brushed back from forehead, or brushed forward; longer sideburns, similar to those used before the American Revolution, 1840's, fringe-like whiskers around lower line of face; upper lip usually clean-shaven, although mustache worn by some; longer chin beard worn by dignified man.

3. **Headdress:** high hat; gray hat for daytime, and black beaver or silk hat for evening; stove pipe hat similar to that worn in the 1830's; hat with curved and flowing brim, 1848-49; flat-crowned, wide-brimmed *Quaker hat* by conservative man; also round-topped, stiff felt cap; *chimney pot hat;* nightcap.

4. **Footwear:** ankle-high shoe, or short boot worn under trousers; evening pump with bow or buckle; elastic-sided shoe popular; front lacing or buttoned at outer side; pointed shoe having light cloth top worn by extremist; square-toed shoe; gaiter.

5. **Accessories:** walking stick or small light cane; *monocle* worn instead of quizzing glass; light-colored glove, white kid glove for evening; boutonnière; use of snuff out of style, pipe not fashionable, cigar popular.

6. **Jewelry:** ring; cuff links; shirt studs; scarf pin; chain worn with watch instead of watch fob.

7. **Typical Colors:** gray-blue, bright blue, brown, green, or plum-colored coat with black velvet collar; light-colored trousers, gray or black for evening, 1840's, almost always black, after 1840; black frock coat; light-colored waistcoat and top coat; gray or light-colored hat.

8. **Typical Materials:** broadcloth for formal coat; serge for other costumes; woolen waistcoat matching suit, or made of cashmere or white cotton.

9. **Make-up:** perfumed macassar oil used on hair by fashionable man, tallow, by backwoodsman.

C. WOMEN

1. Garments:

Outer upper: Louis Philippe costume; smooth bodice; light bodice often worn with dark skirt, 1837; dark blouse still worn as in the early part of the 19th century; bodice worn sewed or fastened on top of skirt band; sloping shoulder, very low neckline, 1835-50, low in back and on shoulder, or medium low neckline, often filled in with chemisette or tucker; ruff sometimes used; sleeve tighter, 1837; long sleeve extending to below elbow or to wrist, bouffant just below shoulder; amadis sleeve; sleeve smaller and set in below shoulder to emphasize low sloping shoulderline; evening dress with

1. Bertha   2. Crispin   3. Antique Bodice   4. Pardessus

long bishop sleeve of lace or gauze in 1840's; *Pompadour sleeve* with ruffles of lace, 1841; plain tight sleeve extending to below elbow or to wrist in vogue, 1841, continued for about fifteen years; sleeves of various types, 1842, long or short, tight, some puffed to wrist; short puffed sleeves for evening; sleeve with bell opening in 1844; undersleeve visible, 1846; *pagoda sleeve;* waist round in back, slender and somewhat shorter at first of period, *corsage en corset* for evening, 1837; bodice opening in front, 1839, pointed, tighter and longer at waist; round with belt and buckle or wide ribbon at side, 1839; *corsage à la Maintenon,* 1840's; round waist with fullness in front, also pointed in front and laced up back; long waist in vogue for fifteen years; outside watch pocket in fold of waist; pleat from shoulder to waist, emphasizing small waist; *bertha* to waistline, 1845; caraco, 1845; *waistcoat corsage,* 1846; plain gown opening in front, 1848; bodice lined and boned with 3 bones placed fan-like, one extending to the armpit, 1840; evening bodice tight and pointed, 1845; bodice longer and pointed, 1848; *passementerie; antique bodice.*

Outer lower: skirt increased in importance yearly during this period; gored skirt out of style; longer skirt, 1837, long evening dress with half-train; long, full, bell skirt; often open over underskirt, 1839, similar to those of the 18th century; wider skirt gathered or pleated into waist band, 1840; large pocket in fold of skirt; *brandenbourgs;* flounce often differing in color from main dress; 1 flounce at bottom of skirt, 1840; 5 to 9 flounces, 1846; crinoline lining for skirt and wide strip used in hem during the late 1840's; woolen or dark silk skirt untrimmed; much trimming on ball-room dress; instep length, for street or house skirt, then to ground, by 1843; woolen dress left untrimmed.

Under: linen underclothing very important, 1837; high-necked and long-sleeved chemise or chemisette changing to one with short full sleeve and knee-length skirt, 1849; vest and drawers of cotton and wool trimmed with embroidery and lace, used by well-to-do; sometimes long pantalettes showing beneath skirt, introduced by Empress Eugénie; many petticoats worn at one time, 1 of flannel, 1 padded with horsehair, 1 of calico stiffened with cord, and 1 of starched muslin; flounced petticoat visible through open skirt; shaped bustle extending around sides and back, worn sometimes, 1841; *demi-corset;* stays or corset with tight lacing, 1840's; *chemisette garters* sometimes attached to corset; *camisole* in 1840's.

Cloak and overgarments: mantle, 1837; *zouave jacket; robe redingote;* cape with pointed hood; cashmere shawl; shaped shawl; mantlet or mantelette; *crispin; crispin cloche; bournouse, burnous* or

1. Bishop Sleeve   2. Pelerine   3. Bonnet
4. Pelisse Robe   5. Bonnet Babet   6. Pelisse Mantle

burnus; paletot; camail; polonaise; *pardessus;* palatine; pelerine; caraco; *opera cloak;* capuchon or *carmeillette,* 1837; mantle with velvet or fur collar and without hood, 1839; canezou and spencer, 1840; *pelisse mantle; visite;* lace scarf or shawl; cardinal; *casaweck; polka,* 1844; many varieties of jackets, 1846; *marquise; caprice; montpensier mantle,* 1847.

Neckwear and wristwear: fraise for carriage dress, 1836; narrow turnover collar, 1840; low neckline filled in with tucker, ruff also worn; V-neckline with lace vest and fichu, popular again; bertha.

Additional garments: pelisse robe; round dress, *peignor;* redingote style of dress; tunic dress; *fichu pelerine;* riding habit with pantaloons; bathing suit with long bloomers and skirt worn with hose and shoes.

2. **Hair:** low coiffure with curls or loops over each ear, by 1836; *coiffure à l'Agnes Sorel,* 1839, for evening; hair parted in middle and drawn over temples, emphasizing height of forehead, 1840; long curls or ringlets on each side of face, 1840's; braided loop on each side; hair sometimes drawn back in smooth fashion; side view of face usually concealed by hair; circular contour of face emphasized by headdress, pad worn under hair at side; general shape of head appearing more round, by 1849; net held mass of hair at back.

3. **Headdress:** cap worn indoors with negligee, and with evening dress, by older woman; hat with high crown not fashionable; brim more flaring; poke bonnet with open brim framing face, 1935-40; *bonnet Babet; bonnet* trimmed with feathers; *Pamela hat,* 1837; huge hat after 1839; ornamental veil in general use, 1840; veil hanging from crown of bonnet, sometimes drawn over face, horizontal line formed by crown and brim; crown less deep, 1843; lining of gauze kept hair from being disarranged by straw; bonnet smaller in front and less flaring, 1846; shallow-crowned gypsy hat; small *cabriolet bonnet* tied under chin with narrow ribbon, 1848; cap or turban worn by older woman; *bavolet; Bishop's knot;* Mary Stuart bonnet, 1849; nightcap.

4. **Footwear:** heelless slipper for indoors; ankle boot worn out-of-doors; shoe with small heel and pointed toe, 1840; elastic boot; gaiter, 1843; galosh; overshoe.

5. **Accessories:** mitten with day or evening dress, 1838; glove considered important, worn indoors except at dining table, light-colored short glove, evening glove with lace, swansdown, ribbon or other trimming, long, buttoned, or laced glove, 1840; large muff; very small parasol; walking-stick parasol, 1840's, adjustable parasol; black silk, or cotton umbrella; aprons for all occasions, special types for dressmaker, maid, and cook, satin apron for morning dress; small

folding fan, becoming very large, 1839; reticule; fancy silk buttons, 1837, porcelain buttons, 1840; brass or wire-drawn hook and eye as well as solid-headed pin, 1843; richly embroidered and lace-trimmed pocket handkerchief, 1847; large bouquet of real or artificial flowers carried; high comb worn in back of hair.

6. Jewelry: less jewelry worn; coral ornament; single gold bracelet on right arm above glove; matched set of jewelry including brooch or breast pin, bracelet and locket often set with cameos; pierced ears, after 1840, earrings not in style, 1848; very little jewelry, by 1847, some massive jewelry; large gold watch pinned at waist or worn on long chain; mourning jewelry; arrows set with diamonds or strands of pearls occasionally worn in the hair.

7. Typical Colors: soft secondary and tertiary colors used after 1839, delicate grayed tones, violet, tan, gray, silver-blue; changeable black moire for evening; pink crepe or net, used over satin; white or colored glove for evening; outer garment contrasting harmoniously in color with dress, 1840, for example, a green mantle worn over a yellow dress; black, colored silk, or gold hair net.

8. Typical Materials: gauze, lace, dimity, percale, and rich silk material for summer dress; serge, flannel, camel's hair, merino, and plaid cashmere for winter dress; dress of muslin printed in small pattern, also, plaid, checked, or striped gingham and calico used for working dress; silk net, tulle, crepe, grenadine gauze, satin, or velvet evening dress; silk mantle; satin cloak; embroidered silk scarf; sable, chinchilla, gray squirrel, or mink fur; chinchilla muff; linen or cotton for underwear; crinoline for lining; Chantilly, Brussels point, Maltese, and Spanish lace.

9. Make-up: paint, powder; artificial ringlets; eyebrow thickener; hair dye; lotion for making eyes sparkle; perfume or scent; dentifrice; depilatory.

SIGNIFICANT MOTIFS

Designs from the past: the floral motif, Grecian and Roman borders, a miniature Gothic spire in jewelry.

INFLUENCES ON LATER COSTUMES

Bertha reappeared, 1880 and early 20th century and in 1950-52; flounces on dresses, 1920; full 3-quarter sleeve, mittens, 20th century.

BOOKS OF REFERENCE

(See BOOKS OF REFERENCE, Part I, *19th Century*, p. 268, and GENERAL BIBLIOGRAPHY, p. 433)

ARTISTS FOR COSTUME REFERENCE

(See p. 269)

GLOSSARY

Amadis Sleeve—refer to *Chap. 16.*

Antimacassar—an ornamental, washable covering used to protect chair back from the oil used on hair. A tidy.

Antique Bodice—long-waisted bodice with long, sharp point in front. *Pl. XXXIX, 3.*

Apron—refer to *Chaps. 2, 11, 12, 13, 14, 15.*

Bavolet—drapery resembling a curtain worn on back of hat.

Bertha—cape-like collar of cloth or lace. *Pl. XXXIX, 1.*

Bishop Sleeve—refer to *Chap. 15. Pl. XL, 1.*

Bishop's Knot—2 ends of ribbon attached to bonnet which fell almost to shoulder.

Bonnet—close-fitting headdress often tied under chin with ribbon strings. Refer to *Chaps. 8, 9, 10. Pl. XL, 3.*

Bonnet Babet—very small bonnet with pleated ruffle, worn extremely far back on head. *Pl. XL, 5.*

Bournouse, Burnous, or Burnus—evening mantle influenced by Arabian garment of same name.

Boutonnière—flower worn in the buttonhole. Refer to *Chap. 16.*

Brandenbourgs—cording and tassels used to decorate the skirt in military style.

Cabriolet Bonnet—type of bonnet having an extension in front resembling a calash or movable carriage top.

Camail—waist-length, cape-like cloak with falling collar, having armslits edged with lace or fringe.

Camisole—cover worn over corset, also known as waistcoat.

Canezou—refer to *Chaps. 15, 16.*

Caprice—loose evening jacket having armholes, but no sleeves.

Capuchon or Carmeilette—short evening mantle having long close sleeves and wired hood. Refer to *Chaps. 5, 8, 9, 11, 12, 13.*

Caraco—refer to *Chaps. 13, 14.*

Cardinal—collarless and sleeveless cape worn in morning and evening. Refer to *Chap. 13.*

Carmeilette—refer to *Capuchon.*

Casaweck—short-sleeved mantle with collar made of velvet, or silk, and trimmed with fur, velvet, or lace.

Chemise—refer to *Chaps. 6, 7, 8, 9, 10, 11, 12, 13, 14, 15, 16.*

Chemisette—refer to *Chap. 16.*

Chemisette Garter—vertical supporter for hose, attached to corset.

Chimney Pot Hat—hat with scarcely any brim, worn by man.

Coiffure à l'Agnes Sorel—hair arranged with bands in front and knot on back.

Corsage à la Maintenon—shaped bodice with ribbon knots extending down the center front.

Corsage en Corset—tight-fitting evening bodice with seams corresponding to those of a corset.

Corset—inner, laced bodice or waist, used to shape or support the body. Refer to *Chaps. 8, 9, 10, 11, 12, 13, 14, 15, 16.*

Cravat—refer to *Chaps. 12, 13, 14, 15, 16.*

CHAPTER 17: GLOSSARY

Crispin—short mantle worn close around shoulder and neck, sometimes with sleeves and a small cape. *Pl. XXXIX, 2.*

Crispin Cloche—knee length crispin which was bell-shaped.

Demi-corset—a short corset.

Fichu—refer to *Chaps. 13, 14, 15, 16.*

Fichu Pelerine—cape with long hanging ends in front which extend to the knee.

Fraise—scarf of embroidered muslin folded across breast and held in place by ornamental pin.

Frock Coat—refer to *Chap. 16.*

Gaiter—refer to *Chaps. 13, 14, 15, 16.*

Galosh—refer to galoche, *Chaps. 9, 10,* and to *Chap. 13.*

Gypsy Hat—refer to *Chaps. 13, 14, 15.*

Louis Philippe Costume—ensemble of dress with wide, drooping shoulder accentuated by cape, bertha, or scarf, ruffles, and tucks, and a wide-banded skirt. This was worn with a very elaborate straw hat.

Mantle—refer to *Chaps. 2, 3, 7, 8, 9, 10, 15.*

Mantlet or mantelette—outer garment composed of a rounded shoulder cape with long knee-length ends in front which were passed under the belt. Refer to *Chaps. 12, 13, 14, 15, 16.*

Marquise—type of mantlet with short ends in front, short sleeve and a deep flounce in back.

Mary Stuart Bonnet—refer to *Chap. 10.*

Monocle—eyeglass for one eye.

Montpensier Mantle—black velvet cloak trimmed with sable.

Nightcap—refer to *Chaps. 10, 11, 12, 13, 14, 15, 16.*

Opera Cloak—full cape for evening wear.

Pagoda Sleeve—sleeve shaped like a funnel, tight above and gradually widening at wrist with several ruffles.

Palatine—shoulder cape of fur usually longer in front than in back. Refer to *Chap. 12.*

Paletot—cape-like outdoor garment hanging in stiff pleats from shoulder to flounce of dress, with flap over armhole and a stiff short cape, sometimes with several capes.

Pamela Hat—type of gypsy hat made of coarse straw.

Pantalettes—refer to *Chaps. 15, 16.*

Pardessus—any 3-quarter length outdoor garment with sleeves, and shaped at waist. *Pl. XXXIX, 4.*

Passementerie—trimming of braid, cord, beads or tinsel.

Peignor—dress with boneless bodice and bishop sleeve.

Pelerine—refer to *Chaps. 12, 13, 15, 16. Pl. XL, 2.*

Pelisse Mantle—garment with shoulder cape, upper part closed, and with very large sleeve. *Pl. XL, 6.*

Pelisse Robe—pelisse-like garment sometimes trimmed down the front with ribbon knot; worn open over a petticoat, 1839. Refer to *Chap. 16. Pl. XL, 4.*

Petticoat—refer to *Chaps. 9, 10, 11, 12, 13, 14, 15, 16.*

Poke Bonnet—refer to *Chap. 16.*

Polka—short, fitted mantle with sleeves.

Polonaise—outdoor garment with sleeves, upper part close-fitting. Refer to *Chaps. 13, 14.*

Pompadour Sleeve—elbow-length sleeve edged with ruffles; worn during the time of Mme Pompadour.

Quaker Hat—low crowned, wide brimmed hat, adopted by the Quakers.

Quizzing Glass—refer to *Chaps. 15, 16.*

Reticule—refer to *Chaps. 13, 14, 15, 16.*

Robe Redingote—dress with lapel on bodice, and skirt with front opening.

Ruff—refer to *Chaps. 10, 11.*

Spencer—refer to *Chaps. 15, 16.*

Stays—refer to *Chap. 15.*

Stock—close-fitting neckband. Refer to *Chaps. 13, 14, 15, 16.*

Tucker—refer to *Chap. 16.*

Veil—refer to *Chaps. 3, 4, 5, 6, 7, 8, 9, 10, 15, 16.*

Vest—knitted underskirt, also waistcoat for man.

Visite—close-fitting coat which resembled the polonaise, having V-neckline fastened with bow, and full cutaway skirt heavily trimmed with lace.

Waistcoat—refer to *Chaps. 11, 12, 13, 14, 15, 16.*

Waistcoat Corsage—bodice resembling a man's waistcoat which fastened at the waist, and sloped to below hip in back.

Zouave Jacket—resembling bolero jacket with 3-quarter length sleeve, tight, or bell-shape; braided in military style.

19th Century

PART III

1850-67

CHRONOLOGY

Clayton-Bulwer Agreement on Central American Canal, *1850.*

Slave trade not permitted in the District of Columbia, *1850.*

First successful underseas cable between Dover, England to Calais, France, *1851.*

New York Central Railroad completed between New York and Albany, *1851.*

Great exhibition in Crystal Palace, London, England, *1851.*

Commodore M. C. Perry commissioned to deliver message from President of United States to Japan, to open ports for trade, *1851.* Perry arrived in Japan in *1853,* response of Japanese, antiforeign. Negotiations for commerce between United States and Japan, *1854.*

Napoleon III proclaimed Emperor of France, *1852.*

Exposition Universelle, France, *1853.*

Paris World Exhibition, *1855.*

Invention of machine for sewing soles to shoes by Lyman Blake, Massachusetts, *1858.*

Garibaldi's Sicilian expedition, *1860.*

National Exhibition of Industry and Art of the Dutch at Haarlem, and of Belgium at Brussels, *1861.*

United States' Civil War, *1861-65.*

Homestead Act, United States, *1862.*

The Morrill Act passed by Congress providing grants of land to help establish agricultural colleges, *1864.*

Municipal Board of Health established, New York City, *1866.*

Alaska purchased from Russia by the United States for $7,200,000, *1867.*

CHAPTER 18

19th Century

PART III

1850-67

HISTORY

The first International Exhibition of Art and Industry, held in the Crystal Palace in London in 1851, awakened England and many other countries to the importance of trade and manufacturing. Internal strife and the need for external expansion were seen to have their bases in the need for development of trade and new resources.

After four years as a republic, France again became a monarchy with Napoleon III as Emperor in 1852. The new ruler, at first looked upon with distrust, but accepted later, was the last of the royal rulers of France.

The Prussian monarchy overthrew the brief all-German parliament of 1849, and this event caused many Germans then in disfavor to emigrate to the United States. It was about this time that Otto von Bismarck, Minister of Prussia, persuaded Austria to side with Prussia in a military intervention against Denmark in which the latter was defeated. A conflict with Austria followed to decide the possession of the spoils. Prussia eventually was victorious and became the head of the North German Confederation, excluding Austria. Prussia thus became the dominant state of Germany and a leading military power.

The Crimean War which lasted from 1855 to 1856 was a combined and successful struggle on the part of England, France, Sardinia and Turkey to prevent Russia from gaining influence in Europe. About the same time a united Italy was founded, with Victor Emmanuel as the first King, in 1861.

Napoleon III named Archduke Maximilian of Austria, the Emperor of Mexico in 1864, and sent troops in an attempt to establish an empire in that country. But with the end of the Civil War in the United States in 1865, and this country reunited, French imperialists were faced with a new problem: war with the United States or withdrawal of their armies from Mexico. The troops were withdrawn and Maximilian left alone to face the hostile Mexicans, was shot in 1867.

Discord developed in the United States between the North and the South in regard to slavery. The Civil War that followed lasted for four years and ended in a reunited United States of America. After the war the emancipated Negro became dependent on his own resources which brought about an economic problem to the country.

With the rise of the middle class in the United States, cheap labor, and the machine age, good taste was lacking in architecture and furniture. Veneer and glued-on ornaments showed the artificiality of the period. These years were marked by the development of sports activities: mountain climbing, horse racing, and ice skating were very much in vogue after the middle of the century.

Mrs. Sarah Josepha Hale, as editor of *Godey's Lady's Book*, for seventeen years had campaigned vigorously for a Day of Giving Thanks and was rewarded for her efforts in 1863. The last Thursday in November was established by Abraham Lincoln, President of the United States, as the day for the national observance of Thanksgiving. Mrs. Hale also carried out successful campaigns for the recognition of women doctors, physical training for women, and equal opportunity for education. Across the sea, another feminine voice was being heard —through the influence of the French Empress Eugénie, women were first employed in public service in 1865.

From 1852 conventions for woman's rights were held in various parts of the world. There was much opposition from the church, and from many men, the idea being that woman's place was fixed by divine decree in the home and that she should remain there. The Civil War in the United States delayed the progress toward equality of rights for women since public thought was turned to the question of slavery and preserving the union. Nevertheless, woman was becoming independent of man, and family life was changing to one of comradeship. As early as 1864 women found employment in governmental departments in Washington, and was working in industry and clerical work in other parts of the country.

Occupations of men of the period included agriculture and fishing as well as industry. The effect of the Industrial Revolution everywhere was shown in the growth of cities. Whereas in 1770 only half of the population of England lived in towns, about 100 years later, almost two-thirds of the people were located in cities.

In the domain of costume, Empress Eugénie has been given credit for instigating many styles and new fashions which were not of her invention. She was very conservative and did not like to be the first to launch a new style. However, she did bring about the popularity of the Spanish mantilla for this had been an attractive accessory in her native land of Spain.

Charles Frederick Worth, who was destined to be a very important figure in dress designing, left London in 1850 at the age of twenty. Soon after his arrival in Paris, he became associated with a firm by the name of Gagelin, the first concern to handle ready-to-wear coats and shawls. In this shop he began to revolutionize fashion and to transform the business of dressmaking into the art of the couturier.

It is true that in the 1850's, the dressmaking industry did not exist. If a woman wished to have a coat made, it was necessary for her to purchase the material, take it to a seamstress and have it made following the lines of the coat she had been wearing for the previous five or ten years. Competition existed in the price but not in a new idea, nor in the beauty and art of the costume. In 1850 there were 158 dressmaking establishments; this number increased over 12 times within half a century.

With the assistance of the Empress Eugénie, Worth gave the silk industry in Lyons new life. After this beautiful queen appeared in a dress designed by the House of Worth and made in Lyons of silk brocade, that city again regained the glory it had had formerly, as manufacturer of beautiful fabrics. Later statistics showed that the looms in Lyons had increased from 57,500 to 120,000.

A lady during this period had many changes of costume: she would not appear twice in succession in the same dress. Empress Eugénie is said to have taken 250 dresses with her at the time of the opening of the Suez Canal.

The sewing machine continued to have a great influence on fashion. This new invention also initiated the fad of braiding, pleating, and tucking. The beautiful hand-sewn costumes went out of style.

In the United States, Mrs. Amelia Bloomer in 1851, attempted to bring a reform in woman's costume by popularizing Oriental bloomers, a style introduced by Mrs. Elizabeth Smith Miller at Seneca Falls, New York. The fad was short-lived.

During this time, known as the Crinoline Period, 1852-70, attention was again concentrated upon the skirt of the costume. It began to widen in 1840, and by 1860 measured about ten yards around. It is no wonder that the inventor of the steel wires or hoops which took the place of the many petticoats, became a very wealthy man. Steel hoops were even worn in the sleeves! The number of flounces on the skirt continued to increase up to fifteen or more. At this time the custom of a man offering his arm to the lady in his company, was discontinued, to be resumed when dresses again became narrower. By the end of this period Worth decided that the crinoline had become absurd and designed a gored skirt.

DRESS

A. *Sources of information:* costumes, paintings, illustrations, and literature.

B. **MEN**
1. **Garments:**
> *Outer upper:* feminine effect not popular, after 1850; fairly tight coat with flared skirt; collar rather flat, sometimes of velvet, and bound with braid; dress coat with wide lapel, sport coat with short lapel; tail coat, double-breasted or single-breasted, buttoned rather high; sleeve set smoothly into armscye; dropped shoulder, at first of period, padding, by end of period; sleeve wider at wrist than in preceding period; square shoulder, by 1860; pocket in tail of evening coat and in skirt of frock coat; pocket below waistline in frock coat; frock coat single-breasted and buttoned low not popular, after 1860; *sack coat* for informal or sports wear becoming very important; morning coat, resembling the cutaway, 1865; double breasted waistcoat cut high, 1850's, cut low, late 1850's, fairly high, 1860; collar rolled or with notched lapel on waistcoat; gilet or inner vest sometimes worn; small watch pocket.
> *Outer lower:* trouser leg a little wider at hem than at hip, 1850's; rather short, 1850, longer, 1860, neither creased nor cuffed; strap under foot used only for dress, rarely worn, 1860's.
> *Under:* shirt with large sleeve, dropped shoulder, ruffle on front, 1850's, also worn for evening dress; starched or pleated shirt front, 1860; stiff cuff showing below wide coat sleeve; drawers.
> *Cloaks and overgarments:* cape with velvet collar for evening; loose overcoat with long skirt almost to heel, cape sleeve, 1850's; semi-fitting topcoat, 1860; *Inverness cape.*

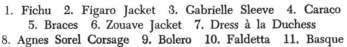

1. Fichu 2. Figaro Jacket 3. Gabrielle Sleeve 4. Caraco
5. Braces 6. Zouave Jacket 7. Dress à la Duchess
8. Agnes Sorel Corsage 9. Bolero 10. Faldetta 11. Basque

Neckwear and wristwear: turnover collar with a wrapped cravat, often tied in large bow, 1850's; *Gladstone collar,* 1852; stand-up collar; soft shirt collar with narrow string tie, until 1860; lower collar, later in century; starched turnover collar for evening, 1865, upstanding points for formal wear; sometimes a wide, wrapped cravat with no tie in front or simple bow of flat silk or satin; white tie used for evening.

2. **Hair:** fairly long hair curled and brushed upwards, sometimes parted; mustache; long and bushy mustache, at first worn by judge or notary, later drooping mustache; *Dundrearys, Dundreary whiskers* or piccadilly weepers; *Newgate fringe,* beard worn later; imperial beard introduced by Napoleon III's barber.

3. **Headdress:** high, round-topped stiff felt hat, 1850's; *bowler* or *derby;* chimney-pot hat; stiff straw hat introduced, *c.* 1854; beaver and silk hat of dark color, 1860; top hat; wide-brimmed, flat-crowned hat; felt hat with soft crown and wide brim; crush hat for opera; cloth or fur cap with ear flaps for travel; nightcap by older man.

4. **Footwear:** little change in footwear; pump for court wear reintroduced by Napoleon III, 1853; square toe and heavy sole worn by conservative; pointed toe by extremist; front lacing adopted, 1860's; heel revived, 1860; cloth top shoe buttoned at side; short Wellington boot; low shoe for tennis and croquet; gaiter.

5. **Accessories:** monocle instead of quizzing glass; boutonnière fashionable; snuff box out of style; *braces;* glove important, white for dancing, light for street; small walking stick.

6. **Jewelry:** rings; scarf pin; cuff links; shirt studs of gold, gems, pearl and coral; watch chain across vest from one pocket to the other or extending from one buttonhole to a pocket.

7. **Typical Colors:** somber colors, grayed shades, 1850's; blue, black, or gray for coat; white, light-colored Scotch plaid or check for waistcoat; sometimes waistcoat of same fabric as coat or trousers; gray, tan, gray blue, plaid, check, striped, or black trousers for ordinary wear, black for dress; gray or black evening trousers, always black, after 1860.

8. **Typical Materials:** khaki cloth introduced from India, 1849; broadcloth coat for formal wear; serge suit; white, washable fabric for waistcoat; also light wool checked or plaid waistcoat; coarse material for sackcoat.

9. **Make-up:** perfume used.

C. WOMEN

1. **Garments:**

Outer upper: Second Empire costume, 1852-70; *Isabeau style;* bodice adjusted by front or back lacing; high, medium, or low neck-

1. Maintenon   2. Casaque   3. Rotonde
4. Garibaldi Shirt   5. Redingote

line; V neckline filled in with lace *chemisette à jabot* or fichu, 1850's; fairly elaborate daytime dress, often with low neckline; deep, wide, low neck framed with bertha, trimmed with flowers, feathers, ribbon, ruching, lace, embroidery, or jewels, 1855; tight sleeve changed to bell shape, 1850's, occasionally of 3-quarter length; bishop sleeve; long sleeve with turnover cuff; engageant; pagoda sleeve with lace weepers; funnel-shaped sleeve, 1850; large bell-shaped sleeve with white detachable undersleeve gathered into narrow band or lace undersleeve, 1855-60; immense sleeve out of style when crinoline became unfashionable; very short, puff sleeve for evening, 1855, also deep bertha over upper arm; Gabrielle sleeve, 1859; amadis sleeve with epaulette, 1859; epaulette worn generally, after 1863; tight-fitting, pointed bodice, 1850's; small waist emphasized by pleat extending from each shoulder to point at waist; *Agnes Sorel corsage*, 1851; round waist with wide belt reappeared, 1860's, sometimes wide buckle; corsage named *à la Louis XV, à la Grecque,* or *à la du Barry;* dress with separate blouse, having short, round waist; waistcoat adopted, 1851, replaced by caraco body and basquine body, 1853; *Watteau body;* bodice often fastened in back, frequently not boned, 1854; bodice trimmed with revers, cape, or *braces,* 1854; waist longer, 1860, short, by 1865; pink *Fontange trimming;* open jacket bodice with tabbed skirt, bell sleeve and puffed undersleeve; Watteau pleat, early 1860's; *basque; bretelles* on basquine bodice, 1866; *Garibaldi shirt,* 1860, forerunner of *shirtwaist; Russian vest;* watch-pocket hidden in fold in the front of waist; increasing amount of lace and trimming used.

Outer lower: dress to floor, 1850; *Empire jupon,* 1851; Oriental *bloomers,* 1851; skirt fitting hip more snugly, 1853; looping up of skirt revived, 1853; skirt became larger, 1857, 10 to 25 yards for a single skirt; plain skirt of heavy material, early 1850's, or flounced skirt, usually with 2 flounces of heavy material, 3 flounces of medium weight material, or 6 flounces of light weight material; flounces trimmed with ruches; 15 flounces, 1852, and 25, 1858; ball dress with 103 tulle flounces worn by Empress Eugénie, 1858; flounces in style for 20 years; fewer flounces worn toward end of period; ball dresses with much trimming; heavy material, plain or pleated, 1858, maximum size 1860; fullness of skirt moved to back and skirt gored, 1860; velvet braid used as trimming on skirt; shorter walking dress, 1859; length of street dress to ground, 1860; day dress with braided hem; skirt lined; skirt looped up for walking, 1862, *page;* dress not looped up, after 1866; *fourreau skirt,* 1864; peplum or short tunic, 1865-66; straighter lines at sides of skirt, 1867; dress fell straight to

1. Pagoda Sleeve   2. Manon Robe   3. Fanchon Cap
4. Mantilla   5. Fourreau Skirt

ground without fold, 1868; later drawn up in pannier fashion around hip and puffed out at back.

Under: embroidery or lace trimming on underclothing; years of *crinoline*, 1852-65; bustle still used, 1854; bodice adjusted by front or back lacing; chemise, corset, and long drawers trimmed in lace or embroidery, worn by middle class, 1856, but not worn universally; corset with front or back lacing; jupon or petticoat; at first numerous petticoats worn at one time: red flannel petticoat with underpetticoat 3½ yards wide, petticoat wadded or quilted to knees and stiffened with whalebone, white starched petticoat with 3 stiffly starched flounces, 2 muslin petticoats, and finally the dress; 2 or 3 petticoats on the same band; *patent-tilter,* or *tournure* cage-like frame of light steel wires used, 1855-58; hoop petticoat, used generally by all classes, by 1859, maximum size, 1860; only 1 petticoat worn by lady when fashion changed, after Empress Eugénie appeared without her crinoline, with hoops below knee suspended by tape from waist, after 1860; *crinolette;* steel hoops discontinued, after 1867; woolen undergarment and drawers of chamois or bloomers gathered at the knee; also quilted petticoat; *pannier puff,* 1860; gored petticoat, 1863; very elaborate petticoat often showed beneath outside skirt, 1861-66.

Cloaks and overgarments: shawl or cape because of size of sleeve; Paisley or cashmere shawl; *rotonde; mantlet Matilda;* spencer, sometimes knitted or crocheted, 1850's; *hug-me-tight* and tight jacket with mannish detail, peplum, collar and cuff for skating; shawl often shaped; casaweck, 1851; *chambord mantle; Colleen Bawn cloak,* 1851; *faldetta; Victoria mantle; talma mantle* becoming a rotonde, 1854; *surtout;* caraco double-breasted, 1855; *sortie de bal; figaro jacket;* bolero; cloak enormous or fitted, 1860; *casaque,* mantelette; *Maintenon;* sealskin coat an innovation of Worth, previously fur worn on outside only by coachman; pelisse robe became the redingote; bournouse; Spanish lace mantilla, 1853, *Garibaldi jacket;* canezou; polonaise, 1860; *zouave jacket* after 1860; *Tallien redingote; Russian jacket; waterproof coat,* 1870.

Additional garments: polonaise princess dress; *Watteau robe; Albanian robe;* peignor; waistcoat or gilet, 1852-53; *Jenny Lind costume; dress à la duchesse; manon robe,* 1860; unsuccessful attempt in France to revive the Empire dress, called *Gabrielle dress,* 1864.

2. **Hair:** worn madonna-like over ear and with large coil or chignon in back; loop or side ringlets worn over ear, 1850; curls often extending around to back of head, 1850; band sometimes on forehead, 1850-55, originated with wife of Worth; center parting, 1853; hair drawn away from ears with curls at back by a few, 1855-65; waved

bands; knot in back and curls on neck; *cache-peigne;* chignon lower on neck, 1860; mixture of red and yellow hair dye used, 1860, in imitation of the Empress Eugénie, who had auburn hair; puffs at top of head and chignon, 1865-70; catogan; hairdress revealed the ears, 1865; 2 long curls lying upon the neck for formal wear; much artificial hair; puffs; massive curls, and a rose by the ear, 1866; ringlets over the head in manner of Directory period.

3. **Headdress:** caul of beaded net or gold thread set with jewels worn over chignon; poke bonnet became smaller, set farther back on head, then worn horizontally, 1850; capote; cabriolet bonnet; bavolet; cap worn only by matron and worn farther back on head; bonnet very small, 1855; coal-scuttle bonnet or broad shallow bonnet still in use, 1855; round hat, 1856; large veil; small hat tilted forward when worn with large chignon; bonnet strings very wide and elaborately trimmed, late 1860's, sometimes tied or held with a small bunch of flowers; bonnet made without a back and fitting around the chignon after 1860; bonnet tall and pointed in front, 1863; bonnet more like cap, 1864; hat becoming more popular than bonnet; flat leghorn hat trimmed with tulle, flowers, and ribbon, often held on by ribbon under the chin, 1860's; small black bonnet with black veil worn by widow; Mary Stuart cap, pillbox or *pork pie hat,* sometimes worn at an angle on the forehead; *fanchon cap;* handkerchief-like cap; lace veil worn, 1850's; knitted or crocheted, Spanish or Brussels lace scarf for evening; strands of pearls, real or artificial, flowers and lace worn for evening; nightcap not fashionable.

4. **Footwear:** small or *Baby French heel,* 1853; evening shoe with bow; toe of shoe square at first, then round, or pointed; kid boot buttoned or laced at side, 1858; button shoe more common than laced shoe; slipper; heelless sandal, 1860; boot 3 inches above ankle, bow and tassels at top of boot; small, low curved heel, 1860's; black kid boot, scarlet heel, 1863; high heel, square toe, large rosette, 1864; laced over the instep; *croquet boot,* 1865; 1½ inch heel and square toe with rosette, 1866; boot with cloth top to match costume, 1867-75, toe square, round, or pointed, upper part of white, colored, or bronze; ankle boot with elastic; shorter dress brought more attention to stocking; hose with lace inset for evening; hose with horizontal stripes or of color, complementing dress and shoe; stocking for day, with plaid or circular stripes, worn with boot, 1864; plain silk hose with clock worn with shoe.

5. **Accessories:** hook and eye used; ornamental button of metal, glass, or sometimes covered with fabric; steel or silver button, set with colored stones fashionable as fastenings for blouse, after 1865;

cameo, pearl, or jet button, by 1867; elaborate small parasol, pagoda style, or fringed, some adjustable, with shorter handle, 1850's, somewhat longer handle, 1860's; folding fan of gauze or painted silk, inlaid mother-of-pearl, ivory with spangles, painted feathers, or painted in imitation of famous masterpieces; velvet band around neck for evening, 1851; velvet bracelet or velvet cuff to protect wrist from sunburn; evening hand bouquet carried in silver or gold bouquet holder, until 1854, then scent bottle; pearls and gems to hold flounces and festoons; comb with diamonds; gilt leather sash with ends in front, worn with dress of light material; girdle decorated with precious stones; pocket handkerchief, considered fashionable to weep violently into beautiful handkerchief when attending the theatre even though the plot was a fairytale; ring to hold handkerchief; wrist-length glove with long sleeve, mitt or glove even worn for breakfast at house party or tea, although head uncovered; glove removed only at the table, when worn to evening dinner, worn indoors during daytime visit, considered improper to even unbutton glove in church; much longer glove, 1864; apron for all kinds of work, small black apron worn by school teacher; small round or flat muff of silk, after 1850; reticule.

6. Jewelry: much jewelry, 1852; amber, crystal, and Venetian glass beads; Roman pearls; coral beads for day jewelry; many bracelets, 2 or more worn on 1 arm, 1850; large gold watch on heavy chain and pinned at belt; dog collar, c. 1863; small or large locket; all kinds of stones including quartz, agate, garnet, turquoise, seed pearls and jet set in large brooch or breastpin; tiny picture frame with hair of beloved person very popular; set of jewelry popular consisting of very long earrings, bracelets, and brooch; wide wedding ring; beautiful mounting for diamonds, 1868; bandeau and jewelry for hair; poor taste sometimes shown in the wearing of jewelry; black mourning jewelry consisting of brooch, earrings, and bracelets.

7. Typical Colors: dark shades and harmonious tones, 1850's and 1860's, for day dresses; usually brilliant or strong colors, after 1856; delicate grayed colors for evening; everything matched; magenta, named after Magenta, Italy, solferino, named after Solferino, Italy, the first analine dyes, 1860; contrast in use of dark and light, and complementary colors; light blouse with dark skirt; colored skirt in vogue, 1857; delicate tones of lavender, silver-gray, crimson, maroon, violet, or magenta for gown; black and purple worn in England at time of Queen Victoria's mourning; white or light-colored stocking, gray silk with red clock, colored hose, 1862-63, stocking and shoe of same color, 1867-75; bright-colored walking shoe, *c.* 1860; colored glove, white for evening, lemon, or fawn for daytime.

8. **Typical Materials:** rich fabric; lace used more commonly on daytime dress, 1850's; cashmere shawl of Paisley weave; velvet hat; taffeta ribbon; crepe silk of exceptionally fine grade; silk popular for day dress, 1860's; shot silk, lace universally used for shawl, collar, entire dress, parasol, and handkerchief; merina, grenadine, alpaca, rep, camel's hair, flannel, serge, broadcloth, grosgrain, or velvet for winter dress; velvet often beaded or cut to represent flowers; percale, dimity, or embroidered muslin for summer dress; light fabric including silk net, tulle, or organdy for evening dress; gold or silver brocade, crepe, jaconet, and taffeta used after the Civil War; merino and lamb's wool used for drawers and vest in winter, gauze, cambric and muslin for summer; black taffeta evening shoe; kid boot, 1858, later, kid or patent leather shoe; lisle or other cotton for stocking, also expensive silk stocking; straw, velvet, silk, crepe, or lace for hat; more silk used in England, 1840-70, due to rise in prosperity; fur of ermine, mink, seal, beaver, or astrakhan; jet trimming introduced, 1855 by Worth.

9. **Make-up:** powder; hair dye.

SIGNIFICANT MOTIFS

There were no typical motifs at this time. Fragments of designs of different centuries were often assembled in one pattern. Checks, plaids, and stripes were always in vogue although large floral patterns led in popularity. Additional influences included styles taken from costumes of the periods of Louis XIV and Louis XV.

INFLUENCES ON LATER COSTUMES

Basque, 1916, similar to that of this period; hoops in evening dress, 1940's and '50's; madonna-like hair style worn by some, first half of the 20th century; bright-colored shoe, 1930's, '40's, and '50's; Empress Eugénie hat worn, 1931; pin with glass or silver bouquet holder, 1940's and '50's; fancy petticoat showing beneath skirt, 1930's and '40's; topless or backless hat, late 1940's.

BOOKS OF REFERENCE

(See Books of Reference, Part I, *19th Century*, p. 268, and General Bibliography, p. 433)

ARTISTS FOR COSTUME REFERENCE

(See p. 269)

GLOSSARY

Agnes Sorel Corsage—bodice with medium-high, square neckline and bishop sleeve. *Pl. XLI, 8.*

à la du Barry Corsage—corsage with stomacher-shaped front.

à la Grecque Corsage—low square neckline extending off the shoulder with vertical pleats coming to a point in front.

à la Louis XV Corsage—corsage which extended from shoulder to waist and had the shape of a stomacher.

Albanian Robe—garment with flounces having colored stripes woven into the edging.

Amadis Sleeve—sleeve having pleat at top of armhole, the pleat hidden beneath the epaulette. The lower sleeve was tight from elbow to wrist where there was a row of buttons. Refer to *Chaps. 16, 17.*

Apron—refer to *Chaps. 2, 11, 12, 13, 14, 15, 17.*

Baby French Heel—small, low heel with an inward curve near the lower part.

Basque—outer part of dress sewed onto a boned bodice. *Pl. XLI, 11.*

Basquine—refer to *Chap. 10.*

Bavolet—flounce sewed at back of bonnet, covering back of hair and neck. Refer to *Chap. 17.*

Bertha—refer to *Chap. 17.*

Bishop Sleeve—refer to *Chaps. 15, 17.*

Bloomers—loose Oriental trousers gathered at the knee, popularized by Mrs. Amelia Bloomer in 1851.

Bolero—small jacket with rounded corners in front. Refer to *Chap. 12. Pl. XLI, 9.*

Boot—shoe that came to above the ankle. Refer to *Chaps. 9, 10, 12.*

Bournouse—fringed, knee-length mantle with hood, worn in the 1850's. Refer to *Chap. 17.*

Boutonnière—refer to *Chaps. 16, 17.*

Bowler or Derby Hat—stiff, felt hat with low, round crown, and narrow brim; bowler the British term for the derby hat has a slightly wider brim and roll at the sides.

Braces—suspenders worn by men, suspender-like straps extending from waist belt in front over shoulder to belt in back on one type of dress worn by women. *Pl. XLI, 5.*

Bretelles—refer to *Chap. 16.*

Bustle—device of various materials, sizes, and construction, worn to hold costume away from the body in a planned shape at the back. Refer to *Chaps. 12, 15.*

Cabriolet Bonnet—refer to *Chap. 17.*

Cache-peinge—headdress of net and ribbon to hold the mass of hair in the back.

Canezou—at first, sleeveless outdoor garment developed from the spencer, later, a neckpiece. Refer to *Chaps. 15, 16, 17.*

Capote—elaborate mid-Victorian bonnet with ribbon bows tied at side or in front. Refer to *Chaps. 15, 16.*

Caraco—loose-fitting jacket, often with wide revers. Refer to *Chaps. 13, 14, 17. Pl. XLI, 4.*

Casaque—close-fitting jacket fastened or buttoned up to neck, with skirt fringed or edged in lace. *Pl. XLII, 2.*

CHAPTER 18: GLOSSARY

Casaweck—refer to *Chap. 17*.

Catogan—hair arrangement formed of loose curls, and plaits tied at top of head with ribbon. Refer to *Chaps. 12, 13, 14*.

Caul—refer to *Chaps. 4, 8, 9, 10*.

Chambord Mantle—hooded cloak of velvet or satin which resembled a shawl having deep folds in back.

Chemise—refer to *Chaps. 6, 7, 8, 9, 10, 11, 12, 13, 14, 15, 16, 17*.

Chemisette à Jabot—pleated or embroidered jabot visible in opening of redingote between neck and waist. Refer to *Chemisette, Chap. 16*.

Chignon—heavy twist or knot of natural or false hair worn high or low. Refer to *Chaps. 10, 14*.

Chimney-Pot Hat—refer to *Chap. 17*.

Colleen Bawn Cloak—cloak of white grenadine with large cape held up by rosettes in back.

Corset—refer to *Chaps. 8, 9, 10, 11, 12, 13, 14, 15, 16, 17*.

Cravat—refer to *Chaps. 12, 13, 14, 15, 16, 17*.

Crinolette—small crinoline or pannier of steel.

Crinoline—stiff unpliable material used to support or stiffen the costume; name given also steel springs which formed a type of cage or hoop used to extend the skirt, sometimes used in entire petticoat.

Croquet Boot—footwear with wide lacing, and tassels in front and back.

Derby—refer to *Bowler*.

Dog Collar—refer to *Chaps. 3, 7*.

Dress à la Duchesse—dress with square, low-necked bodice edged with ruching made of fabric of dress. *Pl. XLI, 7*.

Dundrearys, Dundreary Whiskers or Piccadilly Weepers—long side whiskers worn by Lord Dundreary a character in *Our American Cousin* by Tom Taylor, 1858.

Empire Jupon—petticoat with gores, and with 2 or 3 steel frames at the bottom.

Engageant—flounce of lace showing below a bell-shaped, or loose sleeve. Refer to *Chaps. 12, 13, 14*.

Epaulette—refer to *Chap. 10*.

Faldetta—small, colored, taffeta mantle. *Pl. XLI, 10*.

Fanchon Cap—small cap of lace, worn in daytime. *Pl. XLIII, 3*.

Fichu—refer to *Chaps. 13, 14, 15, 16, 17. Pl. XLI, 1*.

Figaro Jacket—close-fitting short jacket with epaulette on shoulder, and cut away at side in a bolero style. *Pl. XLI, 2*.

Fontange Trimming—gathered ribbon or band through which a colored ribbon was passed.

Fourreau Skirt—gored skirt. *Pl. XLIII, 5*.

Frock Coat—refer to *Chaps. 16, 17*.

Gabrielle Dress—princess dress with box pleat in back, and with bodice and skirt of dress cut in one piece.

Gabrielle Sleeve—sleeve with many puffs from top to bottom. Refer to *Chap. 16. Pl. XLI, 3*.

Gaiter—refer to *Chaps. 13, 14, 15, 16, 17*.

Garibaldi Jacket—military type of jacket made of scarlet cashmere. This name was also given to a separate blouse which was buttoned up the front and tucked into skirt. Named after General Giuseppe Garibaldi of Italy.

Garibaldi Shirt—shirt of bright scarlet merino decorated on the front with black braid and buttons; named after the prominent Italian hero. *Pl. XLII, 4*.

Gilet—vest or short waistcoat.

Gladstone Collar—standing collar with flaring sides, worn with a silk scarf-like tie. This collar was worn by Willam Ewart Gladstone, at one time Prime Minister of England.

Hoop—circular framework used to expand a woman's skirt. Refer to *Crinoline*.

Hug-me-tight—hand-knitted or crocheted under jacket usually with cape-like sleeves.

Imperial—refer to *Chap. 11.*

Inverness cape—a full, sleeveless cape which fitted closely around the neck, from Inverness, Scotland.

Isabeau style—dress with bodice and skirt cut in one piece.

Jupon—underskirt of the same fabric as the skirt or of contrasting material. Refer to *Chaps. 9, 14.*

Jenny Lind Costume—dress having an off-shoulder neckline, and hoop skirt with 3 lace ruffles. This type of dress was worn by the singer, Jenny Lind who became known as "The Swedish Nightingale."

Maintenon—embroidered garment resembling shawl with broad, pleated flounce. *Pl. XLII, 1.*

Manon Robe—garment with the front cut in 1 piece and a pleat in back resembling the Watteau pleat, which extended from under the collar to the bottom of the skirt. *Pl. XLIII, 2.*

Mantelette—outdoor garment consisting of a long, shaped scarf, which came to a deep point in the front, and was held in place by an inner belt attached at the back. This garment was trimmed in fringe, 1850's. Refer to *Chaps. 12, 13, 14, 15, 16, 17.*

Mantilla—refer to *Chap. 16. Pl. XLIII, 4.*

Mantlet Matilde—shawl-like garment, which had trimming of fringe or taffeta in front.

Mary Stuart Cap—refer to *Mary Stuart Bonnet, Chap. 10* and to *Chap. 17.*

Monocle—refer to *Chap. 17.*

Newgate Fringe—short whiskers forming a fringe around the chin.

Nightcap—refer to *Chaps. 10, 11, 12, 13, 14, 15, 16, 17.*

Page—elastic band used to loop up the skirt.

Pagoda Sleeve—refer to *Chap. 17. Pl. XLIII, 1.*

Paisley Shawl—refer to *Chap. 16.*

Pannier Puff—the puff formed by looping the upper skirt.

Patent-tilter—graduated rounds of steel wire held together with tape, and run into the muslin or calico petticoat. Only 1 heavy petticoat was necessary with this invention, in place of the numerous padded skirts used previously.

Peignor—refer to *Chap. 17.*

Pelisse Robe—refer to *Chaps. 16, 17.*

Peplum—refer to *Chaps. 11, 12, 13.*

Petticoat—refer to *Chaps. 9, 10, 11, 12, 13, 14, 15, 16, 17.*

Piccadilly Weepers—refer to *Dundrearys.*

Poke Bonnet—refer to *Chaps. 16, 17.*

Polonaise—at first an outdoor garment. This term was later used for a dress with fullness at back, above which the sash was tied in a bow. Refer to *Chaps. 13, 14, 17.*

Pork Pie Hat—hat worn with dish-shape fold in the crown.

Quizzing Glass—refer to *Chaps. 15, 16, 17.*

Redingote—in this period term referred to pelisse robe with horizontal trimming. Refer to *Chaps. 14, 15, 16. Pl. XLII, 5.*

Reticule—refer to *Chaps. 13, 14, 15, 16, 17.*

Rotonde—short circular mantle matching the dress. *Pl. XLII, 3.*

Russian Jacket—sleeveless, short coat.

Russian Vest—loose blouse resembling Garibaldi jacket.

Sack Coat—loose fitting coat with high short lapels.

Second Empire Costume—type of garment worn during the time of Louis Philippe. This garment had a broad silhouette, tight-fitting bodice and small waistline, pagoda sleeve, and full bouffant skirt.

Shirtwaist—masculine type of waist with high collar and cuffs.

Sortie de Bal—cashmere cloak with satin or silk quilted lining similar to the Talma.

Spencer—refer to *Chaps. 15, 16, 17.*

Surtout—similar to paletot but having peplum pointed in back.

Tallien Redingote—similar to *Polonaise.*

Talma Mantle—circular, occasionally hooded cloak of velvet or satin which somewhat resembled a shawl, sometimes with cape or collar.

Tournure—type of French bustle which replaced many petticoats; steel springs passed through shirring across the back, secured in front by strings.

Veil—refer to *Chaps. 3, 4, 5, 6, 7, 8, 9, 10, 15, 16, 17.*

Vest—refer to *Chap. 17.*

Victoria Mantle—knee-length mantle with collar, and wide hanging sleeve. A deep colored border was u ed as decoration on this garment.

Waistcoat—forerunner of the present day vest. Refer to *Chaps. 11, 12, 13, 14, 15, 16, 17.*

Waterproof Coat—outdoor garment with or without cape; worn as a protection from the rain.

Watteau Body—dress with low square neck, a series of ribbon bows down the front, and elbow sleeve with deep ruffles.

Watteau Pleat—refer to *Chap. 13.*

Watteau Robe—ball dress having a low square neckline and a series of ribbon bows down the front.

Wellington boot—refer to *Chap. 16.*

Zouave Jacket—short, loose jacket which showed military influence. Usually the chemisette showed at the neck and below the 3-quarter sleeve of this jacket. Refer to *Chap. 17. Pl. XLI, 6.*

19th Century

PART IV

1868-89

CHRONOLOGY

Convention of National Woman's Suffrage Party in Cleveland, *November, 1868.*

Civil Rights Bill passed by Congress, *1868.*

Official opening of Suez Canal, *1869.*

The Union Pacific and Central Pacific Railways, constituting the first transcontinental railroad in the United States completed in *1869.*

Franco-Prussian War, *1870.* France, a republic for the third time, *1870.* Adopted a republican constitution, *1875.*

German Empire established, *1871.* King William of Prussia, first German Emperor.

Public Health Act in England, *1875.*

Invention of telephone by Alexander Graham Bell, United States, *1876.*

Queen Victoria proclaimed Empress of India, *1876.*

Inventions by Thomas Edison, United States: Phonograph patented, *1877;* incandescent electric lamp perfected, *1879,* first system of central station power production for generating electricity put into operation, *1882;* invention of motion picture, *1887;* new "kinetoscope," motion picture perfected, *1889.*

Immunization against disease through vaccination discovered by Louis Pasteur, *1881.*

Organization of American Red Cross, *1881.* Clara Barton founder and first president.

Successful automobile made by Gottlieb Daimler, Germany, *1886.*

Pneumatic rubber tire invented by John Boyd Dunlop, Scotland, *1888.*

First Pan-American Congress convened in Washington, *1889.*

Collapse of Panama Company (French company with Ferdinand de Lesseps as president), first to attempt the digging of a canal through Panama, *1889.*

CHAPTER 19

19th Century

PART IV

1868-89

HISTORY

In this period various countries continued to carry on exploration, and most of the continent of Africa was, by 1900, under the control of the important European powers: England, France, Germany, Belgium, Portugal, Italy, and Spain. The Monroe Doctrine protected the American continent from further exploration.

In France, Napoleon III continued his reign and under the Second Empire, Paris was a dazzling social center for foreigners. In Germany, the influence of Bismarck together with the growing army and navy, the universities and nationalism, marked the rise of the German Empire.

England continued to expand her empire. She became dependent upon the raw products secured from India, many of which in turn were returned to that country in the form of manufactured products. In 1876, Queen Victoria became sovereign of India. The Indians studied abroad, chiefly in England and in the United States. They absorbed Western ideas and became nationalistic to such an extent that the British government changed its autocratic attitude toward India and by 1882 invited a small amount of participation in local government. This was not enough for the intelligent Indians and they continued to be dissatisfied and to foment disturbances directed against their rulers.

Canada had already formed a self-governing federation known as the Dominion of Canada in 1867, which proved very successful; the West became settled and as provinces were formed they were absorbed into the Dominion. A similar situation resulted in Australia and the Commonwealth of Australia was created. New Zealand followed the same pattern and the British Empire was gradually becoming the empire upon whose soil the sun never set.

North America continued to be developed, and millionaires were made in spite of the great number of poor people. The United States was psychologically still in its pioneer stage, and the people were adventurous in spirit, setting their hopes on the discovery of gold and silver in the West and on the exploitation of oil wherever they could find it. Even though this was a democratic country, there still were parents who took pride in obtaining titles for their daughters by marrying them to foreigners of nobility.

With democracy on the ascent, people were witnessing the passing of aristocracy. After the appearance of Karl Marx's *Das Kapital,* in 1867, social problems were given more attention, and the labor movement started to grow as an important political power with the influence it wields today. Strikes, better working conditions for labor, socialism versus private enterprise were among the significant issues of the day.

This period showed a further development in scientific discovery: the electric lamp, perfected by Edison in 1879, brought light when and where desired, and turned night into day. As early as 1883, electricity was used as illumination in a number of homes.

While scientific and mechanical discoveries increased, taste declined. Whereas the 18th century was a period of fine craftsmanship and of appreciation of art, these interests vanished with the disappearance of distinct class barriers and the general rise of the middle class. There was lack of taste in costume, architecture, and furnishings: it was the age of red plush, horsehair sofas, heavy mahogany, carved walnut, and mass production. Art was not recognized as "a part of everyday life," but was considered frivolous, and was linked with loose morality.

The position of woman was becoming more important. In England the woman taxpayer was given the municipal franchise in 1869. In the United States, two organizations of interest to women were founded in 1869: one group was known as the National Woman's Suffrage Association, with Mrs. Elizabeth Cady Stanton as president, another group known as the American Woman Suffrage with Henry Ward Beecher as president.

Women looked to careers other than marriage, and that brought about a change in costume. Sports became more important in American life. Tennis, which had been one of the favorite games in France during the 18th century, was now played with much enthusiasm by the middle class in England, and by the men and women of America. Croquet and archery continued to be favorite recreational activities. A more comfortable type of costume permitted some freedom of action. The pastime of tatting, crocheting, and embroidering, was continued by many women.

There was a revival of styles in the costume worn by the man of this period. More originality was shown during the Second Empire in France; color and new ideas again were evident in man's dress for a short time. Waistcoats and ties gave the small accent of color which relieved the monotony of color in his dress. In general, masculine costume was conventional, and man himself, with his adherence to details, represented a model of respectability and correctness. On the other hand, the feminine costume presented an array of luxury, not only in dress but in underclothes.

Cheap fashion magazines and daily newspapers, with photographs of the fashionable woman made it possible for all women to follow the elegant attire of the age. Much credit should be given to Ebenezer Butterick and his wife, Ellen, for the first paper dress patterns which helped the woman of the day in constructing garments.

During the early Victorian age, the crinoline had increased to enormous proportions. Then, following the cycle of most styles, the skirt began to grow narrower, until in the winter of 1869-70 the very tight dress with bustle and draped skirt came into vogue. The corset, always an influence on feminine attire, even went so far as to change the wearer's figure and style of walking. The age of independent dress began at this time, each individual following, to a certain degree, her own taste; many women had costumes designed by the couturier instead of having garments copied from the style of costume they had worn for years. In 1888, the bustle grew smaller and by 1890 it had completely disappeared. Attention which had been given to the skirt now was concentrated on the bodice. Women became more economical and instead of each having a dozen gowns in her wardrobe, four or five dresses were considered sufficient.

In 1874 Jean and Gaston Worth entered the profession of their father, Charles Worth. The House of Worth with Jean Worth as the designer and Gaston as business manager continued in importance and brought about the innovation of many styles and customs; a very important and comfortable custom was inaugurated by Madame Worth when she appeared at the races without a cloak, wearing only a scarf over her shoulders.

DRESS

A. *Sources of information:* costumes, paintings, illustrations, photographs, and literature.

B. **MEN**
   1. **Garments:**

   Outer upper: tail coat still worn for daytime by conservative man; swallow-tailed coat worn for evening only; frock coat or Prince Albert; sack coat; cutaway coat for formal day wear, for church, daytime wedding, tea, garden party, or other formal occasion; coat long, padded shoulder, sleeve with cuff, short lapel, buttoned high; vest cut high in neck, with high-cut coat; vest with V-neckline, collarless or with rolled collar; double-breasted vest, sometimes worn with sack coat or with frock coat; evening waistcoat cut low at neck; striped flannel *blazer* introduced, 1880's; *cardigan; Norfolk jacket,* and *reefer* cut high at neck worn for sports.

   Outer lower: trousers to ankle or instep; knee breeches for court use; also worn by sportsman; trousers light-colored at first; *spring bottom trousers,* 1880's; trousers not creased; for convenience, trousers sometimes turned up to form cuff; *knickerbockers* to below knee.

   Under: stiff-bosomed shirt, 1870's, opened up the back; sometimes with pleated front; false front worn by some; stiff bosom with buttons or removable studs for formal evening wear; drawers.

   Cloaks and overgarments: plaid Inverness cape especially for traveler; black evening cape resembling Inverness cape; short topcoat with velvet collar, 1880's; longer coat following lines of suit; long winter coat; *ulster.*

   Neckwear and wristwear: detachable collar and cuff made of starched cotton fabric, hard white rubber, celluloid, or paper: turned down collar; standing collar or open *wing collar;* collar straight or with spreading tips, closing in front; low turnover collar, narrow string tie; knotted bow, or *ascot tie* with scarf pin; black string or white tie for dress; *Windsor tie* with ends which met or spread apart; *four-in-hand* tie very popular, 1870's, wider in 1880's.

   2. **Hair:** shorter than in preceding period; side part or usually parted in the center from forehead to nape of neck and curled over temples,

1870's; hair smooth down back of head, and parted at side or middle from forehead to crown, 1880's; hair sometimes brushed straight back in a bushy pompadour, or brushed forward from the back, fairly long hair at back; waxed, dyed and perfumed mustache; heavy beard; Dundrearys, Dundreary whiskers or piccadilly weepers not in vogue, after 1870; large beard worn by older man, 1880's; also drooping mustache, 1880's; beard often worn without mustache; smooth-shaven, by 1889.

3. **Headdress:** bowler or derby for business and street; high silk hat for dress; straw hat or cap for sport; visored cap; *fore-and-aft cap,* with ear flap usually tied up; felt hat with flat crown and wide brim; *fedora, slouch hat* of felt popular, the brim turned up or down; *tam-o'-shanter.*

4. **Footwear:** very narrow shoe, called toothpick-toed shoe, cloth-topped shoe, buttoned at outer side, or laced in front; buttoned shoe sometimes with kid top; trousers worn in or out of boot top; elastic-side ankle boot; short gaiter or light-colored *spat;* half shoe or oxford; tennis shoe; bright-colored sock worn by young man, black by older or conservative man; dark woolen stocking and high-buttoned shoe or gaiter worn with knickerbockers.

5. **Accessories:** glove; large, white, cotton, or silk handkerchief; braces; *lorgnette;* walking stick which had a variety of uses, one type known to have been used as ear trumpet.

6. **Jewelry:** watch with emblem or charm on chain which extended across vest or hung from buttonhole down to watch pocket; ring; shirt studs and cuff links; scarf pin used with ascot tie, and occasionally with the four-in-hand.

7. **Typical Colors:** light-colored trousers, topcoat and driving coat; plaid vest; black or white evening vest; white waistcoat for dress; black tail coat for evening; light or dark sack coat; light or dark overcoat; black or checked trousers with cutaway coat; light trousers with frock coat; colored necktie, black or russet oxford; white or brown shoe.

8. **Typical Materials:** rough or smooth fabric for sack coat; black broadcloth for tail coat; rough fabric, tailed coat for sport; twill, homespun or tweed for suit; white piqué or Marseilles for wash vest; silk, ribbed, or brocaded vest; waistcoat and trousers of same material; felt derby.

9. **Make-up:** none.

C. WOMEN

1. **Garments:**

   Outer upper: tight-fitting bodice; lace, ruching, or ruffles used as finishing for open neck; tucker used, 1870's; deep square or round neckline, middle of 1870's; day dress sometimes with high neck; gradually higher neckline; turnover collar on low neck band, or small white collar with ruching above; heart-shaped neckline with point in back, during 1870's, becoming the most popular kind by 1889; high neckline, *c.* 1885; bell-shaped sleeve at first of period; *engageant*; sleeve set into armscye with little or no fullness, often tight and long; Gabrielle sleeve, 1869; pagoda sleeve, 1870; melon puff revived, 1873; sleeve with *mousquetaire cuff;* gathered top, 1888; sloping shoulder out of style; sleeve puffed at top; evening dress with elbow-length sleeve, small puff, or ruffle; round belted bodice early in period, then long pointed corsage; *turret bodice;* basque with smooth, unbelted waistline and peplum to hip, 1874-76; plastron in front and back, 1877; shorter basque, 1880's; very small or wasp waist, 1882; waistline of evening dress pointed in front and back; longer waist, 1885-89; more attention given to bodice, after 1886; *ruching à la Medici.*

Outer lower: upper skirt draped and looped up over a gored under-skirt; skirt lined with horsehair cloth; dress with train, 1865-75; more attention focused on hip, 1870; elaborately draped skirt, drawn or tied back, known as the *tie-back skirt* and for which this period was named *tied-back time;* the bouffant skirt less exaggerated, *c.* 1872; *tablier,* 1872, used more than ever, by 1875; front of skirt sometimes with fringe; also gored skirt with little fullness in front; length of dress to instep, 1874; skirt tight over hip, 1874, with elaborate drapery in back; many flounces and a yard or two of train worn by fashionable lady even for semiformal and daytime wear; dress with bustle discarded for dress with short tunic, *c.* 1876; several tunics often worn; large pocket on inside of skirt, until 1876, sometimes invisible pockets in seams of skirt; sometimes large elaborate pocket worn in skirt toward the back, after 1876; *balayeuse, dust ruffle* or *street sweeper,* skirt tight and ankle length in 1878 because long dress was considered unsanitary; fish-tail train; short skirt with pannier almost revived, 1878-79; skirt often pleated at waist; much variation in drapery, 1881; bustle-type dress with drapery and full-ness higher at hip revived, *c.* 1882; *curtain drapery;* skirt just touch-ing the ground, 1882; *waterfall back,* 1883, *zouave puff;* width of hip increased by pannier folds; trimming of puffs, frills, and ruches in light-weight fabric; pannier and drapery gradually replaced by pleated skirt and plain skirt; tie-back arrangement discarded in day dress, 1886; enlarged bow in back, final appearance of the pouf; change to simplicity, 1889; evening dress with trailing overskirt; floor- or instep-length skirt; divided skirt introduced for sports wear but not popular.

1. Jabot 2. Polonaise 3. Skirt with Bustle 4. Jacket 5. Engageant

Under: ankle-length underskirt or jupon with pleated flounce; gored underskirt tight in front; exquisite petticoat worn during entire period; hoop skirt of wire, or whalebone petticoat, flat in front, late 1860's; small wire crinoline, 1870, also combination of small pannier and crinoline or crinolette; *tilter;* tournure; bustle replacing pannier, *c.* 1870; *Eugénie petticoat;* side of bustle extending over hip and above waist, 1871; bustle narrow and longer, 1873; petti-coat with no fullness around hip, 1873; tournure and bustle disap-pearing, 1874, because of the new tight-fitting dress; bustle return-ing, 1882, at its height in popularity, 1885, *hip bag;* cage bustle discontinued, 1886; *cushion pad* stuffed with horsehair, worn, 1888; long corset high at bust, 1875, tight lacing; garters or supporters attached to corset; chemisette; camisole; vest or chemise worn be-neath corset; a combination of chemise and drawers with tucks, real lace insertion and frills, 1877; union suit introduced; drawer open-ing fastened down by button, 1876; flannel drawers sometimes worn under a cotton type, 1876; drawers not worn by lower class, until the 1880's; number of petticoats increased, 1889.

Cloaks and overgarments: mantle; *jacket* and other overgarments often with *dolman sleeve,* made to fit over bustle; mantilla; casaque and paletot, 1868; *petit casaque;* considered indecent to appear on the street without a mantle concealing outline of figure; Talma-shaped mantle with heavy jet fringe, 1868; figaro jacket or bolero; long cape with capuchon; *Garrick; dolman* with fringe; 3-quarter length shoulder cape of fur; previous to this time fur coat worn by coachman only; Garibaldi jacket, 1868; mantle, 1870's; long cape with hood for evening; waterproof coat; ulster; *Mother Hubbard cloak;* paletot; pelerine, *capuchin* or *capucine;* sacque or zouave jacket worn over indoor dress; *Directoire coat; camargo,* slipover *jersey sweater* introduced, 1880's; *Eton jacket; Hussar jacket.*

Neckwear and wristwear: narrow upright collar or fold of linen; frill of lace; fichu; bertha; Elizabethan ruff; jabot.

Additional garments: dress for indoors, walking, morning visiting, afternoon, garden, dinner, and evening; comfortable sport costume with short skirt; bloomers, riding breeches, bicycling skirt; bathing suit with knee-length bloomers; long or short sacque of wash mate-rial used when working about the house; *dressing gown; shawl dress,* 1870, also *frou-frou dress; Dolly Varden dress;* jersey or guernsey dress of knitted silk or wool; *pinafore dress,* 1879; tunic dress; *Watteau costume; Regency costume; princess dress; Empire dress;* tailor-made costume; negligee with Wateau back; *princess polonaise;* polonaise; *Directoire gown;* mannish tailored suit; thin nightgown profusely trimmed, 1876.

2. **Hair:** chignon very large, 1860-70; ears revealed by 1865; hair combed straight up, coiled high on top of head, bang or fringe on forehead; coiffure seeming to slant from top of head to forehead, by 1870; much false hair; cascades of loops, braids, ringlets, and curls, after 1870; chignon smaller with only a few curls in the back, 1872; *Récamier hair style,* 1873; small chignon, 1873 worn with a Spanish comb which was visible from the front; not as much false hair as formerly, by 1875; 2 long curls worn on the neck with formal hairdress; artificial hair and padding discontinued, 1878; *Alsatian bow* pinned on front of head by young woman, 1875-80; hair parted in middle, 1878-80; coiffure changed, 1880's, waved, curled, or frizzed bang over forehead with flat coil at back; curls on neck for evening not worn, by 1884; coiffure with a fringe and coil on top of head introduced by Alexandra, Princess of Wales; hair worn low on neck, 1886; pompadour with knot on top and ears revealed, 1888.

3. **Headdress:** hat sometimes used in place of bonnet, 1868; *chignon strap;* nightcap, 1870; small hat worn tipped forward or on back of head because of hairdress; large hat profusely decorated; Charlotte Corday cap; *Dolly Varden bonnet,* 1870; small face-veil pulled over chin and tied in back, replacing heavy draped veil worn earlier; bonnet flatter and worn on back of head, 1878; hat very large, by 1879; poke bonnet revived, 1880's; wide bonnet strings used; *Russian bonnet;* Gainsborough hat, 1880; flowerpot hat; *Henry II toque; Langtry bonnet,* 1882; bonnet small and flat, end of 1880's; turban, *sailor hat,* and tam o' shanter, masculine fedora; stuffed birds used as decoration, aigrette, ostrich plume; cap worn in house by married woman; bonnet with long black veil by widow; horse-hair bonnet; toque worn, *c.* 1888.

4. **Footwear:** *Cromwell shoe,* 1868; button or elastic-sided shoe with broad square toe, also high heel and pointed toe; front lacing; high heel and high toque worn, 1885-86; oxford for outdoor costume, patent-leather toe; heavy sport shoe; colored silk stocking; white stocking, until 1880, then black, or black and white striped stocking, after 1880; ribbed stocking, 1886; fine lisle stocking; silk hose unusual and considered a luxury.

5. **Accessories:** neck ribbon; *officer collar;* chatelaine bag or pouch; card case; glove, short for day, long for evening, 3-quarter length glove with short sleeve; mitten, 1879; *brassard;* at first, pleated, folding fan for afternoon and evening, not used, 1870's, gauze and ostrich-feather fan, 1880's; jeweled comb; silk or cotton umbrella; elaborate parasol larger than in previous period, and with walking stick handle, smaller, 1885, larger again, 1886, Japanese sunshade; small

round muff and *tippet;* bouquet; puffed sash; pocket handkerchief with colored border; hair net, 1877; ribbon, flowers or wreath worn in hair; ribbon bow in small topknot, 1880; apron extending around back of dress; utilitarian apron; pocket of dress instead of reticule; flat purse or cardcase carried; smelling salts.

6. **Jewelry:** mourning jewelry; friendship circle; sentimental jewelry; large drop or hoop earrings, until middle of 1870's, studs, after 1875; several shades of gold; precious and semiprecious stones; cameo in vogue; jet enameled brooch with emblem or motto; wide, gold wedding ring, before 1885, narrow later; fairly heavy, long, gold chain with watch or lorgnette; watch on chatelaine; Danish safety pin, 1878; jeweled ornament used in small topknot, 1880.

7. **Typical Colors:** color harmony important; skirt of plain or flowered material, 2 bright colored skirts, outer and under, never used together, but black skirt often worn with colored one; skirt having stripes in various widths, made of the same material; several colors often used in 1 costume, at least 2 contrasting colors; bodice and skirt often of different colors; *verdigris,* marine blue, and pale blue used, before 1880; electric blue, scarlet, crimson, magenta, purple, plum, green, and saffron yellow used, after 1880; also subdued colors, flower prints, checks, stripes, and plaids; mourning costume of black; colored material plain or print used for underwear instead of white.

8. **Typical Materials:** crepe, crepon, poplin, batiste, piqué, silk, lawn, mousseline-de-laine, grenadine, organdie, crepe lisse, voile, gauze, lace, or gold tinsel for dress; satin and taffeta for mantle and walking dress; additional fabrics including: velvet, cotton, linen, net, dotted swiss, dimity, mohair, goat's hair; tarlatan for dance dress; entire costume of silk not common; chemicals used to increase weight of silk, 1870's; revival of silk dress, 1884; new materials introduced including jaconet, pompadour sateen, foulard and jersey; Indian prints; bridal dress of rich silk and lace; wool for vest; plain or brocaded kid, often cloth or satin top, for shoe.

9. **Make-up:** practically none, curling tongs used.

SIGNIFICANT MOTIFS

Sprigs of flowers, checks, plaids, and stripes, the latter often very wide or alternating with a floral design. Beautiful silk prints in Oriental patterns were sold at Liberty's in London as early as 1875.

INFLUENCES ON LATER COSTUMES

Heart-shaped neckline, worn in 1880's, 1940's and '50's; profuse use of buttons, 1950's; high coiffure, 1947; special type of dresses for every kind of

CHAPTER 19: GLOSSARY

occasion, such as those for street wear, walking, bicycling, tennis, etc., in following periods; gored and circular skirt, 1948-52; scarf duplicated in 1952.

BOOKS OF REFERENCE

(See BOOKS OF REFERENCE, Part I, *19th Century,* p. 268, and GENERAL BIBLIOGRAPHY, p. 433)

ARTISTS FOR COSTUME REFERENCE

(See p. 269)

GLOSSARY

Aigrette—refer to *Chaps. 3, 16.*

Alsatian Bow—large ribbon bow worn in hair.

Ascot Tie—scarf tied in knot, with horizontal ends then crossed diagonally.

Balayeuse, Dust Ruffle or Street Sweeper—ruffle on innerside of hem of skirt or petticoat to protect it from the ground.

Basque—refer to *Chap. 18.*

Blazer—light-weight sport jacket.

Bowler or Derby—refer to *Chap. 18.*

Brassard—ribbon bow worn on the arm.

Bustle—whalebone or steel strips put in top of back of petticoat or in separate arrangement to hold the puff of the pannier skirt, often called tournure, pannier, or crinoline. Refer to *Chaps. 12, 15, 18. Pl. XLIV, 3.*

Camargo—jacket with pannier.

Camisole—refer to *Chap. 17.*

Capuchin or Capucine—cloak resembling garment worn by Capuchin monk.

Capuchon—refer to *Chaps. 5, 8, 9, 11, 12, 13, 17.*

Cardigan—collarless sweater with front opening.

Casaque—outdoor jacket having bodice with long basque extending down the front. Refer to *Chap. 18.*

Chatelaine—refer to *Chaps. 14, 16.*

Chatelaine Bag—refer to *Chatelaine.*

Chemise—refer to *Chaps. 6, 7, 8, 9, 10, 11, 12, 13, 14, 15, 16, 17, 18.*

Chemisette—refer to *Chap. 16.*

Chignon—refer to *Chaps. 10, 14, 18.*

Chignon Strap—ribbon band worn beneath hair at back to hold woman's hat in place.

Corset—refer to *Chaps. 8, 9, 10, 11, 12, 13, 14, 16, 17, 18.*

Crinolette—refer to *Chap. 18.*

Crinoline—refer to *Chap. 18.*

Cromwell Shoe—shoe with tongue and buckle became fashionable; resembled the type worn during 17th century.

Curtain Drapery—name given in North America to pannier folds.

Cushion Pad—very small bustle stuffed with horse hair.

Derby Hat—refer to *Bowler.*

Directoire Coat—woman's ankle-length coat having a skirt in the back and cut straight across above the waistline in front.

Directoire Gown—coat-like dress with broad lapel, sash, and gauntlet cuff.

Dolly Varden Bonnet—bonnet of beaver, tied with a plush ribbon and decorated with a crystal and silver bird.

Dolly Varden Dress—revival of the polonaise of 18th century with panniers of printed chintz and buttons or bow at back of waist.

Dolman—3-quarter length, out-of-door wrap made of brocade, silk or woolen fabric, with sleeves cut in 1 piece with the body of the blouse.

Dolman Sleeve—sleeve cut in 1 piece with the body of the blouse.

Dressing Gown—loose garment worn at breakfast which was the forerunner of the tea gown worn later.

Dundrearys, Dundreary Whiskers or Piccadilly Weepers—refer to *Chaps. 17, 18*.

Dust Ruffle—refer to *Balayeuse*.

Empire Dress—dress with high waisted, full bodice, puffed sleeve and a narrow gathered skirt.

Engageant—refer to *Chaps. 12, 13, 14, 18. Pl. XLIV, 5*.

Eton Jacket—short jacket with side lapels, first worn by students of Eton College, England.

Eugénie Petticoat—petticoat with steels, or attached bustle, worn in the early 1870's.

Fedora—velour hat with fairly high, slightly tapering crown.

Fichu—refer to *Chaps. 13, 14, 15, 16, 17, 18*.

Figaro Jacket—short, sleeveless jacket with scallops in the back. Refer to *Chap. 18*.

Fore-and-aft Cap—cap having visor in front and back, worn with Inverness cape.

Four-in-hand—kind of necktie, tied in a slipknot.

Frock Coat or Prince Albert Coat—refer to *Chaps. 16, 17, 18*.

Frou-frou Dress—dress with low corsage, and light pink underskirt with many small flounces.

Gabrielle Sleeve—refer to *Chaps. 16, 18*.

Gainsborough Hat—refer to *Chap. 14*.

Gaiter—refer to *Chaps. 13, 14, 15, 16, 17, 18*.

Garibaldi Jacket—refer to *Chap. 18*.

Garrick—long velvet mantle trimmed with fur, 1870-80.

Henry II Toque—fairly large toque with ostrich feathers.

Hip Bag—slang name given in North America to pannier fold.

Hussar Jacket—jacket with braiding and frog fastening and was worn with waistcoat. The return of English troops from Egypt influenced this fashion.

Inverness Cape—large, plaid, woolen coat with elbow length cape of same material. Refer to *Chap. 18*.

Jabot—ruffles of lace or fabric extending down front of blouse. Refer to *Chap. 13*. *Pl. XLIV, 1*.

Jacket—short jacket, sometimes with flared skirt to fit over bustle. *Pl. XLIV, 4*.

Jersey Sweater—slipover sweater, close-fitting overgarment, copied from a seaside fisherman's sweater.

Jupon—refer to *Chaps. 9, 14, 18*.

Knickerbockers—full, knee-length breeches gathered in at knee, named after Father Knickerbocker who came to New Amsterdam, *c*. 1674.

Langtry Bonnet—small close-fitting bonnet.

Lorgnette—eyeglasses with handle.

Mantilla—refer to *Chaps. 16, 18*.

Mantle—shawl-like garment with long points in back and front, and with side piece forming sleeve. Refer to *Chaps. 2, 3, 7, 8, 9, 17*.

Marseilles—refer to *Chap. 16*.

CHAPTER 19: GLOSSARY

Mother Hubbard Cloak—loose-fitting cloak.

Mousquetaire Cuff—cuff having wrinkled effect.

Nightcap—refer to *Chaps. 10, 11, 12, 13, 14, 15, 16, 17, 18*.

Norfolk Jacket—jacket with box pleats or straps of same material passing over belt, and extending from shoulder to hem in front and back; worn for sport.

Officer Collar—band of fur worn around the neck.

Pagoda Sleeve—refer to *Chaps. 17, 18*.

Paletot—jacket with open-cuffed sleeve. Refer to *Chap. 17*.

Pannier—loop formed over hip by draping of upperskirt. Refer to *Chaps. 12, 13, 14*.

Pelerine—refer to *Chaps. 12, 13, 15, 16, 17*.

Petit Casaque—name given to the polonaise in Paris.

Petticoat—refer to *Chaps. 9, 10, 11, 12, 13, 14, 15, 16, 17, 18*.

Piccadilly Weepers—refer to *Dundrearys, Chaps. 17, 18*.

Pinafore Dress—low-necked, sleeveless overdress worn over a princess dress.

Plastron—trimming for front of a woman's dress from shoulder to center waist, sometimes of a different material from the costume. Refer to *Chap. 9*.

Poke Bonnet—refer to *Chaps. 16, 17, 18*.

Polonaise—formerly an outdoor garment with a straight front; then a dress with bodice and looped-up tunic made in one; later a negligee. Refer to *Chaps. 13, 14, 17, 18*. *Pl. XLIV, 2*.

Pompadour—style of hairdress formed by drawing hair straight up and back from forehead. Refer to *Chap. 13*.

Pouf—fullness formed at back of costume by looping up the skirt; this word is used in connection with hairdress in *Chap. 14*.

Prince Albert Coat—double-breasted frock coat with flat collar, often of velvet. Became fashionable in the United States after the visit of Prince Albert of England in 1876. Refer to *Frock Coat*.

Princess Dress—costume having bodice and skirt cut in one, fitted from shoulder to hip or beyond.

Princess Polonaise—princess-shaped polonaise.

Récamier Hair Style—hair arrangement with high chignon and curls at neck.

Reefer—double-breasted, close-fitting jacket.

Regency Costume—garment with upper skirt and petticoat of satin, and jacket of velvet.

Reticule—refer to *Chaps. 13, 14, 15, 16, 17, 18*.

Ruching à la Medici—ruching or ruff similar to that worn in the time of Catherine de' Medici.

Russian Bonnet—type of bonnet with large bow tied under the chin, steel embroidered crown and lace brim; another kind, a scarlet velvet hat trimmed with black feathers.

Sack Coat—refer to *Chap. 18*.

Sailor Hat—stiff hat with medium size brim and crown.

Shawl Dress—dress made from shawls.

Slouch Hat—felt hat with soft crushable crown.

Spat—short covering for ankle and instep, usually made of felt and buttoned.

Spring Bottom Trousers—trousers which flared at the bottom.

Street Sweeper—refer to *balayeuse*.

Swallow-tailed Coat—formerly a riding coat with front corners of skirt buttoned back to keep the coat lining from touching the horse. Refer to *Chap. 15*.

Tablier—horizontal trimming on front of skirt.

Talma-shaped Mantle—refer to *Talma Mantle, Chap. 18*.

Tam-o'-shanter—round flat cap with tight-fitting headband.

Tie-back Skirt—type of skirt with a drawstring to pull it back and loop it up.

Tied-back Time—period when skirt was looped up.

Tilter—bustle resembling the tournure except that the shirring containing the springs was in a separate piece, and was adjustable.

Tippet—scarf covering neck and shoulders. Refer to *Chap. 15.*

Toque—small close-fitting hat without a brim. Refer to *Chaps. 2, 10, 16.*

Tournure—refer to *Chap. 18.*

Tucker—fabric used to cover the neck above the very low bodice. Refer to *Chaps. 16, 17.*

Turban—refer to *Chaps. 9, 13, 14, 15, 16.*

Turret Bodice—bodice with tabs.

Ulster—fitted double-breasted coat having several capes; at first made of frieze, a coarse woolen cloth with shaggy mat on one side made in Ulster, Ireland.

Veil—refer to *Chaps. 3, 4, 5, 6, 7, 8, 9, 10, 15, 16, 17, 18.*

Verdigris—greenish-blue pigment.

Vest—synonym for waistcoat, used after latter part of 19th century; also used for women's knit undershirt.

Waterfall Back—style of dress in which back of skirt was caught up at intervals with strings beneath the dress.

Waterproof Coat—refer to *Chap. 18.*

Watteau Costume—dress with Watteau pleat in back, and bodice with fichu-like front.

Windsor Tie—large flowing bow tie.

Wing Collar—high stiff collar with turned back corners.

Zouave Jacket—jacket which was tight in back, but loose and open in the front. Refer to *Chap. 18.*

Zouave Puff—1 or 2 horizontal pouch-like puffs at back of skirt which was made of thin material.

19th Century

PART V

1890-99

CHRONOLOGY

United States Silver Purchase Act, *1890*. Repealed, *1893*.

Panic in *1890* and in *1893* in the United States.

Social service activities during entire period. Hull House, Chicago, founded by Jane Addams and Ellen Gates Starr, *1891;* great success of settlement due to perseverance of Jane Addams.

Passage of German militiary bill, *1893*.

Columbian Exposition in Chicago, *1893*.

Independent Labor Party founded in England, *1893*.

Development of socialism and the labor movement in France, *1893*.

Trade Union Congress in France, *1895*.

Invention of the Diesel engine by Rudolf Diesel, German inventor, *1895*.

Cinematographe, invention of Louis and Auguste Lumiere of France; also invention of vitascope by Thomas Armat, *1895*.

Rush for gold in the Klondike, Alaska, *1896*.

Antityphoid inoculation introduced by Sir Almroth E. Wright, England, *1896*.

Prosperity again in the United States, *1897-1901*.

Spanish American War, *1898*.

Trade Unions developed during this period.

Principle of rigid airship developed by Count Ferdinand von Zeppelin of Germany, *1898*.

CHAPTER 20

19th Century

PART V

1890-99

HISTORY

I n France the Third Republic continued. Considerable effort was being expended toward colonial expansion; all of the countries seemed
intent upon having their share.

Alliances were made in Europe between various countries based
on a struggle to maintain a balance of power. The South African war
from 1899-1902 resulted in the whole of South Africa being added to
the British Empire and in 1909 the Confederation of South Africa
states under the British crown was established. An act had federated
Canada in 1867 and the commonwealth of Australia in 1900. Although
England produced literature of merit, the thought of the times stressed
materialistic ideas.

The German theatre under Max Reinhardt led in the development
of the modern stage. Art students selected either Paris or Munich as
the center in which to study, and even now the stamp of these influences is found on the work of present-day artists. The greatest cultural contribution made by France at this time was in Impressionistic
Painting.

There was social conflict in Russia, and its subjects, Poles, Finns,
Jews, and the liberal thinkers who were being persecuted, sought refuge in America. The Russians became active in the development of
their arts. The Moscow Art Theatre was an example of this accomplish-
ment in the field of the drama.

Immigration to the United States increased. Northern Europe was
well represented, as usual, but people from other countries, Slavs,
Italians, Portuguese and Jews came to start life anew in the growing
democracy.

The McKinley Tariff Bill of 1890 in the United States helped to raise the duties on numerous household articles, including cotton cloth, tinware, tools and many articles of food. The rise in prices brought much protest from the consumer. During the same year, the Sherman Silver Act was passed but later was repealed at a special session of Congress.

As a result of the hard times experienced, especially in Kansas, the homesteaders were forced to sell their homes and return to the east. The great distress they experienced brought about the people's party or Populists as the members were called.

The prosperity that the United States had been experiencing was followed by a severe financial panic in 1893. The following year, General Coxey with an army of civilians went from Ohio to Washington to demand money and work for the men who were idle. The demonstration was stopped when they were arrested for trespassing on the Capitol lawn.

The Hawaiian Islands and the Philippines were annexed by the United States in 1898, the latter following the Spanish-American War. Puerto Rico also became an American possession.

Architecture and furnishings continued to be influenced by the inartistic Victorian period with heavy carving, massive draping and upholstered furnishings.

Women continued their efforts for equality in suffrage; as early as 1890 suffrage had been in force in some sections of the United States. Mrs. Emmeline Pankhurst and her daughter, Cristabel, organized a society in England in the early 1890's, known as Women's Social and Political Union. They adopted militant methods and created more ill-will than support for their cause.

Fashion continued to be eclectic. More periods of the past were represented in costume than ever before. The general silhouette changed, the bustle of the 1880's having disappeared. The sleeve at first extended above the shoulder line, and then the balloon-like and leg-of-mutton sleeve reappeared. Although the skirt was not as exaggerated as the sleeve, it came in for its share of attention, with its gores, godets, and many yards of stiffening and lining, evolving into a bell-shape. Rustling silks and muslin petticoats trimmed with lace and embroidery, were important. The huge sleeves and bell skirt required a pompadour and large hat to balance the figure.

Women of all classes desired and were able to copy the rich and fashionable attire since fashion illustrations and patterns were available, as were the sewing machine and the seamstress. Pictures of society women that appeared in magazines and daily papers were helpful as style clues.

The increase of couturier establishments in Paris was so great that in the year 1898, there were 1932 couturier salons. Worth's was a by-word for fashionable and creative costume; those who could afford it had their clothes made by this designer. Among Worth's clients was J. P. Morgan, who took the women of his family to the famous House of Worth for the distinctive clothes they wore.

Some men attempted to play the part of the "dude," "dandy," "masher," or "swell" with their close-buttoned frock coats, buttonhole flowers, spats, patent leather shoes, and tall silk hats. Professional men including ministers, professors, doctors, and lawyers, wore the frock coat and silk hat.

DRESS

A. *Sources of information:* costumes of the time, photographs, advertisements in magazines, newspapers, and posters, paintings, murals, sculpture, illustrations.

B. MEN
   1. Garments:
      Outer upper: illustrations by Charles Dana Gibson crystallizing the popular idea of the handsome man with square jaw and square-shouldered silhouette; cutaway or frock coat with high lapel; frock coat or Prince Albert with long satin-lined lapel worn by professional man; cutaway or tail coat worn for weddings; loose and boxy suit; fairly long, loose sack coat with long lapel, becoming more popular; *tuxedo;* coat sleeve similar to that of the present day; vest followed style of coat; single or double-breasted vest, occasionally with a collar; deep oval neckline on evening waistcoat; black vest with tuxedo, white with tail coat; vest omitted with light-weight summer *suit* and sportswear; Norfolk jacket; knitted cardigan; slipover sweater; blazer for college, sport, and summer wear.
      Outer lower: tight trousers with cutaway frock coat; fuller trousers with sack coat; cuffs on trousers of informal suit, front crease on fuller trousers; business suit usually with trousers and coat of same material; knickers for sport.

Under: shirt with stiffly-starched front, opening at back, with formal coat or formal business suit; some shirts with pleated and slightly starched shirt-front; detachable cuff; soft shirt with attached collar and cuffs worn by working man, shirt collar usually left open at the neck; *rough rider shirt;* drawers.

Cloaks and overgarments: coat extending to knee, or occasionally a little longer; short coat with velvet collar, narrow at shoulder and wider in the skirt; evening coat with velvet collar; Inverness cape for traveler; caped overcoat.

Neckwear and wristwear: very high, standing collar, with or without corners bent back, wing, or turnover; soft collar worn by cyclist; stiff, cardboard-like band; detachable cuff which showed an inch below the coat sleeve; soft Windsor tie for sport; bow tie; four-in-hand; *ascot tie;* white bow tie for evening dress and sometimes for afternoon wear; black bow tie with tuxedo; black string tie considered conservative.

2. **Hair:** parted in middle or on left side; often brushed backward, fairly long in back; many men clean shaven; mustache turned up and sometimes waxed; *walrus mustache;* pointed and clipped beard worn by a few; sideburns and *mutton chops.*

3. **Headdress:** low-crowned straw hat, sometimes secured by elastic cord to coat lapel; top hat varying in height, curled brim; slouch hat; round felt hat; fedora of velour; bowler or derby; fore-and-aft or visor cap; tam-o'-shanter.

4. **Footwear:** pointed toe worn by fashionable man; shoe to ankle, laced or buttoned; black patent leather shoe with kid or cloth top; patent leather pump with bow of grosgrain ribbon; gaiter discontinued, although light or white spat used with formal dress; woolen hose, black sock worn by most men, sock with colored stripes worn by young man.

5. **Accessories:** umbrella; crook-handled bamboo cane fashionable; monocle worn by a few men; nose glasses or pince-nez on cord; gold-bowed spectacles used by older man; white kid glove for dancing; washable leather or chamois glove worn out-of-doors; belt or suspenders; folding pocket book with small compartments held shut by strap; gold toothpick in pencil-like case.

6. **Jewelry:** very little jewelry worn; watch in vest pocket, watch chain with trinket or emblem, chain often extended across vest, from pocket to pocket, or from pocket to higher buttonhole.

7. **Typical Colors:** gray or tan summer coat, dark winter coat, plaid coat; light, checked or striped trousers worn with dark, formal coat; somber colors with accent of gray-colored necktie and waistcoat; plain, plaid, or checked waistcoat, sometimes of same color as coat;

328

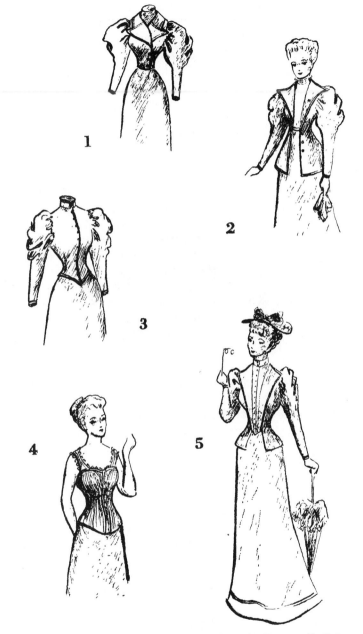

1. Eton Jacket   2. Blazer   3. Reefer   4. Corset   5. Suit

white vest with tail coat, black with tuxedo and sometimes for formal wear; dark informal coat worn with white trousers; black or brown derby; black or striped sock; white, black, or russet-colored shoe; white or light tones for spat.

8. **Typical Materials:** serge, twill, homespun or tweed for suit, blue serge popular; same material used for coat and trousers of business suit; mohair, gray flannel, linen, duck, heavy pongee, and seersucker for summer suit, dark-colored suit for winter; white flannel trousers with dark jacket for summer; stitched, leather glove.

9. **Make-up:** apparently none.

C. WOMEN

1. Garments:

Outer upper: high narrow shoulder line replacing drooping shoulder of the 1880's; close-fitting gown; high neckline for day wear; 1- or 2-inch band of velvet, or white fold, or ruching around neck, sometimes very elaborate ruching; bow often worn at back of neck; illustrations by Charles Dana Gibson influenced styles; severe, starched, turnover collar resembling that worn by man for sport, sailor-collar with bathing, yachting and cycling outfits; square, or heart-shaped neckline for evening dress, or pointed both in back and front, 1892; lace-edged neckline for evening, *c.* 1895; less elaborate neckline at end of century; *Empire style* in 1892; *Princess style* for evening and tea from 1893; huge sleeve and wide shoulder, 1890; *puffed sleeve* in 1892; full sleeve often lined with crinoline or with whalebone hoops; transferable sleeve-bustle; accordion pleating from shoulder to elbow, long cuff below; gigot sleeve, sometimes pointed at wrist; leg-of-mutton sleeve with puff to the elbow, then tight to the wrist, 1893, width obtained in all kinds of ways, gathers, 2 puffs forming a kind of cape; extremely long sleeve, 1895-96; huge sleeve extending off of shoulder or shoulder strap for evening, 1895; sleeve changed, 1896, puff on shoulder with remainder close-fitting; narrow sleeve, by 1898; wasp-waist in this period; very tight lacing, 1891, various kinds of girdles and sashes, some sashes boned; round waistline, 1892, slightly pointed, 1896; lacing in front and in back, 1897; entire dress sometimes accordion pleated, 1896; trimming on bodice with bretelles, ruffles or cascades; draped, pleated or gathered blouse; shirtwaist modeled after man's shirt; separate waist or basque with binding on lower edge, fitting outside of skirt, peplum often used instead of belt.

Outer lower: bustle and drapery disappear, early in the 1890's; plain skirt, no drapery, gores in front with fullness in back, 1890; length to ankle or instep; formal gown to floor, sometimes with train; skirt sometimes open in front showing elaborate petticoat;

1. Umbrella Skirt   2. Balayeuse   3. **Pelisse**   4. Princess Style
5. Pelerine   6. Knickers, Knickerbockers

very tight lacing emphasizing size of hip; gores and *godet pleats* set in below the hip, giving flare to skirt from hip downward; skirt lined 12 inches up from hem with stiff lining, lining in entire skirt, 1891; *Victorian skirt,* 1891; *bell-shaped skirt* in vogue, 1892-1907; widest dimensions of skirt reached, 1896, when skirt with godet pleats measured 9 yards around the bottom, *godet skirt* not so popular toward end of period; pleats often all around the skirt from knee to hem; fullness in back; lined with silk or sateen; ruffles used beneath bottom of dress skirt to make skirt rustle; mohair braid and bias velvet sewed inside of hem of woolen or silk skirt as protection from wear; skirt carried over arm in order to show ruffles, but at the same time considered improper to show ankle; flounces on gored skirt, 1898; sport skirt narrower than regular skirt; waterfall drapery or fan-pleated train; *la Pliante; yoke-skirt; sun-ray skirt;* attention to hip and emphasis on rounded hip, toward end of period; pocket sewed in day skirt inside the front or side-back just above knee; suit skirt usually plain or trimmed with braid; *Rainy Daisy skirt; umbrella skirt; balayeuse,* dust ruffle or street sweeper.
Under: underwear very fine; knitted vest, chemise, or union suit worn under corset, until 1905; very elaborate muslin drawers with lace flounces as wide as petticoat; knickers or bloomers also worn; short muslin or flannel petticoat; 2 starched, white, ruffled petticoats worn; petticoat edged with knife-pleated ruffles, cambric skirt also with lace-edged ruffles; dust ruffle or streetsweeper; small bustle or pad; beautiful corset with shorter stays; excessive lacing to retain waist at 21 inches; tight corset worn high in front in order to give upward tilt to bust; lacing declined by end of period; *bust improver;* corset cover; petticoat bodice; camisole; *figure improver.*
Cloaks and overgarments: very long, circular mantle with high puffs at shoulders, 1890's; pelerine or shoulder cape; *Tudor cape;* pelisse; redingote, also a short coat of similar cut; coat with 2 capes; capuchon hood on cape used for travel; evening coat with puffed sleeve or loose dolman sleeve; semicircular reversible golf cape, plaid on 1 side and plain on other, also, very popular for traveling; *reefer;* blue serge jacket over starched white shirt front; knee-length or hip-length jacket; figaro jacket, 1892; zouave jacket; vest in 1893; *Prince Rupert;* jacket with sleeves became possible because of smaller sleeve in dress; some jackets with short cape over each sleeve; cardigan; sweater; jersey sweater; Norfolk jacket; Eton jacket; bolero; frog fastening on coats.
Additional garments: coat suit very popular in early part of 1890's, hip-length, box coat fashionable, or coat with fitted back; suit hav-

1. Gigot Sleeve   2. Bell-shaped Skirt   3. Bolero
4. Sun-ray Skirt   5. Puffed Sleeve   6. Polonaise

ing coat with balloon sleeves worn for semiformal; negligee; tea jacket; tea gown with Watteau pleat; day gown; walking dress; trim, tailor-made costume in first of period; visiting dress; afternoon dress; seaside frock; cycling dress; tennis dress; jersey dress; riding dress; bathing suit with high neckline, short skirt and bloomers; yachting costumes with sailor collars; ankle-length skirt or bloomers for bicycling; transparent overdress decorated with spangles, 1896; polonaise; tunic dress, 1899.

2. **Hair:** catogan not popular, 1890's; hair worn back from forehead; psyche knot, a Grecian style; sometimes hair parted smoothly with flat knot on top; knot at back or French twist at back, lower part of ears showing; in general, head appearing small, until *c.* 1896; looser coiffure, after 1894; hair pad used late in period; aigrette worn in hair for evening; flowers or bow; jeweled combs at sides and back of top knot.

3. **Headdress:** hat worn for all occasions, traveling, yachting; bonnet with wide ribbon at first; later, day cap worn only by elderly woman; tam-o'-shanter; leghorn hat for summer; toque; hat small at first with upright trimming, perched on head, then slanted forward on brow, after 1897; height emphasized, after 1894; hat large, *c.* 1895; occasionally marquis or 3-corner hat; plain, mannish, straw hat for severely tailored outfit introduced, end of 1880's, continuing very popular; mannish fedora for sport; other styles with all kinds of elaborate decoration adding to height of hat, flowers, especially roses, ostrich plumes, Mercury wings, aigrettes, other feathers or entire bird, ribbon bows, lace, chiffon frills; very large hat later in the period; toque in vogue but not the bonnet; face veil popular and worn across the face covering the chin.

4. **Footwear:** tight, long-pointed shoe, very high French heel, especially for evening; gilt leather slipper often for evening; high shoe of patent leather or kid with light kid or cloth upper for street; slipper with tongue and buckle, or bow used, 1895, sometimes a strap; high, laced or buttoned shoe; low-heeled, black or tan, laced boot, or half-shoe with *legging* worn for sport; gaiter worn with walking dress; stocking with silk foot and cotton top, 1890's; black stocking with black, russet, or white shoe; brown or white stocking with shoe of same color, after 1896; perpendicular stripes woven in stocking for evening; sometimes embroidery or lace insertion on instep, after 1895; stocking of lisle or wool; silk hose a luxury.

5. **Accessories:** *chatelaine bag* or hand purse hooked to belt; lorgnette for smart woman; muff, small or large and flat; fur necklet, feather boa; 4-button glove with long sleeve, long glove with short sleeve,

334

card case; buckled belt with shirtwaist; sash for white or light-colored dress; small, delicate fan, folding wheel-shaped fan; long-handled umbrella, the handle tipped with gold and mother-of-pearl; small parasol, often of lace and elaborate; very elaborate long hatpin; gold pen with mother-of-pearl holder.

6. Jewelry: gold or silver watch with fob, worn in pocket at belt, or hooked on fleur-de-lis or bow knot ornament of same metal on left shoulder; elaborate and rather large locket on chain, sometimes heart-shaped, very delicate locket on short chain for evening; earrings not in style; turquoise and paste ornaments, 1895; dog collar of precious stones for evening; delicate pin of brilliants, diamonds, or pearls used to fasten high collar or as an ornament; very narrow wedding ring; diamond solitaire engagement ring; bracelet of links fastened by small heart-shaped padlock; bangle bracelet.

7. Typical Colors: special thought given to color harmony; bright plaid, checks, stripes; Persian designs on India silk; flowers printed on white or pastel color; small figures on black, white or colored background; deep, strong colors as well as delicate; silver-gray and pink; black, white or colored, thin fabric worn over brilliant color, as blue, red, green, peach, and orange; dark skirt with brilliantly colored blouse; plain red jacket with striped skirt; suit with colored facing; bodice contrasting in color with skirt; black or bright red umbrella; light-colored parasol.

8. Typical Materials: crepe, crepon, poplin, batiste, piqué, or silk dress; wool vest; voile, silk gauze, lace for sleeve and flounce; gold tinsel; satin, velvet, piqué, or heavy fabric for skirt; fur, satin, taffeta, faille, or chiffon cape; seal, mink, Persian lamb, sable, chinchilla, or ermine fur; suede glove, washable leather glove for summer, haircloth or crinoline for lining; additional materials: lawn, mousselaine-de-laine, grenadine, organdie, crepe lisse; foulard, taffeta, velvet, tarlatan, gingham, linen, muslin, seersucker, pongee, duck, dotted swiss, net dimity, mohair or cloth made of goat's hair; silk or cotton umbrella; chatelaine bag of pin-seal.

9. Make-up: starch used as face powder.

SIGNIFICANT MOTIFS

The motifs of this period were not as unique as they were taken from all previous periods, the favorite influence being that of Louis XVI.

INFLUENCES ON LATER COSTUMES

Petticoat with pleated ruffles, 1948; bell skirt, 1948 and '52; suits in all later periods; bloomers worn for gymnastic exercises, first of 20th century; black, white, or colored transparent fabric used over bright-colored silk, 20th century.

BOOKS OF REFERENCE

(See Books of Reference, Part I, *19th Century*, p. 268, and General Bibliography, p. 433)

ARTISTS FOR COSTUME REFERENCE

(See p. 269)

GLOSSARY

Accordion Pleating—refer to *Chaps. 2, 8.*
Aigrette—refer to *Chaps. 3, 16, 19.*
Ascot Tie—wide hanging tie with 1 end twisted and thrown over the other end.
Balayeuse, Dust Ruffle or Street Sweeper—refer to *Chap. 19. Pl. XLVI, 2.*
Basque—refer to *Chaps. 18, 19.*
Bell-shaped Skirt—very full skirt shaped like a bell. *Pl. XLVII, 2.*
Blazer—refer to *Chap. 19. Pl. XLV, 2.*
Bolero—refer to *Chaps. 12, 18. Pl. XLVII, 3.*
Bowler or Derby—refer to *Chaps. 18, 19.*
Bretelles—refer to *Chaps. 16, 18.*
Bust Improver—device used to make the bust appear larger.
Bustle—refer to *Chaps. 12, 15, 18, 19.*
Camisole—refer to *Chaps. 17, 19.*
Capuchon—refer to *Chaps. 5, 9, 11, 12, 13, 17, 19.*
Cardigan—refer to *Chap. 19.*
Catogan—refer to *Chaps. 12, 13, 14, 18.*
Chatelaine Bag—pouch bag of pin-seal, attached to belt. Refer to *Chatelaine, Chaps. 14, 16.*
Chemise—refer to *Chaps. 6, 7, 8, 9, 10, 12, 13, 14, 15, 16, 17, 18, 19.*
Corset—refer to *Chaps. 8, 9, 10, 11, 12, 13, 14, 15, 16, 17, 18, 19. Pl. XLV, 4.*
Dog Collar—refer to *Chaps. 3, 7, 18.*
Dolman Sleeve—refer to *Chap. 19.*
Derby—refer to *Bowler.*
Dude—man with certain affectations; a dandy.
Dust Ruffle—refer to *Balayeuse.*
Empire Style—close-fitting dress with high waist, similar in style to garment worn by woman during the Empire period.
Eton Jacket—refer to *Chap. 19. Pl. XLV, 1.*
Fedora—refer to *Chap. 19.*
Figaro Jacket—close-fitting jacket with an epaulette on each shoulder. Refer to *Chaps. 18, 19.*
Figure Improver—form of small bustle.
Fleur-de-lis—refer to *Chap. 8.*
Fore-and-aft Cap—refer to *Chap. 19.*
Four-in-hand—refer to *Chap. 19.*

CHAPTER 20: GLOSSARY

Frock Coat or Prince Albert Coat—refer to *Chaps. 16, 17, 18, 19.*

Frog Fastening—refer to *Chap. 16.*

Gaiter—refer to *Chaps. 13, 14, 15, 16, 17, 18, 19.*

Gigot Sleeve—full sleeve with more fullness at elbow than at shoulder or wrist. Refer to *Chap. 16. Pl. XLVII, 1.*

Godet Pleats—fluting held in place by a fine steel in the hem, used on back and sides of skirt.

Godet Skirt—skirt with pleats at back and sides.

Inverness Cape—refer to *Chaps. 18, 19.*

Knickers, Knickerbockers—full breeches, gathered or pleated into kneebands and buckled at the knee. Refer to *Knickerbockers, Chap. 19. Pl. XLVI, 6.*

La Pliant—invention of 1896, consisting of pieces of steel, encased in cotton or silk ribbon tapes, which held out the stiff and heavy skirt in the back, much lighter than numerous petticoats. It was possible to transfer these steels to different skirts.

Leggings—fitted coverings for the legs, usually fastened with a strap under the shoe, and extending above the knee or to the waist.

Leg-of-mutton Sleeve—refer to *Chaps. 9, 10, 16.*

Mutton Chops—whiskers on lower sides of face.

Norfolk Jacket—refer to *Chap. 19.*

Pelerine—refer to *Chaps. 12, 13, 15, 16, 17, 19. Pl. XLVI, 5.*

Pelisse—refer to *Chaps. 13, 14, 15, 16. Pl. XLVI, 3.*

Peplum—refer to *Chaps. 11, 12, 13, 18.*

Petticoat—refer to *Chaps. 9, 10, 11, 12, 13, 14, 15, 16, 17, 18, 19.*

Polonaise—refer to *Chaps. 13, 14, 17, 18, 19. Pl. XLVII, 6.*

Prince Albert Coat—refer to *Frock Coat.*

Prince Rupert—velvet or plush jacket worn open at front, and resembling the long Louis XV coat.

Princess Style—refer to *Princess Dress, Chap. 19. Pl. XLVI, 4.*

Psyche Knot—refer to *Chap. 4.*

Puffed Sleeve—sleeve having large puff from shoulder to elbow. *Pl. XLVII, 5.*

Rainy Daisy Skirt—nickname given to a woman who belonged to the Rainy Day Club, and who wore a rainy daisy or walking skirt 2 or 3 inches from the ground. The dress was worn usually during rainy weather.

Redingote—outdoor garment which often had fitted back and semi-fitted open front. Refer to *Chaps. 14, 15, 16, 18.*

Reefer—close-fitting jacket, often double-breasted. *Pl. XLV, 3.*

Rough Rider Shirt—khaki shirt similar to that worn by Theodore Roosevelt and his cavalry in Cuba during the Spanish-American War in 1898.

Spat—refer to *Chap. 19.*

Street Sweeper—refer to *Balayeuse.*

Suit—separate coat and skirt worn as dress or outdoor garment. *Pl. XLV, 5.*

Sun-ray Skirt—skirt with accordion pleating. *Pl. XLVII, 4.*

Tam-o'-shanter—refer to *Chap. 19.*

Toque—*refer to Chaps. 2, 10, 16, 19.*

Tudor Cape—short, circular cape having pointed yoke in front and back, and an epaulette on each shoulder.

Tunic Dress—close-fitting dress.

Tuxedo—informal dinner jacket introduced from England; name given to this coat is of American origin.

Umbrella Skirt—full, bell-shaped skirt. *Pl. XLVI, 1.*

Veil—refer to *Chaps. 3, 4, 5, 6, 7, 8, 9, 10, 15, 16, 17, 18, 19.*

Victorian Skirt—skirt with fullness at back, and flaring out around the knee.

Walrus Moustache—drooping and somewhat large moustache.

Waterfall Drapery—refer to *Waterfall Back, Chap. 19.*

Watteau Pleat—refer to *Chap. 13.*

Windsor Tie—refer to *Chap. 19.*

Wing Collar—refer to *Chap. 19.*

Yoke Skirt—skirt which had a shaped piece in front and 2 side pieces which extended around hips, and joined in the back. The lower part of the skirt was attached to this yoke.

Zouave Jacket—refer to *Chaps. 18, 19.*

20th Century

PART I

1900-13

CHRONOLOGY

Subway in New York City in *1900* preceded by subways in London, Budapest, and Paris.

Currency Act in the United States, *1900.*

First wireless message sent across the Atlantic by Guglielmo Marchese Marconi, Italy, *1901.*

Separation of Church and State in France due to Dreyfus case with defeat for clergy, monarchists and army, but victory for the republic, *1901-5.*

Education Act for elementary and secondary schools in England, *1902.*

French rights of Panama canal bought by United States, *June 28, 1902.*

First successful airplane flight with a motor-driven plane made by Wilbur and Orville Wright, at Kitty Hawk, North Carolina, *1903.*

Russo-Japanese War, *1904-5.*

Night work by women prohibited, *1906.*

United States Pure Food and Drug Act, *1906.*

Manufacture of inexpensive automobile by Henry Ford making it possible for many people to have individual transportation, *1909.*

North Pole claimed to have been discovered by Robert Edwin Peary, *April 6, 1909.*

China declared a Republic, *1911.*

Revolution in Mexico, *1911.*

United States Federal Income Tax, *1913.*

Federal Reserve Bank in United States, *1913.*

Law for decrease of military service, France, *1913.*

CHAPTER 21

20th Century

PART I

1900-13

HISTORY

The United States through these years was becoming an important power in international affairs. The Treaty of peace between Russia and Japan was settled with the help of the United States. The latter country negotiated for the Canal in the Isthmus of Panama, which had been started by the Lesseps company; in 1902 the completion of this Canal was authorized by Congress, provided the President could obtain the rights from the New French Canal Company for the price of $40,000,000, and the consent of the Colombian government to proceed. After the Colombian government refused to ratify the agreement, Panama revolted, and became independent. The Panama Canal was built in the ten-mile canal zone and was opened in 1904.

Theodore Roosevelt, the President of the United States, had become an influential figure both at home and abroad. This era has been called the age of "muck-raking." Periodicals carried articles pertaining to corruption in politics and enterprises, and suggested reforms. The Sherman Antitrust Law that had been passed in the latter part of the 19th century was enforced against trusts.

France became interested in territorial expansion in both Asia and Africa, and signed an agreement with Italy which gave a free hand to France in Morocco and the same privilege to Italy in Tripoli. Italy was experiencing growth in socialism and organization of labor.

In England there was continued interest by both the Conservative and Liberal parties in territorial expansion. Egypt came under the power of Great Britain.

The second Naval Law in Germany provided for an extensive building program over a period of seventeen years. Germany decided that her naval power should rank second only to England. The Army and Finance bills of 1913 provided for enormous increases: an addition of 4,000 officers and a large number of noncommissioned officers and men was made in order to extend the number of the peacetime army to 870,000 men.

Germany was leading the world in education and scientific research. Furthermore, she was becoming a manufacturing and trading power. The Hohenzollern dynasty inflated the patriotic vanity of the Germans, and controlled the teachings in the schools and colleges until the young German thought that he was of a chosen race. Nationalism developed in England and France, but not to the extent that it did in Germany.

The cinema became popular in the United States during this period and was beginning to have an influence on the youth of the day. Likewise, the automobile shows of 1900 attracted much attention and many wealthy people owned the new conveyance which would become a necessity in a couple of decades. Various cars were used—gasoline, steam and electric, the latter being popular among the ladies.

Social and Political Unions for women were founded in 1913. In England, woman demanded her rights through force and at times set fire to property and even fought the police. There was scarcely any suffrage for woman except in the United States and England, although in some parts of Europe a woman could own property. Woman was becoming economically independent as her number increased in the clerical, trade, and professional groups.

The inartistic architecture and furnishings of the preceding period showed new variations in the ugly, turreted houses, rooms with fussy trimmings, golden oak furniture and interior trim, parlors with drawn curtains, and heavy overdrapes.

France was still the fashion leader. In 1900, the display of models of dresses on wax figures was introduced. The hour-glass silhouette continued in the first years of the century. The new corset of 1902 brought about a new silhouette, completely disguising the curves of abdomen and hip. Although there was still an emphasis on the correct costume for the occasion, there was much incongruity. For example, the hobble skirt of 1914 was worn even on long walking excursions. The slit skirt of the same year brought protests from bishops and ministers. Sport clothes proved to be a more useful attire. The tailored suit was a favorite of many women, and a severe type known as the shirtwaist suit was in fashion.

CHAPTER 21: DRESS

The costume of the man changed also, and emphasis was placed on the high, padded shoulder. Less formality was shown in masculine attire than in the preceding periods of dress. Clothing now gave a man an athletic appearance. Peg-top trousers were worn with a longer coat. A shorter coat came into style about 1912. The majority of suits worn were ready-made.

DRESS

A. *Sources of information:* costumes of the period, fashion magazines, paintings, photographs, movies, and literature.

B. **MEN**

1. Garments:

Outer upper: loose coat; broad, padded shoulder greatly exaggerated, by 1910; man's silhouette resembling an athlete or a prizefighter; sleeve with button at wrist; long-waisted shapeless sack coat with rather high lapel, fairly long, 1900-10, then shorter coat with soft roll lapel worn by older man of distinction, until First World War; cutaway coat for formal tea, garden party, reception, and other daytime social function; tuxedo worn for formal or semi-formal occasion; low-cut vest matching business suit, low, buttoned lapel; sometimes double-breasted vest with rolled collar for frock coat; evening vest cut very low; black vest with tuxedo, white vest with tail coat; lounge suit; V-neck, slip-on sweater; heavy, high-neck, or *turtle-neck*, jersey sweater; cardigan; *Norfolk jacket.*

Outer lower: trousers short enough to show the ankle, after 1908; sometimes cuff on informal trousers, after 1908; *peg-top trousers,* pleated at waist with trouser leg creased at back and front, 1911-13; trousers with matched coat or sometimes coat of lighter color; knickers for sport.

Under: red flannel underwear still worn for very cold weather; dress shirt with stiffly-starched shirt front; gloss-starched shirt bosoms; stiff, finely-pleated shirt front worn with dinner jacket, or tail coat; silk shirt, 1912-14; soft-bosomed, colored, striped shirt with attached collar and cuff for informal wear.

Cloaks and overgarments: duster; Mackintosh for wet weather; woolen or fur coat; long overcoat or top coat; driving coat; short, plaid, or tweed coat with *Raglan sleeve;* Inverness cape discontinued; black coat with waist-length cape, for evening wear.

Neckwear and wristwear: very high, uncomfortable collar; round,

343

turnover, or wing; white bow tie for evening; black tie with dinner jacket; ascot tie; four-in-hand tie very popular; string tie worn occasionally by older man; cambric frilled or pleated shirt front seldom worn, after 1910; black satin stock worn with dress suit by few; stiff cuff worn for day as well as evening dress, less of cuff showing beneath coat sleeve than formerly.

2. **Hair:** usually parted in middle or brushed from sides across temples, until 1905; side part popular, after 1905; hair cut closer than formerly; middle part discontinued, 1910; pompadour fashionable, after 1910; bald-headed man often wearing toupee; Van Dyck beard worn by doctor or lawyer; clipped beard; walrus mustache worn by middle-aged man, waxed mustache by young man, 1900-15; or mustache clipped close to upper lip by older man; usually clean shaven.

3. **Headdress:** *Panama,* or stiff straw hat worn from beginning of month of May until Labor Day or the end of summer in the United States; higher crown and broader brim than 1890's; felt hat shaped similar to straw hat worn by young man; small collegiate cap with visor; · *opera hat;* fedora with higher crown; slouch hat; cap; bowler or derby; *Homburg.*

4. **Footwear:** beginning of modern shoemaking, 1900; round toe, *bulldog toe,* 1910, especially worn by college man; then fairly long vamp with pointed toe; high, laced shoe for winter, white canvas, for summer, and with rubber sole for tennis; button shoe; patent leather pump for dancing, patent leather oxford, by 1912; sock with design of dots, circles, squares, or horizontal or vertical stripes; spat worn with cutaway coat; woolen stocking with knickers; garter.

5. **Accessories:** large black umbrella with curved handle; large, heavy walking stick; bamboo cane, 1900-10; nose glasses sometimes with heavy cord and loop over ear or around neck; monocle; *muffler;* glove worn for every occasion, white glove for formal wear, until 1914; pipe, especially for college man; belt used instead of suspenders; cigarette case a necessity due to general use of cigarettes; pocketbook opening with clasp.

6. **Jewelry:** tie pin for daytime, sometimes the only jewelry worn; signet ring; cuff links, waistcoat buttons and shirt studs of gold or silver in sets ornamented with enamel or semiprecious stones, such as lapis lazuli or jade; fraternity pin; watch and watch fob usually with lodge or school emblem; wristwatch, 1914.

7. **Typical Colors:** black, white, dark blue, gray, brown, and green; either blue or gray with white pin stripe for suit; black frock coat worn with light gray striped trousers and pearl gray vest; black vest

with dinner jacket; white vest with tailed coat; salt and pepper mixture, or black and white for less formal cutaway; dark blue serge sack coat with white trousers for summer; black or brown derby, the latter considered flashy; white, tan, or black oxford; bright-colored sock; light-colored or black spat.

8. **Typical Materials:** all types of fabric in vogue; broadcloth for formal suit; serge or tweed sack suit; palm beach, linen or seersucker for summer; duck, or white flannel trousers with blue serge or pin-striped coat; cashmere, piqué, corded silk, or checked vest, buttons on vest often of gold with semiprecious stones to match cuff links and shirt studs; tweed or homespun knickers; tan or black shoe; black, white, or gay-colored sock; pearl gray spat with formal wear, white sometimes for other occasions, also worn with low shoe in winter.

9. **Make-up:** None.

C. WOMEN

1. Garments:

Outer upper: hourglass silhouette in early 1900's; continuation of influence of the Gibson Girl; bertha; informal gown with neckline to base of throat; high collar on street dress, until 1910; collar to base of throat, 1912; low V-shaped neckline, by 1914; bateau neckline; drop shoulder and strap instead of sleeve for evening dress, 1900-8, square or round neckline instead of drop shoulder, remainder of period; shoulder emphasized with horizontal lines; drop shoulder disappeared entirely, by 1914; low V-neckline in front and back worn by extremist, also heart-shaped, square, or bateau neckline, 1910; fine lace and fine fabric of guimpe displayed at neck; sleeve narrow from shoulder to elbow, then full, and gathered at wrist, 1901-3; tight from cuff to elbow, with fullness blousing on upper arm, 1903; leg-of-mutton sleeve; bishop sleeve, 1904-6; sometimes bell-shaped sleeve with full undersleeve; puff sleeve, 1908; *kimono sleeve* introduced, 1910; long, snug, set-in sleeve worn, until 1914; 3-quarter length sleeve or ruffle from elbow, for afternoon and evening; waistline dipped in front, 1900-5, due to pull of tape which fastened waist and skirt, narrow belt worn with this type of costume; 1-piece dress sometimes worn; round waistline with wide girdle, from 1900-3; belt about 2 inches wide with no dip, a transition to a higher waistline; pleated and tucked shirtwaist very popular, 1906-7; scanty dress with narrow shoulder, high waist with no evidence of boning, and narrow sleeve, similar to Empire period, 1908-10; sashed waistline; tunic dress with straight up-and-down silhouette, 1912; waistline of 1-piece dress higher than normal; basque worn again, 1912; loosely bloused waist, 1900-8; fullness in waist making figure appear large in the bust; thin white blouse often worn with an underwaist of pale pink, blue China silk, or muslin, Irish crochet used as trimming, until 1912; *Gibson Girl blouse; Gibson pleat;* blouse with kimono sleeve worn with suit, 1912; white wash-waist or waist of dark silk or thin chiffon; *peek-a-boo* waist; waist often fastened down the back with visible buttons or with buttons under a flap.

Outer lower: skirt smooth at top, flaring from hip to ground, until 1908; *morning-glory* or *serpentine skirt,* until 1908; skirt also with fullness at waist and with a graceful flair to floor, 1904; fullness at back of skirt; gores set in pleats and stitched part way down, 1905-9; skirt clearing the ground, by 1908; ankle-length skirt worn by most women, by 1909; circular skirt; sometimes gored or circular skirt on yoke but without emphasis on hip, after 1909; full skirt discontinued, 1910; *hobble skirt,* 1910-14; very tight clothing brought about *harem skirt,* 1911; train worn on evening dress and some calling dresses, until 1912; train looped up by cord when dancing; *slit skirt; peg-top skirt,* c. 1914; dress gradually became fuller, even the housedress with fuller lines; bell-shape flounces over hobble skirt, a prediction of crinoline, 1913-14.

Under: knitted chemise or sleeveless vest and knee-length drawers, or union suit until 1905 and later; corset and corset cover; pink and blue ribbon used in lingerie; muslin drawers; *pettibockers;* short muslin or flannel petticoat; then combination of corset cover and short petticoat; drawers and corset cover superseded by chemise in 1905; combination still worn by some women; circular, *umbrella drawers,* 1908; 1 petticoat used instead of 6 or 7; petticoat of taffeta with a number of ruffles from the knee down, or muslin skirt with lace trimmed flounces, and flannel petticoat, until 1910; starch not used for linen, and softer fabrics, by 1910; silk underwear worn by some; straight-front corset with wasp or very small waist, 1900, low-busted corset, length to below hip; corset pulled down by supporters, giving an oblique front line, and making the person seem to lean forward when walking; wide-boned girdle coming only to waistline, 1906; lower-busted and very long-skirted corset, 1908; starched ruffles worn to make the bust appear larger; *bust extender* in 1909; bust smaller and flattened with brassière, 1910; rigid figure changed to a drooping, spineless pose, affected, 1911; shorter girdle often worn; corset discontinued by many girls, 1912.

Cloaks and overgarments: short snug-fitting jacket of beaver, seal, squirrel, and other short-haired fur, 1900-5; figaro jacket worn until 1907; other coats with collar, lapel and cuff of masculine

346

1. Kimono Sleeve   2. Four-in-hand Tie   3. Bishop Sleeve, Bertha
4. Umbrella Drawers   5. Dog Collar

type; pelisse; cape, box coat; semifitting coat; hip-length tailored jacket, longer in back, 1907, straight around lower edge, 1909-10; snug-fitting evening jacket before 1910; dolman, 1910-12; cardigan; Norfolk, or jersey sweater; turtle-neck sweater; Eton jacket; *Balkan blouse;* traveling coat with Raglan sleeve; natural linen duster for driving and motoring; Mackintosh.

Neckwear and wristwear: stock made of black ribbon, worn with shirtwaist and street suit, 1901-6; thick ruching at neck, *c.* 1905; cascade of lace, or puffs of chiffon on high collar; fairly low, starched, turnover collar, 1900-5; high, starched collar, until 1910, boned collar, after 1905, high in back and on sides; mannish turn-over collar with tailored shirtwaist, 1908-11; bow at back, 1900-5, then large bow in front; *Buster Brown collar; Peter Pan collar;* Windsor or four-in-hand tie; pleated frill or jabot, 1908-11; collar not high, 1912.

Additional garments: English influence on sports wear, 1904-14; severely tailored suit; severe jacket with short flare a little below hip, worn with peg-top skirt; *Napoleon costume;* negligee with high neckline until 1905, low neck and short sleeve, after 1908; pajama worn at end of period; *X-ray dress;* tea gown; dressing sack; *Mother Hubbard; kimono; wrapper; bungalow apron,* 1910-20; bathing suit designed for swimming; *Gym bloomers.*

2. **Hair:** hair ornaments, including ribbon bows, and jewels during entire period; wide pompadour at first, protruding over forehead, 1900-8; looped over one eye and flatter on sides with back hair in psyche knot, figure-of-eight, or in a French twist on top, 1903-5; parted in the middle, 1904; puffed at sides, with knot on top, 1906-10; much false hair switch, or *rat* of artificial or real hair, or of fine wire netting used, or own hair snarled; many puffs; sometimes braids; *Marcel wave;* curling iron used, before 1907; puff or psyche knot worn in back, 1910-12; pompadour with cluster of curls, 1911; false hair, such as a braid, *switch,* curls or puffs continued to be popular; hairdress smaller, by 1914, parted in middle with knot in back, or braids over ears or crossed in back.

3. **Headdress:** sunbonnet of colored fabric, trimmed in ruffles; bonnet or round hat; trimming of feathers or flowers and ribbon; Gains-borough hat; *Merry Widow hat* with plumes, *c.* 1907-8; large beaver hat, 1909-11; small sailor set straight on the head, or farther back when worn with pompadour; large hat set forward on head; hat of huge dimensions with uncurled ostrich feathers continued to be worn for 5 or 6 years, then small hat with trimming of a few flowers or heron plumes; tricorne hat; *mushroom style hat,* 1909; higher crown and drooping brim because of smaller hairdress, after 1910;

1. Leg-of-mutton Sleeve   2. Kimono Sleeve   3. Peg-top Skirt
4. Slit Skirt   5. Morning-glory Skirt

scant but elegant trimming; toque; opera toque or lace head-covering for evening because of law against wearing large hat in theatre; brim narrow and turned-up, 1911; crown lower, by 1913, law passed making it illegal to sell plumage of wild birds unless imported prior to October 3, 1913; very little trimming on hat, 1914; woolen stocking cap for sport; comb, ribbon, bow, flowers or other kind of decoration worn with top-knot hairdress; even a diadem worn with the psyche knot; small face-veil pulled down over chin, 1900-9, tied at back of hat; sometimes long, loose veil draped back over hat; veil completely encasing head, 1909-11; curtain veil, 1912; automobile veil, necessary because of open cars, 1900-12; some veils extended only to below the nose, 1913-14.

4. **Footwear:** high, buttoned or laced boot; patent leather shoe with cloth top; spat often worn with oxford or pump, after 1908; pump for summer, worn by young lady, 1908-14; low-heeled walking shoe; *Baby Louis heel* or high heel on evening pump; long vamp, pointed toe; Colonial pump; ballet-type slipper; white canvas shoe for summer, with rubber sole for tennis; beaded slipper; dress shoe with silk or thin kid top; pump with strap, after 1910; cotton or lisle stocking for everyday use until 1912; elaborate open-work in silk stocking worn with party slipper; silk hose considered a luxury during most of period; overshoe; toe rubber; fur-trimmed carriage boot for evening; leggings.

5. **Accessories:** long hatpin of elaborate and fancy design, 1907-10, shorter and less elaborate hatpin after 1910; shell hairpin; *barette* and fancy side combs to hold hair in place; ribbon bow worn in hair; muffler; *fascinator;* chiffon, lace or silk scarf worn over head for evening or party, also when driving in motor car, the latter type of veil, very long and tied under chin; long fluffy *boa* and large fur muff, 1905, sometimes boa of ostrich feathers; large muff carried and held up against low-necked coat for warmth, 1909-11; barrel-shaped muff, 1912-13, sprig of holly worn on muff, loop of ribbon or shell bracelet attached to muff for convenience in carrying, sometimes *marabou* muff and neckpiece; long-handled, large, dark blue or black umbrella; fluffy parasol of silk or pongee; ballroom fan sometimes hung by chain around the neck or carried in hand, 1900-12; party bag; slipper bag containing evening slipper by those who walked to party, or went by street car; corsage for evening sent by escort; real or artificial flowers for evening and daytime wear; glove important, white unwashable glove worn with suit during last of period, long glove with 3-quarter length sleeve, glove fitting hand snugly, often worn with hand of glove rolled back through wrist opening, sometimes longer glove wrinkled

350

1. Hobble Skirt   2. Wing Collar   3. Bateau Neckline
4. Derby   5. Jabot   6. Baby Louis Heel   7. Bishop Sleeve

down at wrist, long white glove with evening dress, chatelaine bag hooked to belt, 1906; bag or purse of varied style and color, after 1906; hand-tooled leather bag, 1906-8; *mesh bag* for evening, 1908-9; tapestry; brocade, alligator, or silver or gold mesh bag, 1912-14.

6. **Jewelry:** dog collar; exquisite small pins, after 1906, sunburst diamond breast pin, or other pin worn in lace trimming of waist, bar pin or bow at collar, delicately shaped clover leaf, wreath, horseshoe, or crescent pin, heavy breast pin out of style, fraternity or sorority pin, baby pins single or grouped together, on high collar; silver or gold, linked bracelet, until 1909, hinged circular bracelet about 1911; bangle bracelet, *friendship bracelet*, hinged lockets of various shapes including heart-shape; gold cross; lavalliere; watch worn on shirtwaist or blouse, in pocket of jacket, or in belt, attached to fob; long watch chain, after 1907, short chain, 1909-12, wrist watch, *c.* 1912; narrow wedding ring; usually a diamond, set very high in solitaire ring, worn by graduate or engaged girl; jewels worn in hair.

7. **Typical Colors:** usually subdued colors, 1900-10; baby blue, shell pink, maize, and orchid for evening dress; sometimes white, black and white, navy blue, tan, brown, or steel gray with accents of bright or pastel color; beautiful combinations of brown in a costume; shepherd's plaid or small checks in black and white; Scotch plaid, 1908-9; and after 1912, gay colors including American beauty, cerise, bright blue, blue-green, and orange; light colors for summer; black, bronze, white, or colored shoe to match evening dress; black hose and white canvas shoe.

8. **Typical Materials:** broadcloth tailored suit; serge or tweed dressmaker suit; light wool summer suit; fringe trimming, 1907; monkey fur, red or blue fox, or marabou neckpiece and muff; underwear knitted of cotton considered more healthful than that of wool, 1910; batiste and organdy, pineapple gauze, silk muslin, marquisette, raw silk or pongee for summer dress; taffeta, satin, silk crepe, velvet, and brocade popular for evening; soft silk for church and reception; slenderness emphasized with clinging material, 1908-9; alpaca, pongee, natural linen for automobile duster; velvet, satin, silk, straw, or lace hat; calf, patent leather, or kid pump; satin evening slipper sometimes beaded, trimmed with rosette or bow; white canvas or buckram shoe; black and gun metal shoe; rubber-soled white canvas shoe for tennis; lace and embroidery, muslin, or fine linen for lingerie, until 1910; handkerchief linen, dimity, dotted Swiss for dress and blouse; open work embroidered cotton cloth for waist and dress; softer, finer cotton fabric available, after 1910;

352

CHAPTER 21: DRESS

Irish lace, 1910, Cluny lace, 1911; velveteen or dark blue serge for suit after 1911; silk for dress worn under coat in winter.

9. **Make-up:** practically none, although used secretly by some; emphasis on cultivating beauty from within; cornstarch powder, 1910; make-up considered too worldly by respectable middle class.

SIGNIFICANT MOTIFS

Motifs continued to be drawn from preceding periods.

INFLUENCES ON LATER COSTUMES

Friendship bracelet, early 1940's; the Gibson Girl, 1948 and 1952; slit skirt, 1948-49; silk underwear which has continued to the present; dog collar, 1949, reminiscent of this period; real and artificial flowers worn, 1940's and '50's.

BOOKS OF REFERENCE

(See also GENERAL BIBLIOGRAPHY, p. 433)

Bell, Quentin, *On Human Finery* (New York, A. A. Wyn, Inc., 1949)

Downey, Fairfax, *Portrait of an Era* (as drawn by Charles Dana Gibson) (New York, Charles Scribner's Sons, 1936)

Fifty Years of Fashion (New York, Fairchild Publications, 1950)

Lhuer, Victor, *Le Costume Breton de 1900 jusqu'à Nos Jours* (Paris, Au Moulin de Pen Mur, 1943)

Hall, Carrie A., *From Hoop Skirts to Nudity* (Caldwell, Ida., The Caxton Printers, 1938)

Hoes, Rose Gouverneur, *The Dresses of the Mistresses of the White House* (Washington, D. C., Historical Publishing Co., 1931)

Kerr, Rose Netzorg, *100 Years of Costumes in America* (New York, The Davis Press, 1951)

Laver, James, *Taste and Fashion: From the French Revolution Until Today* (London, George C. Harrap and Co., Ltd., 1945)

Men's Wear; Sports Wear Guide (New York, Fairchild Publications, 1949)

Price, Julius M., *Dame Fashion, Paris-London* (New York, Charles Scribner's Sons, 1912)

Ryan, Mildred Graves, *Your Clothes and Personality* (New York, Appleton-Century-Crofts, Inc., 1949)

———, and Phillips, Velma, *Clothes for You* (New York, Appleton-Century-Crofts, Inc., 1947)

Stote, Dorothy, *Men Too Wear Clothes* (Philadelphia, J. B. Lippincott Co., 1950)

Worth, Jean Philippe, *A Century of Fashion* (Boston, Little, Brown and Co., 1928)

Young, Agnes Brooks, *Recurring Cycles of Fashion, 1760-1937* (New York, Harper & Bros., 1937)

ARTISTS FOR COSTUME REFERENCE

Alexander, John White (1856-1915)

Bellows, George (1882-1925)

Benson, Frank Weston (1862-   )

Bonnat, Léon Joseph Florentin (1833/4-1922)

Bréton, Jules Adolphe Aimé Louis (1827-1906)

Carolus-Duran, Charles Émile Auguste (1838-1917)

Cassatt, Mary (1855-1926)

Cézanne, Paul (1839-1906)

Chase, William Merritt (1849-1916)

Degas, Edgar Hilaire Germain (1834-1917)

Duveneck, Frank (1848-1919)

Fantin-Latour, Ignace Henri (1836-1904)

Glackens, William J. (1870-1938)

Hawthorne, Charles Webster (1872-1930)

Henri, Robert (1865-1929)

Homer, Winslow (1836-1910)

Hopkins, James R. (1878-   )

Huntington, Daniel P. (1860-1906)

Johansen, John Cristen (1876-   )

Kroll, Leon (1884-   )

Orchardson, (Sir) William Quiller (1832-1910)

Orpen, (Sir) William Nevenham Montague (1878-1931)

Parcell, Malcolm Stevens (1896-   )

Paxton, William McGregor (1869-   )

Renoir, Pierre Auguste (1841-1919)

Robinson, Theodore (1852-1896)

Rousseau, Henry Julien Félix (1844-1910)

Sargent, John Singer (1856-1925)

Soutine, Haim (1894-   )

Speicher, Eugene Edward (1883-   )

Sterne, Maurice (1877-   )

Stevens, Alfred Émile Léopold Victor (1828-1906)

Tarbell, Edmund Charles (1862-1938)

Thayer, Abbott Handerson (1849-1921)

Tito, Ettore (1859-   )

Ufer, Walter (1876-   )

Weir, Julian Alden (1852-1919)

Whistler, James Abbott McNeill (1834-1903)

Zorn, Anders Leonard (1860-1920)

Zuloaga y Zabaleta, Ignacia (1870-   )

GLOSSARY

Ascot Tie—refer to *Chap. 20.*

Baby Louis Heel—incurved heel of medium height. *Pl. L, 6.*

Balkan Blouse—low bloused bodice with belt girding the hip.

Barette—small bar pin used to hold the hair in place.

Basque—refer to *Chaps. 18, 19, 20.*

Bateau Neckline—wide, fairly low, neckline. Refer to *Chaps. 8, 9, 14. Pl. L, 3.*

Bertha—refer to *Chaps. 17, 18. Pl. XLVIII, 3.*

Bishop Sleeve—sleeve fairly full from shoulder to wrist, gathered into snug wristband. Refer to *Chaps. 15, 17, 18. Pl. XLVIII, 3; Pl. L, 7.*

Boa—long or short cylindrical neck scarf of fur or feathers.

Bowler or Derby—refer to *Chaps. 18, 19, 20.*

Brassière—band worn around the bust, usually as a support.

Bulldog Toe—high, rounded and blunt toe of shoe.

Bungalow Apron—simple, straight-line dress.

CHAPTER 21: GLOSSARY

Buster Brown Collar—wide, starched collar worn with a Windsor tie and identified with the character, Buster Brown, in the comic strip of the Sunday newspapers of the period.

Bust Extender—ruffles used in 1909 and in later years.

Cardigan—refer to *Chaps. 19, 20.*

Chatelaine Bag—refer to *Chap. 20.*

Chemise—refer to *Chaps. 6, 7, 8, 9, 10, 11, 12, 13, 14, 15, 16, 17, 18, 19, 20.*

Corset—refer to *Chaps. 8, 9, 10, 11, 12, 13, 14, 15, 16, 17, 18, 19, 20.*

Corset Cover—undergarment which covered the corset.

Derby—refer to *Bowler. Pl. L, 4.*

Diadem—refer to *Chaps. 3, 4, 5, 6, 7.*

Dog Collar—refer to *Chaps. 3, 7, 18, 20. Pl. XLVIII, 5.*

Duster—coat of panama, pongee, alpaca, or natural linen used for driving and motoring.

Eton Jacket—refer to *Chaps. 19, 20.*

Fascinator—lacey, woolen, square or triangular head covering.

Fedora—refer to *Chaps. 19, 20.*

Four-in-hand Tie—refer to *Chaps. 19, 20. Pl. XLVIII, 2.*

Friendship Bracelet—consisted of similar links given by various friends, later put together to form a bracelet.

Frock Coat—refer to *Chaps. 16, 17, 18, 19, 20.*

Gainsborough Hat—refer to *Chaps. 14, 19.*

Gibson Girl Blouse—blouse with high neck, turnover collar, small black tie and sleeves with large puff at shoulder.

Gibson Pleat—single pleat which extended over each shoulder, front and back, hiding armscye of shirtwaist.

Gym Bloomers—bloomers worn in the gymnasium.

Harem Skirt—divided skirt.

Hobble Skirt—very narrow skirt. *Pl. L, 1.*

Homburg—felt hat with rolled brim and creased crown, usually worn by older man. Edward VII, who visited Bad Homburg, Germany, many times before his death in 1910, is given credit for the design of this hat.

Inverness Cape—refer to *Chaps. 18, 19, 20.*

Jabot—refer to *Chaps. 13, 14. Pl. L, 5.*

Jersey Sweater—short, loose coat made of jersey. Refer to *Chap. 19.*

Kimono—loose gown. This indoor garment showed the new interest in Japanese art and culture.

Kimono Sleeve—sleeve and waist cut in 1 piece. *Pl. XLVIII, 1; Pl. XLIX, 2.*

Knickers—refer to *Chap. 20.*

Lavalliere—delicate ornament worn on short neck-chain.

Leggings—refer to *Chap. 20.*

Leg-of-mutton Sleeve—refer to *Chaps. 9, 10, 16, 20. Pl. XLIX, 1.*

Mackintosh—waterproof coat bearing the name of the originator of rubberized cloth garments.

Marabou—trimming made from feathers of a certain species of stork; also, a kind of raw silk or fabric made from it.

Marcel Wave—type of artificial waving of the hair devised by Marcel of France, 1907.

Merry Widow Hat—extremely large hat, named for musical show of same name.

Mesh Bag—bag made of interwoven metal links.

Morning-glory or Serpentine Skirt—skirt which fitted snugly at the hip, and flared bell-like, at the hem. *Pl. XLIX, 5.*

Mother Hubbard—loose-fitting, housedress, not beautiful, but very comfortable.

Muffler—small, knitted scarf.

Mushroom-style Hat—hat suggesting a mushroom in shape.

Napoleon Costume—woman's dress, 1905, having straight standing collar with deep turnover, wide revers, and braid trimming.

Norfolk Jacket—refer to *Chaps. 19, 20.*

Opera Hat—tall silk hat that folded flat.

Pajama—loose trousers and jacket worn as a sleeping or lounging garment.

Panama Hat—handwoven hat of fine straw from Ecuador and Colombia, South America.

Peek-a-boo Waist—very thin blouse.

Peg-top Skirt—skirt with fullness and drapery around hip and very narrow at the hem. The name peg-top originally applied to a boy's cone-shaped spinning top. *Pl. XLIX, 3.*

Peg-top Trousers—trousers wide and pleated at the top and narrow at the ankles.

Peter Pan Collar—small, soft, turnover collar. The collar was named from the costume worn by Maude Adams in *Peter Pan* by James M. Barrie.

Pettibockers—ankle-length, silk jersey pantaloons worn by a woman.

Petticoat—refer to *Chaps. 9, 10, 11, 12, 13, 14, 15, 16, 17, 18, 19, 20.*

Pompadour—hair combed back from forehead. Refer to *Chaps. 13, 19.*

Psyche Knot—refer to *Chaps. 4, 20.*

Raglan Sleeve—sleeve with an extremely large opening at the armscye, the 2 seams at front being continued upward to the neckline; named for Lord Raglan, an English general.

Rat—padding worn to make the hair extend outward from the head.

Serpentine Skirt—refer to *Morning-glory Skirt.*

Slit Skirt—narrow slit upward from hem to facilitate walking. *Pl. XLIX, 4.*

Slouch Hat—refer to *Chap. 19.*

Spat—short gaiter worn to protect the ankle as well as to add a dashing touch or a lighter value to the ensemble worn. Refer to *Chap. 20.*

Stock—refer to *Chaps. 13, 14, 15, 16, 17.*

Suit—refer to *Chap. 20.*

Switch—separate tress of real or artificial hair bound at 1 end.

Toque—refer to *Chaps. 2, 10, 16, 19, 20.*

Tricorne—refer to *Chaps. 9, 12, 13, 14, 15.*

Turtle-neck Sweater—slip-on sweater with high turnover collar.

Tuxedo—refer to *Chap. 20.*

Umbrella Drawers—very full, bell-shaped drawers. *Pl. XLVIII, 4.*

Van Dyck Beard—refer to *Chap. 11.*

Veil—refer to *Chaps. 3, 4, 5, 6, 7, 8, 9, 10, 15, 16, 17, 18, 19, 20.*

Walrus Moustache—refer to *Chap. 20.*

Windsor Tie—refer to *Chaps. 19, 20.*

Wing Collar—refer to *Chaps. 19, 20. Pl. L, 2.*

Wrapper—name given to an unshapely housedress, 1905.

X-ray Dress—dress of transparent fabric.

20th Century

PART II

1914-27

CHRONOLOGY

World War I, *1914-18.*

United States officially opened the Panama-Pacific International Exposition, *1915.*

Czar Nicholas of Russia abdicated, *March 15, 1917.* Soviet Republic established on *November 17, 1917.*

United States entered World War I, *April 6, 1917.*

Virgin Islands purchased by the United States from Denmark, *1917.*

Armistice signed, *November 11, 1918.*

Fourteen Points for world peace issued by President Woodrow Wilson, *1918.*

Republic established in Germany in *1918.*

First Peace Conference in Paris, *1919.*

Signing of the Treaty of Versailles, *1919.* The United States Government did not sign but made a separate peace treaty with Germany.

Fascist party in Italy established, *1919.*

Transcontinental air mail service between New York and San Francisco, *1920.*

Woman suffrage in U. S. provided by Nineteenth Amendment, *1920.*

First meeting of the Assembly of the League of Nations, January, *1920.*

Washington Naval Conference, *November 12, 1921* to *February 6, 1922.*

Mussolini became premier of Italy, *1922.*

Talking movies successful, *1925.*

Locarno Pacts giving European powers sense of security for a few years, *1925.*

Transatlantic telephone service, *1927.*

Transatlantic flight from New York to Paris by Charles A. Lindbergh, *1927.*

CHAPTER 22

20th Century

PART II

1914-27

HISTORY

World War I, which began in 1914, involved all the important powers of the world, lasted four-and-a-quarter years and brought about great disaster. On January 8, 1918, President Wilson delivered his famous speech that included the "Fourteen Points," the terms for a peace and for a better world. On November 11, 1918, the Armistice was signed. The many disagreements showed that the world was not ready for the proposed world organization of President Wilson.

In December, 1918, President Wilson went to Paris. He was the first American President ever to go abroad while in office. He was received with great ovation, because the people of Europe looked to the American President to solve the international problems of the time. Later, in March, a Council of Four, representing the four leading powers, United States, Great Britain, France, and Italy, was held. In the Fourteen Points, President Wilson included the Covenant of a League of Nations but to get this he had to compromise on the remaining thirteen points. President Wilson predicted a second war if the Germans were not given a reasonable national existence and the right to participate in world affairs but the other members of the Council demanded severe revenge upon Germany. The Treaty of Versailles was signed on June 18, 1919 by representatives of Germany, and those of the British Empire, France, Italy, Japan, Belgium and twenty-one other countries. The United States made a separate peace treaty with Germany on August 25, 1921.

The end of the war left the world with a great desire for peace and prosperity, for an improved social order, and for better labor conditions. By 1920, the United States had become a leading industrial and financial power. The European nations looked to her for credit and for relief and reconstruction of their war-torn countries. During the war and afterwards there was a great growth of industries in the United States and labor unions gained in power. Many Americans were employed in war activities, especially in the making of munitions. With the cessation of hostilities sharp changes took place in the social order: returning soldiers were given educational and other advantages by the government which they otherwise might not have had; women achieved a new importance through their contributions to the war effort; businessmen had to make the adjustment to private enterprise free of governmental restrictions that had been in effect during the conflict. But except for a short economic recession during the early '20's the country was in a prosperous condition—i.e. until prosperity, unhampered by any sensible controls, came to a sudden end in the stock market crash of 1929.

The war brought an end to most of the monarchial houses of Europe—notably the Austrian imperial house, the Hohenzollerns in Germany (Emperor William II abdicated November 8, 1918), and the Romanovs in Russia where a communist government was established in 1917. The Fascists gained strength in Italy and were becoming very important in Germany.

In consequence of woman proving her usefulness during the war, she was granted more freedom and privileges, especially by the nations that had participated in the conflict. After 1918 various countries had written a new equality for women and men in their constitutions. In 1917 a bill was passed in England permitting women to vote but limiting the age to thirty years. Having received a little freedom, the woman of the day desired more; she was on the march. Women were admitted to practice law in England in 1919. In 1914 Constance Lytton in England went so far as to disguise herself as a poor dressmaker and visited different sections of England to observe that there was discrimination in treatment of various social classes of prisoners. The Woman's Federal Bureau was created in the United States Department of Labor in 1920 by Congress to conserve the woman power of the nation and protect the interests of the woman worker. In 1927 economic independence was enjoyed by many women. The National League of Women Voters, founded in 1920, to replace the National Suffrage Association, made a great contribution to the good of womankind.

During the period there was a great increase in the number of women in the clerical, trade and professional groups. Some of the most important occupations for woman were in the field of ready-to-wear garments. To stimulate interest in fashion design, the designers of North and South America were sent to Paris to bring back word of the latest styles. American designers were encouraged by contests; the first to be held was sponsored in New York City by the Art Alliance of America in 1916. More and more women took up teaching and nursing which still remained the special fields of woman.

Costume changed slightly at the beginning of the period, although the "debutante slouch" or "boneless pose" created a different type of silhouette. Strict economy in materials of all kinds, a definite influence of the war, was apparent in dress. A dignity and simplicity of style was the result; lines were simple, colors subdued. Costume became more practical, influenced by the fact that during the war women worked in factories and on the railroads. Due to their more active lives women required underclothes that permitted freedom of movement; the numerous interior clothes with frills and ruffles of previous periods were discarded. Nineteenth-century curves, as set off by rigid corseting, were no longer fashionable. An important factor that influenced the more simple type of costume, was the shortage of labor which made it impractical to wear clothes that required special care. Simplicity in style continued until the end of this period when a change of importance occurred in formal dress: panels of fabric and sashes were draped below the hem of the skirt. Another innovation of the times was that of costume jewelry. Experimentation in dye stuffs and textile design became important in the United States.

The costume worn by man in previous periods had become increasingly uncomfortable each year as was evident in the choke collars, stiff hats, and shoes with pointed toes. After World War I, a casualness was reflected in dress—vests often were discarded, and the increased sport activities made the change to simpler clothing almost a necessity.

Beauty shops flourished after 1918 and became practically a necessity for the well-groomed professional and society woman. The man of this period also became more interested in his appearance. Cosmetics were now used without reserve. Bobbed hair was introduced. In general "comfort" was the aim of fashion, not carelessness in costume.

DRESS

A. *Sources of information:* fashion magazines, costumes of the time, photographs, paintings, the cinema, and literature.

B. MEN
   1. Garments:

   Outer upper: Prince Albert or frock coat for formal wear; tail coat for evening; very low lapel, high waisted; tuxedo; coat often left open in front; vest with low lapel and cut with inverted V on lower edge; influence of jazz shown in styles of 1918; high-waisted, 1-button coat; *pinch back coat;* sweater with large turnover collar, buttoned down the front; extreme styles in 1920 followed by those less formal; *crew-neck sweater,* turtle-neck sweater; blazer; *Lindbergh jacket; windbreaker;* sport costume for various occasions.

   Outer lower: ankle-length trousers; bell-bottom trousers, 1924-26; tight trousers in 1926; cuffs.

   Under: shirt sometimes of silk; sleeved or sleeveless vest and shorts extending to above the knee; long knitted underwear of wool, cotton or mixture of the two.

   Cloaks and overgarments: coat with fur collar, also longer overcoat, occasionally of raccoon or camel's hair; also short topcoat; *Raglan; balmacan,* 1920's; double-breasted military coat, 1924; raincoat.

   Neckwear and wristwear: high, tight, white collar, sometimes high collar even worn for active sport; large wing collar; collar extending above coat collar in back, cuff extending below coat sleeve; cotton or string tie, four-in-hand tie with large knot, also narrow four-in-hand tie.

   2. Hair: conventional and similar to present day hairdress, parted on side, in middle, or combed in pompadour; *crew-haircut;* large drooping or waxed mustache in early part of period, smooth-shaven later.

   3. Headdress: bowler or derby; high-crowned derby in 1916; stiff straw hat; *Panama straw hat; planter's punch,* soft felt hat; Homburg; motoring cap with visor; lower-crowned derby, 1917; fedora; young man often going bareheaded.

   4. Footwear: oxford displacing high shoe, spat, comfortable shoe for sport; bright-colored sock; black sock worn by conservative; garter.

   5. Accessories: umbrella carried by a few older men; walking stick at first of period; knitted muffler; buttons and studs for dress shirt; glove; pearl-handled knife worn on watch chain later in period;

362

1. Draped Skirt   2. Cowl Neckline   3. Turtle-neck Sweater
4. Derby   5. Accordion Pleated Skirt   6. Middy Blouse

garter; belt or suspender; *wallet* or billfold; fountain pen and pencil; key case.

6. **Jewelry:** signet ring, fraternity pin; watch chain from 1 vest pocket across to the other pocket; wrist watch worn by a few men, considered effeminate.

7. **Typical Colors:** somber colors, including dark blue, brown, black, and gray.

8. **Typical Materials:** serge or other woolen fabric; duck, or light flannel for summer.

9. **Make-up:** none.

C. WOMEN

1. Garments:

Outer upper: definite waistline, above normal or a little below; ample fullness in waist of dress; basque similar to that of the 19th century worn, 1916; decided change in costume after our entrance into World War I, 1917, regulation uniform worn by woman serving government; tunic or 1-piece dress; *chemise dress, apron tunic, handkerchief tunic,* 1917; dress giving illusion of a slim figure due to limit in amount of fabric in a dress, 1918; *Hoover apron;* also loose dress, giving freedom of movement; debutante slouch or drooping pose was popular; high collar across back of both dress and coat; cascade of black beads used as decoration; short or long sleeve; soft shirtwaist blouse with four-in-hand tie; soft ruffled collar, and tight-fitting sleeve, 1918; braid or pleated trimming; healthy appearance important; return to normal costume slow after close of war, 1918; *sailor collar;* fichu over neck and shoulder, jumper showing influence of the Middle Ages; new Paris styles again popular; *ensemble* becoming important; *cowl neckline;* bateau neckline, 1920's; waistline to hip, 1922; short skirt; lines more simple, cap sleeve cut in one with garment, collar with pointed tabs in front; *shawl collar;* daring, low-necked, sleeveless slip dress; *one-hour dress;* tight, wide belt, 1927; low-waisted dress with very low neckline for evening; sleeve short, 3-quarter length or longer; shapeless *sash blouse,* 1917; *step-in-blouse* in 1920; *bolero blouse,* 1926; *sash blouse; middy blouse.*

Outer lower: ankle-length day dress; long evening dress with a train ending in a point resembling a serpent's tail, or a tassel; skirt full at waist and hip, with many flounces suggesting the crinoline period of the 19th century, whalebones and pannier drapery, in 1916; *pocket cascade,* 1916; tubular silhouette, *c.* 1918; *draped skirt,* long skirt with slit at side; accordion pleated skirt; skirt 8 inches from floor, 1919; short and scant skirt, 1920-21; *Kiki skirt;* shorter skirt, 1924, to middle of calf, 1925; fur border on hem of skirt; uneven hemline, 1925; quaint touches of Victorian period on skirt; nearly full length flounce or overtunic on dress; very short skirt, 1926; full skirt, 1927.

Under: long, knitted underwear for winter, short for summer, or light-weight chemise; camisole; brassière; light-weight, cotton underwear with lace and ruffles; full lingerie garment with shoulder strap and skirt with slit side; *Ferris waist; teddies,* straight and clinging *combination,* or drawers and short petticoat worn under the clinging modes of the day, 1925; corset or girdle from hip down, straight front, tight brassière.

Cloaks and overgarments: cape popular; dolman, jacket, and wrap; box coat, open in front with turnback fold, or with lapel and large *patch pocket* on each side; short bolero; coat with chin collar; coat with full skirt and very large sleeve; *blouse coat,* 1926; fur coat with two kinds of fur, large collar and cuff; coatee or redingote of tulle with crossway bands of net and silver tassels; cape coat; Raglan; raincoat; cardigan jacket over low-waisted, straight dress, 1921; blazer; loose slip-on silk sweater; crew-neck or turtle-neck sweater, 1920's.

Additional garments: ensemble consisting of suit with 3-quarter length coat; coat suit; casual belted suit, 1921; semitailored or tailored suit; *tailored dress;* sleeping pajama; many new and comfortable styles for sport activities; 1-piece bathing suit introduced by Annette Kellerman, 1916.

2. **Hair:** long, worn in simple style at first, covering the ears and part of sides of face; low on forehead with roll or psyche knot at back of head, curls around face, 1918; *Irene Castle bob, boyish bob,* 1918, various types of bob suitable to individual; *shingle bob;* sometimes high headdress; Marcel wave; permanent waving in general use, by 1920; bobbed hair worn by most women, by 1924; straight bob with bang; close-waved hairdress; *transformation* and pompadour still used by elderly woman, 1925.

3. **Headdress:** very small *cloche,* toque, or bonnet worn low over head covering ears, back of head and most of forehead, narrow brim; helmet with stiff feathers; tricorne or 3-cornered hat of various shapes, 1915; cockade on hat, 1916; wide band worn around the head, 1924; very wide-brimmed hat, often with much ribbon and lace trimming; *Peter Pan hat;* tam-o'-shanter or beret; flowers on hat made of metal or porcelain; band of silk; wreath of flowers, roses and camelias; large evening headdress of ribbon and flowers, later in period; veil.

4. **Footwear:** very high, laced or buttoned shoe popular at first; next, moderate or Baby Louis heel and very pointed toe; strapped sandal,

slipper with large buckle over high tongue; slipper or pump with high heel; *saddle shoe;* comfortable shoe for sport and street wear; ankle-strap slipper; very high heel in 1918; spat; wool and cotton, ribbed, or pure woolen hose with clocks, 1915, silk or rayon worn generally later.

5. **Accessories:** short-handled umbrella; apron; large old-fashioned handkerchief of rare lace for dress, large floral handkerchief for daytime and tailored costume; vanity case or *compact* containing powder, rouge, and lipstick; different fad in accessories each year; sash with streamer; large plume fan; many combs, tortoise shell hairpins; glove, soft gauntlet glove, 1915; knitted, woolen, long silk, or tulle scarf; muff early in the period; large *Algerian purse* hung on arm by large ring; fountain pen and pencil; key case.

6. **Jewelry:** pearls and other jewelry; dangling strings of beads and pendant earrings; antique coral, or crystal beads, the latter with balls of amber, jade, or antique crystal Buddha pendant; mother-of-pearl, carved ivory, vegetable ivory, or amber bead necklace; costume jewelry introduced about 1922; rhinestones, semiprecious and precious stones; gems in rings matching jewels around neck and on bodice; vegetable ivory and synthetic stones used in brooch, clip, ring, bracelet, and pendant.

7. **Typical Colors:** colors bright at first, then dull, during the war, due to poor American dyes; beige very popular, also delicate tints of pink in muslin with inset motifs of *Mechlin lace;* ochre-tinted tulle with designs in gold thread; snow-white dress embroidered with white beads; colored bead designs on black or colored dress; brighter colors after the war; pearl gray, tan, bronze, or blue for shoe and slipper; white, black, brown, champagne, peach, light blue, or gray, for hose in 1916.

8. **Typical Materials:** muslin, cambric, and tulle resembling fabrics of 1840; transparent and clinging fabrics such as chiffon and georgette, also charmeuse, messaline, silk mull, moire, gabardine, taffeta, corded silk, crepe and velvet; colored satin; Mechlin lace; *neckline lace;* scarcity of wool, some wool jersey; strict conservation of wool due to four years of war; silk, chiffon, and crepe used for the changing styles; silk hose a luxury and very expensive at first, production showing an increase of 25 per cent, 1919-28; rayon and silk hose and underwear worn by everyone for the first time; elaborate furs; combinations of fur and fabric.

9. **Make-up:** evidences of "the vamp" of the movies in the make-up as well as in the costume of many girls and some women; patch worn sometimes; beauty parlors coming into vogue, practically becoming a necessity, absurd amount of powder, rouge, lipstick and mas-

cara; powder, cream, tissue builder, astringent, mask, rinse, and perfume; emphasis placed on being well groomed, especially in the business world; less rouge used toward end of period.

SIGNIFICANT MOTIFS

The motifs were not significant in this period, but were combinations of many periods. The following chapters will include motifs only when they are indicative of the period.

INFLUENCES ON LATER COSTUMES

New synthetic materials continued in the periods which follow; very short skirt, 1945-47; extremely informal styles which became exaggerated, 1940-45; short bob returning, 1949; influence of styles of 1925 shown in costume, 1949, in long-waisted dress and full skirt; middy blouse, 1952.

BOOKS OF REFERENCE

(See Books of Reference, Part I, *20th Century*, p. 353, and General Bibliography, p. 433)

ARTISTS FOR COSTUME REFERENCE

(See p. 354)

GLOSSARY

Accordion Pleated Skirt—skirt made of pressed pleats. Refer to *Accordion Pleating*, *Chaps. 2, 8, 20. Pl. LI, 5.*

Algerian Purse—purse made of leather from Algiers, usually tooled and embossed, sometimes in colors or in gold.

Apron—refer to *Chaps. 2, 11, 12, 13, 14, 15, 17, 18.*

Apron Tunic—tunic having an overskirt, cut away in the back and forming an apron in front.

Baby Louis Heel—refer to *Chap. 21.*

Balmacan—type of loose, flaring overcoat with raglan sleeve.

Basque—refer to *Chaps. 18, 19, 20, 21.*

Bateau Neckline—boat-shaped neckline, high in front and back and wide at the sides. Refer to *Chaps. 8, 9, 14, 21.*

Beret—refer to *Barret, Chaps. 10, 11.*

Blazer—bright-colored jacket, originally vertically striped. Refer to *Chaps. 19, 20.*

Blouse Coat—coat with bloused effect, formed by blousing coat fabric on lining at the waistline; usually with dolman sleeve.

Bolero—refer to *Chaps. 12, 18, 20.*

Bolero Blouse—long-waisted blouse with an additional overlapping section that formed a bolero.

Bowler or Derby—refer to *Chaps. 18, 19, 20, 21.*

Boyish Bob—extremely short bob worn, *1925-30.*

Brassière—undergarment shaped to support the bust. This word has often been shortened to bra. This garment has also been called an uplift or bandeau. Refer to *Chap. 21.*

Camisole—*refer to Chaps. 17, 19, 20.*

Cardigan—refer to *Chaps. 19, 20, 21.*

Chemise Dress—1-piece dress which was slipped on over the head. It had short sleeves, long waist and narrow belt and became the basic style for all dresses of the time; also called the tube dress or pillowslip dress.

Cloche—close-fitting, bell-shaped hat.

Cockade—refer to *Chaps. 13, 14, 15.*

Combination—chemise and panty in one garment.

Compact—small ornamental box containing powder and rouge.

Corset—refer to *Chaps. 8, 9, 10, 11, 12, 13, 14, 15, 16, 17, 18, 19, 20, 21.*

Cowl Neckline—loose neckline of dress falling in graceful curves across the chest; draping of fabric resembling soft folds of monk's cowl. *Pl. LI, 2.*

Crew-haircut—hair cut short and combed upward, resembling a brush on top.

Crew-neck Sweater—sweater with flat, close, round neckline.

Derby—refer to *Bowler. Pl. LI, 4.*

Draped Skirt—long narrow skirt with draped fabric extending in folds from front to back; similar to the peg-top skirt of the previous period. *Pl. LI, 1.*

Dolman—refer to *Chap. 19.*

Ensemble—usually a suit with harmonizing top coat.

Fedora—refer to *Chaps. 19, 20, 21.*

Ferris Waist—trade name given to fitted waist which had buttons on tabs to hold the supporters. It was worn mainly by young girls.

Fichu—refer to *Chaps. 13, 14, 15, 16, 17, 18, 19.*

Frock Coat or Prince Albert Coat—refer to *Chaps. 16, 17, 18, 19, 20, 21.*

Four-in-hand Tie—refer to *Chaps. 19, 20, 21.*

Handkerchief Tunic—tunic made from a square of material, the center of which was cut out for the waistline, the corners falling in graceful folds at the side of the skirt.

Helmet—close-fitting cap worn toward the back of head and with sides extending over ears. Refer to *Chap. 2.*

Homburg—refer to *Chap. 21.*

Hoover Apron—wraparound, cover-all apron with sleeves. It originated during World War I, when Herbert Hoover was Food Administrator, and it has continued to be worn until the present day.

Irene Castle Bob—hair cut, loosely waved, and combed back from the forehead. This hair style was introduced by Irene Castle, the dancer.

Kiki Skirt—extremely tight, knee-length skirt which became popular after it was worn by Lenore Ulric in the play *Kiki.*

Lindbergh Jacket—heavy, warm, woolen or leather jacket with large pockets and elastic, fitted waist and wrist bands. It was worn by Charles A. Lindbergh on his solo flight across the Atlantic Ocean, 1927.

Marcel Wave—refer to *Chap. 21.*

Mechlin Lace—kind of pillow lace originally made in Mechlin, Belgium.

Middy Blouse—straight blouse with braid-trimmed sailor collar, bearing the nickname of the English midshipman (the 3 stripes on the collar represent the three great naval battles of Lord Nelson); worn by young girls. Refer to *Pl. LI, 6.*

CHAPTER 22: GLOSSARY

Muffler—refer to *Chap. 21.*

Neckline Lace—filmy, Flemish lace edging in which the floral pattern was usually outlined by silk thread on dainty net of hexagonal weave.

One-hour Dress—straight line dress with kimono sleeve and plain skirt. It was possible to make this dress in one hour.

Panama Hat—refer to *Chap. 21.*

Patch—refer to *Chaps. 5, 10, 11, 12, 13, 14.*

Patch Pocket—pocket sewed on outside of garment and made of the same fabric.

Peter Pan Hat—small hat with a feather at the side.

Petticoat—refer to *Chaps. 9, 10, 11, 12, 13, 14, 15, 16, 17, 18, 19, 20, 21.*

Pinch Back Coat—coat with inverted pleats in the back which were stitched into the belt.

Planter's Punch—firm straw hat, shaped like a fedora, which originated in Jamaica *c.* 1923; with creased crown and wide pleated ornamental band; later a hat of dyed Panama or other fiber.

Pocket Cascade—pocket formed in fold and draped section at the side of the skirt.

Pompadour—refer to *Chaps. 13, 19, 21.*

Prince Albert Coat—refer to *Frock Coat.*

Psyche Knot—refer to *Chaps. 4, 20, 21.*

Raglan—coat with sleeve which ran from armscye to neckline. Refer to *Raglan Sleeve, Chap. 21.*

Raincoat—waterproof coat worn by man or woman over suit or costume as a protection against the weather.

Redingote—refer to *Chaps. 14, 15, 16, 18, 20.*

Saddle Shoe—2-tone oxford with an ornamental strip of leather across the instep.

Sailor Collar—V-neckline collar, square and deep in the back and trimmed with braid, resembling the collar worn by sailor.

Sash Blouse—blouse with wide pieces, crossing in front like a surplice with attached ends forming a sash or girdle, which was tied or fastened in the back.

Shawl Collar—attached collar having a rounded, unbroken outline, often extending to the waistline.

Shingle Bob—mode of cutting the hair very close to the head in the back, showing the natural contour of the head.

Shorts—short cotton pants worn under trousers.

Spat—refer to *Chaps. 20, 21.*

Step-in Blouse—garment with blouse attached to step-in.

Suit—refer to *Chaps. 20, 21.*

Tailored Dress—close, well-fitted, beautifully and simply made dress.

Tam-o'-shanter—Scotch cap having a flat, round top. Refer to *Chaps. 19, 20.*

Teddies—straight garment, combining a shapeless brassière and straight skirt with a wide strap separating garment into two separate parts or legs.

Toque—refer to *Chaps. 2, 10, 16, 19, 20, 21.*

Transformation—naturalistic wig occasionally worn by a woman afflicted with thin hair.

Tricorne Hat—refer to *Chaps. 9, 12, 13, 14, 15.*

Turtle-neck Sweater—refer to *Chap. 21. Pl. LI, 3.*

Tuxedo—refer to *Chaps. 20, 21.*

Veil—refer to *Chaps. 3, 4, 5, 6, 7, 8, 9, 10, 15, 16, 17, 18, 19, 20.*

Wallet—purse for coins and bills.

Windbreaker—jacket similar to the Lindbergh jacket.

Wing Collar—refer to *Chaps. 19, 20, 21.*

20th Century

PART III

1928-39

CHRONOLOGY

Kellogg Peace Pact signed in Paris, *1928*.

Stock market crash, United States, *1929*.

Kellogg-Briand Anti-War Treaty renounced aggressive war, *1929*.

Flight around the world by the German dirigible, Graf Zeppelin, *1929*.

Trip to the South Pole by Commander Richard E. Byrd, United States, *1929*.

King Alfonso fled from Madrid, *April 14, 1931*. Spain proclaimed a republic, *1931*.

First venture into the stratosphere in a hermetically-sealed aluminum balloon by Auguste Picard, *1931*.

First flight around the globe by airplane made by Wiley Post and Harold Gatty, United States, *1931*.

Withdrawal of Germany from Disarmament Conference and the League of Nations, *October 14, 1933*.

New Deal Policies under President Franklin Roosevelt, social betterments in the United States, *1933-40*.

Hitler and the Nazi party in power in Germany, *1934*.

Popular Front in France, *1936*.

Locarno Pacts of 1925, denounced by Germany, *March 7, 1936*.

Pan-American Conference for maintenance of peace held in Buenos Aires, *1936*, in Lima, *1938*, in Panama in *1939*.

Stalin began purge in Russia, *1937*.

Japan attacked Shanghai, *1937*.

Open warfare between Russia and the Japanese, *1938*.

German invasion of Austria, *March, 1938*. Czechoslovak Crisis, *1938*.

England and France declared war on Germany (after latter invaded Poland) *September 3, 1939*, starting Second World War.

Golden Gate Exposition in San Francisco and New York World's Fair, *1939*.

CHAPTER 23

20th Century

PART III

1928-39

HISTORY

The mechanical and industrial progress of the United States was stupendous in this period: labor-saving devices reached a peak in development. North America experienced an unheard-of prosperity after the First World War but this was followed by "The great depression of 1929." Economic depression was world-wide, however, and although it affected certain countries more than others, it produced a situation about equally grave everywhere. There was an excess of products in the United States in 1929. Farmers were left stranded with their crops due to the inability of an increasing number of jobless people in urban centers to purchase their products. The cost of manufactured materials became very high, while the value of farm products fell.

There had been a wave of great speculation in 1928 and 1929. Stock prices went to unbelievable heights, far higher than earnings of corporations, and in October, 1929 the American financial market crashed. Both agriculture and industry were in a deplorable condition. Emergency measures were passed during the depression by congress, which brought money into the hands of the people, while appropriations were made for public works and for relief. Projects were created whereby unemployed persons could engage in useful work, and at the same time earn a livelihood. The Congress of Industrial Organizations was initiated in 1934. By 1937 there was a spectacular advance in labor organizing in meat-packing plants, the rubber industry, electrical machinery and automobile manufacture.

England was experiencing a certain amount of unrest at home and abroad, but kept supervision and control over Egypt and India. The number of employed workers in England decreased. King George V

EUROPE
January, 1939

died in 1936, his son, King Edward VIII ascended the throne later abdicating, to be succeeded by his brother, George VI.

France had retained her republican form of government but there was a constant disturbance due to the many political parties. After much confusion, the Socialist Prime Minister Blum resigned, followed by Chautemps, a Radical Socialist. The latter was succeeded in 1938 by Daladier who had a conservative point of view. During the latter's first year in office, Hitler's armies marched into Austria, and the crisis over the Sudetenland turned French attention from domestic problems to foreign affairs.

Economic conditions had improved in Italy under the Fascist party between 1922 and 1928, but by 1934 everything was changed. Labor received extremely low wages and many people were unemployed. The government became so powerful that individual liberties practically disappeared.

Germany had become a republic after the First World War, but the National Socialist or Nazi party in a few years seized power as a result of the chaotic economic and social conditions in the country. Adolf Hitler, leader of the Nazis, was appointed chancellor in 1933. Very soon after he became dictator of Germany and his rule resulted in racial oppression and loss of freedom of speech and all other democratic privileges.

In 1931 a republican form of government was established in Spain. Democracy was short-lived here too. Fascist forces in the country, encouraged by Germany and Italy, openly opposed the Loyalists (government party) and civil war broke out in 1936, a bitter struggle that proved to be the prelude to World War II. On September 1, 1939 Poland was invaded by the Nazi armies and a few days later England and France declared war on Germany. For a second time in a generation war had engulfed the world, affecting all phases of life, including costume.

In the early part of the period dresses became so skimpy that manufacturers in 1928 grew alarmed at the small amount of material sold and influenced designers to create costumes that would require more materials. At first, the above-knee-length costume was lowered by the use of small pendants several inches long, attached to the hem. Dresses soon reached a more attractive length, coming down to below the calf of the leg. By 1931 all unnecessary detail was eliminated. Sleeves became larger and the shoulderline was raised by the use of shoulder pads, skirts became longer, and by 1935 a new silhouette was devel-

376

oped. This style did not last; it was not as comfortable as the shorter skirts had been and was not popular. Again, in the fall of 1935, the shorter skirt was in vogue and continued in popularity until it reached the knee again by 1940. During this period the Fashion Originators Guild was organized in 1931 to protect the designs of American stylists who came into prominence at this time.

Previous to the outbreak of World War II woman had made real gains in her status. For one thing, modern conveniences in the home had released her from much of the drudgery of housework. In most countries women's suffrage existed, resulting in more personal independence and greater influence in public affairs. Through the activities of the National Woman's Party and other groups in the United States greater legal equality with men had been achieved.

But during the depression American women again suffered from the competition with men. Jobs became very scarce and men were generally given the preference. In 1934 women, especially public employees, were dismissed from their positions if they married. In spite of this situation there were in 1930 more than ten and three-fourths million women in the United States who were gainfully employed. In the same year the number of women in clerical work was three times as great as in 1910, and by 1937 one-fourth of the women of the United States worked for a living.

DRESS

A. *Sources of information:* costumes of the day, paintings, photographs, magazines, pattern books, newspapers, and the cinema.

B. MEN
1. Garments:
Outer upper: influence of the automobile and active sport life showed an influence in dress, comfort considered very important; few changes in costume; informality in dress; styles set by the Prince of Wales; padded shoulder; double-breasted jacket having 4 to 6 buttons; 2 or 3 button, single-breasted coat, lower button left unbuttoned; evening tail coat changed in style, becoming shorter and wider, fullness under arm; tuxedo or dinner jacket, silk shawl collar; white suit for less formal evening suit; V-neckline sweater; windbreaker; *bush jacket;* cardigan.
Outer lower: trousers with or without cuff, about 1937; length to

break at the instep; striped trousers for dress; shorts for sport cut a little high-waisted, with pleats at belt.

Under: narrow-bosom dress shirt; sport shirt with wide collar; *polo shirt;* attached or separate collar and cuff; soft or starched collar; *tab collar shirt;* white or colored shirt; underwear of wool or cotton for winter; knit vest and cambric shorts for summer.

Cloaks and overgarments: coat with *raglan sleeve, convertible collar* or rolled lapel; narrow or wide lapel; belted, polo coat; double-breasted camel's hair coat; knee-length top coat with broad shoulder and set-in sleeve; fitted overcoat with slight flair in skirt, and length to a little below knee; loose and full, belted coat; raincoat.

Neckwear and wristwear: four-in-hand tie; cotton tie; *foulard* scarf tied in ascot style, worn with sport shirt; bow tie for formal and semiformal wear.

Additional garments: raincoat; *dressing robe* with shawl collar; heavy brocaded *housecoat; pajama;* shorts; *jodhpurs; parka;* knickers, *slacks,* often without cuffs.

2. **Hair:** pompadour; side or middle part.
3. **Headdress:** *Homburg,* bowler or derby, pork pie, *snap brim,* Panama or *planter's punch;* hat with creased crown, resembling felt fedora; Alpine or *Tyrolean hat,* with cord and feather at the side; silk opera hat with 5¾ inch crown; straw sailor or cap for informal and sports wear.
4. **Footwear:** cloth-top shoe worn occasionally, 1932; black or brown oxford; pump for evening; 2-tone shoe for semisport; *saddle oxford;* gaiter, *jodhpur boot;* sport shoe with rubber sole; sandal; galosh or *zipper.*
5. **Accessories:** umbrella carried by a few older men; tobacco or pipe pouch of pigskin; muffler with or without fringe; boutonnière; belt; leather suspenders or braces, also, elastic suspenders with leather tips; glove; *ear muff;* letter and key case; wallet or billfold; fountain pen, and pencil.
6. **Jewelry:** cuff links, tie clasp, ring, shirt studs, wrist watch.
7. **Typical Colors:** subdued colors, dark or light colors; gray or tan for coat; dark blue or white dinner jacket; dark gray, brown, or tan business suit; colorful tie and sock worn by young man; gray or *mocha glove* for evening; gay colors later in period; pastel-colored border of handkerchief, often matching color of suit; black, brown, saddle, or white oxford shoe.
8. **Typical Materials:** serge suit; seersucker, linen or Palm Beach cloth for summer suit; raccoon fur, or camel's hair for overcoat; cashmere reefer; suede, capeskin or pigskin glove; felt or straw hat;

cotton or silk tie; wool cravat; diamond weave, tweed, dotted or checked pattern.

9. Make-up: none.

C. WOMEN

1. Garments:

Outer upper: Grecian, Medieval, French Empire, 17th and 18th Century influences in costume; shapeless dress, no definite waist-line; over-all beaded and spangled sheath evening dress; curved lines emphasized, 1929; Balkan blouse, 1930; high waistline with ruffles or bow in back; princess dress in 1930; unnecessary detail eliminated, 1931; long, tight sheath dress with huge sleeve, 1932; *jumper dress;* cowl neckline; formal costume with high neckline in front and extremely low in back; high shoulder raised with padding and shoulder wing, 1932; shoulder pads worn in most garments, 1935 and later; wide molded shoulderline introduced by designer Adrian; waistline normal, also princess silhouette; *halter-top;* Gay Nineties influence, 1933; soft draped or bias-cut dress, 1934; sloping shoulderline on some dresses, squared shoulder on suit; *bustle-type dress* influenced by paintings of Monet, Renoir, and Boldini; Gibson girl influence; emphasis on correct garment for the occasion; *monastic silhouette,* 1938; *sack dress;* wrapper; *camisole neckline;* black dress or suit with jewelry on lapel; sequin encrusted jacket; sequin-trimmed dress often worn under plain tailored coat; fashions changed by war in Europe.

Outer lower: very short skirt, 1928, pleated, gored and flaring; pendants on lower edge of costume to lengthen skirt, 1929; skirt 2½ inches below knee, 1930; long skirt for evening, sometimes with short train; slim narrow skirt, 12 inches from floor, 1932; skirt a little below the calf, by spring, 1935, then shorter by fall, and a little shorter each year until knee-length, 1940; skirt with apron-like overpanel, 1938; *swing skirt.*

Under: corset practically discontinued; girdle of rubber woven into fabric; *combination; envelope combination; slip,* one kind with *Hollywood top slip;* petticoat; brassière.

Cloaks and overgarments: fitted coat, 1929; short fur jacket; *swagger coat,* 1930, *box coat;* redingote; *evening wrap; opera cape;* cardigan sweater; raincoat.

Additional garments: ensemble of print dress and print-lined wool coat, 1933; print suit, 1935; quilted *lounging robe;* kimono or house-coat; hostess and sleeping pajama, 1936 and later; *bed jacket;* housedress; *shirtwaist dress; culotte;* shorts; jodhpurs; parka.

2. Hair: long hair popular, 1929; long bob, 1930, hair worn in most becoming style for the individual; pompadour type, 1934; styles influenced by actresses; long bob and *page boy bob,* 1937; very long bob worn by young girl, hair shorter and arranged in neater coiffure by woman.

3. **Headdress:** hat with *nose veil* popular, 1930's; veil worn on hat; *Empress Eugénie hat* with feather decoration and *pill box hat,* 1930; turban for evening, later worn for daytime wear; high-crowned hat with small brim worn over one eye, 1932; sailor hat; *off-the-face hat* showing influence of Zulu native of South Africa; low crown, with wide brim, 1934; *halo hat,* very small hat with veil; heart-shaped hat, and toque similar to that of the Renaissance, 1935; usually without hat, 1937; *Breton sailor, Dutch hat,* half-hat, flower-crowned hat, mushroom style hat, *profile hat, short back sailor, skimmer sailor, harlequin hat, Bethlehem headdress, doll hat,* turban and *coolie hat,* 1938; veil, flowers and various hat decorations, 1939; small hat with *bustle back, pancake beret, sequin calotte, tiara,* and *babushka,* 1940, pill box hat.

4. **Footwear:** slipper with short vamp and spike heel, 1929; colored slipper; evening sandal with straps crossed in back and fastened in front; cut-out sandal, 1934; wedge-shaped heel, 1939; clog; platform shoe; saddle oxford; flat shoe in general popular; jodhpur boot; galosh or zipper; very transparent hose, 1933-38; lisle hose worn frequently in 1938-39, due to war between Japan and China; nylon hose becoming popular, *c.* 1939.

5. **Accessories:** short, stubby, and gay umbrella, black glove worn with colored dress; *free finger glove;* hand bag to match shoe and hat; compact; fountain pen and pencil; rattail comb; floral handkerchief; key case; scarf worn in many different ways; ear muff; flowers or ornaments worn as hair decoration; apron.

6. **Jewelry:** hatpin; *clip;* antique jewelry, 1929; very small wrist watch; tiara for evening, 1933; pearl necklace; North American Indian influence in silver jewelry, and woven bead necklace; diamond bracelet; *bangle bracelet;* sport pins; costume jewelry of wood, metal, bone, colorful seeds, and many other natural materials.

7. **Typical Colors:** new and daring combinations, brown and gray, brown and black, cameo pink and wine, turquoise and brown; shocking pink and fiesta colors showing Mexican influence, *c.* 1936; stylized prints often showing pen lines or brush strokes, designs of flowers or architecture, occasionally designs of animals, including horses and dogs; printed fabrics used in spring and summer, plain colors, in fall and winter.

8. **Typical Materials:** various fabrics including cotton, linen, seer-

1. Shirtwaist Dress   2. Chin Collar   3. Evening Wrap
4. Combination   5. Sequin Callotte   6. Pancake Beret   7. Platform Shoe

sucker, silk and wool; rayon, and other *synthetic materials;* jersey and sculptured jersey weaves common.

9. **Make-up:** rouge, and carmine lipstick; red color less obvious and confined only to lips by many, after 1930; nail polish of various shades; hair brushed carefully and frequently by the young girl.

BOOKS OF REFERENCE

(See BOOKS OF REFERENCE, Part I, *20th Century*, p. 353, and GENERAL BIBLIOGRAPHY, p. 433)

ARTISTS FOR COSTUME REFERENCE

(See p. 354)

GLOSSARY

Apron—refer to *Chaps. 2, 11, 12, 13, 14, 15, 17, 18, 22.*

Babushka—scarf worn around the head, tied under the chin. This is the Russian word for grandmother.

Balkan Blouse—blouse with full, loose sleeve, and gathered into wide band around the waist. This garment came into fashion during the Balkan War in 1912.

Bangle Bracelet—bracelet worn for sports wear, having various dangling figures. This ornament was worn first by the East Indian peoples.

Bed Jacket—short jacket worn while resting in bed.

Bethlehem Headdress—hat shaped like a truncated cone, decorated with veil and jewels or coins.

Boutonnière—refer to *Chaps. 16, 17, 18.*

Bowler or Derby—refer to *Chaps. 18, 19, 20, 21, 22.*

Box Coat—loose coat often short, often box-like in shape.

Brassière—refer to *Chaps. 21, 22.*

Breton Sailor—wide-brimmed sailor hat resembling the type worn in France.

Bush Jacket—belted, hip-length jacket with tailored collar and 2 sets of pockets, worn by hunter in African jungle.

Bustle-type Dress—gown having fullness in the back.

Bustle Back—puffs, bows, or ribbon at the back of the hat.

Calotte—refer to *Chap. 10.*

Camisole Neckline—evening dress with neckline resembling that of camisole-top slip which was straight above the bustline with a strap over each shoulder.

Cardigan—refer to *Chap. 19, 20, 21.*

Chin Collar—flaring collar that concealed the chin. *Pl. LII, 2.*

Clip—ornament with hinged clip as a fastener instead of the usual pin.

Clog—sandal-type shoe with wooden or cork sole; worn usually at the beach. Refer to *Chaps. 8, 9, 10, 11, 12, 13, 16.*

Combination—brassière or shirt and panty in 1 piece. *Pl. LII, 4.*

Convertible collar—collar worn low or buttoned close and high.

Coolie Hat—adaptation from the Chinese hat with a peaked crown and slanting sides.

Corset—refer to *Chaps. 8, 9, 10, 11, 12, 13, 14, 15, 16, 17, 18, 19, 20, 21, 22.*

CHAPTER 23: GLOSSARY

Cowl Neckline—Refer to *Chap. 22.*

Culotte—trouser-like garment which resembled a full skirt. Refer to *Chap. 12.*

Derby—refer to *Bowler.*

Doll Hat—very small hat resembling a doll's hat.

Dressing Robe—loose lounging robe worn with or without a belt.

Dutch Hat—adaptation of a Dutch hat.

Ear Muff—adjustable covering for the ear, worn as a protection from the cold.

Empress Eugénie Hat—small hat worn tilted forward.

Ensemble—coat and dress that harmonized in color and fabric.

Envelope Combination—shirt and drawers combined, the latter having an open fold in the back.

Evening Wrap—cloak for evening wear. *Pl. LII, 3.*

Fedora—refer to *Chaps. 19, 20, 21, 22.*

Foulard—thin, soft material of silk, or silk and cotton.

Four-in-hand Tie—refer to Chaps. *19, 20, 21, 22.*

Free Finger Glove—trade name given to glove with a strap sewn along both sides and across ends of fingers.

Galosh—overshoe worn as a protection from rain and snow. Refer to *Galoche, Chaps. 9, 10,* and to *Chaps. 13, 17.*

Halo Hat—hat worn toward the back of the head and framing the face.

Halter-top—strap or band around the neck to hold the bodice of the backless evening dress.

Harlequin Hat—hat with wide, turned-up brim and oblique at the sides.

Hollywood Top Slip—fitted slip with single or double V-top.

Homburg—refer to *Chaps. 21, 22.*

Housecoat—long coat usually full-skirted, opening down the front, worn informally indoors.

Jodhpur Boot—shoe-height boot, open on either side, plain vamp held snugly by strap and buckle.

Jodhpurs—breeches used by equitant; designed with fullness above the knee, close-fitting below, cuff at ankle, and often with strap under instep.

Jumper Dress—sleeveless overdress.

Kimono—refer to *Chap. 21.*

Knickers—refer to *Chaps. 20, 21.*

Lounging Robe—comfortable house coat.

Mocha Glove—glove of a dark brownish, coffee color.

Monastic Silhouette—dress resembling the monk's robe, hanging loosely from shoulder, with fullness held in place by a belt at the waistline.

Muffler—knitted or fabric scarf, made of silk, wool, or synthetic material. Refer to *Chaps. 21, 22.*

Mushroom Style Hat—refer to *Chap. 21.*

Nose Veil—short veil that extended about to the lips.

Off-the-face Hat—similar to the halo hat which formed a frame for the face.

Opera Cape—elaborate loose cloak worn for formal wear.

Opera Hat—refer to *Chap. 21.*

Page Boy Bob—long shoulder-length bob with ends turned under, resembling the head-dress of a page boy in the Middle Ages.

Pajama—1-piece, or 2-piece lounging or sleeping garment consisting of coat and pants, made of silk or cotton fabric.

Panama Hat—refer to *Chaps. 21, 22.*

Pancake Beret—small flat cap. *Pl. LII, 6.*

Parka—long-skirted woolen garment having an attached hood, often fur-lined. This garment was used for winter sports and originally was the outer garment of animal skins worn by the Alaskan and Siberian.

Petticoat—refer to *Chaps. 9, 10, 11, 12, 13, 14, 15, 16, 17, 18, 19, 20, 21, 22.*

Pill Box Hat—hat shaped like a pill box and usually worn slightly tilted, often worn with detachable wimple. Refer to *Wimple, Chap. 8.*

Planter's Punch Hat—refer to *Chap. 22.*

Platform Shoe—slipper with sole made of several layers, making it possible to wear a higher heel. Refer to *Clog, Chaps. 8, 10, 11, 12, 13. Pl. LII, 7.*

Polo Shirt—sport shirt with an open collar, and short sleeve.

Pork Pie Hat—low-crowned felt hat with creased top. Refer to *Chap. 18.*

Princess Dress—close-fitting dress with bodice and skirt in 1-piece. Refer to *Chap. 19.*

Profile Hat—hat worn on one side of head forming a background for the profile of the wearer.

Raglan Sleeve—refer to *Chap. 21*, and to *Raglan, Chap. 22.*

Raincoat—refer to *Chap. 22.*

Redingote—refer to *Chaps. 14, 15, 16, 18, 20, 22.*

Sack Dress—loose-fitted garment, resembling the Watteau type of the 18th century.

Saddle Oxford—sport shoe having white leather in front and back and brown or colored leather over instep; worn by man and woman. Refer to *Saddle Shoe, Chap. 23.*

Sandal—refer to *Chaps. 1, 2, 3, 4, 5, 6, 7, 8.*

Sequin Calotte—small hat decorated with sequins. *Pl. LII, 5.*

Shirtwaist Dress—1-piece, belted tailored dress having a tucked shirtwaist. *Pl. LII, 1.*

Short Back Sailor—hat with narrow brim or no brim in back.

Shorts—very short pants worn on beach or for active sport; also worn as an undergarment.

Skimmer Sailor—flat-crowned sailor with heavy, wide straight brim.

Slacks—loose trousers worn for informal wear.

Slip—combination of brassière and skirt.

Snap Brim—hat with brim pulled down in front.

Suit—refer to *Chaps. 20, 21, 22.*

Swagger Coat—coat having very loose skirt, or flare from the shoulder to the hem.

Swing Skirt—circular skirt with gores which gave a swing motion when the wearer walked. This skirt became popular in the 1930's when swing music was in vogue.

Synthetic Material—cloth made of artificial materials.

Tab Collar Shirt—collar with long point on each side extending down the front.

Tiara—refer to *Chaps. 3, 4, 15.*

Toque—refer to *Chaps. 10, 16, 19, 20, 21, 22.*

Turban—refer to *Chaps. 9, 13, 14, 15, 16, 19.*

Tuxedo—refer to *Chaps. 20, 21, 22.*

Tyrolean Hat—hat resembling type worn by people in the highlands of Austria and Germany.

Veil—refer to *Chaps. 3, 4, 5, 6, 7, 8, 9, 10, 15, 16, 17, 18, 19, 20.*

Wallet—refer to *Chap. 22.*

Windbreaker—lined leather or closely woven, cloth jacket, having convertible leather collar and a zipper. Refer to *Chap. 22.*

Wrapper—revival of the loose informal garment worn at first in the home. The lines of this garment resembled the monastic silhouette. Refer to *Chap. 21.*

Zipper—metal slide fastener; also high boot with zipper fastening called zipper or galosh.

20th Century

PART IV

1940-46

CHRONOLOGY

Pan-American Conference in Havana, *1940*.

Three-power alliance formed by Germany, Italy, and Japan, *1940*.

Selective Service in the United States for conscription of Army with potential strength of 4,000,000, *1940*.

Atlantic Charter, with joint declaration of peace aims, of United States and Great Britain, *1941*.

National emergency proclaimed by the President of the United States, *May 27, 1941*.

Surprise attack on Hawaii and Philippines, *December 7, 1941*. War declared by the United States on Japan, *December 8, 1941;* on Germany and Italy, *December 11, 1941*.

Lend-lease Act passed by Congress, *1941*, providing financial and material aid to Allies, *1941*.

Service Men's Readjustment Act providing education for returning veterans, *1944*. After war colleges and universities crowded.

United Nations, world peace organization of Allies, established at San Francisco, *1945*.

V-E Day, end of war in Europe, *May 8, 1945*.

Demonstration of release of atomic energy for explosive purposes in bombing of Hiroshima, Japan, *1945*.

V-J Day, end of war with Japan, *August 14, 1945*.

Labor government in England, *1945*.

Germany and Austria occupied by United States, England, France, and Russia, *1945*.

France adopted a new constitution, *1946*.

Permanent site in midtown New York for headquarters of the United Nations given by John D. Rockefeller, Jr., *1946*.

Italian republic proclaimed, *1946*.

Philippine independence, *1946*.

CHAPTER 24

20th Century

PART IV

1940-46

HISTORY

Political unrest in Europe and the war which began in 1939, over-shadowed all countries at this time. The war that eventually included the major powers of the world began on September 1, 1939 when Poland was invaded by the Germans. Two days later, Great Britain and France declared war on Germany and in 1941 the United States was forced into World War II by the Japanese attack on Pearl Harbor. A four-year war ensued. The "Four essential human freedoms —freedom of speech, freedom of religion, freedom from want, and freedom from fear," were listed as the war aims by President Roosevelt. In 1945, the collapse of Germany and Japan brought about the end of the fighting.

The phrase "One World" that became very popular was coined at this time by Wendell Willkie, a prominent Republican candidate for the presidency. There seemed to be an advancement in international thought. The Fulbright Act has made it possible for a reciprocal exchange of students, teachers, specialists, and professionals. The Defense Department of the United States has given technical assistance to many countries. Schools in countries other than the United States likewise have granted scholarships to students in other countries. This international exchange of persons has also been assisted by various organizations that have contributed financially to the program.

Great discoveries and inventions continued during this time. The most important of these were the atomic bomb and radar which would have an effect on the future of all nations, in peace or in war.

During the war the garment industry experienced great changes as world conditions became more grave. The United States became a temporary center of fashion and many designers established their salons in New York City. For centuries French fashions had influenced the North American costume. Sometimes new designs by United States dressmakers were included with the Parisian designs, with no mention made of the original designer or of his nationality. Women were still fascinated by the term "Parisian design."

The movie stars have exerted a tremendous influence on the styles for many years. Many play clothes, sport styles, and summer fashions originated in California. The French costumers have long been famous for making exclusive costumes for wealthy women. The United States has excelled in the mass production of low-priced, ready-to-wear garments.

The sewing machine continued to be an aid to women of all classes in the United States in following the latest fashion trends. Modification of this invention speeded the production of garments during the war. Special electrical machines were designed which increased the rapidity of all operations, some machines were capable of making 3,000 stitches a minute. In this way civilian and war needs for garments and other sewed articles were met.

The participation of women in farm and factory work necessitated the use of adequate safety garments. The costumes for women in the war services were designed by leading dress designers of the day: Philip Mangone helped design the costume of the woman in the American army, Mainbocher designed garments for the woman in the navy, and Helen Cookman made the design for the apron worn by the nurse's aide.

Before the interruption by war, there were general rules for formality in dress. The shiny silk or grosgrain topper, or collapsible hat was worn by the man for dress occasions in 1940. The length of the tail coat had to end just below the bend of the knee. It was not considered correct if the white vest showed below the lapel points. The coat sleeve tapered to hold the shirt cuff snugly. Below the coat cuff, about one inch of linen was displayed. The same amount of linen extended above the back of the coat collar. The points of the high, broad-winged collar showed beyond the bow tie. The trousers for the tail coat were always decorated with a double braid on each side, and were long enough to break at the instep. The wing collar was worn for semiformal occasions if ladies were present; for other types of parties the turnover starched collar was acceptable.

The War Production Board changed all this. The regulations for the man's clothes affected every garment: there was a shorter jacket and elimination of patch pockets, belt, vent pleat, tucks, yoke, and any kind of frill. The vest or waistcoat was permitted with the single-breasted jacket, although none was allowed with the double-breasted jacket.

Changes in woman's dress occurred also due to the restrictions placed by the War Production Board on the use of material. This order saved 15 per cent of yardage. Certain categories were exempted from restrictions: infants' apparel, for child from one to four years of age, bridal gowns, maternity dresses, vestments for religious orders, and burial gowns. Some of the dress features which were dispensed with were the balloon sleeve, the turned-over cuff, double yoke, matching sash, patch pockets, attached hood, and shawl. The width of the skirt ranged from 72-80 inches according to size of garment, the depth of hem and belt was reduced to two inches.

There was a constant drive to "conserve your clothes" as a part of the national effort for victory. Woman's Clubs featured style shows of "made-over" clothing. Not only was care of the garment emphasized, but the prevailing mode in the cut of new garments was maintained. Adequate shoulder line, high armscye, and adequate looseness of the garments of this period gave room for movement of the wearer and reduced the strain on the fabric.

Another wartime regulation included restrictions of gasoline and tires which in turn resulted in a change in living habits: people became accustomed to walking and going places by bus or street car, and more interest was shown in the home. Travel was also limited because of the transportation of the military forces and supplies. The civilian learned to share and to give his time and effort to the major goal of winning the war.

Many customs of long standing were changed. Gas rationing restricted deliveries, and made it necessary for the woman in all walks of life to carry packages and purchases. The woman of the United States found herself almost devoid of domestic help, since the factory offered a higher wage to household worker. The role of the housewife during the war included not only her homemaking chores but the planning and care of a victory garden, canning of vegetables and fruits, and the careful budgeting of ration points as well as funds. Volunteer work for the Red Cross and work as a nurse's aide were equally important for the woman, old or young. The OCD (Office of Civilian Defense) and other similar organizations were supported by thousands of volunteer workers.

All of these conditions had an effect on the entire dress. Silk and nylon hose were practically unobtainable because of the need for nylon in war production and the lack of silk importation. Leg make-up was used by the young woman in place of hose. The bathing suit, consisting of a brassière and brief shorts, was a sharp contrast to the two-piece, Buster Brown type of suit, worn during the early part of the 19th century.

Habits formed as a result of military experience often result in a new style in civilian life. After the First World War a man wore a soft, detachable collar instead of the separate starched collar attached to the shirt. Experimentations in the fabrics and garments used by the American Armed Forces made the soldiers of the United States the most comfortably clothed of any military service in the world. These experiments aided in the production of civilian material and garments for use in all kinds of weather. The suit worn by the paratrooper of the United States army, was made of rayon and cotton twill cloth which was first tested in the football suit.

DRESS

A. *Sources of information:* costumes, photographs, fashion magazines, daily papers, and the cinema.

B. MEN
1. Garments:
> *Outer upper:* coat with padded shoulder; medium-length lapel; medium-length coat; white washable suit for summer, 1940; formality shown in informal and formal dress; single- or double-breasted vest matching coat, 1942; coat rather long, with square shoulder, and long lapel, 1945; *American blade;* natural waistline; 2- or 3-button coat with lower button left unfastened, also double-breasted coat, longer coat, 1946; vest not a costume necessity as before the war, not showing above coat, 1946; formal coat reappeared for evening; white tuxedo coat with black trousers for semi-formal wear; *lumber jacket; sport jacket;* blazer; cotton *golf jacket;* turtle-neck sweater, sweater worn in place of vest on college campus.

Outer lower: trousers to instep, lower line slanted from front to back; single braid down side of semiformal trousers, double braid on formal trousers; cuffless trousers.

Under: shirt for formal wear, with white, pleated bosom, 1940-41; difficult to obtain white shirt during the war and the year that followed; undershirt; shorts.

Cloaks and overgarments: knee-length topcoat, checked tweed ulster; long, loose-fitting coat with large pockets and convertible collar; patch pocket and diagonal, slash pocket, before and after the war; *reefer;* raincoat.

Neckwear and wristwear: attached, or separate collar for business; attached collar for campus and country; low turnover; ascot and four-in-hand ties for formal and semiformal day wear; white piqué, pointed, or butterfly shape, for formal evening wear; four-in-hand, or bow with points, or butterfly tie for business; four-in-hand also for sport.

Additional garments: dressing robe and *housecoat;* pajama; bathing suit consisting of trunks only; jodhpurs; sport jacket; slacks; shorts for sport.

2. **Hair:** usually parted on the left, or right side, combed to side, or straight back; pompadour; crew-haircut often worn by college man.
3. **Headdress:** black silk or opera hat for formal, at first; Homburg and derby for both formal and informal wear; pork pie hat; snap brim for business; semisport or tweed cap for campus; rough felt for semisport; town hat with brim turned down in front, fairly low, creased crown; straw hat for general wear in summer, planter's punch.
4. **Footwear:** shoe pointed, before the war, then rounded toe following the shape of the foot; shoe of calf hide; *Blücher;* moccasin; rubber sole for sport; saddle shoe; huarache; monk shoe; sandal; patent-leather shoe for formal and semiformal wear; white, or 2-toned saddle oxford for summer; high rubber boot worn usually on outside of trouser leg; jodhpur boot; shoes rationed during war, due to scarcity of leather; plain, or ribbed black hose for dress, striped and colored hose usual for informal wear; sport sock to knee; sock worn loose or held by garter.
5. **Jewelry:** *tie holder,* gold-initialed tie clip; collar pin, key chain, wrist watch; cuff links; gold cuff links and pearl studs for dress.
6. **Accessories:** boutonnière, and white handkerchief for dress, with colored border for other occasions; muffler, white for formal, black for semiformal; also fringed muffler; white kid glove for formal, light gray for semiformal, natural color pigskin for day wear; umbrella

carried by few; hand-tooled leather or plastic belt; broad ribbon or knitted braces or suspenders; blue, silk cummerbund; billfold; wallet and letter case; fountain pen, and pencil.

7. **Typical Colors:** black, dark blue, oxford gray, and tan for topcoat; blue, brown, gray, and green for suit; pin stripe woolens; blue, gray, maroon, white, ivory, yellow, tan, brown, or green for shirt; white or matching collar on shirt; blue gray, gold, maroon, yellow, copper, brown, green, plain, striped, figured, or plaid for tie; sometimes small figured ascot tie; blue, maroon, green, yellow, tan, ivory, copper, or gray for handkerchief; gray, brown, blue, olive green, drab green, tan, or black hat; maroon, blue, gray, yellow, brown, tan, or gold suspenders, color often repeated in tie; black or dark, rich brown shoe and saddle oxford; maroon, blue, dark gray, black, brown, and green sock; black worn by conservatives; gray for formal day wear; light gray glove.

8. **Typical Materials:** worsted or Cheviot, with or without finish; flannel, Saxony tweed for business; Shetland, gabardine or other lightweight wool for sport; seersucker suit for summer; black and gray striped, worsted or Cheviot for jacket; fleece, tweed, and covert for topcoat; flannel blazer; soft pliant plastic material for raincoat; white piqué waistcoat; vest matching jacket; broadcloth, madras, chambray for shirt; flannel, gabardine, or mesh shirt for semisport; chamois, capeskin, or mocha glove for formal wear, pigskin, knitted, or goatskin for semiformal and campus; pure silk tie, and pajama occasionally; suede, or knitted, sleeveless pullover sweater for semisport, campus, and country; calf, patent leather, or braided leather shoe.

9. **Make-up:** none, good grooming.

C. WOMEN

1. Garments:

Outer upper: basque-type, or full-bloused bodice; *moat collar;* high, round neck for day, fairly low and deep décolletage for evening; sleeve with fullness pleated, or gathered at armscye; leg-of-mutton sleeve; tight, long, or full sleeve; sleeve to just below elbow, full at top, tight or full at lower opening; small cap sleeve, full short sleeve; waist occasionally extremely tight, with wide waistband; fairly high-waisted princess dress, 1940; long formal and semiformal dresses; U. S. War Production Board imposed L-85 restrictions, 1942, same styles in vogue for the duration of the war; the following items discontinued: balloon sleeve, cuff, patch pocket, flap on pocket, yoke, long suit jacket, hood, cape, and sash over 2 inches wide; simple practical costume emphasized; heavier costume for warmth because of fuel conservation; wider and lower neck-

1. Breton Sailor 2. Dutch Cap 3. Matching Slipover Sweater and Cardigan
4. Alpine or Tyrolean Hat 5. Cummerbund 6. Turtle-neck Sweater
7. Homberg 8. Snap Brim 9. Sport Jacket

line in vogue; nipped-in and molded waist; slight change to normal costume, 1946, L-85 restrictions lifted; Paris market opened, showing French styles with a generous use of fabrics which had been limited since the opening of the war; heavily padded, rounded shoulder; modified shoulder width, basque lines, and longer jacket by end of period; embroidered sweater, 1941 and later.

Outer lower: shorter skirt, to knee, by December, 1940; front drapery, and bow on evening skirt; skirt plain in order to conserve fabric, stitching used to suggest patch pockets, narrow skirt, width of hem about 2 inches, regulated by War Production Board; *sarong;* dress to middle of knee, and above, by 1946, very full and flared skirt, with fullness toward the front; hoop skirt revived for evening, 1940; *dirndl,* broomstick skirt.

Under: slip; foundation garment; brassière; and 2-way-stretch girdle; corset; combination of brassière and panty; step-ins; *briefs;* difficult to obtain desirable girdle, 1942, and after, due to restrictions on materials, rayon and nylon lingerie available after the war, 1946; petticoat.

Cloaks and overgarments: fingertip *Mandarin jacket; traveling coat* with gathers across shoulders in back; *reversible coat;* raincoat; plain, fur-trimmed, or fur coat; fur-lined coat introduced by Mainbocher; coat with invested pleat in back; ulster; reefer; Chesterfield coat, 1942; less material used in coat, after 1942, and until end of war; *coat with zip-in lining; boy coat;* turtle-neck sweater; *matching slipover sweater and cardigan; mixed-match separates.*

Additional garments: housecoat; nightgown; sleeping pajama, lounging pajama; street suit with hip-length jacket, high lapel, and patch pocket; dinner suit with bead embroidery; suit very severe, 1942, due to war restrictions; *cocktail dress; sun dress* or *sunback dress; blue jeans* and *Sloppy Joe* styles worn by high school and college girl, 1940; slacks worn by all women (necessary for war work); some long pants tight at ankle; jodhpurs.

2. **Hair:** long hair for girls, 1940, later pompadour on top, close to head at sides, roll or curls at back of neck; hair also worn with knot or curls on top of head; page boy bob; high school and college girl with bob to shoulder, tapering in back, loose and wavy; large waves and simple bobbed coiffures; shorter hair and neater coiffure worn by mature woman; coiffure about the same, until 1947.

3. **Headdress:** cloche or small hat; *Alpine or Tyrolean hat;* large hat; off-the-face hat; hat usually side-tilted, 1946; draped hat for winter; fur hat to match glove; ribbon turban hat influenced by war restrictions on materials; half hat or hat with open crown; cotton hat of

1. Boy Coat 2. Chesterfield 3. Reefer
4. Jodhpurs 5. Saddle Oxford 6. Housecoat 7. Moccasin

same fabric as dress; Dutch hat; Breton sailor; hat not worn as often as in preceding periods; veil worn on hat, also face veil.

4. **Footwear:** pump; *monk shoe;* low- or high-heeled Oxford for every occasion; saddle shoe; *wedgies;* platform sole, medium heel, very narrow, extremely high heel; ration stamps necessary when buying shoes during the war; comfortable play shoe; moccasin; huarache; sandal; jodhpur boot; rayon and nylon hose very expensive during the war because of scarcity, available after the war.

5. **Jewelry:** costume jewelry of plastic, tinted mother-of-pearl, or translucent glass mounted on metal, shell or ceramic; pearls; dog collar, 1944; precious stones not used widely; at first of period, many small bracelets or 1 heavy bracelet.

6. **Accessories:** short-handled umbrella; sequin-trimmed accessories; lapel insignia; Allied Pin, tricolor design; narrow belt, 1942 due to restrictions on materials; apron; cummerbund; muff occasionally; handbag; compact; fountain pen and pencil, rattail comb; floral handkerchief; key case.

7. **Typical Colors:** variety of colors for dress; dark, rich shades for street dress; gray, brown, or black dress; delicate colors for summer; vivid shades in winter; restrictions on colors during war years; large and small prints.

8. **Typical Materials:** alligator, calf, or suede shoe, 1940; all kinds of cotton, rayon, wool fabrics, until 1942; restrictions on materials by War Production Board; wool, rayon, silk, nylon, and leather very scarce; plastic sheeting for shoe, and bag; cotton for evening dress; wool lining in suit prohibited, 1942; black cotton gabardine shoe not rationed; experimentation in materials during the war, new windproof, wool-backed rayon, and sunback rayon developed for flying suit.

9. **Make-up:** scarcely any rouge; emphasis on lipstick and nail polish, care taken to match make-up to dress.

BOOKS OF REFERENCE

(See BOOKS OF REFERENCE, Part I, *20th Century*, p. 353, and GENERAL BIBLIOGRAPHY, p. 433)

ARTISTS FOR COSTUME REFERENCE

(See p. 354)

GLOSSARY

Alpine or Tyrolean Hat—small felt hat with brim and usually with a feather at the side. *Pl. LIII, 4.*

CHAPTER 24: GLOSSARY

American Blade—coat with broad shoulder, and with fullness at upper arm and back to prevent strain and wear on the fabric.

Apron—refer to *Chaps. 2, 11, 12, 13, 14, 15, 17, 18, 22, 23.*

Blazer—light-weight jacket, usually bright colored, blue a popular color. Refer to *Chaps. 19, 20, 22.*

Blue Jeans—overalls or trousers made of denim, a heavy twilled cotton cloth, and formerly worn only by the working man and country boy.

Blücher—shoe with long vamp and strap across instep, derived from the style of boot worn by General Blücher during the battle of Waterloo.

Boutonnière—refer to *Chaps. 16, 17, 18, 23.*

Boy Coat—short coat resembling that worn by a small boy. *Pl. LIV, 1.*

Braces—colorful, patterned suspenders which held the trousers. Refer to *Chap. 18.*

Brassière—refer to *Chaps. 21, 22, 23.*

Breton Sailor—refer to *Chap. 23. Pl. LIII, 1.*

Briefs—close-fitting, short panties.

Broomstick Skirt—refer to *Chap. 1.*

Chesterfield—refer to *Chaps. 13. Pl. LIV, 2.*

Cloche—refer to *Chap. 22.*

Coat with Zip-in Lining—coat with lining worn in cold weather; lining removed for mild weather.

Cocktail Dress—party dress appropriate for wear in the late afternoon, and usually longer than a daytime dress.

Corset—refer to *Chaps. 8, 9, 10, 11, 12, 13, 14, 15, 16, 17, 18, 19, 20, 21, 22, 23.*

Cummerbund—sash of soft material worn for dress by man; adopted by woman also; originated from costume of man in Afghanistan. *Pl. LIII, 5.*

Derby—refer to *Chaps. 18, 19, 20, 21, 22, 23.*

Dirndl—very full gathered skirt resembling the skirt of the Tyrolean peasant.

Dog Collar—refer to *Chaps. 3, 7, 18, 20, 21.*

Dutch Cap—refer to *Dutch Hat, Chap. 23. Pl. LIII, 2.*

Four-in-hand—refer to *Chaps. 19, 20, 21, 22, 23.*

Golf Jacket—comfortable jacket in light weight or heavy fabric; made in various colors.

Homburg—refer to *Chaps. 21, 22, 23. Pl. LIII, 7.*

Housecoat—refer to *Chap. 23. Pl. LIV, 6.*

Huarache—refer to *Chap. 1.*

Jodhpur Boot—refer to *Chap. 23.*

Jodhpurs—refer to *Chap. 23. Pl. LIV, 4.*

Leg-of-mutton Sleeve—refer to *Chaps. 9, 10, 16, 20, 21.*

Lumber Jacket—short, heavy, plaid, wool jacket, belted and with patch pockets.

Mandarin Jacket—loose-fitting jacket resembling a Chinese Mandarin coat.

Matching Slipover Sweater and Cardigan—both garments of same yarn, weave and color, worn together or separately. *Pl. LIII, 3.*

Mixed Match Separates—jacket and skirt of unlike but harmonizing fabrics worn interchangeably.

Moat Collar—narrow standing collar worn around high broad neckline.

Moccasin—refer to *Chaps. 1, 3, 8. Pl. LIV, 7.*

Monk Shoe—low shoe, plain across instep and fastened with buckle.

Opera Hat—refer to *Chaps. 21, 23.*

Page Boy Bob—refer to *Chap. 23.*

Pajama—refer to *Chap. 23.*

Petticoat—refer to *Chaps. 9, 10, 11, 12, 13, 14, 15, 16, 17, 18, 19, 20, 21, 22.*

Planter's Punch—refer to *Chaps. 22, 23.*

Platform Sole—sole and heel made in 1 piece, built up solidly under instep and heel.

The slipper of the 16th century had a type of platform sole. Refer to *Chap. 23,* **and** to *Clog, Chaps. 8, 9, 10, 11, 12, 13, 16, 23.*

Pork Pie Hat—refer to *Chaps. 18, 23.*

Raincoat—refer to *Chaps. 22, 23.*

Reefer—single or double-breasted, tailored coat. *Pl. LIV, 3.*

Reversible Coat—coat which may be worn with either side out, sometimes waterproof**ed** beige gabardine on 1 side, bright plaid, usually wool, on the other.

Saddle Oxford—refer to *Chap. 23. Pl. LIV, 5.*

Sandal—refer to *Chaps. 1, 2, 3, 4, 5, 6, 7, 8, 23,*

Sarong—wraparound skirt of colorful fabric; similar to wraparound skirt, *Chap. 1.*

Slacks—refer to *Chap. 23.*

Slip—refer to *Chaps. 23.*

Sloppy Joe—costume including man's shirt, usually several sizes too large, worn on the outside, and blue jeans rolled up carelessly, 1 trouser leg higher than the other.

Snap Brim—soft felt hat having a medium crown and medium brim, pulled down in front in a jaunty fashion. Refer to *Chap. 23. Pl. LIII, 8.*

Sport Jacket—informal jacket worn when playing golf. *Pl. LIII, 9.*

Suit—refer to *Chaps. 20, 21, 22, 23.*

Sun Dress or Sunback Dress—backless dress.

Tie Holder—chain or other type of ornament worn to hold the four-in-hand tie in place.

Traveling Coat—woman's long, full, flaring coat worn when traveling.

Turtle-neck Sweater—refer to *Chaps. 21, 22. Pl. LIII, 6.*

Tuxedo—refer to *Chaps. 20, 21, 22, 23.*

Tyrolean Hat—refer to *Alpine Hat* and to *Chap. 23.*

Ulster—large, loose-fitting overcoat, originally from Ulster, Ireland. Refer to *Chap. 19.*

Veil—refer to *Chaps. 3, 4, 5, 6, 7, 8, 9, 10, 15, 16, 17, 18, 19, 20, 21, 22, 23.*

Wallet—refer to *Chaps. 22, 23.*

Wedgie—shoe having a very thick sole and a wedge-shaped heel.

20th Century

PART V

1947-52

CHRONOLOGY

Russia absorbs satellite states in Europe, *1946-52.*

Large sums appropriated by United States Government for European recovery, military assistance, Point IV (technical aid) Programs, *1947-52.*

Cranston Print Works, Rhode Island, introduced method of double printing giving effect of tropical worsteds and heavy tweed to cotton fabric, *1948.*

Frame that spins cotton yarn directly from drawn staple, introduced by Nastrofil Company, Milan, Italy, *1948.*

Textiles, second largest industry in United States, *1948.*

Inter-American Conference concluded treaty-charter of Organization of American States, *1948.*

Berlin Blockade by Russia against three other occupying powers (United States, England, France), *1948-49.*

North Atlantic Pact signed by twelve nations, *1949.*

German Federal Government established in Western portion, *1949.*

War in Korea broke out, *June, 1950.*

United States ends the state of war with Germany, *October 19, 1951.*

Independent Kingdom of Libya inaugurated, *October 24, 1951.*

Japanese Government completed ratification of World War II Peace Treaty signed at San Francisco and the parallel Security Pact with the United States, *November 18, 1951.*

Fluorescent fabrics attained nationwide popularity, *1951.*

Queen Elizabeth II of England ascended the throne on death of her father, George VI, *February 6, 1952.*

First moves made toward a federal union of west European countries, growing out of Schuman Plan for pooling iron and coal supplies, *1952.*

CHAPTER 25

20th Century

PART V

1947-52

HISTORY

Very soon after the war it became evident that the dream of One World of peace and prosperity was not to become a reality—at least in this generation. The chief stumbling block in achieving international co-operation was Russia who by her misuse of the veto in the United Nations and her ruthless conquest of satellite countries divided the world into two camps: the Communist nations and those still free and independent. To counter Russia's aggressiveness the United States launched vast programs of military, economic, and technical aid to the nations of the West to build up their own internal and military strength as a defense against the threat of Russia. To implement this unity the North Atlantic Pact was signed by twelve countries in 1949 and a European Army organized under the American general, Dwight Eisenhower.

When the Communist armies broke across the 38th Parallel in South Korea in June, 1950 the free peoples of the world showed their resolve to oppose aggression by immediately backing up President Truman's order to meet the attack with military and naval force. For the first time in history many countries fought in Korea under one standard—the flag of the United Nations.

In contrast to the enslavement of millions by Russia, many peoples won their independence during this period—India, Burma, Israel, and Indonesia. A German Federal Government was established in 1949 in the Western portion of the country. Forty-eight non-Communist nations signed a World War II peace treaty with Japan in September, 1951.

In the United States, because of the huge sums needed for defense and for foreign aid, taxes were very high and prices soared. But the country was generally prosperous. Employment was at a high peak and many more young people were receiving the advantages of higher education, a great many under the GI Bill of Rights. The international exchange of students and teachers contributed to a better understanding among western countries. Scientific research made great strides. The U. S. Government laid plans to construct a hydrogen bomb much deadlier than the uranium type. Jet-propelled airplanes, guided missiles, artificial rainmaking were a few of the achievements of science. Television became a household word as millions of TV sets in American homes brought entertainment and education right into the living room, thereby changing many habits of living.

Women all over the world, even a few in Russia, won new prestige in this period. Political equality with men was established in fifty-two countries. Several women served their countries as ambassadors, Mme Pandit of India was an outstanding figure as head of her delegation in the United Nations. More and more American women were obtaining key positions in business and the professions.

Fashion experts predicted a revolutionary change in dress after the war. According to some authorities garments would be made from new designs, new materials, and be completely original. But when the *New Look* appeared in 1947 it was nothing more than a hodge-podge of previous styles. The Gibson Girl of the early 20th century reappeared with her shirtwaist, large sleeves, black ribbon around the collar, and full skirt. The X silhouette of 1830 was duplicated. The swishing petticoat of the late Victorian period returned. Fashions of the Empire and other periods were copied.

In the New Look emphasis was placed on the hips and rounded shoulderline. The silhouette achieved was not flattering to anyone, although an attempt was made to emphasize femininity by the use of drapery and frills. Even the men came in for a share of the movement. For them it was a *New Bold Look* with more variety in their costumes and brighter colors and patterns in their shirts and ties.

While a few faddists took to the New Look in all its absurdities with avidity it was not generally popular. Women were too used to the convenience of the simpler garments of previous years and they resented the expense the radical change caused them since none of their older, shorter dresses could be made over to comply with the new style. Moreover there was a justified moral indignation in the use of so much more material when so many people in the war-torn world were still in

402

CHAPTER 25: DRESS

desperate need of clothing. Only the manufacturers of dress materials whole-heartedly supported the trend. By 1949 the New Look, although it left traces of its influence, had faded away and styles once more were adapted to the requirements of modern living. Slacks came into general use, although frowned upon by some critics who felt they were an exclusively male garment. Girls also adopted the mannish tailored suit, the Chesterfield, the raincoat with the raglan sleeve, and the post-boy vest.

DRESS

A. *Sources of information:* costumes, fashion illustrations, photographs.

B. MAN
1. Garments:

Outer upper: suit well-fitted; in first of period, coat with padded shoulder and long lapels, single-breasted with 2 or 3 buttons, lower button left unfastened, also double-breasted coat with upper or lower button left unfastened; patch or slash pocket; American blade; coat longer, to below hip, 1948; New Bold Look, fall, 1948; suit designed for seasonal comfort; vest of same material and color as of suit, often omitted in very warm weather; cutaway coat; 1949, coat rather long, collar low and fitted snugly about the neck showing some shirt collar, sleeve to above the break in the wrist showing shirt cuff, low or fairly high lapels; coat with center back or 2 side vents; single- or double-breasted coat; buttons of double-breasted coat set high to give height, broad lapel, or peaked lapel giving height; tuxedo with wide lapel; long lapels still worn by many; change in silhouette, 1950-52: natural-width shoulders, straight hanging jacket, full sleeve tapered to cuff; 3-button coat, fall of 1952; tail coat, 1952; vest usually of same fabric as suit, bright colors and checks by the young man; pullover sweater, or *sleeveless blazer* worn in place of vest; cardigan with plaid front; mesh-knitted shirt of British influence for sport; *Cowichan* or *Siwash sweater;* army jacket; sports coat buttoned high, with convertible collar and patch pockets; sports jacket with belted back, 1952.

Outer lower: first of period, trousers with fullness pleated in around the waist; length to break at instep; cuffs; 1952, tapered trousers to give slenderizing effect.

Under: white shirt again available, collars and cuffs usually attached, collar with hidden loop fastening; knit and mesh-knitted undershirt and shorts; briefs.

Cloaks and overgarments: knee-length topcoat; Chesterfield with fly front; coat for all seasons with slip-in lining; single- or double-breasted coat, rolled, notched or peaked lapel; length of overcoat, 3 inches below break of knee, 1949; *Chester;* pile fabric lining in tweed or gabardine coat; winter coat with *mouton* collar; coat with raglan sleeve; synthetic material; *processed raincoat* with patch pockets; single- or double-breasted ulster.

Neckwear and wristwear: wing, or low turnover collar, com-*mand collar* or *forward collar* worn open or closed, spreading shirtcollar, rounded collar pinned beneath tie, 1949-50; *Pierpont* or *pin point collar,* 1950; similar styles continuing, through 1952; linen showing less than an inch above collar and under cuffs, 1947-49, less amount, 1950-52; tie colorful, plain 1-figure per tie, 1950-51, stripes popular, fall, 1952; bow tie with pointed or straight ends, very narrow, 1951-52; narrow four-in-hand tie with pointed or straight ends; piqué bow tie for dress.

Additional garments: lounging robe with rolled lapel, sometimes peaked lapel, length to 3 inches below knee; pajama with long pants, or shorts, light weight for summer, heavier for winter; before 1949, long shorts resembling those worn by the British in North Africa in World War II; bathing suit; nylon trunks for beach; *beach coat;* lumber jacket; *"TV" lounging jacket,* 1952; slacks; knickers; jodhpurs; *Levis,* 1951-52; processed jackets with mouton collars, fall, 1952.

2. **Hair:** hair parted on left or right side and combed to side or straight back; pompadour worn by a few; crew-cut by young men; Marcel wave by a few men.

3. **Headdress:** hat with wide crown, until 1951; Homburg, snap brim hat, pork pie hat, hat with brim flat on side and front and pencil curl in back; planter's punch or Panama hat with double-pleated *puggree* around crown; *Tremont hat,* 1950; visored cap for sport; January, 1950, tapered crown with medium brim; cap with visor showing influence of French legionnaire; semi-Homburg; hat with punched crowns, and other types previously mentioned, 1952; fore-and-aft cap, fall, 1952.

4. **Footwear:** shoe following shape of foot, low heel; Blücher; saddle oxford; straight, plain, or wing top shoe; moccasin loafer with strap, tailored moccasin; all-over perforated shoe; woven leather oxford; crepe-soled shoe; sandal; previous styles continued in 1952, shoes less bulky, raffia, blue denim, or linen shoe for beach sports wear; patent-leather oxford with plain tip, 2-eyelet or pump for dress;

1. Balerina Skirt   2. Suit   3. Greatcoat   4. Petticoat   5. Feminine Blouse

wooden clog for beach; jodhpur boot; short boot for campus, for winter or rainy weather; rubber overshoe; black sock for formal wear, colorful sock for other occasion; garter.

5. **Jewelry:** ring worn by some; wrist watch; watch on chain; identification bracelet; key chain; collar pin or bar; gold initial *tie clip* or tie holder; money clip; white or gray pearl studs, and gold cuff links for dress, sometimes set with stone to match color of suit, 1950.

6. **Accessories:** boutonnière, sometimes a red carnation for dress; white handkerchief for dress, with colored border, or plain color for informal wear, the latter folded in a rather carefree manner and worn with points extending from left chest pocket of coat; neckerchief or muffler; cummerbund; pigskin and mocha glove; garter; braces and sock of same design and color; belt; letter and cigarette cases, the latter sometimes of gold; penknife; wallet; key case; umbrella; walking stick carried by some; leather buttons used on sport jacket; chef's apron worn when preparing food for picnic.

7. **Typical Colors:** gayer than in preceding period; cool colors in spring, warm colors in fall; pastel and deep shades; colors coordinated in suit, fall, 1948, for example, blue, gray, brown, or black suit, and harmonizing accessories; white or pastel color for shirt, border of handkerchief harmonizing with stripe in shirt; white dinner jacket for dress, also white handkerchief and white glove; light to dark gray flannel suit for the young man, fall, 1952; brown, black, or dark blue shoe; natural-colored light tan glove for informal wear; during entire period beautiful and well-designed ties, all colors used, stripes and small patterns popular, white piqué tie for dress; green, charcoal gray, blue gray, dark blue, brown, or black hat; various patterns including stripes, checks, and large bold figures, used for lounging robe, and pajama; all colors for sports wear, jacket, sweater, beach robe, shorts, and slacks.

8. **Typical Materials:** suits designed for comfort, porous fibers, light weight and cool wrinkle-resistant cloth including dacron; striped or plaid suit, by young men, flannel, worsted or gabardine suit, herringbone tweed, especially for sport; spun rayon tropical suit for summer; herringbone tweed cashmere or worsted coat; cotton, linen or gabardine sport shirt, also silk shantung, piqué, broadcloth, or nylon shirt, 1952; noncrushable, striped rep, wool, foulard, twill silk ribbon, or pure silk tie, 1950-52; nylon, or ribbed, woolen sock; felt hat, smooth, or rough-textured straw hat for summer, light weight fiber hat and Baku, 1950-52; also Milan, Panama, and cocoa straw hat; capeskin, mocha or deerskin glove; patent-leather dress shoe; buckskin moccasin, leather, or crepe rubber sole; alligator,

1. Peasant Blouse   2. Basque Jacket   3. Camisole Top
4. Square Dance Dress   5. Sleeveless Blazer   6. Stole

calf, cordovan, or pigskin belt; mesh, or knitted braces; matching braces and garter; worsted slacks for sport; pure silk pajama; silk foulard lounging robe; cotton and terry cloth beach jacket; corduroy, or woolen jacket for winter; processed, or plastic raincoat, rubber galosh.

9. **Make-up:** cologne used; many kinds of shaving luxuries; good grooming emphasized.

C. WOMEN
1. Garment:

Outer upper: basque bodice, many frills, high, or extremely low neckline, 1947; silhouette with rounded shoulder line, with smaller shoulder pad, and emphasis on larger hipline, 1947-49; extreme styles outmoded by spring, 1949, rounded or bottle shoulder disappearing, padding used after 1949; sleeve pushed up forming the shape of a Chinese lantern and styles of preceding period, 1949; many changes in silhouette, by summer, 1950, wider shoulder, straight fullness, long torso, small waist emphasized by exaggerated fit at waist; 1951, stiff lining in peplum of jacket emphasized the rounded or arched hipline; summer, 1952, jackets briefer, peplum of jacket less arched, also short flaring peplum; 1947-48, small turned-up collar resembling those of the 15th century, *Puritan collar,* Peter Pan collar, sailor collar, *Gibson girl collar, winged collar or revers, flyaway collar, sling neckline;* styles of collar of 1949 included those of 1947 and *scoop neckline, plunging neckline,* open, low neckline, shoulder-cuff neckline; bare shoulder and *midriff;* various types of necklines, 1950-52, including those of preceding years, also bertha, draped, fore-and-aft neckline that was the same in front and back, *halter-top,* tank top, slashed neckline, and high wide neckline, turtle-neck, band neckline, wide décolleté, and low draped or cowl neckline; bare look, spring and summer, 1952; fall, 1952, emphasis placed on the contrast of the color of the skin with a black dress; sleeve with very full shoulder to wrist, leg-of-mutton sleeve, short or cap sleeve, 1947-49; many types of sleeves, 1951-52, including raglan, bracelet-length, medium full sleeve in dress and suit, dress with or without strap for formal wear, 1950-52; many beads and sequins, elaborate decoration on blouse during entire period, *peasant blouse,* Mexican blouse, *stocking bodice* often sleeveless, 1949-52; middy blouse for sports wear at first, by 1952, popular for dress, costume sweater, *tailored* or *feminine blouse* during entire period, also plain blouse with ruffled sleeve; fall, 1952, costume less extreme, beautiful lines, silhouette neither full nor slim, shoulder with little padding, waistline varied, high-waisted for the *Empire style,* low-waisted for the middy style; length of dress

1. Plunging Neckline   2. Little Boy Shorts   3. Cobbler's Apron
4. Beach Coat   5. Jester Pants   6. Gaucho Pants
7. Toreador Pants, Cinch Belt   8. Duster   9. Stocking Bodice

or coat emphasized with higher collars, lower waistlines, long torso, straight skirt, accent in back through bloused back and back-dipping waistline.

Outer lower: 1948, skirts extremely long; *balerina skirt,* ankle-length pleated skirt; full quilted skirt; tight, slit skirt with emphasis placed at hip; bustle resembling that worn, 1862, sometimes draping in front showing Egyptian influence; narrow silhouette, spring, 1949, tiers, back fullness, panels of all kinds including triangular and *flying panels;* very large pocket on each hip; slim skirt wrapped on 1 side, and spiral wraparound; crushed pleating to give effect of slim skirt; next, bouffant skirt; dirndl; fullness in back of draped skirt with draping extending beyond silhouette on 1 side or fullness gathered all around the waist; arched peg-top tucks; the length for the New Look being 12 to 14 inches for the daytime dress, although usually worn much longer by most girls, 8 to 12 inches for the late day, and dinner dress, and 6 inches from the floor for the formal short-length evening dress, and semiformal dresses; 1949-51, suit length shorter, 13 to 14 inches from floor, and the dress a little shorter than the suit; after 1949, length worn that was becoming to the individual; day-length dinner dress; various types of skirts included, handkerchief draped skirt, loose panel pleats, 1947-49; *trumpet silhouette skirt, harem hem skirt,* skirt with low placed fullness, cotton dirndl with straw and haircloth, or straw pockets, *Guatemalan skirt, circle skirt,* 1951-52; fall, 1951, back flare or side pleats, pleated skirt, quilted skirt, 10-gored skirt, bell-shaped skirt, flared skirt, dirndl, skirt with inversed center pleat, half-circle skirt, and a narrow 1-yard skirt; little change in length of skirt, fall, 1952, waltz length, 7 inches from floor, cocktail dress, 7-10 inches from floor, and street dress, 11-14 inches off floor, sometimes slightly dipped hemline in the back.

Under: foundation garment emphasizing waist, although not nipped in, 1949-50; short corset to nip-in waist, 1951; panty girdle, plain girdle, 1949-52; long line corset, 1952, also high waistline girdle; *bra* to emphasize high, well separated and pointed breasts, bandeau bra, long line bra, and strapless wired bra; one style, black satin with imitation chip diamonds to be worn with sheer dress, 1950-52; slip, strapless bra-slip with organdy petticoat; elaborate petticoat; petticoat or half-slip; chemise or camisole with trunk panties, sometimes top of camisole to fill in low neckline, worn with matching petticoat, with or without blouse and sheer outside skirt; underwear becoming more elaborate and elegant; short bloomer-band leg panty, elastic leg briefs, 1949-52.

Cloaks and overgarments: Chesterfield; greatcoat or large, long, full

1. Sheath Dress   2. Stocking Bodice   3. Chemise Dress   4. Cloche
5. Scoop Neckline   6. Flyaway Jacket   7. Flyaway Collar
8. Wraparound Skirt   9. Sleeveless Look   10. Duster   11. Bertha

coat; wraparound coat and coat with dolman sleeve, 1949, showing influence of 1920's; fur coat with cuffed bellow or cuffed balloon sleeve, 1949-52; 3-quarter or ankle-length coat; duster with large bracelet-length sleeve and large turned-back cuff, 1950-52; long or short coat resembling those of the 18th century; versatile cape that could be transformed to buttoned jacket or coat, *pyramid coat,* boxy coat, narrow coat with convertible collar and capelet, pushup sleeve and melon sleeve on some coats, belted straight coat, fitted coat with zip-in lining, fitted coat with deep armhole, and raglan topper of fur or cloth, 1950-52; coat showing influence of Mexican poncho, 1951; redingote; cape in the spring, 1951; fall coats of 1952 included untrimmed cloth coat in novelty fabric with high collar, sometimes edged in Persian lamb, fitted coat with *princess silhouette,* narrow loose coat, straight coat and slightly flared coat, silk coat with soft sleeve detail, coat with raglan sleeve, short double-breasted coat, coat with bloused back, cloak with *martingale belt* suggesting low-dipping waist, Norfolk jacket with lowered martingale belt; among the short jackets of this period were: short or fingertip topper, swagger coat, and reefer, or short jacket with flared back, *flyaway jacket,* bolero with flyaway back or with straight back, boy coat, cardigan jacket, Cowichan or Siwash sweater, sport jacket influenced by Middle Ages, cloth or knit sleeveless blazer, basque jacket, *weskit,* spencer, Eton jacket; raincoat. **Additional garments:** *camisole top* sun dress, 1947-52; suit during entire period, bloused back, *Directory suit* with cutaway bolero, middy suit with hip-length jacket and pleated skirt, fall, 1952; convertible *separates* very popular, 1950-52, formal separates, 1952; dress worn with long coat having same fabric as dress, dress with bolero or capelet, 1952; short evening dress with camisole top, fall, 1952, *convertible jumper* and *four-way dress* popular, fall, 1952; *coat dress,* 1949-52; after 1949, baretop dress worn with matching jacket, sun dress, sunback dress with belted stole, *Empire-line sunback dress* with upper part ending above *midriff,* shirring used across bosom, dress with *sleeveless look; square dance dress,* 1947-52; *classic shirt frock;* dress with *side long look,* 1951; *petticoat dress, sheath dress,* quick-to-sew print, *chemise dress, trumpet coat dress,* halter-top dress, fall, 1952; raincoat with flaring back, often with hood, 1 type reversible, having plain color on 1 side and checks or stripes on the other; dress with tunic type of skirt tied as apron, and used as a cape when needed; short beach coat, sometimes with ruffles, 1952, swim suit with halter or bra, or bra top and shorts, swim suit with elasticized *cinch belt* or self drapery; lumber jacket blouse; *shrug jacket, reversible jersey blouse,* twin

1. Poncho   2. Weskit   3. Sun Dress, Stole   4. Shrug Jacket
5. Balerina Skirt   6. Convertible Jumper for Sports Wear
7. Convertible Jumper for Evening   8. Convertible Jumper for Daytime

set of jersey sweaters; slacks; *pedal pushers;* jodhpurs; *little boy shorts;* shorts and halter-top or bra, for summer play, shorts longer, 1949; play co-ordinates, 1949-52, 1-piece play suit, 1951; novelty play suits, 1951-52; quilted jacket with slacks, lounging suit for entertaining, 1951-52; more feminine type of costume after summer, 1951; hostess gown or coat; sweater blouse and velvet calf-length pants or long trousers, sometimes *toreador pants, jester pants, gaucho pants* or *cabin boy breeches; "TV sets";* elastic midriff sleeping gown, shortie gown, shortie pajama, also long sleeping gown, and long pajama.

2. **Hair:** close to head; often short with ringlets; 1949, very short hair resembling coiffure of 1920; long hair worn by a few; chignon, 1949-52; *horse's tail, poodle cut* and other short coiffures, 1952.

3. **Headdress:** until 1950, the following styles were worn: crushed beret, Scotch tam-o'-shanter; cloche; close-fitting crown resembling that of 1920 helmet; bonnet-type of hat, similar to that worn by men of the Renaissance period; wide-brimmed hat; draped crown; Victoria bonnet; veil designed after type used in Middle Ages, sometimes tied in quaint bow resembling those used in Victorian age; ribbon trimming, bow, rosette or flowers, often hanging down in back or over one ear; half hat and close-fitting feather hat for midseason, 1948-49; close-fitting felt hat; tricorne with one corner caught up with small ornament; tilted large hat; woman often bareheaded in summer and winter, especially for informal and evening wear, during entire period; 1950, varied styles, including braid-trimmed pill box, tricorne, feathered helmet, casual slouch, flowered bonnet, jersey calotte with chin strap, matador hat, Churchill hat with Homburg brim, and pork pie crown; hat worn forward in 1950-52, 2-tone combination in hats; visor-type hat, sailor, Breton sailor, flower trimmed hat, 1951; hat worn straight, 1951-52; hat with chignon shape in back, cloche, silhouette hat, and styles of preceding years, 1952; veil on hat worn during entire period; hat with shallow, round crown with narrow turned down brim, fall, 1952, also, hat with small crown, worn straight on top, or far back on head.

4. **Footwear:** nearly every kind of shoe worn during the entire period, very high thin heel, or low heel, platform sole, pump with toe and heel, but instep free, sandal with double strap circling from back of shoe and encompassing front of foot, open-work sandal with cotton lace vamp and colorful embroidery, Roman sandal with cleverly designed vamp, buskin, huarache, clog, saddle oxford, *ballet slipper,* winged flap covering back of heel and front of foot with very plain, open toe, bright-colored shoe, low heel for casual wear; revived interest in comfortable shoe, 1949, low heel for

1. Coat Dress 2. Coat Dress with Cape 3. Helmet
4. Dirndl 5. Flying Panels 6. Spencer Jacket
7. Cabin Boy Breeches 8. Pedal Pushers

daytime, high heel for dress; jodhpur boot; 1949-52, hose or stocking in 4 proportioned leg sizes; during entire period nylon hose almost exclusively, often very thin, attention given heel of stocking, black heel worn with black shoe for dress, colored heel to match dancing dress, 1949, gold or lace heel, or designs of arrows and dots in 1952; textured hose of silk and cotton, silk and lisle, or ribbed hose to be worn with tweeds and casual fabrics; bare leg with leg make-up; sock for teenage and college girl; galosh.

5. Jewelry: elaborate and beautiful costume jewelry of fine texture worn throughout the period; *scatter pins,* 1948-52; jewelry of pearls, sapphires, emeralds, brilliants of many colors, and rhinestones, beautifully cut and carved metal arranged in large delicate floral design, lacy, metal bib or pearl necklace, 1949; heraldic and antique styles, 1949-52; necklace, earring and bracelet set, fashioned of metal-backed brilliants elaborately arranged, dog collar of porcelain beads, pearl necklace of from 1 to 6 and more strands, back interest in necklace, 1949-52; pin clip and earring set, fashioned of tiny shells, buttons or sequins, often made by the wearer; jewels worn in hair, chignon pins, 1950-52; jet with rhinestones, fall, 1952; pins worn on the skin, 1951-52.

6. Accessories: during the entire period, varied accessories; beautiful aprons, party apron worn as an overskirt, *cobbler's apron;* umbrella and parasol with long handle reminiscent of the early 20th century, short umbrella continuing in popularity; shoulder sling bag showing influence from the ancient Chinese, Middle Ages, and Latin America, tooled leather bags from Italy, Central and South America; bag or purse with short handle, framed bag, envelope bag, underarm bag, oversized dress bag, transparent, plastic box-like bag, bag of calf, suede, reptile, alligator, imitation leather, or faille; 1952, clutch bag of leather, plastic, faille, or over all pearls, rhinestones, or jet accents, cane bag having a cane through center of bag, reticule, handpainted basket carried as handbag; card case; wallet; beautiful compact; comb and comb case; gold kid, saddle leather, or colorful knotted string belt, 1949; narrow or wide belt, cummerbund, *cinch belt;* short or long glove, short gauntlet glove, cuffed glove, cuff sometimes draped or made of puffs, 1949-52, glove designed with polka dots or stripes and ascot to match, 1951-52; black suede gloves with black dyed fox cuffs, fall, 1952; water-repellent scarf, beautiful scarf, plain, silk screen printed, handblocked, or hand-painted with landscapes, or abstract designs, used as decoration for head, neck, or waist, square, short, or long narrow scarf, or ascot, 1949-52, also mantilla; ribbons with several ends hanging worn at neckline of blouse or dress, 1950; stole, straight or triangular sometimes of veiling or net and decorated with rhinestones, black velvet, or handwoven, often fringed, and with pockets, 1950-52; mink band that resembled collar of turtle-neck sweater, also very small fur neckpiece; muff of fake fur, 1952; *cache-chignon;* artificial flowers worn on scarf, on purse, in pocket and on dress at neck, shoulder, or waist; a rose on belt, collar or stole very popular, 1952; fresh flowers in glass or silver vial pinned on dress, sometimes glass vial with rubber pocket pinned on small bag for party wear; lingerie neckwear not frilly but softly tailored and low cut in the first years of this period; capelet or very short jacket to cover bare-shoulder or to dress-up a costume; embroidered crest on jacket, 1950-52; white linen collar and cuffs on suit, fall, 1952; many buttons (some of rhinestone) and bows, 1949, showing influence of late 19th century and lifted to prominence by the popular song, "Buttons and Bows"; rhinestone buttons increasing in favor, 1949-52; white or floral handkerchief, also wide bordered lace handkerchief; fans of ostrich feathers, fake aigrettes, white velvet or pleated black lace fan, 1950-52, also handbag size fan of lace.

7. **Typical Colors:** colors with distinctive names, and new color combinations throughout the period: avocado green, meadow green, romance pink, luggage tan, and maize; pastel tones and deep shades for dresses; yellow, sky blue, turquoise, navy, black, green, red, gray, or white shoe, colorful print; light luminous colors for spring, 1949; deep-toned gingham plaid, colorful costume, 1949-52; fall, 1950, taupe, brown, forest green, or dark navy coat; dress of red, copper tones, navy blue, slate, teal blue, or shades of blue, and charcoal gray worn for fashionable evening wear, 1950-52; natural skin tone, pink, or oyster white for glove; light neutral colors for hats in spring and summer and deeper shades for fall and winter, 1949-52; colors especially popular, fall, 1952, black combined with brilliant color, black and white, coppery tones, gold, brown, dark red, magenta, plum, all shades of blue, such as slate blue, navy, and teal, shades of gray such as charcoal gray, slate gray, stone gray, gay plaids, and prints; fall, 1952, coat light in color, gray and blond camel hair; strong colors for hats, fall, 1952; light-colored hose for spring and summer, dark colors for fall and winter.

8. **Typical Materials:** varied materials during entire period; wrinkle-resistant fabrics; synthetic materials for all types of garments including raincoat, also taffeta, or gabardine raincoat; coats of wool including *poodle cloth,* synthetic furs, camel, black Alaskan seal, muskrat, mink, Russian broadtail, squirrel, *mouton;* nylon glove, blouse, pleated skirt, dress, bed jacket or negligee, underwear and girdle; nylon lace for slip and petticoat, sometimes nylon lace over

nylon sheer; woolen and worsted fabrics for winter and overgarments; wool jersey, corduroy or felt skirt; seersucker, plain organdy, shadow stripe organdy, bemberg rayon sheer, piqué, terry cloth, batiste, or gingham for summer, also *butcher linen,* rayon crepe, taffeta, paper taffeta, *toile,* silk crepe sheer, shantung, gabardine, and a variety of cottons and newly treated cottons, cotton and linen or pure linen fabrics in light medium or heavy weight; gabardine suit for summer and winter, 1947-52; flannel or worsted fabric of various weight for suit or dress; velveteen or tweed suit; fine lace, net or chiffon for dance dress, 1950-52; gabardine for shirt or sport jacket; leather, plastic, or elastic cinch belt; glazed chintz for skirt; piqué, jersey, other fabric or straw for hat, also felt, velour, or velvet, fall, 1952, softly textured furry surface, and fabrics of preceding period; suede, calf, kidskin, or snakeskin for shoe, cotton and straw for summer play shoe; cotton lisle anklet; gold kid, pigskin, capeskin, broadcloth, cotton string, or nylon glove; sequins, beads, jewels, jet trimming, or gold decoration on formal glove; straw, sailcloth, plastic, bead, faille, leather, or black patent-leather for bag; velvet or braid trimming popular; emphasis on texture in garment, 1951-52; fall, 1952, washable winter fabrics, including tweed, printed corduroy, cotton, calico, denim, linen, jersey in wool, silk, or rayon, also coated fabrics, felt, wool jersey that appeared to be handknitted, rayon suiting with a texture resembling wool; angora ascot, stole, and hat; silk, cotton, or wool stole; rhinestones on bodice, cuffs, and pockets of hostess coat; texture emphasized in trimming, metallic thread, and lustrous yarns used, also chenille with flat yarn; fringe often used for trimming; black faille capelet with passementerie braid trimming; embroidery combined with jet; mink tails used as decoration on garments.

9. **Make-up:** scarcely any rouge, lips emphasized, brilliant and dark-colored nail polish, 1947-50; delicate rouge, lipstick, and nail polish typical of the New Look, 1949; beauty shops continued in popularity; experimentation in new methods of permanent waving; light powder, rouge by some, deep-colored lipstick, light, or dark-colored nail polish, 1950-51; light or bright colored lipstick, and nail polish, dark powder, tanned skin popular, especially for summer, 1947-52, by fall, 1952, light creamy skin emphasized.

SIGNIFICANT MOTIFS

A significant change in the motifs of 1949 used on printed fabrics, cotton, silk, or synthetic material, for dresses and draperies was from naturalistic flowers, stripes or checks to the reproductions of pen or crayon drawings of still life, animals, people, buildings, or pastoral scenes, mostly classic in type. These prints were followed by others having simple, and pleasing arrangements of lines and brush strokes, faithfully portraying the sparkling water colors used in the original designs of the artist. Sun glasses, the bird cage, the Paisley pattern and cross-stitch designs were featured in popular prints. Pinhead dots usually black and widely spaced on a light-colored background, and small checks, and cross-barred patterns were frequently used. Additional designs were Greek, 1951, Tartan designs, 1950-52; terraced figures or stripes, especially for men's socks, braces, and garters; and African tribal designs in 1952.

BOOKS OF REFERENCE

(See Books of Reference, Part I, *20 Century,* p. 352, and General Bibliography, p. 433)

ARTISTS FOR COSTUME REFERENCE
(See p. 354)

GLOSSARY

Aigrette—refer to *Chaps. 3, 16, 19, 20.*
American Blade—refer to *Chap. 24.*
Apron—refer to *Chaps. 2, 11, 12, 13, 14, 15, 17, 18, 22, 23.*
Ascot—refer to *Chaps. 20, 21.*
Balerina Skirt—very full, usually ankle-length, gored or flared skirt, sometimes made of 3 or more tiers of ruffles, resembling type worn by a Spanish dancer. *Pl. LV, 1; Pl. LIX, 5.*
Ballet Slipper—flat low slipper laced around the ankle, and worn for casual or evening wear.
Basque—refer to *Chaps. 18, 19, 20, 21, 22.*
Basque Jacket—refer to *Basque. Pl. LVI, 2.*
Beach Coat—short, loose coat of cotton or synthetic fiber used especially for beach wear. *Pl. LVII, 4.*
Bell-shaped Skirt—refer to *Chap. 20.*
Bertha—refer to *Chaps. 17, 18, 21. Pl. LVIII, 11.*
Blazer—refer to *Chaps. 19, 20, 22.*
Blücher—refer to *Chap. 24.*
Bolero—refer to *Chaps. 12, 18, 20, 22.*
Boot—refer to *Chaps. 9, 10, 12, 18.*
Boutonnière—refer to *Chaps. 16, 17, 18, 23, 24.*
Boy Coat—short jacket with collar and cuffs; resembling type worn by a small boy. Refer to *Chap. 24.*
Bra—short name given to brassière.
Braces—refer to *Chaps. 18, 24.*
Brassière—refer to *Chaps. 21, 22, 23, 24.*

419

Breton Sailor—refer to *Chaps. 23, 24.*

Briefs—extremely short trunks. Refer to *Chap. 24.*

Buskin—refer to *Chaps. 4, 5, 8, 9, 12.*

Bustle—refer to *Chaps. 12, 15, 18, 19, 20.*

Butcher Linen—strong heavy cloth made of long fiber flax and used for the blue apron worn by butchers, or when white used for dresses and suitings; sometimes made of rayon, or rayon and cotton.

Cabin Boy Breeches—short, tight-fitting pants, laced at the knee. *Pl. LX, 7.*

Cache-chignon—velvet bow used to catch loose ends of hair. A jeweled pin held bow in place.

Calotte—refer to *Chaps. 10, 23.*

Camisole Top—blouse of dress which resembled a camisole. Refer to *Pl. LVI, 3.*

Cardigan—refer to *Chaps. 19, 20, 21, 23.*

Chemise Dress—dress with straight lines and belted at the waist. *Pl. LVIII, 3.*

Chester—big coat with half belt and inverted pleats in the back.

Chesterfield—tailored coat with black velvet collar. Refer to *Chaps. 13, 24.*

Chignon—refer to *Chaps. 10, 14, 18, 19.*

Cinch Belt—tight, wide elastic belt. *Pl. LVII, 7.*

Circle Skirt—skirt cut in the shape of a circle.

Classic Shirt Frock—dress with blouse resembling a shirtwaist.

Cloche—refer to *Chaps. 22, 24. Pl. LVIII, 4.*

Clog—refer to *Chaps. 8, 9, 10, 11, 12, 13, 16, 23.*

Coat Dress—dress that could also be worn as a light-weight coat; sometimes with cape across the back, 1949. *Pl. LX, 1, 2.*

Cobbler's Apron—sleeveless, hip length, belted apron with huge pockets across the front, worn for dress or utility. *Pl. LVII, 3.*

Command Collar—wide spread collar with points almost at right angles.

Convertible Jumper—sleeveless dress worn with sweater for sportswear, with dressy blouse for daytime, and without blouse for evening. *Pl. LIX, 6, 7, 8.*

Cowichan or Siwash Sweater—sweater with striking Indian pattern in black, on white or gray background, made by the Siwash Indians of Vancouver Island, B. C.

Crew Cut—refer to *Chap. 22.*

Cummerbund—refer to *Chap. 24.*

Directory Suit—suit with high midriff and very short cutaway jacket; in general, suit that followed the silhouette of the French Directory period, 1795-99.

Dirndl—refer to *Chap. 24. Pl. LX, 4.*

Dog Collar—refer to *Chaps. 3, 7, 18, 20, 21, 24.*

Dolman Sleeve—refer to *Dolman, Chap. 19.*

Duster—summer-weight coat with bracelet length, full sleeve, sometimes belted and worn as a dress. Refer to *Chap. 21. Pl. LVII, 8, Pl. LVIII, 10.*

Empire-line Sunback Dress—dress with very full, short-waisted bodice.

Empire Style—refer to *Empress Dress, Chap. 19.*

Eton Jacket—refer to *Chaps. 19, 20, 21.*

Feminine Blouse—fairly full blouse with details of lace, tucks and gathers. *Pl. LV, 5.*

Flyaway Collar—collar with points that flared to the sides, similar to winged collar *Pl. LVIII, 7.*

Flyaway Jacket—very short jacket with very full back. *Pl. LVIII, 6.*

Flying Panels—panels floating free over slim skirt. *Pl. LX, 5.*

Fore-and-aft Cap—refer to *Chaps. 19, 20.*

Forward Collar—collar having points about 3½ inches long which spread toward the shoulder and not downward.

Four-in-hand—refer to *Chaps. 19, 20, 21, 22, 23, 24.*

CHAPTER 25: GLOSSARY

Four-way Dress—dress that could be worn for various occasions.

Galosh—refer to *Galoche, Chaps. 9, 10, 13, 17, 23.*

Gaucho Pants—calf-length pants, wrapped across the front, with trouser leg tapered to below the knee; resembling pants worn by the cowboy of Argentina. *Pl. LVII, 6.*

Gibson Girl Collar—shirtwaist collar, worn by the Gibson Girl, early part of the 20th century, usually accompanied by a black ribbon band.

Greatcoat—refer to *Chaps. 13, 14, 16. Pl. LV, 3.*

Guatemalan Skirt—handwoven skirt from Guatemala.

Halter-top—blouse with bare back, having the neckline continued around the back of the neck.

Harem Hem Skirt—soft hem draped to give bloomer effect. Refer to *Harem Skirt, Chap. 21.*

Helmet—refer to *Chaps. 2, 22. Pl. LX, 3.*

Homburg—refer to *Chaps. 21, 22, 23, 24.*

Horse's Tail Hairdress—hairdress of girls and young women in which the long bob was combed upward in one mass at back of head and held with rubber band, ribbon or clip.

Huarache—refer to *Chaps. 1, 24.*

Jester Pants—tight-fitting breeches tied below the knee. *Pl. LVII, 5.*

Jodhpur Boot—refer to *Chaps. 23, 24.*

Jodhpurs—refer to *Chaps. 23, 24.*

Knickers—refer to *Knickerbockers, Chaps. 19, 20,* and to *Chaps. 20, 21, 23.*

Leg-of-mutton Sleeve—refer to *Chaps. 9, 20, 24.*

Levis—tight-fitting denim trousers with a U-shaped crotch worn by boys and younger men; part of western or cowboy outfit, originally known as Levi's and made by Levi Strauss and Company.

Little Boy Shorts—tailored and cuffed shorts. *Pl. LVII, 2.*

Lumber Jacket—refer to *Chap. 24.*

Mantilla—refer to *Chaps. 16, 18, 19.*

Marcel Wave—refer to *Chaps. 21, 22.*

Martingale Belt—half-belt in back of jacket or coat. The word has been long applied to a leather strap extending from the bit of reins of a horse's bridle to the girdle.

Middy Blouse—beach shirt of blue denim with pullover neckline, later became part of a dress and fitted the figure more closely. Refer to *Chap. 22.*

Midriff—designation of the body between lower breastline and waistline.

Moccasin—refer to *Chaps. 1, 3, 8, 24.*

Mocha Glove—refer to *Chap. 23.*

Mouton—processed lambskin.

New Bold Look—introduced by Fashion Staff of a leading fashion magazine for men; an organized program of manufacturers and retailers to assist men to co-ordinate an ensemble and to create a demand for the new types of garments. This service could be compared to a similar one available to women in their various fashion magazines.

New Look—styles for women, introduced in 1947.

Norfolk Jacket—refer to *Chaps. 19, 20, 21.*

Pajama—refer to *Chaps. 23, 24.*

Panama Hat—refer to *Chaps. 21, 22, 23.*

Patch Pocket—refer to *Chap. 22.*

Peasant Blouse—embroidered blouse gathered at the neck, with short puffed sleeves. *Pl. LVI, 1.*

Pedal Pushers—close-fitting pants extending below the knee, made in various colors, usually of blue denim, at first with trouser leg rolled up to the calf of the leg, later with or without cuff. *Pl. LX, 8.*

Peg-top—refer to *Peg-top Skirt, Chap. 21.*

Peplum—refer to *Chaps. 11, 12, 13, 18, 20.*

Peter Pan Collar—refer to *Chap. 21.*

Petticoat—refer to *Chaps. 9, 10, 11, 12, 13, 14, 15, 16, 17, 18, 19, 20, 21, 22, 23, 24. Pl. LV, 4.*

Petticoat Dress—dress with elaborate petticoat that showed beneath sheer dress.

Pierpont or Pin Point Collar—collar ending in sharp points, extending over tie.

Planter's Punch Hat—refer to *Chaps. 22, 23, 24.*

Plunging Neckline—extremely low narrow neckline. *Pl. LVII, 1.*

Pompadour—refer to *Chaps. 13, 19, 21, 22.*

Poncho—overblouse worn as a blouse or jacket. Refer to *Chap. 1. Pl. LIX, 1.*

Poodle Cloth—woolen material with surface of thickly woven loops, popular, 1952.

Poodle Hair Cut—woman's hairdress in which the hair is cut uniformly to about 1½ inches and loosely curled.

Pork Pie Hat—refer to *Chaps. 18, 23, 24.*

Princess Silhouette—refer to *Princess Dress, Chap. 19.*

Processed Raincoat—cloth coat made waterproof.

Puggree—wide, soft band arranged in folds around crown of hat.

Puritan Collar—type of large plain collar resembling that worn by the Puritans in the early part of the 17th century.

Pyramid Coat—cloak narrow at shoulder, and very wide at hem.

Raglan—refer to *Chap. 22,* and to *Raglan Sleeve, Chaps. 21, 23.*

Redingote—refer to *Chaps. 14, 15, 16, 18, 20, 22, 23.*

Reticule—refer to *Chaps. 13, 14, 15, 16, 17, 18, 19.*

Reversible Jersey Blouse—blouse worn with buttons in front or in back.

Saddle Oxford—refer to *Chaps. 23, 24.*

Sailor Collar—refer to *Chap. 22.*

Sandal—refer to *Chaps. 1, 2, 3, 4, 5, 6, 7, 8, 23, 24.*

Scatter Pins—ornamental pins worn in groups on dress, collar, down the front as buttons, on hat, or on gloves. *Pl. LVIII, 10.*

Scoop Neckline—neckline shaped like a scoop. *Pl. LVIII, 5.*

Separates—separate blouses, jackets and skirts, worn in various combinations.

Sheath Dress—tight-fitting dress. *Pl. LVIII, 1.*

Shrug Jacket—very short jacket or sweater with sleeves and body in 1 piece. *Pl. LIX, 4.*

Side Long Look—dress having neckline drapery or panel at side.

Siwash Sweater—refer to *Cowichan.*

Slacks—trousers used for sports, gardening and lounging. Refer to *Chaps. 23, 24.*

Sleeveless Blazer—short sleeveless jacket with pockets, knitted or made of fabric. *Pl. LVI, 5.*

Sleeveless Look—dress or blouse without sleeve or decoration at armhole. *Pl. LVIII, 9.*

Sling Neckline—pointed neckline that extended diagonally and joined side opening of dress.

Slip—refer to *Chaps. 23, 24.*

Slit Shirt—refer to *Chap. 21.*

Snap Brim Hat—refer to *Chaps. 23, 24.*

Spencer jacket—tight-fitting, waist-length jacket, with or without collar. Refer to *Spencer, Chaps. 15, 16, 17, 18. Pl. LX, 6.*

Square Dance Dress—dress with full blouse, sleeveless or puff sleeve, and full skirt. *Pl. LVI, 4.*

Stocking Bodice—knitted woolen tube, to be pulled over head and fastened with draw string or shirred on rubber, worn with shorts, skirts, or dinner dress. *Pl. LVII, 9, Pl. LVIII, 2.*

CHAPTER 25: GLOSSARY

Stole—refer to *Chaps. 5, 6, 7, 8. Pl. LVI, 6. Pl. LIX, 3.*

Suit—refer to *Chaps. 20, 21, 22, 23, 24. Pl. LV, 2.*

Sun Dress or Sunback Dress—refer to *Chap. 24. Pl. LIX, 3.*

Tailored Blouse—plain waist of soft fabric with tucks or tailored detail.

Tam-o'-shanter—refer to *Chaps. 19, 20, 22.*

Tie Clip—long clip to hold tie in place.

Tie Holder—chain or clip to hold tie in place. Refer to *Chap. 24.*

Toile—sheer fabric of silk and cotton.

Toreador Pants—short, tight-fitting pants, buttoned at the knee, resembling those worn by the Spanish bullfighter. *Pl. LVII, 7.*

Tremont Hat—hat with tapered crown and center crease and fairly narrow brim worn up or down; sometimes with pinch crown and snap brim.

Tricorne Hat—refer to *Chaps. 9, 12, 13, 14, 15, 22.*

Trumpet Coat Dress—dress with flare from a little above the knee, worn without a coat.

Trumpet Silhouette Skirt—skirt tight at hip with pleating or fullness from a little above the knee.

Turtle-neck Sweater—refer to *Chaps. 21, 22.*

Tuxedo—refer to *Chaps. 20, 21, 22, 23, 24.*

"TV" Lounging Jacket—loose-fitting jacket worn while viewing the television program.

"TV Sets"—lounging separates worn while viewing the television program.

Ulster—refer to *Chaps. 19, 24.*

Veil—refer to *Chaps. 3, 4, 5, 6, 7, 8, 10, 15, 16, 17, 18, 19, 20, 21, 22, 23, 24.*

Wallet—refer to *Chaps. 22, 23, 24.*

Weskit—waist-length, tight-fitting sleeveless jacket; dialect for waistcoat. *Pl. LIX, 2.*

Winged Collar or Revers—collar with ends which stand out on either side. Refer to *Wing Collar, Chaps. 20, 21, 22.*

Wraparound Skirt—skirt wrapped across the front or the back. Refer to *Chap. 1. Pl. LVIII, 8.*

20th-CENTURY FASHIONS
AND
HISTORICAL INFLUENCES

1900

1910

1914

1916

1918

1920

1926

1929

1931

1935

1939
1941
1945
1947
1948

1949
1950
1951
1952

1810

1840

1952

1952

1895

1895

1952

1952

1922

1928

1952

1952

1928

1928

1928

1952

1952

1952

Appendix

GENERAL BIBLIOGRAPHY

SOURCES OF ILLUSTRATIONS

EUROPEAN RULERS AND
AMERICAN PRESIDENTS

General Bibliography

HISTORICAL BACKGROUNDS

A number of books, periodicals and articles have been helpful as references in recording the events of the times. *Synopsis of History,* a folder issued by the Museum of Fine Arts in Boston gives an excellent chronological chart of the ancient world. *The Customs of Mankind* by Lillian Eichler Watson, *A Handy Book of Curious Information* by William Shepard Walsh and *A History of Industry* by Ellen Louise Osgood have been useful, the first for the customs of the past, and the latter one for the development of industry and its effect upon society.

Historical and political events that have influenced the customs of the times have been found in *A Short History of the Ancient World* by Charles Edward Smith, *The World of the Middle Ages* by John L. La Monte, *A Survey of European Civilization* by Wallace K. Ferguson and Geoffrey Bruun, *The Growth of Western Civilization* by A. E. R. Boak, Albert Hyma, and P. W. Slosson, and *American Political and Social History* by Harold Underwood Faulkner.

Numerous magazines present aspects of daily living, a helpful one being *Weekly World News Digest.* References to historical, economic, and cultural events of other years have been obtained from various sources, such as *Annual* of *The Americana, Book of the Year* of *The Encyclopaedia Britannica, An Encyclopedia of World History* by William H. Langer, *A Dictionary of Contemporaries,* and *Who Was Whom* by Miriam Allen de Ford, *Historical Tables* by S. H. Steinberg, *Famous First Facts,* and *More First Facts* by Joseph Nathan Kane, *Dictionary of Dates* by Helen Rex Keller, and *The Collectors' Reference Books of Dates* by Percy Jackson Higgs.

Many books are available in which reference is made to activities of women in the history of the world, namely: *Womankind in Western Europe* by Thomas R. Beard, "Woman's Place in Industry and Labor Organization," a chapter by Sophie Yudelson, in *Annals of the American Academy of Political and Social Science,* Vol. XXIV, *A Comparison of the Political and Civil Rights of Men and Women in the United States,* a booklet published by the Government Printing Office, *A Short History of Women* by Sir John Langdon-Davies, *Women from Bondage to Freedom* by Ruby Husted Bell, "Sumptuary Legislation and Personal Regulation in England," a chapter by Elizabeth Baldwin, in *Johns Hopkins University Studies in Historical and Political Science,* Vol. XLIV, and *Womankind in Western Europe* by Thomas Wright.

BOOKS ON COSTUME

Adam, Frank, *The Clans, Septs and Scottish Highlands,* by Sir Thomas Innes of Learney (London, W. and A. K. Johnston, Ltd., 1952).

Alexander, Christine, *Jewelry* (New York, Metropolitan Museum of Art, 1928).

French Ministry of War, *Armée Français Uniforms,* Documents Éstables sous les Auspices du Ministère de la Guerre (Paris, "L'Uniform Officiel," 1951).

Baker, Blanch, *Dramatic Bibliography* (New York, The H. W. Wilson Co., 1933).

Barton, Lucy, *Historic Costume for the Stage* (Boston, Walter H. Baker Co., 1935).

Beaulieu, Michèle, *Contribution à l'Étude de la Mode à Paris* (Paris, R. Munier, 1936).

Bertrand de Moleville, Antoine Français, *The Costume of the Hereditary States of the House of Austria* (London, W. Bulmer and Co., 1804).

Blanc, Auguste Alexander Philippe Charles, *Art in Ornament and Dress* (London, Chapman and Hall, 1877).

Blum, André, *Histoire du Costume en France* (Paris, Hachette, 1924).

Boeheim, Wendelin, *Handbuch der Waffenkunde* (Leipzig, H. A. Seemann, 1890).

Boehn, Max von, *Modes and Manners,* 4 vols., translated by Juan Joshua, (Philadelphia, J. B. Lippincott, Co., 1932-36).

Braun, Louis, and others, *Zur Geschichte der Kostüme* (Munich, Braun and Schneider, 1909).

Brooke, Iris, *Western European Costume and Its Relation to the Theatre* (London, G. G. Harrap Ltd., 1939).

Brooklyn Public Library, *A Reading and Reference List on Costume* (Brooklyn, 1909).

Bruhn, Wolfgang, *Das Kostümwerk* (Berlin, E. Wasmuth, 1941).

Brummell, George Bryan (Beau Brummell), *Male and Female Costume* (Garden City, N. Y., Doubleday and Co. Inc., 1932).

Burris-Meyer, Elizabeth, *This Is Fashion* (New York, Harper and Brothers, 1943).

Calderini, Emma, *Il Costume Popolare en Italia* (Milan, Sperling and Kupfer, 1934).

Chalif, Louis Harvey, *Russian Festivals and Costumes for Pageants and Dances* (New York, Chalif Russian School of Dancing, 1921).

Challamel, Jean Baptiste Marie Augustin, *The History of Fashion in France* (New York, Scribner and Welford, 1882).

Chalmers, Helena, *Clothes on and off the Stage* (New York, D. Appleton and Co., 1928).

BIBLIOGRAPHY

Chuse, Anne R., *Costume Design* (Pelham, N. Y., Bridgman Publishers, 1930).

Clifford, C. R., *Period Furnishings* (New York, Clifford and Lawton, 1927).

———, C. R., *The Lace Dictionary* (New York, Clifford and Lawton, 1913).

Colas, René, *Bibliographie Général du Costume et de la Mode* (Paris, R. Colas, 1933).

Crawford, Morris de Camp, *The Ways of Fashion* (New York, Fairchild Pub. Co., 1948).

Cunnington, Cecil Willet, *The Art of English Costume* (London, Collins, 1949).

Cunnington, C. Willet and Phillis, *The History of Underclothes* (London, Michael Joseph, 1951).

Dabney, Edith, and Wise, C. M., *A Book of Dramatic Costume* (New York, Appleton-Century-Crofts, Inc., 1931).

Davenport, Millia, *The Book of Costume*, 2 vols. (New York, Crown Publishers, 1948).

D'Ivori, Joan, pseud. see Vila-Puig, Juan.

Doten, Hazel R., *Fashion Drawing: How to Do It* (New York, Harper and Brothers, 1939).

Downey, John Godwin, "Cosmetics—Past and Present," *Journal of American Medical Association* (June, 1934).

Evans, Mary, *Costume Throughout the Ages* (Philadelphia, J. B. Lippincott Co., 1950).

———, *How to Make Historic American Costumes* (New York, A. S. Barnes and Co., 1942).

Fairholt, Frederick W., *Costume in England: A History of Dress to the End of the 18th Century*, 2 vols. (London, G. Bell and Sons, 1909-10).

———, *Satirical Songs and Poems on Costume from XIII-XIX Century* (London, Pearcy Society, 1849).

Funk, Wilfred J., *So You Think It's New* (New York, Funk and Wagnalls Co., 1927).

Gallois, Émile, *Costumes de l'Union Française* (Paris, Éditions Arc-en-Ciel, 1946).

———, *Costumes Espagnols* (New York, French and European Publications, 1939).

———, *Provinces Français* (New York, French and European Publications, 1936).

Garavito, H., *6 Pinturas de Chichicastenango, Guatemala* (Guatemala, C. A., B. Zadik and Co., Editores, n. d.).

Garcia Boiza, Antonio, *El Traje Regional Salmantino* (Madrid, Spain, Espasa-Calpe, 1940).

Gardilanne Gratiane de, *Les Costumes Regionaux de la France*, 4 vols. (New York, Harcourt, Brace and Co., 1929).

435

——, *The National Costumes of Holland* (London, G. G. Harrapp Ltd., 1932).

Genin, J. N., *An Illustrated History of the Hat* (New York, H. N. Grossman, Printer, 1848).

Giafferri, Paul Louis Victor de, Marquis, *L'Histoire du Costume Féminin Français* (Paris, Editions Nilsson, 1922-23).

——, *The History of French Masculine Costume* (New York, Foreign Publications, 1927).

Gorsline, Douglas, *What People Wore* (New York, The Viking Press, 1952).

Haire, Frances Hamilton, *The American Costume Book* (New York, A. S. Barnes and Co., Inc., 1934).

——, *The Folk Costume Book* (New York, A. S. Barnes and Co., Inc., 1934).

Halouze Édouard, *Costumes of South America* (New York, French and European Publications, 1941).

Hamlin, Alfred Dwight Foster, *A History of Ornament*, 2 vols. (New York, The Century Co., 1916-23).

Hastrel, Adlophe d', *El Pintor y Litógrafo Coleados del Rio de la Plata* (Buenos Aires, Guillermo Kraft, Limitada, 1944).

Heierli, Frau Julie, *Die Volkstrachten der Schweiz*, 5 vols. (Erlenbach-Zurich, E. Rentsch, 1922-32).

Hiler, Hilaire, and Meyer, Helen, *Bibliography of Costume* (New York, The H. W. Wilson Co., 1939).

Hill, Georgiana, *A History of English Dress from the Saxon Period to the Present Day*, 2 vols. (London, R. Bentley and Son, 1893).

Men's Capes and Cloaks, (New York, The Hispanic Society of America, 1931).

Holme, Charles, *Peasant Art in Italy* (London, The Studio, Ltd., 1913).

Hottenroth, F. R., *Le Costume chez les Peuples Anciens et Modernes* (Paris, Armand Guérinet, 1922).

Hubbard, M., and Peck, E., *National Costumes of the Slavic Peoples* (New York, The Woman's Press, 1920).

Hughes, Talbot, *Dress Design* (New York, Pitman Publishing Co., 1932).

Innes of Learney, Sir Thomas, *Tartans of the Clans of Scotland* (New York, Irving Raven, 1952).

Jordan, Nina R., *American Costume Dolls: How to Make and Dress Them* (New York, Harcourt, Brace and Co., Inc., 1941).

——, *Mexican Costumes and Customs* (Pasadena, Calif., c. 1940).

Keim, Aline, *The Costumes of France* (New York, French and European Publications, 1930).

Kelly, Francis M., and Schwabe, Randolph, *A Short History of Costume and Armor, chiefly in England, 1066-1800* (New York, Charles Scribner's Sons, 1931).

BIBLIOGRAPHY

Kerr, Rose Netzorg, *Interpretive Costume Design* (Worcester, Mass., Fairbairn Publishers, 1937).

Klein, Ruth, *Lexikon der Mode* (Baden-Baden, W. Klein, 1950).

Köhler, Karl, and Sichart, Emma von, *A History of Costume* (New York, G. Howard Watt, 1928).

Kredel, Fritz, and Todd, Frederick P., *Soldiers of the American Army* (New York, H. Bittner and Co., 1944).

Kretschmer, Albert, *Deutsche Volkstrachten* (Leipzig, J. G. Bach, 1890?).

Kretschmer, A., and Rohrbach C., *The Costumes of all Nations from Earliest Times to the XIX Century* (London, H. Sotheran and Co., 1882).

Lalasse, Hippolyte, *Costumes et Coiffes de Bretagne* (Paris, H. Laurens, 1932).

Large, Hector, *Le Costume Militaire* (Paris, Éditions, Arc-en-Ciel, n. d.).

Laver, James, *Style in Costume* (New York, Oxford University Press, 1949).

Lebeuf, Jean-Paul, *Vetements et Parures du Cameroun Français* (Paris, Éditions, Arc-en-Ciel, 1946).

Leeming, Joseph, *The Costume Book* (New York, Frederick A. Stokes, 1940).

Leloir, Maurice, *Dictionnaire du Costume* (Paris, Libraire Gründ, 1951).

——, *Histoire du Costume de l'Antiquite à 1914*, 12 vols. (Paris, E. Henri, 1933-49).

Lepage-Medvey, E., *French Costumes* (New York, The Hyperion Press, 1939).

——, *National Costumes, Austria, Hungary, Poland, Czecho-Slovakia* (New York, The Hyperion Press, 1939).

Le Roux de Lincy, Antoine Jean Victor, *Les Femmes Célèbres de l'Ancienne France* (Paris, Le Roi, 1847).

Lesley, Everett P., Jr. and Osman, William, *Conspicuous Waist: Waistcoats and Historical Designs, 1700-1952* (New York, Cooper Union, Museum for the Arts of Decoration, 1952).

Lester, Katherine Morris, *Historic Costume* (Peoria, Ill., The Manual Arts Press, 1942).

——, and Oerke, Bess Viola, *Accessories of Dress* (Peoria, Ill., The Manual Arts Press, 1940).

Lhuer, Victor, *Costume Auvergnat et Bourbonnais* (Paris, Éditions, Arc-en-Ciel, 194—).

Louandro, Charles Léopold, *Les Arts Sompuaires: Histoire du Costume et de l'Ameublement et des Arts et Industries qui s'y Rattachment, sous la Direction de Hangard-Maugé* (Paris, Hangard-Maugé, 1857-58).

Louden, Adelaide Bolton, and Norman P., *Historic Costume through the Ages* (Philadelphia, H. C. Perleberg, 1936).

Luard, John, Lieut. Colonel, *History of the Dress of the British Soldier* (London, William Clowes and Sons, 1852).

Lundquist, Eva Rodhe, *La Mode et Son Vocabulaire* (Göteborg, Wettergren and Kerber, 1950).

Maigron, Louis, *Le Romantisme et la Mode, d'après des Documents Inédits* (Paris, H. Champion, 1911).

Makovskii, Sergiêl Konstantīnovīch, *Peasant Art of Subcarpathian Russia* (Prague, Plamja Edition, 1926).

Manchester, H., *The Evolution of Dress Fastening Devices from the Bone Pin to the Koh-i-noor* (Long Island, N. Y., Waldes and Co., Inc., 1922).

Mann, Kathleen, *Peasant Costume in Europe* (New York, Macmillan, 1950).

McClellan, Elizabeth, *History of American Costume, 1607-1870* (New York, Tudor Publishing Co., 1942).

McIan, Robert Donald, *The Clans of the Scottish Highlands* (London, Ackerman and Co., 1857).

Menpes, Mortimer, and Menpes, Dorothy, *World's Children* (London, A. and C. Black, 1903).

Merida, Carlos, *Carnival in Mexico* (Mexico, Talleres Graficos de la Nacion, 1940).

——, *Mexican Costume* (Chicago, The Pocahontas Press, 1941).

——, *Trajes Regionales Mexicanos* (Mexico, Editorial Atlante, 1945).

Monro, Isabel Stevenson, and Cook, Dorothy E., *Costume Index* (New York, The H. W. Wilson Co., 1937).

Nelson, Henry Loomis, *The Army of the United States,* 3 vols. (New York, B. W. Whitlock Publishers, n. d.).

Northrup, B. and Green, A., *Thirty Historic Plates* (New York, Columbia University, 1925).

Oprescu, George, *Peasant Art in Roumania* (London, The Studio, Ltd., 1929).

Ortiz, Echagüe, José, *España Tipos y Trajes* (Barcelona, Sociedad General de Publicaciones, 1933).

Palliser, B., *History of Lace* (London, S. Low Marston and Co., Ltd., 1910).

Parmentier, A., *Album Historique* (Paris, A. Colin, 1907-10).

Parsons, Frank Alvah, *The Art of Dress* (Garden City, N. Y., Doubleday and Co., Inc., 1921).

Pettigrew, Dora W., *Peasant Costume of the Black Forest* (London, A. and C. Black, Ltd., 1937).

Picken, Mary Brooks, and others, *The Language of Fashion* (New York, Funk and Wagnalls Co., 1939).

Piton, Camille, *Le Costume Civil en France du XIIIe au XIXe Siècle* (Paris, E. Flammarion, 1913).

Planché, James Robinson, *A Cyclopaedia of Costume* or *Dictionary of Dress,* 2 vols. (London, Chatto and Windus, 1876-79).

Plischke, Hans, *Tahitische Travergewänder* (Berlin, Wiedmannsche Buchhandlung, 1931).

Primmer, Kathleen, *Scandinavian Peasant Costume* (London, A. and C. Black, Ltd., 1939).

BIBLIOGRAPHY

Pugin, A. W. N., *Glossary of Ecclesiastical Ornament and Costume*, translated by Rev. Bernard Smith (London, H. G. Bohn, 1846).

Quennell, Marjorie, *A History of Everyday Things in England*, 3 vols. (New York, Charles Scribner's Sons, 1918-35).

Quicherat, Jules, *Histoire du Costume en France* (Paris, Hachette, 1875).

Racinet, Albert Charles, *Le Costume Historique*, 6 vols. (Paris, Firmin-Didot, 1888).

Renan, Ary, *Le Costume en France* (Paris, A. Picard, n. d.).

Rhead, George Woolliscroft, *Chats on Costume* (London, T. F. Unwin, 1906).

Robida, Arthur, *Yester-Year* (London, S. Low Marston and Co., Ltd., 1893).

Rodier, Paul, *The Romance of French Weaving* (New York, Frederick A. Stokes, 1931).

Roediger, Virginia More, *Ceremonial Costumes of the Pueblo Indians* (Berkeley, University of California Press, 1941).

Rosenberg, Adolf, *Geschichte des Kostüms* (Berlin, E. Wasmuth, 1905-23?).

Rudofsky, Bernard, *Are Clothes Modern?* (Chicago, Paul Theobold, 1947).

Ruppert, Jacques, *Histoire du Costume de l'Antiquité au XIXᵉ Siècle* (Paris, Librairie d'Art, R. Ducher, c. 1930-31).

Sage, E., *A Study of Costume* (New York, Charles Scribner's Sons, 1926).

Sellner, Eudora, *History of Costume Design: Portfolios* (Worcester, Mass., Milton Bradley Co., 1920).

Settle, Alison, *English Fashion* (London, Collins, 1948).

Shoes Thru the Ages: The Story of Footwear (St. Louis, International Shoe Co.).

Shover, Edna Mann, *Art in Costume Design* (Springfield, Mass., Milton Bradley Co., 1920).

Smith, H. Clifford, *Jewellery* (London, Methuen and Co., 1908).

Spicer, Dorothy Gladys, *Latin American Costume* (New York, The Hyperion Press, 1941).

Strutt, Joseph, *A Complete View of the Dress and Habits of the People of England* (London, H. G. Bohn, 1842).

Stuart, John Sobieski Stolberg, *The Costume of the Clans with Observation upon the Literature, Arts, Manufactures and Commerce* (Edinburgh, J. Grant, 1892).

Sumberg, Samuel Leslie, *The Nuremberg Schembart Carnival* (New York, Columbia University Press, 1941).

Tilke, Max, *The Costumes of Eastern Europe* (Berlin, E. Wasmuth, Ltd., 1925).

Tonsberg, Nils Christian, *Norske Nationaldragter Tegnede af Forskjellige Norske Kunstnere og Ledsagede med Oplysende Test.* (Christiania, Udgiverens Forlag, 1852).

Traphagen, Ethel, *Costume Design and Illustration* (New York, John Wiley and Sons, Inc., 1932).

Trendell, Herbert Arthur, *Dress Worn at His Majesty's Court* (London, Harrison and Sons, 1912).

Truman, Nevil, *Historic Costuming* (London, Sir Isaac Pitman and Sons, Ltd., 1936).

Uzanne, Louis Octave, *La Française du Siècle* (Paris, A. Quantin, 1886).

Verrill, Alpheus Hyatt, *Perfumes and Spices* (Boston, L. C. Page and Co., 1940).

Vertes, Marcel, *Art and Fashion* (New York, The Studio Publications, Inc., 1944).

Vila-Puig, Juan, *Vestidos Típicos de Espana* (Barcelona, Editorial Orbis, 1936).

Vincent, John Martin, *Costume and Conduct in the Laws of Basel, Bern and Zurich, 1370-1800* (Baltimore, The Johns Hopkins Press, 1935).

Viollet-LeDuc, Eugène Emmanuel, *Dictionnaire Raisonné du Mobilier*, 6 vols. (Paris, Gründ et Maguet, 1854-75).

Wahlen, Auguste, *Moeurs, Usages et Costumes de Tous les Peuples du Monde* (Bruxelles, Librairie Historique-Artisque, 1843-44).

Walkup, Fairfax, *Dressing the Part: A History of Costume for the Theatre* (New York, Appleton-Century-Crofts, Inc., 1950).

Webb, W. M., *The Heritage of Dress* (New York, McClure Co., 1908).

Wilcox, Ruth Turner, *The Mode in Costume* (New York, Charles Scribner's Sons, 1942).

——, *The Mode in Fashion* (New York, Charles Scribner's Sons, 1948).

——, *The Mode in Footwear* (New York, Charles Scribner's Sons, 1948).

——, *The Mode in Hats and Headdress* (New York, Charles Scribner's Sons, 1945).

Wilson, Carrie, *Fashions Since Their Debut* (Scranton, Pa., International Textbook Co., 1939).

Wilton, Mary Margaret, *The Book of Costume* (London, H. Colburn, 1847).

Wingfield, Lewis Strange, *Civil Costume in England from the Conquest to the Regency* (London, William Clowes and Sons, Ltd., 1884).

Wistrand, P., *Svenska Folkdräkter, Kulturhistoriske Studier* (Stockholm, Aktiebolaget Hiertas, 1907).

W. P. A. Museum Extension Project, *Handbook of Military Uniforms of the Revolutionary Period* (Willow Grove, Pa.).

Wright, Marion Logan, *Biblical Costume* (London, Society for Promoting Christian Knowledge, 1936).

Yarwood, Doreen, *English Costume from the 2nd Century* B.C. *to 1950* (New York, Crown Publishing Co., 1952).

Young, Agnes Brooks, *Stage Costuming* (New York, The Macmillan Co., 1927).

Young Women's Christian Association, *National Costumes of the Slavic Peoples* (New York, The Woman's Press, 1920).

Sources of Illustrations

Post cards and reproductions of paintings that depict the costumes of the past and present may be obtained in various museums. Additional reproductions of works of art and costumes of many periods are available in University Prints, Artext Prints, The Perry Pictures, and in photographs of costume dolls obtained from the Metropolitan Museum of Art and the Boston Museum of Fine Arts.

A review of the past and present styles may be made from the following magazines:

PAST FASHIONS

Delineator

Godey's Lady's Book and Magazine

Peterson's Magazine

Flair

Pictorial Review

National Geographic

PRESENT-DAY FASHIONS

Adam: La Revue de L'Homme (Paris)

American Fur Designer

American Gentleman and Sartorial Art Journal

American Ladies' Tailor and les Parisiennes

Art et la Mode (Paris)

Bride's Magazine, The

Butterick Pattern Book

California Apparel News

California Juvenile Trends

California: Men's and Boys' Stylist

California Stylist

California, The

Charm

Élites Françaises (Paris)

English Fashion Forecast (London)

Esquire

Fashion Digest

Famous Paris Models

Fashion Trends

Gaceta Gentleman (Havana)

Glamour

Harper's Bazaar

Jardin des Modes (Paris)

Ladies' Home Journal

Life

McCall Pattern Book

McCall's Magazine

Mademoiselle

Mayfair Magazine

Men's Modes

Men's Wear

Men's Wear of Canada (Toronto, Canada)

Mignon: Revista de la Mujer (Puebla, Mexico)

Millinery Research
Modern Bride
Modern Miss
Modes et Travaus (Paris)
Officiel de la Couture et la Mode de Paris (Paris)
Originator: Sketchbook of Modern Fashion
Professional Models Journal
Qualité: La Revue de l'Élégance (Paris)
Queen: The Lady's Newspaper and Court Chronicle (London)
Seventeen
Silhouette
Simplicity Pattern Book
Style for Men (London)
Tendances de la Mode (Paris)
Today's Woman
Vogue
Vogue Pattern Book
Woman's Home Companion
Woman's Wear Daily

Additional reference material may be obtained from sources for visual aids in art:

Chapman, William McK., Editor, *Films on Art* (Kingsport, Tenn., Kingsport Press, Inc., for the American Federation of Arts, 1952).

Horkheimer, Mary Foley, and Diffor, John W., *Educators Guide to Free Films,* 12th ed. (Randolph, Wis., Educators Progress Service, 1952).

Schreiber, Robert E., *Service Supplement,* V (Mishawaka, Ind., October 15, 1948).

Wehberg, Hilla, *Cultural Groups in American Life: A Film Survey* (New York, Production Committee, Metropolitan Motion Picture Council, 1939).

Williams, Catherine M., *Sources of Teaching Material,* Booklet (The Ohio State University, Columbus, Ohio, Bureau of Educational Research, 1952).

Educational Film Guide, monthly supplements (New York, H. Wilson Co., 1952).

Audio-Visual Guide, XVII (December, 1950), 4.

European Rulers

27 B.C.–A.D. 1953

ROMAN EMPERORS

Augustus, 27 B.C.-A.D. 14
Tiberius, A.D. 14-37
Claudius, 41-54
Nero, 54-68
Vespasian, 69-79
Titus, 79-81
Trajan, 98-117
Hadrian, 117-138
Antoninus Pius, 138-161
Marcus Aurelius, 161-180

Septimus Severus, 193-211
Caracalla, 211-217
Decius, 249-251
Valerian, 253-260
Aurelian, 270-275
Diocletian, 284-305
Constantine I, 307-337
Julian, 360-363
Theodosius I, 379-395

EAST ROMAN AND BYZANTINE EMPERORS

Theodosius II, 408-450
Justinian I, 527-565
Heraclius, 610-641
Leo III, 717-740
Irene, 797-802
Basil I, 867-886

Leo VI, 886-912
Basil II, 963-1025
Romanus IV, 1067-71
Alexius I Comnenus, 1081-1118
Michael VIII, 1260-82
Constantine XI, 1448-53

THE PAPACY

Petrus, 67 (64)?
Linus, 67 (65)-76?
Anacletus (Cletus), 76-91?
Clemens I, 91-100 (97)?
Evaristus, (97) 100-105?
Alexander I, 105-115?
Sixtus I (Xystus), 115-125?
Telesphorus, 125-136?
Hyginus, 136-140?
Pius I, 140-155?

Anicetus, 155-166?
Soter, 166-175?
Eleutherius, 175-189?
Victor I, 189-199
Zephyrinus, 199-217
Calixtus I, 217-222
Urbanus I, 222-230
Pontianus, 230-235
Anterus, 235-236
Fabianus, 236-250

Cornelius, 251-253
Lucius I, 253-254
Stephanus I, 254-257
Sixtus II, 257-258
Dionysius, 259-268
Felix I, 269-274
Eutychianus, 275-283
Cajus, 283-296
Marcellinus, 296-304
Marcellus I, 308-309
Eusebius, 309-310
Melchiades (Miltiades), 311-314
Silvester I, 314-335
Marcus, 336
Julius I, 337-352
Liberius, 352-366
Damasus I, 366-384
Siricius, 384-399
Anastasius I, 399-401
Innocentius I, 401-417
Zosimus, 417-418
Bonifatius I, 418-422
Coelestinus I, 422-432
Sixtus III, 432-440
Leo I, 440-461
Hilarius, 461-468
Simplicius, 468-483
Felix II (III), 483-492
Gelasius I, 492-496
Anastasius II, 496-498
Symmachus, 498-514
Hormisdas, 514-523
Johannes (John) I, 523-526
Felix III (IV), 526-530
Bonifatius II, 530-532
Johannes II, 533-535
Agapetus I, 535-536
Silverius, c. 537
Vigilius, 537-555
Pelagius I, 556-561
Johannes III, 561-574
Benedictus I, 575-579
Pelagius II, 579-590

Gregorius I, 590-604
Sabinianus, 604-606
Bonifatius III, 607
Bonifatius IV, 608-615
Adeodatus I, 615-618
Bonifatius V, 619-625
Honorius I, 625-638
Severinus, 640
Johannes IV, 640-642
Theodorus I, 642-649
Martinus I, 649-653
Eugenius I, 654-657
Vitalianus, 657-672
Adeodatus II, 672-676
Donus, 676-678
Agatho, 678-681
Leo II, 682-683
Benedictus II, 684-685
Johannes V, 685-686
Conon, 686-687
Sergius I, 687-701
Johannes VI, 701-705
Johannes VII, 705-707
Sisinius, 708
Constantius I, 708-715
Gregorius II, 715-731
Gregorius III, 731-741
Zacharius, 741-752
Stephanus II, 752
Stephanus III, 752-757
Paulus, I, 757-767
Stephanus IV, 768-772
Hadrianus I, 772-795
Leo III, 795-816
Stephanus V, 816-817
Paschalis I, 817-824
Eugenius II, 824-827
Valentinus, 827
Gregorius IV, 827-844
Sergius II, 844-847
Leo IV, 847-855
Benedictus III, 855-858
Nicholas I, 858-867

EUROPEAN RULERS

Hadrianus II, 867-872
Johannes VIII, 872-882
Marinus I, 882-884
Hadrianus III, 884-885
Stephanus VI, 885-891
Formosus, 891-896
Bonifatius VI, 896
Stephanus VII, 896-897
Romanus, 897
Theodorus II, 897
Johannes IX, 898-900
Benedictus IV, 900-903
Leo V, 903
Sergius III, 904-911
Anastasius III, 911-913
Lando, 913-914
Johannes X, 914-928
Leo VI, 928-929
Stephanus VIII, 929-931
Johannes XI, 931-935
Leo VII, 936-939
Stephanus IX, 939-942
Martinus II, 942-946
Agapetus II, 946-955
Johannes XII, 955-964
Leo VIII, 964-965
Benedictus V, 964-966 *
Johannes XIII, 965-972
Benedictus VI, 973-974
Benedictus VII, 974-983
Johannes XIV, 983-984
Bonifatius VII, 984-985
Johannes XV, 985-996
Gregorius V, 996-999
Johannes XVI, 997-998 †
Silvester II, 999-1003
Johannes XVII, 1003
Johannes XVIII, 1003-9
Sergius IV, 1009-12
Benedictus VIII, 1012-24
Johannes XIX, 1024-32

Benedictus IX, 1032-44
Silvester III, 1045
Gregorius VI, 1045-46
Clemens II, 1046-47
Damasus II, 1048
Leo IX, 1049-54
Victor II, 1055-57
Stephanus IX, 1057-58
Benedictus X, 1058-59 †
Nicholas II, 1058-61
Alexander II, 1061-73
Gregorius VII, 1073-85
Victor III, 1086-87
Urbanus II, 1088-99
Paschalis II, 1099-1118
Gelasius II, 1118-19
Calixtus II, 1119-24
Honorius II, 1124-30
Innocentius II, 1130-43
Coelestinus II, 1143-44
Lucius II, 1144-45
Eugenius III, 1145-53
Anastasius IV, 1153-54
Hadrianus IV, 1154-59
Alexander III, 1159-81
Lucius III, 1181-85
Urbanus III, 1185-87
Gregorius VIII, 1187
Clemens III, 1187-91
Coelestinus III, 1191-98
Innocentius III, 1198-1216
Honorius III, 1217-27
Gregorius IX, 1227-41
Coelestinus IV, 1241
Innocentius IV, 1243-54
Alexander IV, 1254-61
Urbanus IV, 1261-64
Clemens IV, 1265-68
Gregorius X, 1271-76
Innocentius V, 1276
Hadrianus V, 1276-77

* This or his contemporary was the antipope.
† This may have been an antipope.

Johannes XXI, 1277
Nicholas III, 1277-80
Martinus IV, 1281-85
Honorius IV, 1285-87
Nicholas IV, 1288-92
Coelestinus V, 1294
Bonifatius VIII, 1294-1303
Benedictus XI, 1303-4
Clemens V, 1305-14
Johannes XXII, 1316-34
Benedictus XII, 1334-42
Clemens VI, 1342-52
Innocentius VI, 1352-62
Urbanus V, 1362-70
Gregorius XI, 1370-78
Urbanus VI, 1378-89
Bonafatius IX, 1389-1404
Innocentius VII, 1404-6
Gregorius XII, 1406-17
Martinus V, 1417-31
Eugenius IV, 1431-47
Nicholas V, 1447-55
Calixtus III, 1455-58
Pius II, 1458-64
Paulus II, 1464-71
Sixtus IV, 1471-84
Innocentius VIII, 1484-92
Alexander VI, 1492-1503
Pius III, 1503
Julius II, 1503-13
Leo X, 1513-21
Adrianus VI, 1522-23
Clemens VII, 1523-34
Paulus III, 1534-49
Julius III, 1550-55
Marcellus II, 1555
Paulus IV, 1555-59

Pius IV, 1559-65
Pius V, 1566-72
Gregorius XIII, 1572-85
Sixtus V, 1585-90
Urbanus VII, 1590
Gregorius XIV, 1590-91
Innocentius IX, 1591
Clemens VIII, 1592-1605
Leo XI, 1605
Paulus V, 1605-21
Gregorius XV, 1621-23
Urbanus VIII, 1623-44
Innocent X, 1644-55
Alexander VII, 1655-67
Clement IX, 1667-69
Clement X, 1670-76
Innocent XI, 1676-89
Alexander VIII, 1689-91
Innocent XII, 1691-1700
Clement XI, 1700-21
Innocent XIII, 1721-24
Benedict XIII, 1724-30
Clement XII, 1730-40
Benedict XIV, 1740-58
Clement XIII, 1758-69
Clement XIV, 1769-74
Pius VI, 1775-99
Pius VII, 1800-23
Leo XII, 1823-29
Pius VIII, 1829-30
Gregory XVI, 1831-46
Pius IX, 1846-78
Leo XIII, 1878-1903
Pius X, 1903-14
Benedict XV, 1914-22
Pius XI, 1922-39
Pius XII, 1939-

EAST FRANKLAND

Louis the German, 840-876
Carloman, 876-880
Louis, 876-882

Charles the Fat, Emperor, 876-887
Arnulf, Emperor, 887-99
Louis the Child, 899-911

EUROPEAN RULERS

Post-Carlovingian:
Conrad of Franconia, 911-918

Henry I of Saxony, 919-936
Otto I of Saxony, 936-962

THE GERMANIC-ROMAN EMPIRE

Otto I, 962-973
Otto II, 973-983
Otto III, 983-1002
Henry II, 1002-4
Conrad II, 1024-39
Henry III, 1039-56
Henry IV, 1056-1106
Henry V, 1106-25
Lothair III, 1125-37

Conrad III, 1137-52
Frederick I, 1152-90
Henry VI, 1190-97
Otto IV, 1198-1215
Philip of Swabia, 1198-1208
Frederick II, 1211-50
Conrad IV, 1250-54
William of Holland, 1254-56
Interregnum, 1256-73

THE HOLY ROMAN EMPIRE

Rudolph I, 1273-91
Adolph of Nassau, 1291-98
Albrecht I, 1298-1308
Henry VII, 1308-13
Louis the Bavarian, 1314-47
Frederick of Habsburg, 1314-25
Charles IV, 1347-78
Wenzel, 1378-1400
Ruprecht, 1400-10
Sigismund, 1410-37
Albrecht II, 1437-39
Frederick III, 1440-93
Maximilian I, 1493-1519
Charles V, 1519-56

Ferdinand I, 1556-64
Maximilian II, 1564-76
Rudolph II, 1576-1611
Matthias, 1612-19
Ferdinand II, 1619-37
Ferdinand III, 1637-57
Leopold I, 1658-1705
Joseph I, 1705-11
Charles VI, 1711-40
Charles VII, 1742-45
Francis I, 1745-65
Joseph II, 1765-90
Leopold II, 1790-92
Francis II, 1792-1806

BRANDENBURG-PRUSSIA

Joachim I, 1499-1535
Joachim II, 1535-71
John George, 1571-98
Joachim Frederick, 1598-1608
John Sigismund, 1608-19
George William, 1619-40
Frederick William, 1640-88
Frederick III, 1688-1713 (King as
    Frederick I after 1701)

Frederick William I, 1713-40
Frederick II, 1740-86
Frederick William II, 1786-97
Frederick William III, 1797-1840
Frederick William IV, 1840-61
William I, 1861-88 (merged with
    German Empire in 1871)

GERMANY

(Part of Holy Roman Empire to 1806)
German Confederation, 1815-66
William I (Emperor), 1871-88
Frederick III, 1888
William II, 1888-1918

Republic, 1918-33
Dictatorship, 1933-45
Military occupation, 1945-
   Federal Republic of Germany, 1949-

THE CARLOVINGIANS

Pepin (Mayor of the Palace), *Died* **714**
Charles Martel (Mayor of the Palace), 714-741
Pepin I (Mayor of the Palace), 741-751, King 751-768

Charlemagne and Carloman, 768-771
Charlemagne, King 771-800, Emperor 800-814
Louis the Pious, Emperor, 814-840

FRANCE

Charles the Bald, 840-877
Louis II, 877-879
Louis III, 879-882
Carloman, 879-884
Charles the Fat, 885-887
Odo, 888-898
Charles III (the Simple), 898-922
Robert I, 922-923
Rudolph, 923-936
Louis IV, 936-954
Lothair, 954-986
Louis V, 986-987
Hugh Capet, 987-996
Robert II, 996-1031
Henry I, 1031-60
Philip I, 1060-1108
Louis VI, 1108-37
Louis VII, 1137-80
Philip II, 1180-1223
Louis VIII, 1223-26
Louis IX, 1226-70
Philip III, 1270-85

Philip IV, 1285-1314
Louis X, 1314-16
John I, 1316
Philip V, 1316-22
Charles IV, 1322-28
Philip VI, 1328-50
John II, 1350-64
Charles V, 1364-80
Charles VI, 1380-1422
Charles VII, 1422-61
Louis XI, 1461-83
Charles VIII, 1483-98
Louis XII, 1498-1515
Francis I, 1515-47
Henry II, 1547-59
Francis II, 1559-60
Charles IX, 1560-74
Henry III, 1574-89
Henry IV, 1589-1610
Louis XIII, 1610-43
Louis XIV, 1643-1715
Louis XV, 1715-74

EUROPEAN RULERS

Louis XVI, 1774-92
Republic, 1792-1804 (under Napoleon as First Consul after 1799)
Napoleon I (Emperor), 1804-14
Louis XVIII, 1814-24
Charles X, 1824-30

Louis Philippe, 1830-48
Second Republic, 1848-52
Napoleon III (Emperor), 1852-70
Third Republic, 1870-1940
German occupation, 1940-44
Fourth Republic, 1946-

GREAT BRITAIN AND IRELAND

Egbert, 802-839
Ethelwulf, 839-858
Ethelbald, 858-860
Ethelbert, 860-866
Alfred the Great, 871-901
Edward the Elder, 901-925
Athelstan, 925-940
Edmund I, 940-946
Edred, 946-955
Edwy, 955-959
Edgar, 959-975
Edward the Martyr, 975-979
Ethelred the Unready, 979-1016
Canute of Denmark, 1016-35
Harold I, 1035-40
Hardicanute, 1040-42
Edward the Confessor, 1042-66
Harold II, 1066
William I, 1066-87
William II, 1087-1100
Henry I, 1100-35
Stephen, 1135-54
Henry II, 1154-89
Richard I, 1189-99
John, 1199-1216
Henry III, 1216-72
Edward I, 1272-1307
Edward II, 1307-27
Edward III, 1327-77
Richard II, 1377-99
Henry IV, 1399-1413

Henry V, 1413-22
Henry VI, 1422-61
Edward IV, 1461-83
Edward V, 1483
Richard III, 1483-85
Henry VII, 1485-1509
Henry VIII, 1509-47
Edward VI, 1547-53
Mary, 1553-58
Elizabeth, 1558-1603
James I, 1603-25
Charles I, 1625-49
Republic (as *Commonwealth* and *Protectorate*), 1649-60
Charles II, 1660-85
James II (James VII of Scotland), 1685-88
William III and Mary II, 1689-94 (William III alone to 1702)
Anne, 1702-14
George I, 1714-27
George II, 1727-60
George III, 1760-1820
George IV, 1820-30
William IV, 1830-37
Victoria, 1837-1901
Edward VII, 1901-10
George V, 1910-36
Edward VIII, 1936
George VI, 1936-52
Elizabeth II, 1952-

SPAIN

Ferdinand and Isabella, 1479-1516
Charles I, 1516-56

Philip II, 1556-98
Philip III, 1598-1621

Philip IV, 1621-65
Charles II, 1665-1700
Philip V, 1700-46
Ferdinand VI, 1746-59
Charles III, 1759-88
Charles IV, 1788-1808
Joseph Bonaparte, 1808-13
Ferdinand VII, 1813-33

Isabella II, 1833-68
Republic, 1868-70
Amadeo, 1870-73
Republic, 1873-75
Alfonso XII, 1875-85
Alfonso XIII, 1886-1931
Republic, 1931-39
Dictatorship, 1939-

ITALY

Victor Emmanuel II, 1861-78
  (King of Sardinia, 1849-61)
Humbert, 1878-1900

Victor Emmanuel III, 1900-46
Dictatorship, 1922-43
Republic, 1946-

AUSTRIA AND AUSTRIA-HUNGARY

Ferdinand III, 1637-57
Leopold I, 1658-1705
Joseph I, 1705-11
Charles II (Charles VI in the Holy
  Roman Empire), 1711-40
Maria Theresa, 1740-80
Joseph II, 1780-90
Leopold II, 1790-92
Francis I (Francis II in the Holy
  Roman Empire), 1792-1835 (after
  1806 Emperor of Austria)

Ferdinand I, 1835-48
Francis Joseph, 1848-1916 (after
  1867 Emperor of Austria and King
  of Hungary)
Charles I, 1916-18
Republic, 1918-34
Dictatorship, 1934-38
United to Germany, 1938-45
Republic, 1945-

RUSSIA

Ivan III, 1462-1505
Basil IV, 1505-33
Ivan IV, 1533-84
Theodore I, 1584-98
Boris Godunov, 1598-1605
Michael, 1613-45
Alexius, 1645-76
Theodore II, 1676-82
Ivan V and Peter I, 1682-89
(Peter I, alone, to 1725)
Catherine I, 1725-27
Peter II, 1727-30
Anna, 1730-40

Ivan VI, 1740-41
Elizabeth, 1741-62
Peter III, 1762
Catherine II, 1762-96
Paul, 1796-1801
Alexander I, 1801-25
Nicholas I, 1825-55
Alexander II, 1855-81
Alexander III, 1881-94
Nicholas I, 1894-1917
Republic, 1917
Dictatorship, 1917-

Presidents of the United States

1789-1953

George Washington, 1789-1797
John Adams, 1797-1801
Thomas Jefferson, 1801-1809
James Madison, 1809-1817
James Monroe, 1817-1825
John Quincy Adams, 1825-1829
Andrew Jackson, 1829-1837
Martin Van Buren, 1837-1841
William Henry Harrison, 1841
John Tyler, 1841-1845
James K. Polk, 1845-1849
Zachary Taylor, 1849-1850
Millard Fillmore, 1850-1853
Franklin Pierce, 1853-1857
James Buchanan, 1857-1861
Abraham Lincoln, 1861-1865
Andrew Johnson, 1865-1869

Ulysses S. Grant, 1869-1877
Rutherford B. Hayes, 1877-1881
James A. Garfield, 1881
Chester A. Arthur, 1881-1885
Grover Cleveland, 1885-1889
Benjamin Harrison, 1889-1893
Grover Cleveland, 1893-1897
William McKinley, 1897-1901
Theodore Roosevelt, 1901-1909
William Howard Taft, 1909-1913
Woodrow Wilson, 1913-1921
Warren G. Harding, 1921-1923
Calvin Coolidge, 1923-1929
Herbert Hoover, 1929-1933
Franklin D. Roosevelt, 1933-1945
Harry S. Truman, 1945-1953
Dwight D. Eisenhower, 1953-